Tax Planning for U.S. MNCs with EU Holding Companies

Tax Planning for U.S. MNCs with EU Holding Companies

Goals • Tools • Barriers

Pia Dorfmueller

Kluwer Law International
The Hague/London/New York

Library of Congress Cataloging-in-Publication Data

Dorfmueller, Pia.
  Tax planning for U.S. MNCS with EU holding companies: goals, tools, barriers / by
  Pia Dorfmueller.
    p. cm.
  Includes index.
  ISBN 90-411-9922-5
    1. International business enterprises–Taxation–Law and legislation–Europe. 2. Tax
  planning–Europe. 3. International business enterprises–Taxation–Law and
  legislation–United States. 4. Tax planning–United States. I. Title: Tax planning for US
  multinational corporations with EU holding companies. II. Title.

KJC7259.D67 2003
658.15'3 – dc21

                                                                            200304470X

  ISBN 90 411 9922 5

Published by Kluwer Law International,
P.O. Box 85889, 2508 CN The Hague, The Netherlands.
sales@kluwerlaw.com
http://www.kluwerlaw.com

Sold and distributed in North, Central and South America
by Aspen Publishers, Inc.
7201 McKinney Circle, Frederick, MD 21704, USA

Sold and distributed in all other countries
by Turpin Distribution Services Limited,
Blackhorse Road, Letchworth, Herts,
SG6 1HN, United Kingdom

Printed on acid-free paper

Printed in Great Britain by
Antony Rowe Ltd, Chippenham, Wiltshire

SUMMARY OF CONTENTS

ACKNOWLEDGMENTS

As I complete my graduate training, I am indebted to a number of individuals.

First and foremost, I must offer Prof. Dr. Wolfgang Kessler my deepest thanks. Your guidance and assistance have been invaluable to me and for that I offer my gratitude. Secondly, I wish to thank Prof. Dr. Heinz Rehkugler for his second approval.

I also offer my thanks to Prof. Dr. Dieter Endres of PricewaterhouseCoopers GmbH, Frankfurt, Germany. Your example as an economist, as a teacher, and as a colleague is the one that I strive to match. I am particularly grateful to Prof. Tracy A. Kaye of Seton Hall Law School, Newark, NJ, USA for her superb support.

Finally, I thank my family and friends. My family, especially Ron, as well as my parents, have provided me - once again - with continual support and encouragement during the writing of this book. I appreciate the cheerfulness with which they endured the many hours I spent writing this text. I owe a particular debt to Cindy C. Wilson, Adam B. Freiheit, and Wendy L. Potomski. As my dearest friends, they have helped me to survive the most challenging task I have ever undertaken.

THE EIFFEL TOWER IS THE EMPIRE STATE BUILDING AFTER TAXES.

Anonymous

ABBREVIATIONS

Abs.	Absatz
ACE	Adjusted Current Earnings
ACRS	Appropriate Capital Recovery System
ACT	Advance Corporate Tax
AG	Aktiengesellschaft
AMT	Alternative Minimum Tax
AMTI	Alternative Minimum Tax Income
APA	Advance Pricing Agreement
ApS	Anpartsselskab
Art.	Artikel
AS	Archiv für Schweizerisches Abgaberecht
A/S	Aktieselskab
Aufl.	Auflage
BEK	Bekendtgorelse
BFH	Bundesfinanzhof
BGBl.	Bundesgesetzblatt
BIFD	Bulletin for International Fiscal Documentation
BMF	Bundesministerium der Finanzen
BOE	Boletín Offical del Estado
B.S.	Belgisch Staatsblatt
BStBl.	Bundessteuerblatt
B.V.	Besloten vennootschap met beperkte aanspreakelijkheit
BVerfG	Bundesverfassungsgericht
BVerfGE	Bundesverfassungsgerichts-Entscheidungen
C.B.	Cumulative Bulletin of the Internal Revenue Service
CBT	Common Base Taxation
CCH	Commerce Clearing House
CEPS	Centre for European Policy Studies
CFC	Controlled Foreign Corporation
CFR	Code of Federal Regulations
Cir.	Federal Circuit Court of Appeal
Cl.Ct.	Federal Court of Claims
Cong.	Congress
CTF	Canadian Tax Foundation
C.V.	Commanditaire vennootschap
D.C.	District of Columbia
DCL	Dual-Consolidated Loss
DRC	Dual-Resident Corporation
EBIT	European Business Initiative on Taxation
EC	European Community
ed.	Edition
e.g.	exempli gratia
E&P	Earnings and Profits
et. al.	et alii/alia
etc.	et cetera
ETVE	Entidad de Tenencia de Valores Extranjeros
EU	European Union

EUCIT	European Unitary Company Income Tax
EUFT	Eligible Unrelieved Foreign Tax
F.2d	Federal Reporter Second
FBCI	Foreign Base Company Income
FDIA	Federal Deposit Insurance Act
Fed. Reg.	Federal Register
Fig.	Figure
fn.	Footnote
FPHC	Foreign Personal Holding Company
F.R.	Federal Register
FSA	Field Service Advisory
FSC	Foreign Sales Corporation
FTB	Franchise Tax Board
FTC	Foreign Tax Credit
GewSt	Gewerbesteuer
GmbH	Gesellschaft mit beschränkter Haftung
GmbHG	Gesetz betreffend die Gesellschaften mit beschränkter Haftung
GmbH-Report	GmbH-Report - Recht und Wirtschaft für die GmbH - Sonderteil der Zeitschrift GmbH-Rundschau
HoldCo	Holding Company
H.R.	House Reconciliation
Hrsg.	Herausgeber
HST	Home State Taxation
IBFD	International Bureau of Fiscal Documentation
IFSC	International Financial Services Centre
incl.	inclusive
i.e.	id est
I.R.B.	Internal Revenue Bulletin
IRC	Internal Revenue Code as of January 23, 2002
IRS	Internal Revenue Service
Iss.	Issue
J.O.	Journal Officiel de la République Française
KapESt	Kapitalertragsteuer
KG	Kommanditgesellschaft
KSt	Körperschaftsteuer
lit.	Buchstabe
LLC	Limited Liability Company
LLLP	Limited Liability Limited Partnership
LLP	Limited Liability Partnership
LP	Limited Partnership
Ltd.	Limited
MNC	Multinational Corporation
Mon.B.	Moniteur Belge
n/a	Not applicable
No.	Number
NOL	Net Operating Loss

Nr./No.	Nummer
N.V.	Naamloze vennootschap
Ö-BGBl.	Bundesgesetzblatt (Austria)
OECD	Organization for Economic Cooperation and Development
ÖStZB	Die finanzrechtlichen Erkenntnisse des VwGH und VfGH, Beilage zur Österreichische Steuer-Zeitung
OID	Original Issue Discount
OpCo	Operating Company
p.e.	Permanent Establishment
PFIC	Passive Foreign Investment Company
P.L.	United States Public Laws
PLC	Public Limited Liability Company
P.L.R.	Private Letter Ruling
Pub.L.	Public Laws
R&D	Research and Development
Regs.	Regulations Issued under the Code
Rev. Proc.	Revenue Procedure
Rev. Rul.	Revenue Ruling
SA	Sociétés Anonyme (France, Switzerland)
SA	Società Anonima (Switzerland)
SA	Sociedad Anónima (Spain)
SARL	Sociétes à Responsabilité Limitée
SAS	Société par Actions Simplifiée
SCpA	Sociedad en Comanditaria por Acciones
SE	Societas Europaea
Sec.	Section
Sess.	Session
S.I.	Statutory Instruments
SOPARFI	Société de Participations Financières
SRL	Sociedad de Responsabilidad Lititada
Tab.	Table
TAM	Technical Advice Memorandum
T.C.	Tax Court Reporter
T.D.	Treasury Decision
Temp. Regs.	Temporary Regulations
Trb.	Tractatenblad van het Koninkrijk der Nederlanden
Treas. Reg.	Treasury Regulation
u.a.	und andere
U.K.	United Kingdom
UNICE	Union of Industrial and Employers' Confederations of Europe
U.S.	United States
v.	versus
Vol.	Volume
VwGH	Verwaltungsgerichtshof
WAK-N	Kommission für Wirtschaft und Abgaben des Nationalrates
WL	Westlaw

WTD	Worldwide Tax Daily
WTO	World Trade Organization

LIST OF FIGURES

LIST OF TABLES

SECTION 1: INTRODUCTION TO INTERNATIONAL TAX PLANNING FOR U.S. MNCS

1. INTRODUCTION

U.S. taxpayers often internationalize gradually over time. A U.S. business may operate on a strictly domestic basis for several years, then may begin to explore foreign markets by first exporting its products abroad,[1] and later by licensing its products to a foreign manufacturer[2] or entering into a joint venture with a foreign partner.[3] If its forays into foreign markets are successful, the U.S. business may create a foreign subsidiary[4] and move a portion of its operations abroad by establishing a sales or manufacturing facility. If the foreign operation is carried on through a locally incorporated foreign subsidiary, its earnings will be deferred from U.S. taxation until "repatriated" to the U.S. in the form of dividends, interest, royalties, or other payments.[5] As a result, the U.S. taxpayer has significant control in determining when the earnings of the foreign subsidiaries are included in U.S. taxable income.

In certain situations, however, significant U.S. tax consequences can occur for the U.S. owner under three principal U.S. anti-deferral regimes. One example is the controlled foreign corporation (CFC) provisions (the so-called *Subpart F*),[6] i.e., income of a foreign corporation must

---

[1] Any profits earned on export sales are subject to immediate taxation in the U.S. but remittance of the income may be blocked by exchange control restrictions in the foreign country. In this case, the U.S. taxpayer may elect to defer recognition of the income for U.S. tax purposes until the funds can be effectively converted into U.S. dollars and remitted. Rev. Rul. 74-351, 1974-2 C.B. 144 as modified by Rev. Rul. 81-290, 1981-2 C.B. 108. See Meldman, R. E. and Schadewald, M. S., *A Practical Guide to U.S. Taxation of International Transactions*, 2000, 325.

[2] The character of the license or other contractual relationship, e.g., principal - agent, determines whether the U.S. company is subject to foreign income taxes. If the U.S. company receives royalty income, the foreign country may impose a withholding tax on the income. Many countries, including the U.S., subject certain payments, e.g., royalties, made to foreign persons to withholding tax, even if the foreign person would not otherwise be subject to tax in that country. The determination of whether a U.S. company is subject to tax in a foreign jurisdiction as a result of the licensing agreement depends on the tax law of that country and its application to the agreement. If a double tax treaty exists between the U.S. and the foreign country, the U.S. company will not be subject to income tax in the foreign country unless it has a permanent establishment. Generally, royalty income is not attributable to a permanent establishment and is subject only to withholding tax. See Abrams, H. E. and Doernberg, R. L., *Essentials of United States Taxation*, 1999, 4-74; Isenbergh, J., *International Taxation*, 2000, 226; Bittker, B. I. and Eustice, J. S., *Federal Income Taxation of Corporations and Shareholders*, 2002, paragraph 15.03[1].

[3] See Matthews, K., *Tax Notes International* 1989, 575; Ross, S. G., *Tax Notes International* 1990, 781; Benson, D. M., *The Tax Adviser* 1996, 628. For the U.S. tax treatment of an international joint venture, see Davis, B. N. and Lainoff, S. R., *Tax Law Review* 1991, 165; Flick, H. F. W., *U.S. steuerliche Konsequenzen bei Umstrukturierungen*, 1997, 715; Larkins, E. R., Oakley, E. F. and Winkle, G. M., *The Tax Adviser* 1999, 418.

[4] The enterprise usually will be carried on through a branch when the U.S. company is not sure of the foreign market and does not want to invest permanently in the foreign country, or if substantial losses are expected. The establishment of a foreign subsidiary basically indicates a company's intention to make a long-term investment abroad. See Meldman, R. E. and Schadewald, M. S., *A Practical Guide to U.S. Taxation of International Transactions*, 2000, 333.

[5] See Salmon, J. J. and Gander, F. R., *Tax Notes International* 1990, 99; Endres, D. and Spengel, C., *Steuerstrukturen in Deutschland aus Sicht eines US-Investors*, 1997, 82; Altshuler, R. and Grubert, H., *National Tax Journal* 2001, 788; Engel, K., *Texas Law Review* 2001, 1530. Certain qualifying corporations located in Mexico and Canada must be included in the U.S. consolidated income tax return (IRC § 1504(d)). See Zschiegner, H., *Internationale Wirtschaftsbriefe*, Fach 8, USA, Gruppe 2, 1998 III, 981; Abrams, H. E. and Doernberg, R. L., *Essentials of United States Taxation*, 1999, 2-300; Peroni, R. J., Fleming, J. C. Jr. and Shay, S. E., *SMU Law Review* 1999, 457; American Chamber of Commerce in Germany e.V. and PricewaterhouseCoopers GmbH, *Steuern in den USA*, 2001, 83; Fleming, J. C. Jr., Peroni, R. J. and Shay, S. E., *Florida Tax Review* 2001, 339.

Instead of incorporating a foreign subsidiary to operate the foreign business, the enterprise could be carried on through a branch. Deferral cannot be achieved in such a case. Instead, the branch's earnings are included in the U.S. company's tax returns in the current period in much the same way as are earnings of a U.S. office or division. See Tello, C. P., *Tax Management International Journal* 1998, 11; Engel, K., *Texas Law Review* 2001, 1529.

[6] The U.S. Subpart F provisions were the foundation of many CFC regimes, including Australia, Canada, Denmark, Estonia, Finland, France, Germany, Hungary, Indonesia, Italy, Japan, Korea, Mexico, New Zealand, Norway, Portugal, South Africa, Spain, Sweden, and the U.K. See Schaumburg, H., *Internationales Steuerrecht*, 1998, paragraph 10.8; Smith, M. and Laudan, D., *International Tax Review* 1999, 65; Department of the Treasury, *Subpart F*, 2000, 58; Casna, R., *International Tax Report* 2002, 1; Lang, M., *Internationales Steuerrecht* 2002, 217.

be included, in whole or in part, in the U.S. shareholder's taxable income in the current year.[7] None of the anti-deferral regimes creates any U.S. tax liability for foreign subsidiaries because the U.S. lacks international taxing jurisdiction to tax foreign subsidiaries directly on their foreign income.[8] Instead, they create a U.S. tax liability for the U.S. shareholders of foreign subsidiaries. As a result, any U.S. taxpayer paying foreign taxes must consider the (indirect) foreign tax credit (FTC) provisions.[9] Due to high corporate income tax rates and U.S. restrictions limiting the ability of U.S. taxpayers to fully use FTCs, more attention has been focused on structuring investments through hybrid entities since the introduction of the check-the-box regulations in 1997.[10]

Tax planning involves, in particular, defining the tax base (*conversion*) and arranging the timing of tax payments (*deferral*[11]). These two concepts constitute the Holy Grail of tax planning. The analysis starts here and attempts to design conversion and deferral structures resulting in achieving the main goal of maximizing post-tax profits or, from a tax viewpoint, minimizing the overall tax costs. When developing new structures for U.S. investors, it is necessary to test them in different ways. Firstly, have the goals of the investor been achieved? Secondly, which tools have been used and are they appropriate? Lastly, will the tax savings be permanent or be counteracted by an anti-deferral regime? Assuming an overseas investment, this book will explore the three aspects of tax planning which are critical to the U.S. investor: "Goals · Tools · Barriers".

The examination further focuses on holding companies in Europe, because the European market is a market of importance, growth, and potential.[12] Also, several European jurisdictions provide favorable holding company regimes, which are essential for reducing the global tax burden by (re)organizing or (re)structuring the U.S. operation overseas.[13] Moreover, the approaches made by the European Commission toward an Internal Market without tax obstacles and the related formation of a Societas Europaea (SE)[14] holding company will promote the increased use of European holding companies in the future. Finally, the analysis is presented from a U.S. investors

---

[7] The other two regimes are foreign personal holding companies (FPHCs - IRC §§ 551-558) and passive foreign investment companies (PFICs - IRC §§ 1291-1297). The CFC and the FPHC regimes are applicable to certain types of income earned through a foreign corporation with substantial U.S. shareholdings. In general, these provisions apply basically to investment income and certain types of business income. In contrast thereto, the PFIC rules apply to companies earning investment income, irrespective of the extent of U.S. shareholdings. A discussion of those provisions is beyond the scope of this analysis. See Byrnes, L. A., *Tax Notes International* 1989, 26; Stoffregen, P. A. and Lipeles, S. R., *Tax Notes International* 1994, 1326; Doering, J. A., *Journal of International Taxation* 1995, 209; Brewer, K. P. and Forouhar, M. N., *Tax Management International Journal* 1997, 160; Dagan, T., *Virginia Tax Review* 1998, 409; Jensen, P., Spikes, P. and Carter, D., *The International Tax Journal* 1998, 4; Tello, C. P., *Tax Management International Journal* 1998, 14; Zschiegner, H., *Internationale Wirtschaftsbriefe*, Fach 8, USA, Gruppe 2, 1998 III, 964; Tillinghast, D. R., *Florida Tax Review* 1999, 373; Isenbergh, J., *International Taxation*, 2000, 181; McNulty, J. K., *Brief Look at the Early History of the Unintegrated Corporate and Individual Income Taxes in the U.S.A.*, 2000, 884; Meldman, R. E. and Schadewald, M. S., *A Practical Guide to U.S. Taxation of International Transactions*, 2000, 169; Engel, K., *Texas Law Review* 2001, 1549. For CFCs/Subpart F provisions in detail, see *infra* page 83.

[8] See Meldman, R. E. and Schadewald, M. S., *A Practical Guide to U.S. Taxation of International Transactions*, 2000, 7.

[9] See Larkins, E. R., Oakley, E. F. and Winkle, G. M., *The Tax Adviser* 1999, 416.

[10] A hybrid entity is one organized in a foreign jurisdiction that is treated as a corporation for foreign tax purposes but as a partnership for U.S. tax. For details, see *infra* page 75.

[11] The Department of the Treasury defines deferral as "... the postponement of current taxation on the net income or gain economically accrued by a taxpayer." See Department of the Treasury, *Subpart F*, 2000, ix.

[12] Currently, the EU consists of 15 member states (Austria, Belgium, Denmark, Finland, France, Germany, Greece, Ireland, Italy, Luxembourg, The Netherlands, Portugal, Spain, Sweden, and the U.K.). 13 candidate countries, including Bulgaria, Cyprus, Czech Republic, Estonia, Hungary, Latvia, Lithuania, Malta, Poland, Romania, Slovak Republic, Slovenia, and Turkey are expected join the Union (EU enlargement homepage unter http://europa.eu.int/comm/enlargement/index.htm). See EU, *Enlargement*, 2001, 5; Cussons, P., Cooke, D. and Newton, D., *Journal of International Taxation* 2002, 24.

[13] See Herzig, N., *Die Wirtschaftsprüfung* 1998, 282.

[14] European Company.

viewpoint. Much of the world's economic activity originates in the U.S. and a significant number of business transactions and investments in the world are affected in some measure by U.S. taxation.[15]

The first holding company regime after the implementation of the EU Parent-Subsidiary Directive[16] was introduced in Luxembourg in 1990.[17] Since then, holding companies have been subject to various examinations but analyses focused on tax planning are rare. The first comprehensive review was undertaken by Kessler (1996).[18] This paper was inspired by that publication.

Choosing the U.S. as the home country of the investor requires analysis of a jungle of highly interrelated and complex provisions, regulations and notices of U.S. international tax law. This complexity results from the efforts by U.S. tax authorities to formalize distinctions between legitimate business operations outside the U.S. that generally enjoy full credits for foreign taxes and the deferral of U.S. taxation. The rules are also designed to prevent maneuvers to shift income to corporations considered to be tax haven operations. Isenbergh, for example, describes the U.S. outbound regime as "often nightmarish".[19] Hence, it is no surprise that the "bibles" of U.S. tax law, including, for example, Abrams/Doernberg (1999)[20] and Bittker/Eustice's (2002)[21] run 1,000 pages or even more.

Adding to this complexity, the U.S. Constitution allows individual states and other local governments to impose their own taxes, resulting in more than 60,000 taxing jurisdictions within the U.S.[22] Due to this large number of taxing jurisdictions and because state and local taxation vary tremendously,[23] the primary focus of this monograph is on the structure of U.S. federal tax law.

This paper proposes that the conventional debate concerning international tax planning techniques disregards a crucial point. The conventional debate fails to consider all relevant tax data and tax consequences triggered at each level of a foreign group which invests in the EU. This is immanent as most analyses of international tax planning structures compare the different tax regimes in the EU and design tax beneficial structures based on the comparative examination. Such traditional analyses fail to consider the tax consequences incurred at the level of the ultimate parent company, as they isolate the interposed company from its shareholder. Hence, the conclusions drawn from the results of such traditional examinations might randomly lead to an overall tax beneficial structure. This paper goes beyond the traditional approach and steps on virgin tax soil as it combines the comprehensive analyses of EU tax laws which give rise to tax planning, and U.S. tax law applying at the level of the investor which could potentially deny any tax deferral. Therefore, this paper follows two proposals for future research made by Kessler (1996).[24] First, it includes an analysis of a large variety of countries and, second, the impact of tax planning structures on the ultimate parent company is considered.

---

[15] See Isenbergh, J., *International Taxation*, 2000, 3; Noren, D. G., *Tax Law Review* 2001, 340.

[16] Council Directive No. 90/435 on the Common System of Taxation Applicable in the Case of Parent Companies and Subsidiaries of Different Member States, dated July 23, 1990, *Official Journal of the European Communities*, dated August 8, 1990, L 225. See Taylor, J. C. and Hannum, C. E., *Tax Notes International* 1997, 91; Bolanz, G., *Die EU-Holding als strategisches Gestaltungsinstrument in der Steuerplanung*, 1998, 22; Zois, A., *Cardozo Journal of International and Comparative Law* 1999, 181; EBIT, *Tax Analysis*, 2002, 5.

[17] The so-called *Société de Participations Financières (SOPARFI)*. For details, see *infra* page 125.

[18] Kessler, W., *Die Euro-Holding*, 1996.

[19] See Isenbergh, J., *International Taxation*, 2000, 16. Similar Graetz, M. J., *Tax Law Review* 2001, 264.

[20] Abrams, H. E. and Doernberg, R. L., *Essentials of United States Taxation*, 1999.

[21] Bittker, B. I. and Eustice, J. S., *Federal Income Taxation of Corporations and Shareholders*, 2002.

[22] See Abrams, H. E. and Doernberg, R. L., *Essentials of United States Taxation*, 1999, 1-2.

[23] See Zschiegner, H., *Internationale Wirtschaftsbriefe*, Fach 8, USA, Gruppe 2, 1998 IV, 993; Abrams, H. E. and Doernberg, R. L., *Essentials of United States Taxation*, 1999, 1-4; American Chamber of Commerce in Germany e.V. and PricewaterhouseCoopers GmbH, *Steuern in den USA*, 2001, 98; Lee, P. T. and Kowallik, A., *Internationale Wirtschaftsbriefe*, Fach 8, USA, Gruppe 2, 2001, 1085; Zschiegner, H., *Internationale Wirtschaftsbriefe*, Fach 8, USA, Gruppe 2, 2001, 1135.

[24] See Kessler, W., *Die Euro-Holding*, 1996, 333.

This in-depth examination is divided into 6 sections and is organized as follows: Section 1 analyzes why holding companies are a significant tax planning tool. Further, in order to highlight the importance of tax deferral from a U.S. investor's point of view, the basic concepts of the U.S. federal taxation of corporations and partnerships are compared. Section 2 demonstrates the specific tax planning goals of a U.S. investor. Section 3 considers the tax planning tools available to a U.S. investor that are appropriate to achieve the previously identified tax planning goals. Section 4 discusses the policies of the U.S. investor's jurisdiction that view some tools as tax-abusive and, thus, deny tax deferral. Sections 2 to 4 (the goals, the tools, and the barriers) are the pillars of this paper. Section 5 puts a roof on the three pillars, i.e., considers the interrelation and the counteraction of the different provisions and regimes and demonstrates structures that achieve the greatest benefit by avoiding any restrictions on the use of tax planning tools and the application of any tax provisions which would deny any tax benefits. Section 5 contains an in-depth synopsis of EU holding company regimes implemented under local laws in Austria, Belgium, Denmark, France, Germany, Ireland, Luxembourg, the Netherlands, Spain, and Switzerland. It then demonstrates how the tax planning goals of a U.S. MNC might be achieved by properly using these tax planning tools while avoiding the application of tax planning barriers. The last section, Section 6, considers developments in U.S. tax law and international initiatives on harmful tax competition[25] that might have an impact on the current tax beneficial structures of U.S. MNCs, as demonstrated in the previous section. Section 6 also contains concluding comments.

2. HOLDING COMPANIES AS KEY INTERNATIONAL TAX PLANNING TOOL

Decisions regarding the organization and structure of foreign business activities are influenced by both tax and non-tax reasons. The future structure cannot, therefore, be based solely on tax considerations without considering any and all pertinent non-tax factors. There are a variety of non-tax factors that influence the organizational structure and the choice of location including the stability of the foreign government, the presence of exchange controls or import quotas, restrictions on foreign investment, the risk of property expropriation, the availability of low cost labor, the presence of stable banking facilities, the existence of adequate communication facilities, and the general attitude of the other country toward foreigners.[26]

2.1. Definition and Forms

A "holding company" might be considered one of the more glamorous and promising planning tools used in international tax law. Even though those using the term may often be vague as to its implications, there is no denying its general recognition as the hallmark of creative and sophisticated tax planning for multinational corporations (MNCs).[27]

---

[25] The increased openness of tax policies caused by the increased globalization of trade and investments has resulted in the development of e-commerce and has increased the significance of tax havens. See Runge, B., *Wettbewerb nationaler Steuerrechte*, 1997, 957; Lehner, M., *Steuer und Wirtschaft* 1998, 159.

[26] See Gocke, R. and Baumhoff, H., *Internationale Wirtschaftsbriefe*, Fach 3, Deutschland, Gruppe 1, 1989, 1233; Bremer, S., *Der Holdingstandort Bundesrepublik Deutschland*, 1996, 56; Haidorfer Nikolenkov, A., *Holdingstruktur und Standortwahl*, 1996, 104; Cinnamon, A., *International Tax Review* 1999, 9; Meldman, R. E. and Schadewald, M. S., *A Practical Guide to U.S. Taxation of International Transactions*, 2000, 348; Endres, D. and Dorfmueller, P., *Praxis Internationale Steuerberatung* 2001, 98; Endres, D., Dorfmueller, P. and Urse, M., *International Tax Report* 2001 I, 3; Endres, D. and Eckstein, H.-M., *Steuerrecht International*, 2001, 27.

[27] See Kessler, W., *Die Euro-Holding*, 1996, 5.

Most enterprises, whether they operate on a global basis or remain purely local, seek to keep overall tax costs as low as possible.[28] Indeed, the minimization of the global tax burden is usually one of the main goals with respect to tax, along with ensuring full compliance with all relevant local requirements. Within an international context, holding companies are often suitable vehicles for implementing, controlling, and adjusting tax rate reduction strategies.

In the present context, a holding company is seen as an entity formed with the primary business purpose of holding (long-term) investments in domestic and foreign subsidiaries with independent legal or business personalities.[29] These investments are, therefore, the main assets of a typical holding company, and its predominant activities are, thus, usually restricted to managing, controlling, and financing the relevant business operations.[30] The operations, themselves, are often decentralized.

Bundling investments in different companies under a common holding company serves different purposes and has led to a corresponding array of catchwords to describe the various types of holding companies. Management holdings, finance holdings, divisional holdings, intermediate holdings, family holdings, foreign holdings, and country holdings are examples of holding companies with a single primary purpose.[31] In practice, there are many cases of dual-purpose holding companies such as country-managing holding companies, partially fulfilling more than one aim.[32]

2.2. Location Issues and Tax Attributes

Consolidating shareholdings and other ownership rights in business operations under a single holding company can lead to a variety of significant business benefits. Of course, management must decide if the expected advantages can justify incorporating a holding company in light of the traditions, present circumstances and future plans of the concern.[33] Although management groups may hold differing views as to precisely when in the course of a corporation's development a holding company becomes advantageous or appropriate, most will accept as a general premise that once international operations have reached a certain volume and complexity, centralization of group management becomes a primary issue. A holding company is an ideal vehicle to manage this issue.[34] In most cases, the motive for actually setting up a holding company is the reaction to

---

[28] See Bremer, S., *Der Holdingstandort Bundesrepublik Deutschland*, 1996, 52; Kessler, W. and Dorfmueller, P., *Praxis Internationale Steuerberatung* 2001, 177.

[29] See Bremer, S., *Der Holdingstandort Bundesrepublik Deutschland*, 1996, 6; Kessler, W., *Die Euro-Holding*, 1996, 10; Hintzen, B., *Die deutsche Zwischenholding als Gegenstand der internationalen Steuerplanung*, 1997, 6; Endres, D. and Dorfmueller, P., *Praxis Internationale Steuerberatung* 2001, 94; Fohr, I., *Besteuerungskonzept für Holdinggesellschaften*, 2001, 29.

[30] See Everling, W., *Der Betrieb* 1981, 2550; Arndt, H.-W. and Ringel, E., *Betriebs-Berater* 1988, 2147; Taylor, J. C. and Hannum, C. E., *Tax Notes International* 1997, 91; Bader, A., *Steuergestaltung mit Holdinggesellschaften*, 1998, 15; Zois, A., *Cardozo Journal of International and Comparative Law* 1999, 179.

[31] See Anesini, S., *Die Holding als Instrument der Führung in konzernierten Unternehmen*, 1991, 58; Bühner, R., *Management-Holding in der Praxis*, 1992, 31; Hakelmacher, S., *Die Wirtschaftsprüfung* 1992, 123; Bühner, R., *Der Betrieb* 1994, 437; Haidorfer Nikolenkov, A., *Holdingstruktur und Standortwahl*, 1996, 13; Lutter, M., *Erscheinungsformen und der für dieses Buch maßgebende Rechtbegriff der Holding*, 1996, paragraph A 13; Kessler, W., *Die Euro-Holding*, 1996, 11; Hintzen, B., *Die deutsche Zwischenholding als Gegenstand der internationalen Steuerplanung*, 1997, 9; Bader, A., *Steuergestaltung mit Holdinggesellschaften*, 1998, 13.

[32] See Bühner, R., *Der Betrieb* 1993, 286; Keller, T., *Unternehmensführung mit Holdingkonzepten*, 1993, 56; Hintzen, B., *Die deutsche Zwischenholding als Gegenstand der internationalen Steuerplanung*, 1997, 16.

[33] E.g., a holding company is an essential element in the context of national and cross-border joint ventures and amalgamations. See Hintzen, B., *Die deutsche Zwischenholding als Gegenstand der internationalen Steuerplanung*, 1997, 20.

[34] See Keller, T., *Der Betrieb* 1991, 1633; Bremer, S., *Der Holdingstandort Bundesrepublik Deutschland*, 1996, 40; Hintzen, B., *Die deutsche Zwischenholding als Gegenstand der internationalen Steuerplanung*, 1997, 14.

business needs and circumstances, in particular, when seen from a strategic point of view, although there are cases of holding companies having been formed specifically for legal or tax reasons.[35]

Irrespective of any individual circumstances, structuring a large and wide-spread organization as a chain of individually incorporated businesses owned by a single holding company offers a multiplicity of advantages over a single legal entity operating through a series of divisions or branches. Examples of such advantages include:[36]

- clear business structures with clearly defined responsibilities for results;
- enhanced motivation of management personal;
- the prevention of any feeling of false security in the minds of officers and employees through belonging to a large organization;
- the break-up of old-established resistance to change;
- the ability to bring the products and customers back into the main focus of management energy;
- separation of liabilities and risks;
- simple integration of newly started or newly acquired activities;
- the ability to offer potential investors the opportunity of investing in only some of the group's operations; and
- flexibility to reorganize and to cooperate with other businesses.

Few enterprises will see all the items listed above as desirable, and even fewer will view the list as exhaustive. However, the list does provide a useful and fairly typical indication of the more common motives found in practice. Put more simply, most corporations establish holding companies in the hope of combining the advantages of a large concern (such as its buying power or its general image of being a household name) with the flexibility of decision making and reacting quickly to the demands of the market for which smaller businesses are recognized.[37] This "win-win" result will, of course, only be achieved if management of both the parent company and the subsidiaries are prepared and able to harmonize their objectives to form common goals in an atmosphere of mutual trust.

U.S. MNCs often believe a holding company is a convenient way to own and manage a group of subsidiaries in a particular region such as Europe.[38] There are numerous motives for doing this that are rather more specific than the general items in the list above, and these motives would be extended to include tax planning.[39] Indeed, a foreign holding company vehicle is predominantly identified as a significant tool in international tax planning to increase shareholder value through the minimization of the tax burden on overseas earnings and profits.

Typical criteria for establishing holding companies include:[40]

---

[35] See Arndt, H.-W. and Ringel, E., *Betriebs-Berater* 1988, 2147; Bremer, S., *Der Holdingstandort Bundesrepublik Deutschland*, 1996, 52.

[36] See Bühner, R. and Walter, H., *Der Betrieb* 1977, 1207; Keller, T., *Der Betrieb* 1991, 1633; Wenzl, H., *Holding*, 1996, 8; Hintzen, B., *Die deutsche Zwischenholding als Gegenstand der internationalen Steuerplanung*, 1997, 18; Lettl, T., *Deutsches Steuerrecht* 1997, 1017; Bader, A., *Steuergestaltung mit Holdinggesellschaften*, 1998, 6; Burek, C. J., *Die Besteuerung der Holdinggesellschaft*, 1998, 29; Marantelli, A., *Steuer Revue* 2000 II, 92; Streu, V., *Der Einsatz einer inländischen Zwischenholding in der internationalen Konzernsteuerplanung*, 2000, 170. For example, for 2002, Bayer AG has set two major goals: a complete group restructuring and a clear improvement in profit. Bayer plans to reorganize itself into a management holding company with four pillars that will have the legal status of stock corporations, plus three services companies. The new structure provides greater independence and flexibility to the subsidiaries. See Handelsblatt, 52/2002, 13.

[37] See Wenzl, H., *Holding*, 1996, 7.

[38] See Hintzen, B., *Die deutsche Zwischenholding als Gegenstand der internationalen Steuerplanung*, 1997, 15.

[39] See Bader, A., *Steuergestaltung mit Holdinggesellschaften*, 1998, 29; Endres, D. and Eckstein, H.-M., *Steuerrecht International*, 2001, 70.

[40] See Flick, H., *Deutsches Steuerrecht* 1989, 557; Grotherr, S., *Betriebs-Berater* 1995, 1512; Bader, A., *Steuergestaltung mit Holdinggesellschaften*, 1998, 30; Zois, A., *Cardozo Journal of International and Comparative Law* 1999, 179; Kluge, V., *Das Internationale Steuerrecht*, 2000, B 44; Fohr, I., *Besteuerungskonzept für Holdinggesellschaften*, 2001, 36; Endres,

- tax exemption of domestic and foreign dividends received;
- tax exemption of capital gains arising from the disposal of both domestic and foreign shares;
- the ability to deduct capital losses from the disposition of investments;
- the ability to deduct financing costs;
- liberal debt-to-equity ratio;
- wide treaty network with low rates of withholding taxes on dividends and interest;
- unlimited loss carry forwards;
- tax consolidation regimes; and
- no capital taxes on formation or (intragroup) transfer of shares.

3. BASIC CONCEPTS OF U.S. FEDERAL INCOME TAXATION

This section presents an overview of the U.S. federal taxation provisions for U.S. domestic corporations and partnerships since the check-the-box elections, a significant tool of U.S. international tax planning, are based on the application of different tax approaches for corporations and partnerships (branches). As holding companies are the focus of this paper, the taxation of dividend and capital gains as well as the tax-deductibility of interest expenses will be examined.

3.1. Taxation of Corporations and Corporate Shareholders

Under U.S. tax law, corporations[41] are generally treated as separate and distinct entities from their owners.[42] In general, a corporation is subject to federal income tax, regardless of whether any current or subsequent profit distributions are made to its shareholders (the so-called *classical method of taxation*).[43] Those profits are taxed in the hands of the individual shareholders when received as dividends.[44] Thus, profits earned and distributed are usually subject to double taxation, as no tax credit can be claimed at the level of the individual shareholders.[45] Taxation occurs at the corporate

D. and Dorfmueller, P., *Praxis Internationale Steuerberatung* 2001, 98; Endres, D., Dorfmueller, P. and Urse, M., *International Tax Report* 2001 I, 3; Endres, D. and Möller, M., *Corporate Taxation* 2001, E 63; Kessler, W., *Steuer Revue* 2001, 768; O'Grady, E., *Tax Notes International* 2002, 1063.

[41] According to IRC § 7701(a)(3), the term "corporation" means associations, joint-stock companies, and insurance companies but does not include partnerships.

[42] See Abrams, H. E. and Doernberg, R. L., *Essentials of United States Taxation*, 1999, 2-1; McDaniel, P. R., McMahon, M. J. Jr. and Simmons, D. L., *Federal Income Taxation of Business Organizations*, 1999, 375; Moussallem, S., *Die Besteuerung einer US-corporation*, 2001, 31.

[43] See Brumbaugh, D. L., *Tax Notes International* 1992, 235; McNulty, J. K., *Limited Liability Companies*, 1995, 684; Moussallem, S., *Die Besteuerung einer US-corporation*, 2001, 31.

[44] IRC § 61(a)(7). A dividend is included in the shareholder's gross income when received, regardless of whether the cash receipts or accrual method is used. See *Commissioner v. American Light & Traction Co.*, 156 F.2d 398 (7th Cir. 1946); *Caruth Corp. v. United States*, 865 F.2d 644 (5th Cir. 1989). See Moussallem, S., *Die Besteuerung einer US-corporation*, 2001, 32.

[45] See McNulty, J. K., *Limited Liability Companies*, 1995, 684; Haun, J., *Hybride Finanzierungsinstrumente im deutschen und US-amerikanischen Steuerrecht*, 1996, 154; McDaniel, P. R., McMahon, M. J. Jr. and Simmons, D. L., *Federal Income Taxation of Business Organizations*, 1999, 376; McNulty, J. K., *Brief Look at the Early History of the Unintegrated Corporate and Individual Income Taxes in the U.S.A.*, 2000, 874; American Chamber of Commerce in Germany e.V. and PricewaterhouseCoopers GmbH, *Steuern in den USA*, 2001, 71; CCH, *2002 U.S. Tax Master Guide*, 2001, paragraph 201; Lee, P. T. and Kowallik, A., *Internationale Wirtschaftsbriefe*, Fach 8, USA, Gruppe 2, 2001, 1086; Moussallem, S., *Die Besteuerung einer US-corporation*, 2001, 32.

level in the fiscal year during which profits are generated. Then, once the dividend distributions have been made, the distributed profits are taxed in the hands of the individual shareholders.[46]

Under current law, the most important exception to the taxation of a corporation as a separate entity is the election under Subchapter S of the IRC (§§ 1361-1379).[47] Under this provision, a corporation is treated as a flow-through entity with gains and losses reported in the shareholders' tax returns.[48] However, Subchapter S only applies to business corporations with a limited number of shareholders, i.e., not more than 75.[49] A number of restrictive conditions limit the availability of this election to corporations.[50] While Subchapter S is often referred to as an election which, in essence, permits corporations to elect to be taxed as partnerships, the operational effects under Subchapter S differ from partnership treatment.[51] Corporations that do not make the election are referred to as "C corporations";[52] corporations that choose to be treated as flow-through entities are called "S corporations".[53] In the following pages, only C corporations will be subject to examination.

3.1.1. Computation of Taxable Income

Taxable income of a corporation is typically determined by applying the same provisions that govern the taxation of individuals such that the gross income rules, the deduction rules, the accounting provisions, and the capital gains and losses rules are all pertinent.[54] However, there are a number of

---

[46] Or in liquidation. IRC §§ 11 and 301(c). See Doernberg, R. L., *Tax Notes International* 1991, 506; Sieker, K., *Internationale Wirtschaftsbriefe*, Fach 8, USA, Gruppe 2, 1993, 719; Abrams, H. E. and Doernberg, R. L., *Essentials of United States Taxation*, 1999, 2-1; McNulty, J. K., *Brief Look at the Early History of the Unintegrated Corporate and Individual Income Taxes in the U.S.A.*, 2000, 874; Endres, D. and Eckstein, H.-M., *Steuerrecht International*, 2001, 23; Lee, P. T. and Kowallik, A., *Internationale Wirtschaftsbriefe*, Fach 8, USA, Gruppe 2, 2001, 1086.

[47] For an analysis regarding the pros and cons of the election, see Zink, W. J. and Mezzo, L. J., *The Tax Adviser* 1989, 105; Frankel, A. T. and Weichholz, J., *The CPA Journal* 1994, 22; Sprohge, H. and Burt, C. J., *Management Accounting* 1994, 34; Cecil, W., Ciccotello, C. S. and Grant, T., *Journal of Accountancy* 1995, 45; Yanoshak, J., *The Tax Adviser* 1995, 42; Abrams, H. E. and Doernberg, R. L., *Essentials of United States Taxation*, 1999, 2-336.

[48] See Sieker, K., *Internationale Wirtschaftsbriefe*, Fach 8, USA, Gruppe 2, 1993, 721; McNulty, J. K., *Limited Liability Companies*, 1995, 684; McDaniel, P. R. and Ault, H. J., *Introduction to United States International Taxation*, 1998, 29; Zschiegner, H., *Internationale Wirtschaftsbriefe*, Fach 8, USA, Gruppe 2, 1998 III, 961; Abrams, H. E. and Doernberg, R. L., *Essentials of United States Taxation*, 1999, 2-342; McNulty, J. K., *Brief Look at the Early History of the Unintegrated Corporate and Individual Income Taxes in the U.S.A.*, 2000, 884; CCH, *2002 U.S. Tax Master Guide*, 2001, paragraph 301; Bittker, B. I. and Eustice, J. S., *Federal Income Taxation of Corporations and Shareholders*, 2002, paragraph 6.06.

[49] See Sieker, K., *Internationale Wirtschaftsbriefe*, Fach 8, USA, Gruppe 2, 1993, 719; Zschiegner, H., *Internationale Wirtschaftsbriefe*, Fach 8, USA, Gruppe 2, 1997 II, 895; Zschiegner, H., *Internationale Wirtschaftsbriefe*, Fach 8, USA, Gruppe 2, 1998 II, 960; Vorwold, G., *GmbH-Rundschau* 2001, 20; Eustice, J. S. and Kuntz, J. D., *Federal Income Taxation of S Corporations*, 2002, paragraph 1.03[2][b][i].

[50] IRC § 1361(b). See Abrams, H. E. and Doernberg, R. L., *Essentials of United States Taxation*, 1999, 2-336; CCH, *2002 U.S. Tax Master Guide*, 2001, paragraph 305; Bittker, B. I. and Eustice, J. S., *Federal Income Taxation of Corporations and Shareholders*, 2002, paragraph 6.02.

[51] See Zschiegner, H., *Internationale Wirtschaftsbriefe*, Fach 8, USA, Gruppe 2, 1997 II, 895; Stark, K. J. and Zolt, E. M., *European Taxation* 2000, 329; CCH, *2002 U.S. Tax Master Guide*, 2001, paragraph 335; Moussallem, S., *Die Besteuerung einer US-corporation*, 2001, 32.

[52] Corporations are referred to as "C corporations", because they are subject to the provisions of Subchapter C of the IRC (§§ 301-385). See Sieker, K., *Internationale Wirtschaftsbriefe*, Fach 8, USA, Gruppe 2, 1993, 719; Zschiegner, H., *Internationale Wirtschaftsbriefe*, Fach 8, USA, Gruppe 2, 1998 II, 960; American Chamber of Commerce in Germany e.V. and PricewaterhouseCoopers GmbH, *Steuern in den USA*, 2001, 72.

[53] See McDaniel, P. R., McMahon, M. J. Jr. and Simmons, D. L., *Federal Income Taxation of Business Organizations*, 1999, 376; Stark, K. J. and Zolt, E. M., *European Taxation* 2000, 329. For a comprehensive comparison of a S corporation with a LLC, see Jennings, R., *The National Public Accountant* 1997, 25.

[54] IRC § 61(a). See Abrams, H. E. and Doernberg, R. L., *Essentials of United States Taxation*, 1999, 1-13; American Chamber of Commerce in Germany e.V. and PricewaterhouseCoopers GmbH, *Steuern in den USA*, 2001, 79; Bittker, B. I. and Eustice, J. S., *Federal Income Taxation of Corporations and Shareholders*, 2002, paragraph 5.01[1].

significant variations from these basic income tax rules that are applicable only to corporations.[55] For example, in the application of the deduction sections, such as IRC §§ 162(a) and 165(a), the deduction rules for corporations are generally guided by the premise that all corporations are engaged in trade or business.[56] Additionally, there are a number of specific provisions which apply only to corporations, including the dividend received deduction under IRC § 243 for intercorporate dividends that effectively excludes all or part of such dividends from a corporation's taxable income.[57]

The treatment of capital gains and losses recognized by corporations differs as well.[58] According to IRC § 1212(a), capital losses are allowed only to the extent of capital gains, with a three-year carryback and a five-year carryforward of any excess losses.[59]

For most corporations, the non-applicability of the passive activity loss provisions under IRC § 469 is a very significant difference between the taxation of individuals and corporations. Under this rule, the taxpayer's ability to use deductions and credits from passive activities to offset active income, such as income from a trade or business, or from services and portfolio income such as dividends and interest, is limited. IRC § 469 applies to closely held C corporations, defined in IRC §§ 469(j)(1) and 465(a)(1)(B) as C corporations in which more than 50 percent of the stock is held at some time during the last half of the taxable year by five or fewer persons, taking into account certain attribution rules.

Corporate shareholders of U.S. **domestic corporations**, depending on the level of ownership may, in effect, exclude all or a portion of any intercorporate dividend income received, pursuant to IRC § 243 (the so-called *dividend received deduction*).[60] Under current U.S. law, the tax on intercorporate dividends primarily affects investments in public corporations by other corporations. These investments have little to do with corporate operating structures. Without some exclusion, successive taxation of dividends as distributions are made between corporations in a chain would result in multiple taxation of the dividends and would leave very little profit for distribution to the ultimate individual shareholders. If a corporate shareholder has a substantial degree of ownership in or control of the paying corporation, the argument in favor of relief from corporate taxation of dividend income is even stronger.

There are two exceptions which relate to the determination of cascading tax, i.e., the principle of including in income the dividends received at the shareholder level. First, if a corporation owns 80 percent or more of the voting stock and 80 percent or more in value of the stock

---

[55] See Abrams, H. E. and Doernberg, R. L., *Essentials of United States Taxation*, 1999, 2-47; Bittker, B. I. and Eustice, J. S., *Federal Income Taxation of Corporations and Shareholders*, 2002, paragraph 5.01[1]. For a flowchart outlining the determination of a corporation's taxable income, see CCH, *2002 U.S. Tax Master Guide*, 2001, paragraph 62.

[56] See Abrams, H. E. and Doernberg, R. L., *Essentials of United States Taxation*, 1999, 2-48. It should be noted that the IRC does not provide a comprehensive definition of "trade or business". See Meldman, R. E. and Schadewald, M. S., *A Practical Guide to U.S. Taxation of International Transactions*, 2000, 420; Doernberg, R. L., *International Taxation In a Nutshell*, 2001, 28; Bittker, B. I. and Eustice, J. S., *Federal Income Taxation of Corporations and Shareholders*, 2002, paragraph 15.02[2][a].

[57] See Zschiegner, H., *Internationale Wirtschaftsbriefe*, Fach 8, USA, Gruppe 2, 1998 II, 945; Bittker, B. I. and Lokken, L., *Federal Taxation of Income, Estates and Gifts*, 2002, paragraph 90.2.1.

[58] See McDaniel, P. R. and Ault, H. J., *Introduction to United States International Taxation*, 1998, 11; Bittker, B. I. and Lokken, L., *Federal Taxation of Income, Estates and Gifts*, 2002, paragraph 90.2.1.

[59] See Zschiegner, *Die Besteuerung von Gesellschaften*, 1990, 127; American Chamber of Commerce in Germany e.V. and PricewaterhouseCoopers GmbH, *Steuern in den USA*, 2001, 85; CCH, *2002 U.S. Tax Master Guide*, 2001, paragraph 1756; Bittker, B. I. and Eustice, J. S., *Federal Income Taxation of Corporations and Shareholders*, 2002, paragraph 5.03[3].

[60] See Raineri, W. T., *Tax Notes International* 1996, 1719; American Chamber of Commerce in Germany e.V. and PricewaterhouseCoopers GmbH, *Steuern in den USA*, 2001, 80; Moussallem, S., *Die Besteuerung einer US-corporation*, 2001, 179.

of another U.S. corporation, these affiliated companies may file a consolidated tax return[61] which eliminates dividends paid by the subsidiary to the parent in computing consolidated taxable income.[62] Hence, the profit generated within an affiliated group is only subject to corporate tax once.[63] Second, if affiliated companies choose not to file consolidated tax returns, the parent nevertheless may deduct the amount equal to all domestic dividends received from gross income under IRC § 243,[64] subject to the conditions and limitations of IRC § 243(b).[65] In case of a shareholding in excess of 80 percent, all dividends, e.g., 100 percent of the qualifying dividends, are deductible for U.S. federal tax purposes (IRC § 243(a)(3)).[66] In the case of an interest of at least 20 percent but less than 80 percent, 80 percent of the qualifying dividends are deductible for U.S. federal tax purposes.[67] Under IRC § 243(c), the intercorporate dividend deduction is limited to 70 percent for corporations that do not own 20 percent or more of the value and the voting power of the paying company's stock.[68]

In summary, at the current federal corporate tax rate of 35 percent, the maximum tax rate on dividends received by a corporation is 10.5 percent. i.e., the highest corporate tax rate of 35 percent imposed on 30 percent of the distribution included in taxable income for a less than 20 percent owner.

These rules also apply to dividends received from a **foreign corporation** that are paid out of the earnings and profits (E&P) of a taxable U.S. domestic predecessor corporation.[69] Hence, a domestic corporation is entitled to a 70 percent [or 80 percent in the case of a minimum shareholding of at least 20 percent] deduction of the U.S.-source portion of dividends paid by a foreign corporation that is at least 10 percent owned, by vote and value, by the domestic corporation.[70] The U.S.-source portion of the dividend income is the amount that maintains the same ratio to the

---

[61] IRC § 1504(A)(2). See Flick, H. F. W. and Janka, W., *Deutsches Steuerrecht* 1991 I, 1039; Zschiegner, H., *Internationale Wirtschaftsbriefe*, Fach 8, USA, Gruppe 2, 1998 III, 980; Abrams, H. E. and Doernberg, R. L., *Essentials of United States Taxation*, 1999, 2-300.

[62] IRC §§ 1501-1505. See Abrams, H. E. and Doernberg, R. L., *Essentials of United States Taxation*, 1999, 2-302; CCH, *2002 U.S. Tax Master Guide*, 2001, paragraph 237; Lee, P. T. and Kowallik, A., *Internationale Wirtschaftsbriefe*, Fach 8, USA, Gruppe 2, 2001, 1097.

[63] See Moussallem, S., *Die Besteuerung einer US-corporation*, 2001, 179.

[64] A U.S. corporation is generally allowed a 100 percent deduction for any dividends received from a foreign sales corporation (FSC) that are distributed out of E&P attributable to foreign trade income (IRC § 245(c)). In addition, a 70 percent [or 80 percent in the case of ownership of at least 20 percent of the corporation] deduction is provided for dividends received from a FSC that made the distribution out of E&P attributable to effectively connected income received or accrued by a FSC.

[65] Reg. § 1.243-4.

[66] See Zschiegner, H., *Internationale Wirtschaftsbriefe*, Fach 8, USA, Gruppe 2, 1998 III, 965; American Chamber of Commerce in Germany e.V. and PricewaterhouseCoopers GmbH, *Steuern in den USA*, 2001, 80; Lee, P. T. and Kowallik, A., *Internationale Wirtschaftsbriefe*, Fach 8, USA, Gruppe 2, 2001, 1086; Bittker, B. I. and Eustice, J. S., *Federal Income Taxation of Corporations and Shareholders*, 2002, paragraph 5.05[2].

[67] See Zschiegner, H., *Internationale Wirtschaftsbriefe*, Fach 8, USA, Gruppe 2, 1998 III, 965; Abrams, H. E. and Doernberg, R. L., *Essentials of United States Taxation*, 1999, 2-83; CCH, *2002 U.S. Tax Master Guide*, 2001, paragraph 237; Bittker, B. I. and Eustice, J. S., *Federal Income Taxation of Corporations and Shareholders*, 2002, paragraph 5.05[1].

[68] See Abrams, H. E. and Doernberg, R. L., *Essentials of United States Taxation*, 1999, 2-83; American Chamber of Commerce in Germany e.V. and PricewaterhouseCoopers GmbH, *Steuern in den USA*, 2001, 80; CCH, *2002 U.S. Tax Master Guide*, 2001, paragraph 237.

[69] IRC § 245(a). See Zschiegner, H., *Internationale Wirtschaftsbriefe*, Fach 8, USA, Gruppe 2, 1998 III, 965; CCH, *2002 U.S. Tax Master Guide*, 2001, paragraph 241; Bittker, B. I. and Eustice, J. S., *Federal Income Taxation of Corporations and Shareholders*, 2002, paragraph 5.05[4].

[70] See American Chamber of Commerce in Germany e.V. and PricewaterhouseCoopers GmbH, *Steuern in den USA*, 2001, 80; CCH, *2002 U.S. Tax Master Guide*, 2001, paragraph 241; Bittker, B. I. and Eustice, J. S., *Federal Income Taxation of Corporations and Shareholders*, 2002, paragraph 5.05[4][a].

dividends as the ratio of undistributed U.S. earnings to total undistributed earnings (IRC § 245(a)).[71] For example, a 100 percent deduction for dividends received is granted to a domestic corporation for dividends paid by a wholly owned subsidiary out of its E&P for the tax year.[72] In this case, all of the foreign subsidiary's gross income must be effectively connected with a U.S. trade or business (IRC § 245(b)).[73]

In order to prevent any abusive dividend stripping practices, IRC § 246(c) requires a minimum 45-day holding period within a 90-day period for both domestic and foreign shareholdings.[74] The deduction for dividends received creates a difference between E&P and taxable income, thus, potentially triggering the alternative minimum tax (AMT) provisions, even for corporations eligible for the 100 percent dividend received deduction.[75]

In contrast to most European countries,[76] the U.S. imposes tax on **capital gains** recognized on the sale of stock of U.S. **domestic** and **foreign corporations**. Depending on the holding period of the stock, a gain or loss recognized on its sale is characterized as either long-term or short term. Under IRC §§ 1222(3) and (4), capital gains/losses[77] on the disposition of stock held for more than 12 months are classified as long-term capital gains or losses.[78] Conversely, capital gains or losses recognized on the sale of stock held for 12 months or less are treated as short-term capital gains.[79] The excess of net long-term capital gains over net short-term capital losses is considered a net capital gain, which is included in taxable income.[80] Capital losses are permitted only as an offset to capital gains.[81] In the case of an excess of capital losses over capital gains, a three-year carry back and a five year carry forward are granted.[82]

Interest payments are generally deductible for U.S. federal tax purposes when paid or accrued - depending on the taxpayer's method of accounting for expenses - irrespective of the residence of the recipient.[83] However, there are several general limitations on a payor's ability to deduct interest payments and certain limitations on a payor's capacity to deduct interest payments made to specific foreign persons.[84] Under the IRC, related parties are required to charge an arm's length rate of interest for amounts loaned, and if no interest is determined, interest may be imputed

---

[71] See Bittker, B. I. and Lokken, L., *Federal Taxation of Income, Estates and Gifts*, 2002, paragraph 73.3.

[72] See Lee, P. T. and Kowallik, A., *Internationale Wirtschaftsbriefe*, Fach 8, USA, Gruppe 2, 2001, 1086.

[73] See American Chamber of Commerce in Germany e.V. and PricewaterhouseCoopers GmbH, *Steuern in den USA*, 2001, 80.

[74] See Garrett-Nelson, L., *Tax Notes International* 1997, 1287; Zschiegner, H., *Internationale Wirtschaftsbriefe*, Fach 8, USA, Gruppe 2, 1998 III, 965; American Chamber of Commerce in Germany e.V. and PricewaterhouseCoopers GmbH, *Steuern in den USA*, 2001, 80; CCH, *2002 U.S. Tax Master Guide*, 2001, paragraph 237; Bittker, B. I. and Eustice, J. S., *Federal Income Taxation of Corporations and Shareholders*, 2002, paragraph 5.05[7][c].

[75] IRC § 56(g)(ii). For details on the AMT, refer *infra* page 31.

[76] For the prerequisites of the exemptions in the different EU member states refer to *infra* chapter "Country-by-Country Synopsis", page 111.

[77] Stock is considered a capital asset under IRC § 1221, which provides no enumerated category.

[78] IRC § 1222. For purposes of computing the holding period, both the dates of acquisition and sale are considered. See Abrams, H. E. and Dornberg, R. L., *Essentials of United States Taxation*, 1999, 1-52.

[79] IRC §§ 1222(2) and (4). See Abrams, H. E. and Dornberg, R. L., *Essentials of United States Taxation*, 1999, 1-52.

[80] IRC § 1222(11). See Thiele, C., *Einführung in das US-amerikanische Steuerrecht*, 1997, 89; Sellers Smith, R., *West Tax Law Dictionary*, 2002.

[81] IRC § 1211(a). See CCH, *2002 U.S. Tax Master Guide*, 2001, paragraph 1752.

[82] IRC § 1212(a)(1).

[83] See Zschiegner, H., *Internationale Wirtschaftsbriefe*, Fach 8, USA, Gruppe 2, 1998 III, 973; CCH, *2002 U.S. Tax Master Guide*, 2001, paragraph 937.

[84] E.g., IRC § 163(j)(5). See Ruding, H. O., *Journal of International Taxation* 1994, 6; Zschiegner, H., *Internationale Wirtschaftsbriefe*, Fach 8, USA, Gruppe 2, 1998 III, 973; Lee, P. T. and Kowallik, A., *Internationale Wirtschaftsbriefe*, Fach 8, USA, Gruppe 2, 2001, 1095.

on the indebtedness.[85] Special corporate taxes can apply if a corporation accumulates excess profits without distributing them, however, there is no similar requirement that the U.S. corporation distribute a dividend to its shareholder.[86] Even though a transfer from a U.S. transferor may be labeled as an "interest payment", there are several statutory and judicial doctrines that could reclassify the payment as a dividend payment or otherwise, based on the facts and circumstances of the situation.[87]

3.1.2. Tax Rate Structure

Corporate tax rates are nominally progressive, ranging from 15 percent to 35 percent. According to IRC §§ 11 and 1201, the following separate rate structure applies to the taxable income of C corporations:[88]

Tab. 1: U.S. Federal Corporate Tax Rates for 2001[89]

Taxable Income				Of the Amount
Over	But Not Over	Pay	+ ...% on Excess	Over
U.S. $0	U.S. $50,000	U.S. $0	15	U.S. $0
U.S. $50,000	U.S. $75,000	U.S. $7,500	25	U.S. $50,000
U.S. $75,000	U.S. $100,000	U.S. $13,750	34	U.S. $75,000
U.S. $100,000	U.S. $335,000	U.S. $22,250	39	U.S. $100,000
U.S. $335,000	U.S. $10,000,000	U.S. $113,900	34	U.S. $335,000
U.S. $10,000,000	U.S. $15,000,000	U.S. $3,400,000	35	U.S. $10,000,000
U.S. $15,000,000	U.S. $18,333,333	U.S. $5,150,000	38	U.S. $15,000,000
U.S. $18,333,333	...	U.S. $6,416,667	35	U.S. $18,333,333

Source: CCH, Tax Guide, 2001, paragraph 219.

In practice, for all but the very smallest corporations, corporate income is basically taxed at a flat rate of 35 percent.[90]

IRC § 1201 provides that for any year in which the minimum tax rate under IRC § 11 exceeds 35 percent,[91] the minimum corporate tax rate on long-term capital gains is limited to 35 percent.[92] Given that a special tax rate applies to any net capital gain, the taxpayer computes taxable

---

[85] In general, see IRC §§ 482 and 7872.

[86] IRC § 531.

[87] See *Roth Steel Tube Co. v. Commissioner*, 800 F.2d 625 (6th Cir. 1986).

[88] See Zschiegner, H., *Internationale Wirtschaftsbriefe*, Fach 8, USA, Gruppe 2, 1998 III, 965; American Chamber of Commerce in Germany e.V. and PricewaterhouseCoopers GmbH, *Steuern in den USA*, 2001, 91.

[89] IRC §§ 11(b) and 1201(a).

[90] See Abrams, H. E. and Doernberg, R. L., *Essentials of United States Taxation*, 1999, 2-45.

[91] Excluding the five and three percent surtaxes. Under IRC § 11, if a corporation has taxable income exceeding U.S. $100,000, a five percent surtax is imposed on the excess over U.S. $100,000 up to a minimum additional tax of U.S. $11,750, i.e., 39 percent - 34 percent = 5 percent. If the taxable income exceeds U.S. $15,000,000, a three percent surtax is imposed on the excess over U.S. $15,000,000 up to the minimum tax of U.S. $100,000. This surtax is triggered when taxable income reaches U.S. $18,330,000, i.e., 38 percent - 35 percent = 3 percent. See Bittker, B. I. and Eustice, J. S., *Federal Income Taxation of Corporations and Shareholders*, 2002, paragraph 5.01[1].

[92] See Lee, P. T. and Kowallik, A., *Internationale Wirtschaftsbriefe*, Fach 8, USA, Gruppe 2, 2001, 1089; Bittker, B. I. and Eustice, J. S., *Federal Income Taxation of Corporations and Shareholders*, 2002, paragraph 5.01[2].

income, which is taxable at ordinary rates after removing the net capital gain. The full tax liability is determined by adding together these two taxes.[93] Under current law, corporate taxes do not exceed 35 percent, so this provision does not have any impact.[94]

3.1.3. Alternative Minimum Taxation

The alternative minimum tax (AMT) provisions apply to all corporations, other than S corporations and small business corporations.[95] The AMT is a 20 percent tax imposed on an expanded base of income that essentially adjusts the tax base for the determination of the corporation's income tax (IRC § 55(b)).[96] The purpose of the tax is to ensure that taxpayers with high incomes do not avoid significant tax liability by using exclusions, deductions, and credits.[97] Hence, the AMT is a safeguard against the undermining of the progressive tax rate and unfair allocation of the tax burden.[98] Mechanically, under IRC § 55(a), the AMT is an add-on tax but structurally, the AMT is a "shadow" tax system that applies a lower flat tax rate to a more broadly defined tax base than is used in computing the regular corporate tax.

Generally speaking, the tax base for the AMT is the corporation's regular taxable income increased by the tax preferences as required under IRC § 57[99] and adjusted as specified in IRC § 56 by recalculating certain deductions[100] to negate, to some extent, the acceleration of these deductions which is provided under the regular corporate tax provisions.[101] In addition, for AMT purposes, a

---

[93] See Abrams, H. E. and Doernberg, R. L., *Essentials of United States Taxation*, 1999, 1-57.

[94] See Zschiegner, H., *Internationale Wirtschaftsbriefe*, Fach 8, USA, Gruppe 2, 1998 II, 944.

[95] A corporation qualifies as a small business corporation if its average annual gross receipts for the preceding three taxable years do not exceed U.S. $5,000,000. Once a corporation qualifies as a small business corporation under the U.S. $5,000,000 test, it will remain a small business corporation not subject to AMT as long as its average gross receipts for the preceding three taxable years do not exceed U.S. $7,500,000 (IRC § 55(e)(1)(A)). In addition, under IRC § 55(e)(1)(C) any newly formed corporation will be treated as a small corporation in its first taxable year, regardless of the amount of its gross receipts. See Sieker, K., *Internationale Wirtschaftsbriefe*, Fach 8, USA, Gruppe 2, 1993, 720; Djanani, C., Brähler, G. and Lösel, C., *Internationale Wirtschaftsbriefe*, Fach 10, International, Gruppe 2, 2002, 1608.

[96] See McDaniel, P. R. and Ault, H. J., *Introduction to United States International Taxation*, 1998, 13; Zschiegner, H., *Internationale Wirtschaftsbriefe*, Fach 8, USA, Gruppe 2, 1998 III, 966; Abrams, H. E. and Doernberg, R. L., *Essentials of United States Taxation*, 1999, 2-48; CCH, *2002 U.S. Tax Master Guide*, 2001, paragraph 1401; Bittker, B. I. and Eustice, J. S., *Federal Income Taxation of Corporations and Shareholders*, 2002, paragraph 5.08[1].

[97] S.Rep. No. 99-313, 99th Cong., 2d Sess. 518-19 (1986). See Johnsen, K. M., *The CPA Journal* 1993, 81; Haun, J., *Hybride Finanzierungsinstrumente im deutschen und US-amerikanischen Steuerrecht*, 1996, 155; Jensen, P., Spikes, P. and Carter, D., *The International Tax Journal* 1998, 9; Zschiegner, H., *Internationale Wirtschaftsbriefe*, Fach 8, USA, Gruppe 2, 1998 III, 966; McDaniel, P. R., McMahon, M. J. Jr. and Simmons, D. L., *Federal Income Taxation of Business Organizations*, 1999, 380; Bittker, B. I. and Eustice, J. S., *Federal Income Taxation of Corporations and Shareholders*, 2002, paragraph 5.08[1].

[98] See C&L Deutsche Revision AG, *Besteuerung deutscher Unternehmen in den USA*, 1994, 52; Fischl, A. and Schneider, R. A., *Tax Management International Journal* 1997, 571; Anonymous, *Tax Executive* 1999 I, 349; Ernst & Young, *Doing Business in the United States*, 1999, 43; Kroschel, J., *Die Federal Income Tax der Vereinigten Staaten von Amerika*, 2000, 259; Anonymous, *Tax Executive* 2001, 308; CCH, *2002 U.S. Tax Master Guide*, 2001, paragraph 1410; Moussallem, S., *Die Besteuerung einer US-corporation*, 2001, 147.

[99] IRC § 57(a) lists the following items: (1) solid mineral - but not oil and gas - depletion allowances under IRC § 611 to the extent the deduction exceeds the taxpayer's basis for the property at the end of the year; (2) a portion of the amount by which intangible drilling and development costs deducted under IRC § 263(c) for drilling oil, gas or geothermal steam wells exceeds net income from such wells for the year; (3) interest on private activity bonds exempt from tax under IRC § 103; and (4) certain accelerated depreciation taken on property placed in service before 1987. See CCH, *2002 U.S. Tax Master Guide*, 2001, paragraph 1425; Bittker, B. I. and Eustice, J. S., *Federal Income Taxation of Corporations and Shareholders*, 2002, paragraph 5.08[2].

[100] IRC § 56(a)(2) and (3) prescribe other timing adjustments relating to mine exploration and development expenses and long-term construction contracts. See CCH, *2002 U.S. Tax Master Guide*, 2001, paragraph 1401; Bittker, B. I. and Eustice, J. S., *Federal Income Taxation of Corporations and Shareholders*, 2002, paragraph 5.08[1].

[101] See Zschiegner, H., *Internationale Wirtschaftsbriefe*, Fach 8, USA, Gruppe 2, 1998 III, 966.

special net operating loss carryover rule, presented in IRC § 56(d), must be used instead of the normal net operating loss carryover rule of IRC § 172. Under IRC § 56(d)(1), a net operating loss carryover is not permitted to reduce "alternative minimum taxable income" (AMTI)[102] to zero; the minimum AMT net operating loss carryover deduction equals 90 percent of the AMTI without regard to a deduction.[103]

The most complex, and most significant, however, is the "adjusted current earnings" (ACE) adjustment in IRC § 56(g).[104] This provision adds to the AMTI an amount equal to 75 percent of the excess of the corporation's ACE over its AMTI, computed without reference to the ACE adjustment or the AMT net operating loss deduction.[105] If the AMTI exceeds ACE, then the ACE adjustment is negative. ACE is defined in IRC § 56(g)(4) as AMTI with several enumerated adjustments.[106] These adjustments are intended to cause AMTI to more accurately reflect the corporation's economic income, according to the purpose of AMT.[107] The corporation is generally required to pay the greater of the regular income tax or the AMT.[108]

Many of the adjustments in IRC § 56 and tax preferences in IRC § 57 that are taken into account in computing the AMTI reflect timing differences with respect to regular taxable income rather than permanent exclusions from taxable income. Consequently, prior years' AMT is treated to some extent as a prepayment of the current year's regular taxes.[109] To the extent that regular taxable income in any year exceeds tentative AMT as defined in IRC § 55(b), IRC § 53 allows a portion of the AMT liability from prior years as a credit against the regular tax liability.[110] For corporations, the portion of the credit for prior minimum tax paid is limited to a portion of the prior AMT liability attributable to adjustments and preferences included in AMTI.[111] AMT from any number of prior years may be credited against regular tax in a particular year, but the carryforward credit available

---

[102] According to IRC §§ 55(d)(2) and (3), a tax-exemption of U.S. $40,000 is allowed to a corporation, but is reduced by 25 percent of the amount by which the corporation's AMTI exceeds U.S. $150,000. Hence, for a corporation with AMTI of U.S. $310,000 or more, no exemption is available. The amount of tax resulting from this computation is termed "tentative minimum tax" by IRC § 55(b). See McDaniel, P. R. and Ault, H. J., *Introduction to United States International Taxation*, 1998, 14; Abrams, H. E. and Doernberg, R. L., *Essentials of United States Taxation*, 1999, 2-48; Bittker, B. I. and Lokken, L., *Federal Taxation of Income, Estates and Gifts*, 2002, paragraph 111.4.5.

[103] See Zschiegner, H., *Internationale Wirtschaftsbriefe*, Fach 8, USA, Gruppe 2, 1998 III, 966; American Chamber of Commerce in Germany e.V. and PricewaterhouseCoopers GmbH, *Steuern in den USA*, 2001, 92; Bittker, B. I. and Eustice, J. S., *Federal Income Taxation of Corporations and Shareholders*, 2002, paragraph 5.08[3].

[104] See Abrams, H. E. and Doernberg, R. L., *Essentials of United States Taxation*, 1999, 2-50; CCH, *2002 U.S. Tax Master Guide*, 2001, paragraph 1440; Djanani, C., Brähler, G. and Lösel, C., *Internationale Wirtschaftsbriefe*, Fach 10, International, Gruppe 2, 2002, 1610.

[105] See Zschiegner, H., *Internationale Wirtschaftsbriefe*, Fach 8, USA, Gruppe 2, 1998 III, 967; CCH, *2002 U.S. Tax Master Guide*, 2001, paragraph 1401; Bittker, B. I. and Eustice, J. S., *Federal Income Taxation of Corporations and Shareholders*, 2002, paragraph 5.08[5]; Bittker, B. I. and Lokken, L., *Federal Taxation of Income, Estates and Gifts*, 2002, paragraph 111.4.4.

[106] See Djanani, C., Brähler, G. and Lösel, C., *Internationale Wirtschaftsbriefe*, Fach 10, International, Gruppe 2, 2002, 1610.

[107] See Abrams, H. E. and Doernberg, R. L., *Essentials of United States Taxation*, 1999, 2-50; CCH, *2002 U.S. Tax Master Guide*, 2001, paragraph 1440; Bittker, B. I. and Eustice, J. S., *Federal Income Taxation of Corporations and Shareholders*, 2002, paragraph 5.08[5].

[108] See McDaniel, P. R. and Ault, H. J., *Introduction to United States International Taxation*, 1998, 15; Zschiegner, H., *Internationale Wirtschaftsbriefe*, Fach 8, USA, Gruppe 2, 1998 III, 966; Hinchman, G., *Financial Executive* 2001, 67; Bittker, B. I. and Eustice, J. S., *Federal Income Taxation of Corporations and Shareholders*, 2002, paragraph 5.08[1].

[109] See Haun, J., *Hybride Finanzierungsinstrumente im deutschen und US-amerikanischen Steuerrecht*, 1996, 155; Bittker, B. I. and Lokken, L., *Federal Taxation of Income, Estates and Gifts*, 2002, paragraph 111.4.6.

[110] See McDaniel, P. R. and Ault, H. J., *Introduction to United States International Taxation*, 1998, 15; Abrams, H. E. and Doernberg, R. L., *Essentials of United States Taxation*, 1999, 2-49; American Chamber of Commerce in Germany e.V. and PricewaterhouseCoopers GmbH, *Steuern in den USA*, 2001, 92.

[111] IRC § 53(d)(1)(A) and (B)(iv). It should be noted that mechanically AMT is not the entire amount resulting from multiplying AMTI by the AMT rate but only the amount by which the tentative AMT exceeds the regular tax liability for the year.

for future years is, of course, reduced by the amount of the credit claimed.[112] The carryforward credit is available in the first year the corporation incurs a regular tax liability, irrespective of whether or not the items that gave rise to the previous AMT liability were brought back into the regular income tax base in that year.[113]

3.2. Taxation of Partnerships and Corporate Partners

Subchapter K (IRC §§ 701-777) prescribes a coordinated and detailed treatment of partnership transactions.[114] The provisions of Subchapter K are highly interrelated. Few, if any of its provisions can be studied or wholly understood in isolation.[115]

Partnerships[116] are treated as flow-through entities for U.S. federal tax purposes.[117] Thus, they are an aggregate of the partners, not a taxable unit, although the partnership must file a partnership return.[118] Therefore, the partners are each taxed on a pro rata share of the firm's income, whether or not the income is distributed to them.[119] Under the prevailing conduit approach, the character of such items as ordinary income, capital gains and losses, tax-exempt interest, and so forth, passes through to the partners.[120] A corporate partner's distributive share of partnership items is included in its corporate income tax return.

---

[112] IRC § 53(a).

[113] See Bittker, B. I. and Lokken, L., *Federal Taxation of Income, Estates and Gifts*, 2002, paragraph 111.4.6; Joint Committee on Taxation, *Alternative Minimum Tax*, 2002, 4. Presume that in year 01 an accelerated deduction of U.S. $1,000 reduces regular taxable income and is treated as a tax preference item (IRC § 57) subject to the AMT. In a later year, regular taxable income will be U.S. $1,000 higher than it would have been without the deduction.

[114] H.R. Rep. No. 83-1337, 83d Cong., 2d Sess. 65 (1954); S. Rep. No. 1622, 83d Cong., 2d Sess. 89 (1954), 954 WL 6064 (Leg.Hist.).

[115] See Stark, K. J. and Zolt, E. M., *European Taxation* 2000, 327.

[116] According to IRC § 761, a "partnership" includes a syndicate, group, pool, joint venture, or other unincorporated organization that carries on any business, financial operation, or venture, and that is not, within the meaning of the IRC, a trust, estate or corporation. See Zschiegner, *Die Besteuerung von Gesellschaften*, 1990, 134; Zschiegner, H., *Internationale Wirtschaftsbriefe*, Fach 8, USA, Gruppe 2, 1998 IV, 985; CCH, *2002 U.S. Tax Master Guide*, 2001, paragraph 401; Ernst & Young, *The Ernst & Young Tax Guide 2002*, 2002, 175.

[117] IRC § 701. See Pöllath, R., *Unternehmensbesteuerung nach dem DBA-USA*, 1990, 251; Zschiegner, *Die Besteuerung von Gesellschaften*, 1990, 134; Zschiegner, H., *Internationale Wirtschaftsbriefe*, Fach 8, USA, Gruppe 2, 1997 II, 897; McDaniel, P. R. and Ault, H. J., *Introduction to United States International Taxation*, 1998, 28; Abrams, H. E. and Doernberg, R. L., *Essentials of United States International Taxation*, 1999, 306; Isenbergh, J., *International Taxation*, 2000, 25; Stark, K. J. and Zolt, E. M., *European Taxation* 2000, 326; American Chamber of Commerce in Germany e.V. and PricewaterhouseCoopers GmbH, *Steuern in den USA*, 2001, 129; CCH, *2002 U.S. Tax Master Guide*, 2001, paragraph 417; Ernst & Young, *The Ernst & Young Tax Guide 2002*, 2002, 175; Willis, A. B., Pennell, J., Postlewaite, P. F. and Lipton, R., *Partnership Taxation*, 2002, paragraph 9.01[1].

[118] IRC §§ 701, 6031. Annual information reporting on Form 1065 is required regardless of whether the partnership has taxable income for the taxable year. Moreover, the partnership must send a copy of Schedule K-1 (Form 1065) to each partner. See Veltins, A. M., *Das Recht der U.S. partnership und limited partnership einschließlich ihrer Besteuerung*, 1984, 110; Zschiegner, H., *Internationale Wirtschaftsbriefe*, Fach 8, USA, Gruppe 2, 1998 IV, 991; McDaniel, P. R., McMahon, M. J. Jr. and Simmons, D. L., *Federal Income Taxation of Business Organizations*, 1999, 375; CCH, *2002 U.S. Tax Master Guide*, 2001, paragraph 404; Ernst & Young, *The Ernst & Young Tax Guide 2002*, 2002, 175. A partnership return is more than just an information return, however, because audits and adjustments with respect to partnership items must be conducted at the partnership level, not the individual partner level, except in the case of certain small partnerships (IRC §§ 6221-6233). See Willis, A. B., Pennell, J., Postlewaite, P. F. and Lipton, R., *Partnership Taxation*, 2002, paragraph 20.01.

[119] See Veltins, A. M., *Das Recht der U.S. partnership und limited partnership einschließlich ihrer Besteuerung*, 1984, 111; McDaniel, P. R. and Ault, H. J., *Introduction to United States International Taxation*, 1998, 28; Abrams, H. E. and Doernberg, R. L., *Essentials of United States International Taxation*, 1999, 3-15; Stark, K. J. and Zolt, E. M., *European Taxation* 2000, 326; CCH, *2002 U.S. Tax Master Guide*, 2001, paragraph 404.

[120] IRC § 702. See Zschiegner, H., *Internationale Wirtschaftsbriefe*, Fach 8, USA, Gruppe 2, 1997 II, 897; Middleton, C. I., *Journal of Partnership Taxation* 1999, 320; CCH, *2002 U.S. Tax Master Guide*, 2001, paragraph 423; Ernst &

In many instances, however, the IRC treats a partnership as a separate entity. For example, most accounting elections are made at the partnership level, and partnership returns are audited at the entity level (IRC §§ 6221-6231).[121] Additionally, the partnership is treated as a separate entity with respect to transactions between the partnership and a partner acting in a capacity other than as a member of the partnership (IRC § 707(a)).[122] These provisions reflect general legislative preference for a conduit approach, tempered by a variety of separate entity rules designed chiefly for administrative convenience.

But this conduit approach does introduce some accounting complexities in that it requires the separate computation of the various special items of partnership income, gain, loss or credit, and more importantly, creates the problem of determining the amount and character of each partners' distributive share of each of the various items. Determining the character of income can be important because IRC § 1(h) provides a preferential rate for capital gains.[123]

Partnership taxable income is computed following the same provisions that rule the computation of taxable income for any individual engaged in business, with a few specific modifications.[124] IRC §§ 702(a) and 703(a)(1) require certain items that are included in the computation of a partner's income tax liability be segregated and separately stated on the partnership's return.[125] This rule applies to items whose taxable status is affected by the tax situation of the individual partner. Aggregate partnership taxable income or loss, exclusive of the separately stated items and non-allowable deductions, is computed under the general rules regarding gross income and deductions. In this regard, the partnership has its own accounting period and accounting methods, although IRC § 706(b) restricts the partnership's ability to choose a taxable year that does not coincide with the taxable year of a majority of its partners.[126] Although, in general, partnership business income is computed on an entity basis, because of the passive loss limitation of IRC § 469,

---

Young, *The Ernst & Young Tax Guide 2002*, 2002, 175; McKee, W. S., Nelson, W. F. and Whitmire, R. L., *Federal Taxation of Federal Taxation of Partnerships and Partners*, 2002, paragraph 1.01[1]. Individual partners are subject to graduated rates that reach a maximum of approximately 40 percent with respect to ordinary income and 20 percent with respect to certain capital gains. There are other rates for other capital gains. Moreover, as corporations, they are subject to AMT rules that can result in an increase in the overall effective tax rate. See Zschiegner, H., *Internationale Wirtschaftsbriefe*, Fach 8, USA, Gruppe 2, 1998 I, 924; Reimer, M., *Die steuerliche Erfassung privater Veräußerungsgewinne*, 2001, 119; Ernst & Young, *The Ernst & Young Tax Guide 2002*, 2002, 244.

[121] See CCH, *2002 U.S. Tax Master Guide*, 2001, paragraph 415.

[122] See Abrams, H. E. and Doernberg, R. L., *Essentials of United States Taxation*, 1999, 3-111.

[123] For taxpayers in the 15 percent marginal bracket, the maximum rate on capital gains is generally 20 percent. Thus, an individual partner who is otherwise subject to tax at a higher marginal rate receives a significant advantage when capital gains realized by the partnership retain that character when taxed to the partner.

[124] IRC § 703(a)(2). Reg. § 1.703-1(a)(2). A partnership has its own taxable year under IRC § 706(b)(1). IRC § 706(a) provides that a partner includes the distributive share of partnership items in the taxable year in which or with which the partnership year ends. If the partnership's freedom to choose its taxable year were unfettered, this rule would permit significant tax deferral. Individual partners, who almost invariably use a calendar year, could cause the partnership to elect a fiscal year ending January 31. Thus, all of the income of the partnership from February through December would not be reportable by the partners until the next calendar year. To prevent this type of avoidance, IRC § 706(b) restricts the partnership's choice of its taxable year. In general, a partnership must adopt the same taxable year as any one or more of its partners that have an aggregate interest in partnership profits and capital of more than 50 percent. If there is not a partner with more than a 50 percent interest or a majority group with the same taxable year, the partnership must adopt the same taxable year as all of the "principal partners", who are the partners with a five percent or more interest in profits and capital. See Zschiegner, *Die Besteuerung von Gesellschaften*, 1990, 137; Zschiegner, H., *Internationale Wirtschaftsbriefe*, Fach 8, USA, Gruppe 2, 1998 IV, 991; Abrams, H. E. and Doernberg, R. L., *Essentials of United States Taxation*, 1999, 3-234; CCH, *2002 U.S. Tax Master Guide*, 2001, paragraph 416; Fuller, J. P., *Tax Notes International* 2002, 1082.

[125] Regs. §§ 1.703-1(a) and 1.702-1(a)(1)-(8). See CCH, *2002 U.S. Tax Master Guide*, 2001, paragraph 417.

[126] See CCH, *2002 U.S. Tax Master Guide*, 2001, paragraph 416; Flick, H. F. W., *Internationales Steuerrecht* 2001 I, 2; McKee, W. S., Nelson, W. F. and Whitmire, R. L., *Federal Taxation of Partnerships and Partners*, 2002, paragraph 9.04[1]; Willis, A. B., Pennell, J., Postlewaite, P. F. and Lipton, R., *Partnership Taxation*, 2002, paragraph 9.05[2].

it may be necessary for a partnership to separately state the net income or loss from each individual business "activity" that it conducts. This segregation is always required for limited partnerships.[127]

Once the taxable income of the partnership is computed, aside from the special modifications for treating the partnership itself as an accounting entity, the approach shifts. This shift is accomplished by requiring each partner to include a share of income, deductions, or losses in an individual tax return along with any other taxable income for the year. This applies even in cases when partners report using the cash method,[128] and since the partnership uses the accrual method,[129] the partners have not actually received payment of the income item. Because each partner is entitled to a distributive share of separately stated deduction items and credits, as well as any residual losses and deduction items accrued by the partnership, even if not paid, the taxation of a cash method partner is affected.

The partnership losses - including capital losses - that may be recognized by a partner are limited to the amount of the adjusted basis - before reduction by the current year's losses - of a partner's interest in the partnership at the end of the partnership taxable year in which the losses occurred.[130] Any disallowed loss is carried forward to and may be deducted by the partner in subsequent partnership taxable years to the extent that the basis exceeds zero before deducting the loss.[131] Techniques that have been used to increase a partner's basis so that losses that otherwise would not be available can be deducted include:

(1) making additional contributions to the capital of the partnership;[132]
(2) refraining from drawing salary or other distributions from the partnership; and
(3) increasing the partner's share of partnership liability if this is permitted under the substantial economic effect.[133]

Since partnership income is computed on the basis of the partnership's accounting period, the attribution to the partners is normally made only at the end of that period.[134]

3.3. Corporation v. Partnership

In the following paragraphs, distinctions between the facts presented above will be drawn.

---

[127] See CCH, *2002 U.S. Tax Master Guide*, 2001, paragraph 427.

[128] See Zschiegner, H., *Internationale Wirtschaftsbriefe*, Fach 8, USA, Gruppe 2, 1998 II, 944; CCH, *2002 U.S. Tax Master Guide*, 2001, paragraph 439; Vorwold, G., *Steuer und Wirtschaft* 2002, 235.

[129] See Zschiegner, H., *Internationale Wirtschaftsbriefe*, Fach 8, USA, Gruppe 2, 1998 II, 944; CCH, *2002 U.S. Tax Master Guide*, 2001, paragraph 439; Vorwold, G., *Steuer und Wirtschaft* 2002, 236.

[130] IRC § 704(d). See Abrams, H. E. and Doernberg, R. L., *Essentials of United States Taxation*, 1999, 3-175.

[131] Reg. § 1.704-1(d). See Middleton, C. I., *Journal of Partnership Taxation* 1999, 324.

[132] No gain or loss is recognized, either by the partnership or by any of its partners, upon a contribution of property in exchange for a partnership interest (IRC § 721(a)). This is true whether the contribution is made to an existing partnership or to a newly formed partnership, pursuant to Reg. § 1.721-1. See Middleton, C. I., *Journal of Partnership Taxation* 1999, 328; Stark, K. J. and Zolt, E. M., *European Taxation* 2000, 329.

[133] Allocations have economic effect if they are consistent with the underlying economic arrangement of the partners. For example, a limited partner who has no risk under the partnership agreement other than the initial capital contribution generally may not be allocated losses attributable to a partnership recourse liability to the extent such losses exceed the capital contribution. These recourse losses generally must be allocated to the partners - usually the general partners - who bear the ultimate burden of discharging the partnership's liabilities. Non-recourse deductions are deemed to lack economic effect and, consequently, must be allocated according to the partner's interest in the partnership (Reg. § 1.704-2). See Middleton, C. I., *Journal of Partnership Taxation* 1999, 328.

[134] IRC § 706(a). See Veltins, A. M., *Das Recht der U.S. partnership und limited partnership einschließlich ihrer Besteuerung*, 1984, 116; CCH, *2002 U.S. Tax Master Guide*, 2001, paragraph 404.

Organization

Shareholders do not realize gains or losses from contributing property to a C corporation if the shareholder is in a specified control relationship with the corporation.[135] In other cases, the transfer of property induces the shareholder to recognize gains or losses on the contribution. Substantially identical provisions are generally applicable to contributions of property by partners to a partnership.[136] The basis of the property carries over to the partnership[137] and also determines the partner's basis for an interest in the partnership.[138]

Taxable Year

C corporations are able to choose their own taxable years,[139] whereas partnerships must use the taxable year of the majority of partners or the principal partners unless specific business purposes for using differing taxable years are established.[140]

Taxability of Income

C corporations are taxed on the income generated by the corporation. Corporate profits are taxable again when distributed to shareholders.[141] In contrast thereto, partnerships are not taxpayers as such,[142] and partners are taxed on a pro rata share of the partnership's income. Under the flow-through approach, the character of such items as ordinary income, capital gains and losses, tax-exempt interest, etc., passes through to the partners.[143]

Deductibility of Losses

C corporations deduct their own losses, subject to carryback and carryforward rules applicable to net operating losses and capital losses. Shareholders are not able to use excess corporate losses[144] but may, however, deduct losses on worthless stock, usually as capital losses unless the shares are IRC § 1244 stock.[145] Conversely, partners are permitted to deduct partnership losses to the extent of the adjusted basis for each partner's interest in the partnership.[146] The share of partnership liabilities

---

[135] IRC § 351. Under this rule, gains or losses are not recognized unless the taxpayer-transferor (1) transfers property to a corporation; (2) receives stock in exchange; and (3) is in control of the corporation instantly after the transfer along with other transferors, if any. See Shakow, D. J., *The Taxation of Corporations, Partnerships, and Their Owners*, 1997, 28; Abrams, H. E. and Doernberg, R. L., *Essentials of United States Taxation*, 1999, 2-12; Bittker, B. I. and Eustice, J. S., *Federal Income Taxation of Corporations and Shareholders*, 2002, paragraph 3.14.

[136] IRC § 721.

[137] IRC § 723.

[138] IRC § 722. See Abrams, H. E. and Doernberg, R. L., *Essentials of United States Taxation*, 1999, 3-4.

[139] See Bittker, B. I. and Eustice, J. S., *Federal Income Taxation of Corporations and Shareholders*, 2002, paragraph 5.07.

[140] See *supra* note 124.

[141] See Sieker, K., *Internationale Wirtschaftsbriefe*, Fach 8, USA, Gruppe 2, 1993, 719; McNulty, J. K., *Limited Liability Companies*, 1995, 685; Stark, K. J. and Zolt, E. M., *European Taxation* 2000, 329.

[142] IRC § 701.

[143] IRC § 702.

[144] See McNulty, J. K., *Limited Liability Companies*, 1995, 685; Middleton, C. I., *Journal of Partnership Taxation* 1999, 306; Stark, K. J. and Zolt, E. M., *European Taxation* 2000, 329.

[145] For losses on "Section 1244 stock", refer Bittker, B. I. and Eustice, J. S., *Federal Income Taxation of Corporations and Shareholders*, 2002, paragraph 4.24.

[146] IRC § 704(d). See Veltins, A. M., *Das Recht der U.S. partnership und limited partnership einschließlich ihrer Besteuerung*, 1984, 119; Abrams, H. E. and Doernberg, R. L., *Essentials of United States Taxation*, 1999, 3-175.

allocated to the partners increases each partners' bases.[147] Therefore, the use of partnerships might be favorable for start-up business ventures that are expected to initially incur substantial losses.

Non-Liquidating Distributions

Distributions from C corporations to their shareholders are generally taxed as ordinary dividends and do not affect the share's basis. If corporations distribute appreciated property, the difference between the property's FMV and its adjusted basis must be recognized as income by the corporations. By recognizing these amounts, double taxation of corporate income on that property is assured.[148] In contrast thereto, no income is generally recognized by the partners upon receiving distributions from the partnership.[149] In cases in that the value of the distribution exceeds the partners' basis for a partnership interest, the gain is treated as a capital gain.[150] Distributions in kind by the partnerships to the partners do not trigger any tax consequences, i.e., neither gains nor losses.[151]

Liquidations

A corporation generally realizes capital gains or losses upon receipt of liquidating distributions of appreciated or depreciated property.[152] Shareholders usually recognize capital gains or losses on the complete liquidation of a corporation,[153] unless it is the liquidation of a collapsible corporation that gives rise to ordinary income[154] or if a subsidiary, which might be non-recognizable, performs a carryover-basis exchange.[155] When liquidating a partnership, the partners recognize income only if the cash distributed is greater than the basis of their interests.[156] Partners ordinarily recognize a loss only if there is no distribution in kind.[157]

---

[147] IRC §§ 722 and 752. This is not achieved even by S corporations.

[148] IRC § 301. See Abrams, H. E. and Doernberg, R. L., *Essentials of United States Taxation*, 1999, 2-87; Bittker, B. I. and Eustice, J. S., *Federal Income Taxation of Corporations and Shareholders*, 2002, chapter 9.

[149] See Dickenson, H., *The Practical Tax Lawyer* 2001, 12.

[150] IRC § 731(a). See Abrams, H. E. and Doernberg, R. L., *Essentials of United States Taxation*, 1999, 3-7; McKee, W. S., Nelson, W. F. and Whitmire, R. L., *Federal Taxation of Partnerships and Partners*, 2002, paragraph 1.01 [2].

[151] IRC § 731(b). See Veltins, A. M., *Das Recht der U.S. partnership und limited partnership einschließlich ihrer Besteuerung*, 1984, 119.

[152] IRC § 336. See Abrams, H. E. and Doernberg, R. L., *Essentials of United States Taxation*, 1999, 2-181; Stark, K. J. and Zolt, E. M., *European Taxation* 2000, 329.

[153] IRC § 331. See McDaniel, P. R. and Ault, H. J., *Introduction to United States International Taxation*, 1998, 16; Abrams, H. E. and Doernberg, R. L., *Essentials of United States Taxation*, 1999, 2-179.

[154] IRC § 341.

[155] IRC §§ 332, 334(b) and 337. See Abrams, H. E. and Doernberg, R. L., *Essentials of United States Taxation*, 1999, 2-194.

[156] See Ricketts, R. and Masselli, J., *Taxes* 2001, 42.

[157] IRC §§ 731 and 736. See Veltins, A. M., *Das Recht der U.S. partnership und limited partnership einschließlich ihrer Besteuerung*, 1984, 113; Abrams, H. E. and Doernberg, R. L., *Essentials of United States Taxation*, 1999, 3-13; Willis, A. B., Pennell, J., Postlewaite, P. F. and Lipton, R., *Partnership Taxation*, 2002, paragraphs 9.06[4].

SECTION 2: TAX PLANNING GOALS

Many outbound transfers of assets to foreign corporations are to countries with tax rates higher than or equal to the U.S. rate.[158] Thus, tax avoidance is not the motive for such transfers. Nevertheless, all other considerations being equal, a U.S. entity generally would prefer to make its foreign investment in or through a tax haven in order to minimize its global effective tax burden. A tax haven is a jurisdiction where either locally sourced income or residents are subject to no or low taxation.[159]

Taxpayers are permitted under tax law to structure their investments in ways that minimize their tax liability, provided that they do not violate the letter or the intent of the law.[160] To minimize current tax liability, taxpayers often attempt to defer the recognition of taxable income.[161] One way to do this is to shift income-generating activities to a foreign entity that is outside U.S. tax jurisdiction.[162] A foreign corporation is the most suitable entity for such an arrangement because, unlike a partnership, it is not a conduit through which income is taxed directly in the hands of the owner.[163] Foreign taxes increase a U.S. MNC's total tax liability only to the extent they are not subject to a credit for U.S. tax purposes.[164] FTC purports to preserve capital export neutrality by allowing U.S. MNCs to offset their U.S. tax liability with taxes paid abroad.[165] However, as the indirect FTC is limited in both magnitude[166] and type (different baskets),[167] the primary goal of a U.S. MNC with operations abroad is to avoid any excess FTCs, where the foreign tax rate exceeds the U.S. tax rate.[168] With respect to U.S. taxes, the U.S. basically collects any residual U.S. taxes on low-tax foreign-source income.[169] Nevertheless, foreign-source income can give rise to opportunities to defer, or even permanently reduce, U.S. taxes.[170]

As a result of the potential for abuse, U.S. Congress has enacted several provisions to restrict the availability of tax deferral, i.e., deferral is available only on the active business profits of U.S.-owned foreign affiliates which are separately incorporated as subsidiaries abroad.[171]

---

[158] The classification of an entity as a foreign corporation for U.S. tax purposes is an important consideration. IRC § 7701(a)(5) defines a foreign corporation as one that is not domestic. A domestic corporation is a corporation that is created or organized in the U.S. See Lipton, R. M. and Thomas, J. T., *Journal of Partnership Taxation* 1996, 203; Isenbergh, J., *International Taxation*, 2000, 24; Tello, C. P., *Tax Management International Journal* 2001, 163.

[159] See Dreßler, G., *Gewinn- und Vermögensverlagerungen in Niedrigsteuerländer und ihre steuerliche Überprüfung*, 2000, 26; Isenbergh, J., *International Taxation*, 2000, 16; Meldman, R. E. and Schadewald, M. S., *A Practical Guide to U.S. Taxation of International Transactions*, 2000, 345; Mukadi Ngoy, J., *Journal of International Taxation* 2001, 38.

[160] BVerfG, resolution dated April 4, 1959, 1 BvL 23, 34/57, BVerfGE 9, 237; BFH, decision dated March 16, 1993, XI R 52/90, BStBl. II 1993, 564. See Wagner, F. W. and Dirrigl, H., *Die Steuerplanung der Unternehmung*, 1980, 8; Bremer, S., *Der Holdingstandort Bundesrepublik Deutschland*, 1996, 52; Grothern, S., *Grundlagen der internationalen Steuerplanung*, 2000, 7; Meldman, R. E. and Schadewald, M. S., *A Practical Guide to U.S. Taxation of International Transactions*, 2000, 339.

[161] See Kessler, W., *Die Euro-Holding*, 1996, 89; Dagan, T., *Virginia Tax Review* 1998, 409; Sharp, W. M. Sr., *Tax Notes International* 1998, 692; Dilworth, R. H. and Andrus, J. L., *Tax Law and Practice*, 2001, 1096.

[162] See Meldman, R. E. and Schadewald, M. S., *A Practical Guide to U.S. Taxation of International Transactions*, 2000, 340.

[163] See McDaniel, P. R., McMahon, M. J. Jr. and Simmons, D. L., *Federal Income Taxation of Business Organizations*, 1999, 375; Moussallem, S., *Die Besteuerung einer US-corporation*, 2001, 31.

[164] See Newberry, K. J. and Dhaliwal, D. S., *Journal of Accounting Research* 2001, 646.

[165] See Peroni, R. J., *University of Miami Law Review* 1997, 977; Dagan, T., *Virginia Tax Review* 1998, 394; Abrams, H. E. and Doernberg, R. L., *Essentials of United States Taxation*, 1999, 4-3; Wells, B., *Tax Executive* 2001, 366.

[166] For details on the limitation see *infra* page 51.

[167] For details on the basket system see *infra* page 53.

[168] For details on the U.S. federal tax rate structure see *infra* page 30.

[169] See Goldberg, S. H. and Alpert, H. H., *Journal of Taxation* 1994, 5.

[170] See Spudowski, M. A. and Sutro, P. J., *Journal of International Taxation* 1999, 16.

[171] See *infra* page 83.

1. AVOIDANCE AND MINIMIZATION OF FOREIGN WITHHOLDING TAXES

One method of avoiding taxation is to invest through a foreign corporation incorporated in a tax haven. Because the foreign corporation is a resident of the tax haven, the income it earns is subject domestically to no or low taxes.[172] Tax haven countries may also have provisions limiting the exchange of financial and commercial information.[173] A tax haven can, in effect, be created by an income tax treaty. In an optimal tax scenario, under an income tax treaty between Country A, an EU member state, and Country B, a jurisdiction outside the EU, residents of Country A are subject to a withholding tax of zero percent on dividend and interest income sourced in Country B. Country C, the U.S., and Country A have a similar treaty. The U.S. does not have a treaty with Country B or the treaty tax rate on dividend and interest income is higher, e.g., five percent. A U.S. corporation can create a foreign subsidiary in Country A and use that subsidiary to make investments in Country B. If the Country B investment income had been earned directly by the U.S. corporation, it would be subject to a, e.g., 25 percent withholding tax in the event that no income tax treaty exists between Country B and the U.S.[174] As a result of investing through the foreign subsidiary created in Country A, the U.S. parent corporation pays zero percent in foreign taxes on the income earned, that is, zero percent to Country B and zero percent to Country A.

In most cases, it might not be possible to completely avoid paying any foreign withholding taxes. Typically, a five percent withholding tax is imposed on dividend income incurred by substantial shareholders. The definition of the term "substantial shareholding", i.e., the required threshold, is important as, under most existing income tax treaties, a reduced foreign withholding tax rate may be applied, as compared to portfolio investments. Under Art. 10 of the **OECD model tax convention**, a significant shareholding is defined as a direct ownership of at least 25 percent of a company's capital.[175] According to the **1996 U.S. model income tax convention**, a substantial shareholding means a direct participation of at least ten percent of the voting stock of the company paying the dividends.[176] The following table summarizes the **treaty policy** regarding the meaning of "substantial shareholding" and the variations in the levels of withholding tax rates on dividends received by a U.S. MNC.[177]

---

[172] See Meldman, R. E. and Schadewald, M. S., *A Practical Guide to U.S. Taxation of International Transactions*, 2000, 346; Mukadi Ngoy, J., *Journal of International Taxation* 2001, 38.

[173] See Meldman, R. E. and Schadewald, M. S., *A Practical Guide to U.S. Taxation of International Transactions*, 2000, 346; Mukadi Ngoy, J., *Journal of International Taxation* 2001, 39.

[174] See American Chamber of Commerce in Germany e.V. and PricewaterhouseCoopers GmbH, *Steuern in den USA*, 2001, 77.

[175] See OECD, *Model Tax Convention*, 2000.

[176] Art. 10(2)(a) of the 1996 U.S. model income tax convention. See Abrams, H. E. and Doernberg, R. L., *Essentials of United States Taxation*, 1999, 4-74; Isenbergh, J., *International Taxation*, 2000, 224; Doernberg, R. L., *International Taxation In a Nutshell*, 2001, 126; Lowell, C. H. and Governale, J. P., *US International Taxation*, 2002, paragraph 9.01[2][d].

[177] For tax rates on interest and royalties, see Department of the Treasury, *U.S. Tax Treaties*, 2001, 31.

Treaty Withholding Tax Rates on Dividends Received by U.S. MNCs from Substantial Shareholdings in Selected EU Member States plus Japan and Switzerland

Payor's Country of Residence	Actual Rate	Minimum Percentage Required
Austria	5%	10% of the voting stock
Belgium	5%	10% of the voting power
Denmark	5%	10% of the share capital
France	5%	10% of the voting stock
Germany	5%	10% of the voting shares
Ireland	5%	10% of the voting stock
Japan	10%	10% of the voting shares
Luxembourg	0%	25% of the voting stock[178]
	5%	10% of the voting stock
The Netherlands	5%	10% of the voting power
Spain	10%	25% of the voting stock
Switzerland	5%	10% of the voting stock

After the enactment of the EU Parent-Subsidiary Directive,[179] the focus for the reduction or elimination of withholding taxes is on non-EU payors and recipients.[180] Due to nil withholding taxes on dividend routings within the EU, new tax planning strategies were designed for ultimate parent companies located outside the EU.[181] The use of such structures is referred to as "Treaty Shopping" or "Directive Shopping".[182]

When minimizing the overall withholding tax burden, a non-EU parent company must overcome two hurdles. Firstly, it must bundle its EU investments in order to benefit from the tax-neutral flow-through of dividends within the EU. Secondly, it must locate its European holding company in a jurisdiction that does not withhold taxes on any dividends paid outside the EU, e.g., to the U.S.

---

[178] The stock must have been held during an uninterrupted period of at least two years preceding the date of distribution. For details on the new U.S./Luxembourg income tax treaty, refer *infra* page 139.

[179] Council Directive No. 90/435 on the Common System of Taxation Applicable in the Case of Parent Companies and Subsidiaries of Different Member States, dated July 23, 1990, *Official Journal of the European Communities*, dated August 8, 1990, L 225. See Taylor, J. C. and Hannum, C. E., *Tax Notes International* 1997, 91; Bolanz, G., *Die EU-Holding als strategisches Gestaltungsinstrument in der Steuerplanung*, 1998, 22; Zois, A., *Cardozo Journal of International and Comparative Law* 1999, 181; EBIT, *Tax Analysis*, 2002, 5.

[180] See Ruding, H. O., *Journal of International Taxation* 1994, 7.

[181] See Ruding, H. O., *Journal of International Taxation* 1994, 7.

[182] See Windholtz, T. F. and Bernot, J. E., *Journal of International Taxation* 1991 I, 88; Arnold, B. J. and McIntyre, M. J., *International Tax Primer*, 1995, 16; Bader, A., *Steuergestaltung mit Holdinggesellschaften*, 1998, 130; Zettler, H., *Treaty-shopping nach Inkrafttreten des § 50d Ia EStG*, 1999, 20; Hoffmann, W.-D., *Steueroptimales Ausschüttungsverhalten und Repatriierungsstrategien*, 2000, 523; Isenbergh, J., *International Taxation*, 2000, 236; Meldman, R. E. and Schadewald, M. S., *A Practical Guide to U.S. Taxation of International Transactions*, 2000, 345; Spencer, D. E., *Journal of International Taxation* 2000, 62; Kessler, W. and Dorfmueller, P., *Praxis Internationale Steuerberatung* 2001, 178; Kessler, W., Dorfmueller, P., Schmidt, W. and Teufel, T., *Tax Notes International* 2001, 1218.

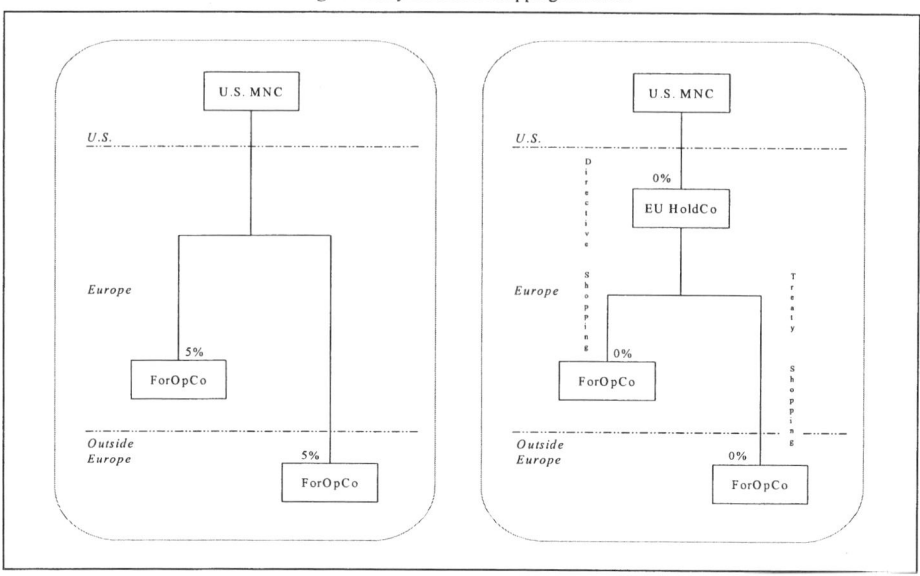

There are two strategies to consider when choosing the best "dividend" location for an EU holding entity. The non-EU investor may analyze the respective double tax treaties and compare the treaty rates, which might be as low as zero. Or the investor can analyze the different local laws and pick the one that does not impose, or provides generous exemptions to, withholding taxes on dividends, as does Denmark, Ireland, Spain, and the U.K.[183] Hence, for dividends, the most attractive jurisdiction, i.e., the one which provides the highest degree of reliance, is one where no withholding tax is levied under local law and, to ensure the tax exemptions persist through changing local law, the treaty rate is nil according to the relevant double tax treaty.

Although withholding taxes on the foreign subsidiary's dividend payments can often be reduced by having the foreign subsidiary owned by a holding company entitled to the benefit of an income tax treaty, an increasing number of income tax treaties contain certain anti-treaty shopping provisions that could deny a reduced rate of withholding tax on dividends and any other types of income.[184] However, despite these adverse results, an intermediate holding company may be beneficial for a U.S. MNC if the structure is intended to be intact for a long period of time and dividend payments from the operating subsidiaries to the interposed holding company are protected from U.S. taxes as the result of the indirect FTC computed on the look-through approach via the holding company and into the operating subsidiaries.[185]

---

[183] See Endres, D. and Dorfmueller, P., *Praxis Internationale Steuerberatung* 2001, 102; Endres, D., Dorfmueller, P. and Urse, M., *International Tax Report* 2001 II, 8; Kessler, W. and Dorfmueller, P., *Praxis Internationale Steuerberatung* 2001, 181. See chapter „Country-by-Country Synopsis" *infra* page 111.

[184] See Arnold, B. J. and McIntyre, M. J., *International Tax Primer*, 1995, 116; Ogley, A., *Journal of International Taxation* 1996, 30; Rsm International Tax Committee and Lorence, R. D., *Journal of International Taxation* 1996, 126; Hintzen, B., *Die deutsche Zwischenholding als Gegenstand der internationalen Steuerplanung*, 1997, 94; Bader, A., *Steuergestaltung mit Holdinggesellschaften*, 1998, 97; Sider, V., Maiorano, R., Beaulne, D. and Zive, J., *Journal of International Taxation* 2000, 39; Graetz, M. J., *Tax Law Review* 2001, 322.

[185] See Hintzen, B., *Die deutsche Zwischenholding als Gegenstand der internationalen Steuerplanung*, 1997, 50.

2. CLAIMING U.S. FOREIGN TAX CREDITS

When a U.S. corporation conducts business in a high-tax foreign jurisdiction, i.e., a U.S. MNC invests in a jurisdiction with statutory tax rates higher than 35 percent, the resulting excess foreign tax credits increase the total tax cost beyond what it would have been if only the U.S. had taxed the foreign-source income. The U.S. foreign tax credit system[186] and potential tax planning strategies to avoid any excess foreign tax credits will be discussed in the following paragraphs.

The U.S. retains the right to tax its citizens and residents on their worldwide taxable income.[187] This approach can result in double taxation, presenting a potential problem for U.S. persons who invest abroad.[188] U.S. international tax policy for foreign-source income[189] has traditionally attempted to provide U.S. investors with capital export neutrality.[190] Under this doctrine, income should be taxed at the same rate in the home country whether it is derived from foreign or domestic investment.[191]

---

[186] Prof. Isenbergh describes the foreign tax credit as "the heart of the system of U.S. outbound taxation". See Isenbergh, *International Taxation*, 2000, 123.

[187] IRC §§ 1, 11. See Johnsen, K. M. and Lipton, J. A., *Tax Management International Journal* 1991, 235; Pugh, E. O. T., *Tax Notes International* 1993, 1429; Anonymous, *Tax Executive* 1996, 246; Benson, D. M., *The Tax Adviser* 1996, 628; Haun, J., *Hybride Finanzierungsinstrumente im deutschen und US-amerikanischen Steuerrecht*, 1996, 154; Martin, W. J., *Tax Management International Journal* 1998, 446; Tello, C. P., *Tax Management International Journal* 1998, 14; Ernst & Young, *Doing Business in the United States*, 1999, 44; Middleton, C. I., *Journal of Partnership Taxation* 1999, 314; Golbert, A. S., *World Trade* 2000 I, 48; Meldman, R. E. and Schadewald, M. S., *A Practical Guide to U.S. Taxation of International Transactions*, 2000, 5; CCH, *2002 U.S. Tax Master Guide*, 2001, paragraph 2401; Engel, K., *Texas Law Review* 2001, 1529.

[188] See Anonymous, *Tax Executive* 1999 I, 349; Larkins, E. R., Oakley, E. F. and Winkle, G. M., *The Tax Adviser* 1999, 416; Crocco, P., *The Tax Adviser* 2000, 480; Huffman, R. and Fischl, A., *The Tax Adviser* 2000, 484; Meldman, R. E. and Schadewald, M. S., *A Practical Guide to U.S. Taxation of International Transactions*, 2000, 55; Rodriguez, A. E., *The International Tax Journal* 2001, 87; Tello, C. P., *Tax Management International Journal* 2001, 162.

[189] The provisions for sourcing income outside the U.S. are not as detailed and specific as those for determining U.S.-source income. Basically, IRC § 862 provides that if dividends, interest, compensation for personal service, income from the use or sale of property, or other income is not U.S. income, then it is foreign-source income. i.e., foreign-source income is generally all non-U.S.-source income. See Golbert, A. S., *World Trade* 2000 II, 45; Meldman, R. E. and Schadewald, M. S., *A Practical Guide to U.S. Taxation of International Transactions*, 2000, 31.

[190] In general, a residence country can choose among three policies to relieve double taxation: the tax credit regime, the tax exemption regime, and the deduction regime. Under the tax credit scheme, domestic corporations are allowed to credit taxes paid against the domestic tax liability generated by foreign-source income. In the simple setting usually considered, capital export neutrality corresponds to a policy of taxing foreign-source income upon accrual and granting unlimited FTCs. Numerous capital exporting countries restrict the tax credit to the domestic tax liability generated by the foreign-source income, so that the corporation pays either the foreign or the domestic tax rate, whichever is higher. See Altshuler, R. and Fulghieri, P., *National Tax Journal* 1994, 353; Arnold, B. J. and McIntyre, M. J., *International Tax Primer*, 1995, 33; Benson, D. M., *The Tax Adviser* 1996, 629; Krehbühl, H.-H., *Das Steueranrechnungsverfahren in den USA*, 1997, 149; Peroni, R. J., *University of Miami Law Review* 1997, 977; Martin, W. J., *Tax Management International Journal* 1998, 455; Schjelderup, G., *International Journal of the Economics of Business* 1999, 93; Meldman, R. E. and Schadewald, M. S., *A Practical Guide to U.S. Taxation of International Transactions*, 2000, 20; Peroni, R. J., *Texas Law Review* 2001, 1609; Wells, B., *Tax Executive* 2001, 366; Vlaanderen, P., *Tax Notes International* 2002, 1098. The IRS emphasized the importance of the principle of capital export neutrality in Notice 98-5, 1998-3 I.R.B. 49. For details on Notice 98-5, see DiMuzio, D. A. and Sheard, T. J., *The Tax Adviser* 1998, 290; Dolan, D. K., DuPuy, C. M. and Bower, D. I., *Tax Management Memorandum* 1998, 143; Zschiegner, H., *Internationale Wirtschaftsbriefe*, Fach 8, USA, Gruppe 2, 1998 VI, 1003. Another notice, Notice 98-11, 1998-6 I.R.B. 18, also discussed the importance of the principle of capital export neutrality to U.S. international tax policy, in particular, regarding Subpart F.

[191] See Ruding, H. O., *Journal of International Taxation* 1994, 4; Krehbühl, H.-H., *Das Steueranrechnungsverfahren in den USA*, 1997, 148; Martin, W. J., *Tax Management International Journal* 1998, 448; McLure, C. E. Jr. and Zodrow, G. R., *National Tax Journal* 1998, 4; Tello, C. P., *Tax Management International Journal* 1998, 21; Hines, J. R. Jr., *National Tax Journal* 1999, 385; Rousslang, D. J., *National Tax Journal* 2000, 590; Aud, E. F. Jr., Benson, D. M. and Garrett-Nelson, L., *Tax Executive* 2001, 53; Gerken, L., Märkt, J. and Schick, G., *Intereconomics* 2001, 245; Graetz, M. J., *Tax Law Review* 2001, 270.

To mitigate the possibility of double taxation, U.S. Congress enacted the FTC provisions.[192] Under these provisions, a qualified taxpayer is allowed a tax credit for foreign income taxes paid. The statutory standard for determining which foreign tax levies are creditable as income taxes is IRC § 901(b)(1) which allows a credit for "the amount of any income, war profits, and excess profit taxes paid or accrued during the taxable year to any foreign country."[193] According to IRC § 903, it is also permitted to credit taxes imposed in lieu of income taxes otherwise generally imposed by a particular foreign country.[194] However, where the tax of a particular foreign jurisdiction is not determined to substantially equal an income tax, it will not qualify for the FTC.

The FTC purports to preserve capital export neutrality by allowing the taxes that U.S. MNCs pay abroad to offset their U.S. tax liability.[195] The credit is a dollar-for-dollar reduction of the U.S. income tax liability.[196]

The FTC is elective for any particular tax year.[197] If the taxpayer chooses not to take the FTC, IRC § 164 allows a deduction for foreign taxes paid or incurred.[198] It is generally more

---

[192] IRC §§ 901-908. Tax Reform Act 1986, P.L. 99-514. See Johnsen, K. M. and Lipton, J. A., *Tax Management International Journal* 1991, 235; Altshuler, R. and Fulghieri, P., *National Tax Journal* 1994, 349; Carr, J. L. Jr. and Moetell, M. C., *Tax Management International Journal* 1995, 219; Benson, D. M., *The Tax Adviser* 1996, 628; Tello, C. P., *Tax Management International Journal* 1998, 14; Hines, J. R. Jr., *National Tax Journal* 1999, 386; Schjelderup, G., *International Journal of the Economics of Business* 1999, 94; Bauman, C. and Schadewald, M., *Journal of International Accounting, Auditing & Taxation* 2001, 181; Rodriguez, A. E., *The International Tax Journal* 2001, 87. Jurisdictions other than the U.S. permitting taxpayers to claim FTCs and to defer home country taxation of foreign-source income include Canada, Japan, Norway, and the U.K. For the Canadian FTC regime, see Jodoin, C. E., *Tax Management International Journal* 1998, 197.

[193] For a foreign levy to qualify for the FTC, it must be a tax, and its predominant character must be that of an income tax in the U.S. sense (Regs. §§ 1.901-2 and 1.903-1). These regulations also provide comprehensive guidance in determining what types of foreign taxes are creditable against U.S. tax liabilities. As the term "income tax" is not defined in the IRC, its meaning was, thus, left to the courts. A levy is a tax if it is a compulsory payment, rather than a payment for a specific economic benefit. A tax's predominant character is that of an income tax in the U.S. sense if it reaches the realized net gain and is not a soak-up tax. i.e., does not depend on being credited against income tax of another country, according to Third Circuit case, *Keasbey & Mattison Co. v. Rothensies*, 133 F.2d 894 (3rd Cir. 1942). See Rosenbloom, H. D. and Booth, C. W., *Case Western Reserve Journal of International Law* 1993, 5; Krehbühl, H.-H., *Das Steueranrechnungsverfahren in den USA*, 1997, 155; Meldman, R. E. and Schadewald, M. S., *A Practical Guide to U.S. Taxation of International Transactions*, 2000, 108; Tello, C. P., *Tax Management International Forum* 2002, 43. A foreign levy that does not meet the prerequisites of Reg. § 1.901-2 may nevertheless be creditable as an in lieu of tax amount under IRC § 903 and the regulations issued there under. See Endres, D. and Spengel, C., *Steuerstrukturen in Deutschland aus Sicht eines US-Investors*, 1997, 84; Tello, C. P., *Tax Management International Journal* 1998, 14; Abrams, H. E. and Doernberg, R. L., *Essentials of United States Taxation*, 1999, 4-115; Doernberg, R. L., *International Taxation In a Nutshell*, 2001, 196.

[194] There is very little authority in the rulings or case law as to what will qualify as an in lieu of foreign tax amount. Under Reg. § 1.903-1(a), a tax will qualify as being in lieu of an income tax if it replaces a foreign income-type tax that would have qualified for the credit. If the tax is in addition to, rather than as a replacement for, an income-type tax, no credit is allowed. See Coven, G. E., *Florida Tax Review* 1999, 116; Golbert, A. S., *World Trade* 2000 II, 42; Andersen, R. E., *Foreign Tax Credits*, 2002, paragraph 3.03.

[195] The rules are driven by capital export neutrality, however, as not all foreign taxes are creditable, the concepts of national neutrality and capital import neutrality are also maintained. See Peroni, R. J., *University of Miami Law Review* 1997, 977; Dagan, T., *Virginia Tax Review* 1998, 394; Lehner, M., *Steuer und Wirtschaft* 1998, 166; Abrams, H. E. and Doernberg, R. L., *Essentials of United States Taxation*, 1999, 4-3; Isenbergh, J., *International Taxation*, 2000, 123; Wells, B., *Tax Executive* 2001, 366.

[196] See Peroni, R. J., *University of Miami Law Review* 1997, 994; Martin, W. J., *Tax Management International Journal* 1998, 446; Abrams, H. E. and Doernberg, R. L., *Essentials of United States Taxation*, 1999, 4-101; Ruchelman, S. C., Asbeck, E. van, Canalejo, G. and et. al., *Journal of International Taxation* 2000, 40; Doernberg, R. L., *International Taxation In a Nutshell*, 2001, 171; Graetz, M. J., *Tax Law Review* 2001, 261.

[197] See Krehbühl, H.-H., *Das Steueranrechnungsverfahren in den USA*, 1997, 156; Abrams, H. E. and Doernberg, R. L., *Essentials of United States Taxation*, 1999, 4-108.

[198] A taxpayer can change from a deduction to a credit - or *vice versa* - in different tax years. See Pugh, E. O. T., *Tax Notes International* 1993, 1429; Endres, D. and Spengel, C., *Steuerstrukturen in Deutschland aus Sicht eines US-Investors*, 1997, 82; Leary, W. F., *Tax Management International Journal* 1998, 346; Kroschel, J., *Die Federal Income Tax der Vereinigten Staaten von Amerika*, 2000, 257.

beneficial to credit foreign taxes than to claim them as deductions.[199] This is due, in part, to the fact that a credit reduces the U.S. tax liability (dollar-for-dollar), while a deduction lowers the U.S. tax costs only by the amount of the deductions multiplied by the marginal tax rate.[200] Also, a credit generates more benefits if foreign income taxes are paid on income that is not subject to tax in the U.S. In this instance, a deduction is not permitted, according to IRC § 265, but there is no limitation on a credit. Deemed foreign taxes paid under IRC §§ 902 or 960 are only creditable and not available as deductions. A taxpayer is not provided with a credit and a deduction for the same foreign income taxes, according to IRC § 275(a)(4)(A).[201] However, a taxpayer can take a deduction in the same year as an FTC for foreign taxes that are not available as credits, e.g., non-income taxes.[202]

2.1. Direct Credit

IRC § 901 provides a direct FTC to U.S. taxpayers who pay or incur any foreign income taxes.[203] For purposes of the direct credit, only the taxpayer who bears the legal responsibility for the foreign tax is eligible for the credit.[204] A check-the-box election to treat a foreign subsidiary as a pass-through entity allows the S corporation[205] - and its shareholders - to claim a direct FTC for taxes paid by the foreign subsidiary.[206]

---

[199] There are instances, however, where it may be favorable to deduct foreign taxes, rather than take them as a credit. One such situation occurs when the taxpayer has a net operating loss. In this scenario, there is no U.S. income tax against which the credit could be taken, but a deduction would increase the net operating loss, which could then be credited back and/or carried forward to reduce taxable income in other years. Taking into account the FTC carryback and carryforward provisions, the present value benefit of a FTC carryback and carryforward must be compared with the benefit of the carryback and carryover of a larger net operating loss, especially since the FTC carryforward period is only five years, whereas the net operating loss carryforward period is fifteen years. See Abrams, H. E. and Doernberg, R. L., *Essentials of United States Taxation*, 1999, 4-108.

[200] See Endres, D. and Spengel, C., *Steuerstrukturen in Deutschland aus Sicht eines US-Investors*, 1997, 82; Abrams, H. E. and Doernberg, R. L., *Essentials of United States Taxation*, 1999, 4-108; Middleton, C. I., *Journal of Partnership Taxation* 1999, 315; Isenbergh, J., *International Taxation*, 2000, 123; Timokhov, V., *Tax Notes International* 2002, 777.

[201] See Krehbühl, H.-H., *Das Steueranrechnungsverfahren in den USA*, 1997, 156.

[202] See Martin, W. J., *Tax Management International Journal* 1998, 461.

[203] See Carr, J. L. Jr. and Moetell, M. C., *Tax Management International Journal* 1995, 219; Benson, D. M., *The Tax Adviser*, 1996, 630; Moetell, M. C., *Tax Management International Journal* 1997, 111; Martin, W. J., *Tax Management International Journal* 1998, 446; Tello, C. P., *Tax Management International Journal* 1998, 14; Middleton, C. I., *Journal of Partnership Taxation* 1999, 312. For creditable taxes, refer *supra* note 193.

[204] See Altshuler, R. and Fulghieri, P., *National Tax Journal* 1994, 351; Endres, D. and Spengel, C., *Steuerstrukturen in Deutschland aus Sicht eines US-Investors*, 1997, 85; McDaniel, P. R. and Ault, H. J., *Introduction to United States International Taxation*, 1998, 90; Abrams, H. E. and Doernberg, R. L., *Essentials of United States Taxation*, 1999, 4-109.

[205] An S corporation is a corporation that meets the requirements of, and elects to be taxed under Subchapter S of the IRC. In general, this type of corporation acts as a conduit, passing through to the shareholders its taxable income or loss, much like a partnership. See Sieker, K., *Internationale Wirtschaftsbriefe*, Fach 8, USA, Gruppe 2, 1993, 719; American Chamber of Commerce in Germany e.V. and PricewaterhouseCoopers GmbH, *Steuern in den USA*, 2001, 72; Bittker, B. I. and Eustice, J. S., *Federal Income Taxation of Corporations and Shareholders*, 2002, paragraph 6.01; Ernst & Young, *The Ernst & Young Tax Guide 2002*, 2002, 176.

[206] See Sieker, K., *Internationale Wirtschaftsbriefe*, Fach 8, USA, Gruppe 2, 1993, 721. For the check-the-box election in detail, see *infra* page 70.

2.2. Indirect Credit

If a U.S. MNC operates in a foreign country through a foreign subsidiary, the direct credit is not available for foreign taxes paid by the foreign corporation.[207] Under IRC § 902, an indirect credit is provided to U.S. corporate taxpayers that receive actual or constructive dividends, e.g., under Subpart F, from foreign corporations that have paid foreign income taxes.[208] Hence, this provision parallels the dividends received deduction of IRC § 243 for dividends paid by U.S. corporations.[209] In general, the first six tiers of foreign subsidiaries are eligible for the indirect FTC provided that certain requirements are met.[210] The foreign taxes are deemed paid by the corporate owners in the same proportion as the dividends actually or constructively included in the foreign corporation's post-1986[211] undistributed earnings and profits (E&P).[212]

Fig. 2: Indirect FTC Formula (sole ownership, without limitation)

$$\text{Indirect FTC} = \frac{\text{Actual or constructive dividend}}{\text{Post-1986 undistributed E\&P}} * \text{Post-1986 foreign taxes}$$

Presuming a U.S. corporation is not the sole owner, the tax credit under IRC § 902 will be calculated with reference solely to the proportionate interest in accumulated profits attributable to the U.S.

---

[207] See Benson, D. M., *The Tax Adviser* 1996, 630; Endres, D. and Spengel, C., *Steuerstrukturen in Deutschland aus Sicht eines US-Investors*, 1997, 85; Zschiegner, H., *Internationale Wirtschaftsbriefe*, Fach 8, USA, Gruppe 2, 1998 III, 976; Middleton, C. I., *Journal of Partnership Taxation* 1999, 315.

[208] The purpose of IRC § 902 is to eliminate the disparity that would otherwise exist between foreign permanent establishments and foreign subsidiaries of U.S. MNCs. *U.S. v. Goodyear Tire & Rubber Co.*, 110 S. Ct. 462 [1989]. See Koifman, L., *The CPA Journal* 1993, 78; Moetell, M. C., *Tax Management International Journal* 1997, 111; McDaniel, P. R. and Ault, H. J., *Introduction to United States International Taxation*, 1998, 93; Pollack, L. A., Porter, D. and Corrie, F., *International Tax Review* 1998 II, 24; Tello, C. P., *Tax Management International Journal* 1998, 15; Meldman, R. E. and Schadewald, M. S., *A Practical Guide to U.S. Taxation of International Transactions*, 2000, 101; CCH, *2002 U.S. Tax Master Guide*, 2001, paragraph 2485; Bittker, B. I. and Eustice, J. S., *Federal Income Taxation of Corporations and Shareholders*, 2002, paragraph 15.21[2][a].

[209] See *supra* page 27.

[210] IRC § 902(b). For the requirements in detail, refer *infra* page 49.

[211] The Tax Reform Act 1986 (H.R. 3838, 99th Cong., 2d Sess) replaced annual matching dividends, taxes, and earnings with a system of pooling foreign earnings and taxes. IRC § 902 now treats dividends from foreign corporations as coming from a single cumulative account of post-1986 earnings. See Green, G. L. Jr., *The National Public Accountant* 1993, 35; Abrams, H. E. and Doernberg, R. L., *Essentials of United States Taxation*, 1999, 4-121; Doernberg, R. L., *International Taxation In a Nutshell*, 2001, 205.

[212] IRC §§ 902 and 951(a). See Pugh, E. O. T., *Tax Notes International* 1993, 1429; Moetell, M. C., *Tax Management International Journal* 1997, 115; Yoder, L. D., *Tax Management International Journal* 1999 I, 340.

The term "earnings and profits" has never been defined in the IRC even though it first appeared in the federal tax law in the Revenue Act of 1916 and it serves as the cornerstone of the U.S. system of taxation of corporate worldwide profits. The concept of E&P has nevertheless evolved over the years in a body of regulations, rulings and case law. Basically, E&P represents a corporation's economic gains and losses and, in, most cases, is quite different from the accounting concept of net income and the corporation's taxable income. E&P is an annual computation and is accumulated from the later of the date of incorporation or February 28, 1913. E&P generally includes all income, expenses, gains and losses realized by the corporation. Thus, it tracks the company's ability to distribute dividends. See Anonymous, *Tax Executive* 1997, 156; Krehbühl, H.-H., *Das Steueranrechnungsverfahren in den USA*, 1997, 157; Abrams, H. E. and Doernberg, R. L., *Essentials of United States Taxation*, 1999, 2-75; McDaniel, P. R., McMahon, M. J. Jr. and Simmons, D. L., *Federal Income Taxation of Business Organizations*, 1999, 563; Meldman, R. E. and Schadewald, M. S., *A Practical Guide to U.S. Taxation of International Transactions*, 2000, 165. For a chart how to compute E&P, see Moussallem, S., *Die Besteuerung einer US-corporation*, 2001, 174.

shareholder.[213] Hence, the ratio of dividend payments to the U.S. shareholder to accumulated profits in excess of income taxes, as well as the amount of mainstream tax paid with respect thereto, will be computed as if the U.S. owner's proportionate interest in accumulated profits were the entire accumulated profits of a corporation of which it was the sole participant. Thus, the amount of FTC will not vary as a result of the status of any other shareholder. It should be noted that this approach reverses the Tax Court's decision in *Vulcan Materials Co. v. Commissioner*[214] and set forth in Rev. Rul. 87-14.[215] In the *Vulcan* case, the court held that it was proper for the taxpayer to compute its deemed paid credit under IRC § 902 using a separate E&P account with respect to its interest in a Saudi Arabian corporation.[216] When a U.S. domestic corporation chooses the FTC for deemed paid foreign taxes, IRC § 78 requires a gross up of dividend income by the amount of deemed paid taxes.[217]

2.2.1. Prerequisites

2.2.1.1. Ownership

Certain ownership requirements must be met before the indirect credit is available to a U.S. domestic corporation. The domestic corporation must own at least ten percent of the voting stock of a **first-tier** foreign corporation.[218] The point in time at which the threshold is determined is the date the dividend is paid, rather than the period during which the underlying income was earned.[219] The deemed paid credit is provided, then, with respect to dividends paid from income earned prior to meeting the shareholding prerequisite.

Furthermore, the credit is available for (a pro rata share of) deemed paid foreign taxes of **second- and third-tier** foreign corporations if the ten percent or more ownership requirement is met at the second- and third-tier levels (the so-called *absolute test*).[220] An indirect shareholding percentage of voting stock down the chain must equal at least five percent (the so-called *relative test*).[221] The indirect credit is also available for foreign taxes paid by **fourth-through-sixth-tier**

---

[213] See Carr, J. L. Jr. and Moetell, M. C., *Tax Management International Journal* 1995, 219.

[214] 96 T.C. 410 [1991].

[215] Rev. Rul. 1987-1 C.B. 181.

[216] See Anonymous, *Journal of Accountancy* 1991, 24; Haris, K. L. and Wirtz, F. J., *Tax Management International Journal* 1991, 464; Lainoff, S. R., *Tax Management International Journal* 1992, 26; Kral, K. H., Serota, J. and Weiss, J., *Journal of Accountancy* 1995, 25; Moetell, M. C., *Tax Management International Journal* 1997, 117; Swanick, M. F. and Leary, W., *Tax Management International Journal* 2000, 299.

[217] Regs. §§ 1.960-1(a) and (3). See Pugh, E. O. T., *Tax Notes International* 1993, 1430; Carr, J. L. Jr. and Moetell, M. C., *Tax Management International Journal* 1995, 219; Zschiegner, H., *Internationale Wirtschaftsbriefe*, Fach 8, USA, Gruppe 2, 1998 III, 977; Yoder, L. D., *Tax Management International Journal* 1999 I, 340; Meldman, R. E. and Schadewald, M. S., *A Practical Guide to U.S. Taxation of International Transactions*, 2000, 102; Bittker, B. I. and Eustice, J. S., *Federal Income Taxation of Corporations and Shareholders*, 2002, paragraph 15.21[2][e]; Kuntz, J. D. and Peroni, R. J., *U.S. International Taxation*, 2002, paragraph B4.09[4].

[218] IRC § 952(a). See Pugh, E. O. T., *Tax Notes International* 1993, 1429; Culbertson, R. E., *Tax Notes International* 1996, 1761; Endres, D. and Spengel, C., *Steuerstrukturen in Deutschland aus Sicht eines US-Investors*, 1997, 85; Martin, W. J., *Tax Management International Journal* 1998, 446; Tello, C. P., *Tax Management International Journal* 1998, 15; Zschiegner, H., *Internationale Wirtschaftsbriefe*, Fach 8, USA, Gruppe 2, 1998 III, 976; Middleton, C. I., *Journal of Partnership Taxation* 1999, 315; CCH, *2002 U.S. Tax Master Guide*, 2001, paragraph 2485; Arnold, B. J., *Tax Notes International* 2002, 1092.

[219] See Kral, K. H., Serota, J. and Weiss, J., *Journal of Accountancy* 1995, 25.

[220] See Culbertson, R. E., *Tax Notes International* 1996, 1761; Anonymous, *Tax Executive* 1997, 159; Tello, C. P., *Tax Management International Journal* 1998, 15.

[221] See Pugh, E. O. T., *Tax Notes International* 1993, 1430; Moetell, M. C., *Tax Management International Journal* 1997, 113; Tello, C. P., *Tax Management International Journal* 1998, 15; Zschiegner, H., *Internationale Wirtschaftsbriefe*,

foreign corporations if the absolute and relative tests apply at each level of ownership.[222] Additionally, the FTC can be used for tiers four through six only if the subsidiary is a CFC and the payee is an IRC § 951(b) U.S. shareholder.[223]

Fig. 3: IRC § 902 Ownership Requirements

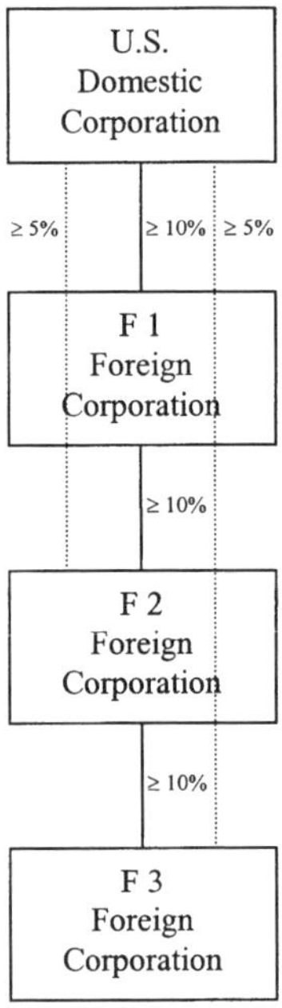

U.S. Domestic Corporation	U.S. must directly own at least 10 percent of the voting stock of F 1 and must indirectly own at least 5 percent of the voting stock of F 2 and F 3.
≥ 5% ≥ 10% ≥ 5%	
F 1 Foreign Corporation	F 1 must directly own at least 10 percent of the voting stock of F 2.
≥ 10%	
F 2 Foreign Corporation	F 2 must directly own at least 10 percent of the voting stock of F 3.
≥ 10%	
F 3 Foreign Corporation	A credit for deemed paid foreign taxes may be claimed for payments from foreign corporations through the sixth-tier if the subsidiary is a CFC and the payee is an IRC § 951(b) U.S. shareholder.

2.2.1.2. Holding Period

A holding period applies for the purpose of crediting foreign income taxes connected to foreign-source dividends.[224] In general, under IRC § 901(k), a credit is denied for foreign withholding taxes paid for dividends if the payee has not held the payor stock at risk for at least 16 days for the

---

Fach 8, USA, Gruppe 2, 1998 III, 976; Meldman, R. E. and Schadewald, M. S., *A Practical Guide to U.S. Taxation of International Transactions*, 2000, 103.

[222] IRC §§ 902(b)(2)(B)(ii) and (iii). See Garrett-Nelson, L., *Tax Notes International* 1997, 1288; Tello, C. P., *Tax Management International Journal* 1998, 15; Zschiegner, H., *Internationale Wirtschaftsbriefe*, Fach 8, USA, Gruppe 2, 1998 III, 976; Kroschel, J., *Die Federal Income Tax der Vereinigten Staaten von Amerika*, 2000, 259.

[223] IRC § 902(b). See Jensen, P., Spikes, P. and Carter, D., *The International Tax Journal* 1998, 7; Meldman, R. E. and Schadewald, M. S., *A Practical Guide to U.S. Taxation of International Transactions*, 2000, 104. An IRC § 951(b) U.S. shareholder is a U.S. person that owns ten percent or more of the total voting power of a foreign corporation. See Tello, C. P., *Tax Management International Journal* 1998, 15; Middleton, C. I., *Journal of Partnership Taxation* 1999, 316; Isenbergh, J., *International Taxation*, 2000, 158.

[224] The holding period prerequisite was added in 1997 in order to prevent taxpayers that could benefit from additional FTCs from buying stock in foreign corporations about to pay dividends from taxpayers who could not use such credits. See Jensen, P., Spikes, P. and Carter, D., *The International Tax Journal* 1998, 8.

dividend-paying common stock or for at least 46 days for certain dividends on preferred stock.[225] The 16-day holding period must be satisfied within the 30-day period beginning 15 days before the ex-dividend date.[226] If the investment is held for 15 days or less during the 30-day period, the FTC for the withholding tax on the dividend is not allowed.[227]

2.2.2. Foreign Tax Credit Limitations

To prevent taxpayers from using foreign taxes as credits against U.S. taxes levied on U.S.-source income, the FTC has been subject to restrictions under IRC § 904.[228] Income earned and taxes incurred in all foreign jurisdictions in which the U.S. taxpayer has operations or subsidiaries paying dividends are combined in computing the limitation. The method is called the overall limitation method.[229] Under the overall limitation method, the FTC for any taxable year cannot exceed the lesser of two amounts:[230]

(1) actual foreign taxes paid or accrued;[231] or
(2) U.S. taxes (before FTC) on foreign-source taxable income.[232]

Under the limitation, the FTC is computed as follows:[233]

[225] See Fischl, A. and Schneider, R. A., *Tax Management International Journal* 1997, 573; Jensen, P., Spikes, P. and Carter, D., *The International Tax Journal* 1998, 8; Zschiegner, H., *Internationale Wirtschaftsbriefe*, Fach 8, USA, Gruppe 2, 1998 III, 977; Abrams, H. E. and Doernberg, R. L., *Essentials of United States Taxation*, 1999, 4-124.

[226] IRC § 901(k)(1)(A)(i). See Fischl, A. and Schneider, R. A., *Tax Management International Journal* 1997, 573; Garrett-Nelson, L., *Tax Notes International* 1997, 1287; Tello, C. P., *Tax Management International Journal* 1998, 16.

[227] Securities dealers holding securities in the active conduct of their securities business in a foreign country are exempt from the holding period rule, according to IRC § 901(k). See Jensen, P., Spikes, P. and Carter, D., *The International Tax Journal* 1998, 7.

[228] See Joyce, T. B. and Parks, S. M., *Tax Management International Journal* 1990 I, 323; Altshuler, R. and Fulghieri, P., *National Tax Journal* 1994, 349; McIntyre, M. J., *Tax Notes International* 1996, 57; Krehbühl, H.-H., *Das Steueranrechnungsverfahren in den USA*, 1997, 151; Martin, W. J., *Tax Management International Journal* 1998, 446; Huffman, R. and Fischl, A., *The Tax Adviser* 2000, 484. For a detailed study regarding the relation between the impact of FTC limitations on the marginal tax benefit of interest deductions and the issuance choices made by U.S. MNCs raising capital in the public markets, see Newberry, K. J., *Foreign Tax Credit Limitations and Capital Structure Decisions*, 1994; Newberry, K. J., *Journal of Accounting Research* 1998, 157. One major result of the study provides evidence that binding FTC limitations can increase the cost of debt financing for the public issuance. This is consistent with current arguments that U.S. foreign tax policy undermines the competitiveness of U.S. MNCs.
    Moreover, a corporation that is subject to the alternative minimum tax (AMT) may claim only 90 percent of its foreign taxes paid to offset the AMT, according to IRC § 59(a)(2). See Flick, H. F. W. and Janka, W., *Deutsches Steuerrecht* 1991 II, 1074; Meldman, R. E. and Schadewald, M. S., *A Practical Guide to U.S. Taxation of International Transactions*, 2000, 85; CCH, *2002 U.S. Tax Master Guide*, 2001, paragraph 1410. For the AMT in detail, refer *supra* page 31.

[229] See Joyce, T. B., *Tax Management International Journal* 1992 I, 55; Carr, J. L. Jr. and Moetell, M. C., *Tax Management International Journal* 1995, 219; McIntyre, M. J., *Tax Notes International* 1996, 57; Krehbühl, H.-H., *Das Steueranrechnungsverfahren in den USA*, 1997, 151; McDaniel, P. R. and Ault, H. J., *Introduction to United States International Taxation*, 1998, 96; Middleton, C. I., *Journal of Partnership Taxation* 1999, 317; Isenbergh, J., *International Taxation*, 2000, 130; Kroschel, J., *Die Federal Income Tax der Vereinigten Staaten von Amerika*, 2000, 258; American Chamber of Commerce in Germany e.V. and PricewaterhouseCoopers GmbH, *Steuern in den USA*, 2001, 85.

[230] See Pugh, E. O. T., *Tax Notes International* 1993, 1431; Ernst & Young, *Doing Business in the United States*, 1999, 47; Isenbergh, J., *International Taxation*, 2000, 126.

[231] See Martin, W. J., *Tax Management International Journal* 1998, 446.

[232] See Altshuler, R. and Fulghieri, P., *National Tax Journal* 1994, 351; *The Tax Adviser* 1996, 630; Siemaszko, D. J. and Windsor, J. G., *The Tax Adviser* 1996, 412; Benson, D. M., Endres, D. and Spengel, C., *Steuerstrukturen in Deutschland aus Sicht eines US Investors*, 1997, 87; Martin, W. J., *Tax Management International Journal* 1998, 446; Zschiegner, H., *Internationale Wirtschaftsbriefe*, Fach 8, USA, Gruppe 2, 1998 III, 977; Larkins, E. R., Oakley, E. F. and Winkle, G. M., *The Tax Adviser* 1999, 416; Rodriguez, A. E., *The International Tax Journal* 2001, 87.

Fig. 4: FTC Limitation Formula

$$\text{FTC Limitation} = \frac{\text{Foreign-source taxable income}}{\text{Worldwide taxable income}} * \text{U.S. tax before FTC}$$

The FTC limitation is computed on a net income basis, i.e., using the ratio of net foreign-source income to net worldwide income. Thus, the allocation of expenses attributed by a U.S. MNC to its gross foreign-source income will have a significant impact on the FTC limitation.[234]

Because the FTC is limited, the amount of the U.S. tax liability will distort the investment choices of corporations with excess credits.[235] Capital export neutrality is compromised for this group of entities, since an investment in a jurisdiction with a low corporate tax rate will be more beneficial than a comparable investment in the U.S. or in a high corporate tax rate jurisdiction.[236] Capital export neutrality is further violated by the deferral advantages available for income earned through foreign subsidiaries that is not subject to U.S. tax until it is remitted to the ultimate U.S. parent. To achieve full capital export neutrality, a FTC system would have to provide unlimited credits for foreign tax payments against the domestic tax liability. This would include issuing U.S. refunds for foreign tax paid that exceeds the U.S. tax burden on the same income.[237] Hence, the country of residence would abandon the right to tax domestic-source income. This feature of the IRC increases the attractiveness of low-tax jurisdictions for all U.S. MNCs, irrespective of FTC positions.[238]

---

[233] See Joyce, T. B. and Parks, S. M., *Tax Management International Journal* 1990 I, 323; Crocco, P. Jr., *The Tax Adviser* 2000, 480; Isenbergh, J., *International Taxation*, 2000, 126; Meldman, R. E. and Schadewald, M. S., *A Practical Guide to U.S. Taxation of International Transactions*, 2000, 70; Newberry, K. J. and Dhaliwal, D. S., *Journal of Accounting Research* 2001, 659; Tello, C. P., *Tax Management International Journal* 2001, 162. Under the overall limitation method, a taxpayer totals the taxes he has paid to all foreign countries and possessions. This total is then subjected to a limitation computed by multiplying the U.S. tax liability by a fraction of which the numerator consists of taxable income from foreign-source income and the denominator consists of the worldwide taxable income. Possessions of the U.S. are, e.g., Virgin Island, Guam, and American Samoa (IRC §§ 927(d)(5), 931-936). See Martin, W. J., *Tax Management International Journal* 1998, 451. For IRC § 936 in detail, see Swanick, M. F., *Tax Management International Journal* 1995, 474.

[234] For the computation of the numerator and the detailed impacts, refer *infra* page 55.

[235] Under the Tax Reform Act of 1986, the corporate tax rate was lowered from 46 percent to 34 percent. Consequently, this increased the likelihood of excess FTCs. See Johnsen, K. M. and Lipton, J. A., *Tax Management International Journal* 1991, 235; Altshuler, R. and Fulghieri, P., *National Tax Journal* 1994, 356; Ruding, H. O., *Journal of International Taxation* 1994, 5; Krehbühl, H.-H., *Das Steueranrechnungsverfahren in den USA*, 1997, 150.

[236] See Martin, W. J., *Tax Management International Journal* 1998, 449; McLure, C. E. Jr. and Zodrow, G. R., *National Tax Journal* 1998, 5; Tello, C. P., *Tax Management International Journal* 1998, 15; Graetz, M. J., *Tax Law Review* 2001, 284.

[237] This could be achieved by adopting a per country limitation to replace the overall limitation represented by the basket regime. See Krehbühl, H.-H., *Das Steueranrechnungsverfahren in den USA*, 1997, 150; Martin, W. J., *Tax Management International Journal* 1998, 449.

[238] In 1962, U.S. Congress enacted the Subpart F rules that restrict deferral on specific types of unrepatriated income. Under Subpart F, income that arises from a subsidiary's passive ownership of assets is denied deferral and is taxed immediately. Income earned from the conduct of a business is generally not subject to Subpart F provisions and can be deferred. See Avi-Yonah, R. S., *Tax Notes International* 1998, 1798; Birnkrant, H. J. and Croker, J. E. Jr., *Journal of Taxation* 1998, 50; Engel, K., *Texas Law Review* 2001, 1538. For a detailed analysis of the Subpart F provisions, see *infra* page 83.

To prevent any cross-crediting[239] of foreign taxes from high- and low-taxed foreign income,[240] the FTC rules provide for several separate limitation baskets.[241] These provisions require that a separate limitation be computed for each specific basket of foreign-source taxable income and the foreign taxes attributable to that income.[242] IRC § 904(d) provides separate limitation baskets for the following:[243]

- passive income;[244]
- high withholding tax interest;[245]
- financial services income;[246]

---

[239] Cross-crediting taxes means using taxes imposed at a high rate to offset the U.S. tax on income subject to a lower rate of foreign tax. See McIntyre, M. J., *Tax Notes International* 1996, 64; Meldman, R. E. and Schadewald, M. S., *A Practical Guide to U.S. Taxation of International Transactions*, 2000, 67; Dilworth, R. H. and Andrus, J. L., *Tax Law and Practice*, 2001, 1100.

[240] *Example for cross-crediting*: Assume two different scenarios for a U.S. corporation: In alternative 1, U.S. corporation generates only U.S. $500,000 of highly taxed (at a rate of 40 percent) foreign-source income. In alternative 2, U.S. corporation has an additional U.S. $100,000 of low-taxed (at a rate of 5 percent) foreign-source income.

	Alternative 1	Alternative 2
Foreign-source income	500,000	600,000
Foreign taxes	**200,000**	**205,000**
U.S.-source income	700,000	700,000
U.S. taxes (35 percent)	420,000	455,000
FTC limitation	**175,000***	**210,000****

(All amounts in U.S. $)
*: 420,000 * (500,000/1,200,000) = 175,000
**: 455,000* (600,000/1,300,000) = 210,000
While U.S. corporation's foreign taxes increased by U.S. $5,000, its FTC limitation increased by U.S. $35,000.

[241] See Joyce, T. B., *Tax Management International Journal* 1992 I, 56; McIntyre, M. J., *Tax Notes International* 1996, 58; Dolan, D. K., DuPuy, C. M. and Bower, D. I., *Tax Management Memorandum* 1998, 143; Martin, W. J., *Tax Management International Journal* 1998, 446; Tello, C. P., *Tax Management International Journal* 1998, 15; McDaniel, P. R. and Ault, H. J., *Introduction to United States International Taxation*, 1998, 98; Anonymous, *Tax Executive* 1999 I, 349; Dilworth, R. H. and Andrus, J. L., *Tax Law and Practice*, 2001, 1097; Wells, B., *Tax Executive* 2001, 366; Bittker, B. I. and Eustice, J. S., *Federal Income Taxation of Corporations and Shareholders*, 2002, paragraph 15.21[4]; Kuntz, J. D. and Peroni, R. J., *U.S. International Taxation*, 2002, paragraph A1.03[4].

[242] See Joyce, T. B., *Tax Management International Journal* 1992 I, 59; Endres, D. and Spengel, C., *Steuerstrukturen in Deutschland aus Sicht eines US-Investors*, 1997, 88; Krehbühl, H.-H., *Das Steueranrechnungsverfahren in den USA*, 1997, 159; Martin, W. J., *Tax Management International Journal* 1998, 446; Abrams, H. E. and Doernberg, R. L., *Essentials of United States Taxation*, 1999, 4-127; Isenbergh, J., *International Taxation*, 2000, 147.

[243] Reg. § 1.904-4. See Joyce, T. B. and Parks, S. M., *Tax Management International Journal* 1990 I, 323; Benson, D. M., *The Tax Adviser* 1996, 630; Tello, C. P., *Tax Management International Journal* 1998, 15; Zschiegner, H., *Internationale Wirtschaftsbriefe*, Fach 8, USA, Gruppe 2, 1998 III, 977; CCH, *2002 U.S. Tax Master Guide*, 2001, paragraph 2480; Tello, C. P., *Tax Management International Forum* 2002, 44.

[244] According to the definition in IRC § 904(d)(2)(A), passive income generally means FPHC as defined in IRC § 954(c) and the amounts included in the gross income under IRC §§ 551 and 1293. Although IRC § 954(c) is part of the Subpart F rules, the application under IRC § 904 is not restricted to CFCs (Reg. § 1.904-4(b)(1)(i)(A)). See Joyce, T. B. and Parks, S. M., *Tax Management International Journal* 1990 I, 323; Endres, D. and Spengel, C., *Steuerstrukturen in Deutschland aus Sicht eines US-Investors*, 1997, 89; Meldman, R. E. and Schadewald, M. S., *A Practical Guide to U.S. Taxation of International Transactions*, 2000, 72; Doernberg, R. L., *International Taxation In a Nutshell*, 2001, 217. For FPHC in detail, see *infra* page 94.

[245] The high withholding tax limitation is designed to prevent the offset of withholding taxes on interest against U.S. tax on other foreign-source income. High withholding tax interest is defined in IRC § 904(d)(2)(a) as interest subject to at least four percent withholding tax or other tax imposed on a gross basis by a foreign jurisdiction or U.S. possession. See Joyce, T. B. and Parks, S. M., *Tax Management International Journal* 1990 III, 452; Endres, D. and Spengel, C., *Steuerstrukturen in Deutschland aus Sicht eines US-Investors*, 1997, 90; Meldman, R. E. and Schadewald, M. S., *A Practical Guide to U.S. Taxation of International Transactions*, 2000, 74.

[246] This limitation was introduced to prevent non-financial entities from establishing financial institutions in low-tax jurisdictions to generate low-taxed financial income that would avoid excess FTC on high-taxed non-financial income. In general, financial services income includes income received or accrued by any person predominantly engaged in the active

- shipping income;[247]
- dividends from **each** IRC § 902 corporation that is not a U.S.-controlled foreign corporation (non-CFC);[248]
- dividends from a domestic international sales corporation (DISC) or former DISC to the extent they are treated as foreign-source income;[249]
- taxable income attributable to foreign trade income under IRC § 923(b); and[250]
- distributions from a foreign sales corporation (FSC) or former FSC out of E&P attributable to foreign trade income or qualified interest and carrying charges under IRC § 263(c).[251]

All other foreign-source income, including most active business income, is included in a (residual) general limitation basket.[252]

---

conduct of a banking, insurance, financing, or similar business, as defined in IRC § 904(d)(2)(C). Prop. Reg. § 1.904-6(e)(1)(iv), which has never been finalized, included a broader definition of financial services income, including incidental income. However, it is anticipated that the definition under the Prop. Reg. should apply. See Joyce, T. B. and Parks, S. M., *Tax Management International Journal* 1990 III, 456; Endres, D. and Spengel, C., *Steuerstrukturen in Deutschland aus Sicht eines US-Investors*, 1997, 90; Meldman, R. E. and Schadewald, M. S., *A Practical Guide to U.S. Taxation of International Transactions*, 2000, 72.

[247] Shipping income used for FTC limitation purposes corresponds to the one under Subpart F (IRC § 954(f)), according to IRC § 904(d)(2)(D). See Joyce, T. B. and Parks, S. M., *Tax Management International Journal* 1990 III, 459; Meldman, R. E. and Schadewald, M. S., *A Practical Guide to U.S. Taxation of International Transactions*, 2000, 72.

[248] IRC § 904(d)(1)(E). i.e., dividends from subsidiaries that are owned at least ten percent but not more than 50 percent by U.S. shareholders (the so-called *10/50 companies*) are included in this basket. See Joyce, T. B. and Parks, S. M., *Tax Management International Journal* 1990 III, 459; Eigenbrode, R., *The Tax Adviser* 1993, 444. For tax years beginning after December 31, 2002, all non-controlled IRC § 902 corporations are treated as **one** entity for this purpose. See Rollinson, M., *Tax Management International Journal* 1998, 522; Tello, C. P., *Tax Management International Journal* 1998, 16; Zschiegner, H., *Internationale Wirtschaftsbriefe*, Fach 8, USA, Gruppe 2, 1998 III, 978; Abrams, H. E. and Doernberg, R. L., *Essentials of United States Taxation*, 1999, 4-131; Meldman, R. E. and Schadewald, M. S., *A Practical Guide to U.S. Taxation of International Transactions*, 2000, 75; Dilworth, R. H. and Andrus, J. L., *Tax Law and Practice*, 2001, 1098; Doernberg, R. L., *International Taxation In a Nutshell*, 2001, 225.

[249] The DISC provisions once provided tax benefits to U.S. exporters with respect to pre-1985 transactions. However, for tax years after 1984, much of this benefit has been eliminated in that a DISC can only operate under the interest charge DISC rules. With an interest charge, DISC income attributable to U.S. $10,000,000 or less of qualified export receipts can be deferred, but the DISC's shareholders are subject to an interest charge based on the amount of tax otherwise due on the deferred income which is computed as if the income were contributed. See American Chamber of Commerce in Germany e.V. and PricewaterhouseCoopers GmbH, *Steuern in den USA*, 2001, 77; CCH, *2002 U.S. Tax Master Guide*, 2001, paragraph 2468; Giuliani, F. M., *The International Tax Journal* 2001, 54.

[250] Foreign trade income includes all of a FSC's gross income attributable to foreign trading gross receipts that are generated from export sales, services, and leases. See Joyce, T. B. and Parks, S. M., *Tax Management International Journal* 1990 III, 462.

[251] U.S. exporters may obtain a tax advantage under the FSC provisions which is designed to encourage U.S. exports and has replaced the system of DISCs. A FSC must be created or organized under the law of a jurisdiction that is outside the U.S. and may be taxed on its income except for its exempt foreign trade income. A portion of foreign trade income is exempt from U.S. tax if the FSC satisfies certain foreign presence, foreign management, and foreign economic process tests. At the same time, a. U.S. corporate shareholder is allowed a deduction for 100 percent of dividends received from the FSC out of E&P attributable to foreign trade income. Thus, there is no corporate level tax imposed on a portion of a FSC's income from exports. The WTO found the FSC provisions to be an illegal export subsidy and the FSC rules were repealed in 2000. See Joyce, T. B. and Parks, S. M., *Tax Management International Journal* 1990 III, 462; Larkins, E. R. and Oakley, E. F. and Winkle, G. M., *The Tax Adviser* 1999, 417; Angus, B. M. and Kies, K. J., *Tax Executive* 2000, 436; Foster, J. D., *Tax Foundation's Tax Features* 2000 I, 7; Foster, J. D., *Tax Foundation's Tax Features* 2000 II, 7; Golbert, A. S., *World Trade* 2000 II, 44; Lang, J. M., Stack, R. B., Charnovitz, S. and Brady, J. T., *Tax Management International Journal* 2000, 566; American Chamber of Commerce in Germany e.V. and PricewaterhouseCoopers GmbH, *Steuern in den USA*, 2001, 78; CCH, *2002 U.S. Tax Master Guide*, 2001, paragraph 2470; Engel, K., *Texas Law Review* 2001, 1548; Franz, N., *Chemical Week* 2001, 14; Lubkin, G., *Tax Management International Journal* 2001, 482.

[252] IRC § 904(d)(1) and Reg. § 1.904-4. See Joyce, T. B. and Parks, S. M., *Tax Management International Journal* 1990 I, 323; Joyce, T. B. and Parks, S. M., *Tax Management International Journal* 1990 III, 464; Tischer, F., *Die Betriebswirtschaft* 1993, 213; McIntyre, M. J., *Tax Notes International* 1996, 58; Endres, D. and Spengel, C., *Steuerstrukturen in Deutschland aus Sicht eines US-Investors*, 1997, 89; Isenbergh, J., *International Taxation*, 2000, 149;

Fig. 5: Categories of FTC Baskets

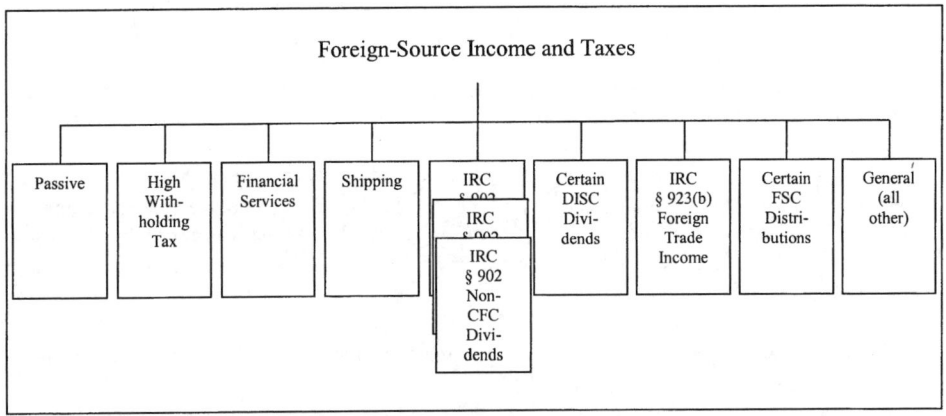

2.2.2.1. Computation of Foreign-Source Taxable Income

The numerator of the FTC limitation formula - foreign-source taxable income - is determined in a two-step computation. The taxpayer must first identify the foreign-source gross income included in the corporation's taxable income. Expenses directly and indirectly incurred in earning this income then reduce this amount.[253] Consequently, it is of utmost importance to precisely determine not only gross income generated from foreign-sources, but also to properly allocate and apportion expenses to foreign-source taxable income.[254] If foreign-source income can be increased, the taxpayer can utilize more FTCs and reduce its U.S. tax liability.[255] The determination of whether income is from sources within or outside the U.S. is made under IRC §§ 861-863 and 865.[256]

IRC §§ 861 and 862 specify the source of income as well as the allocation and apportionment of certain deductions and other business expenses incurred in the U.S.[257] Under these provisions, the taxpayer is allowed to compute the taxable income derived from activities performed within or outside the U.S.[258] and the expenses related to that income.[259] In determining U.S.-source

Meldman, R. E. and Schadewald, M. S., *A Practical Guide to U.S. Taxation of International Transactions*, 2000, 72; CCH, *2002 U.S. Tax Master Guide*, 2001, paragraph 2480.

[253] See Endres, D. and Spengel, C., *Steuerstrukturen in Deutschland aus Sicht eines US-Investors*, 1997, 92; Yoder, L. D. and Kahn, J. H., *Tax Management International Journal* 1999, 533; Meldman, R. E. and Schadewald, M. S., *A Practical Guide to U.S. Taxation of International Transactions*, 2000, 48.

[254] See McIntyre, M. J., *Tax Notes International* 1996, 59; Tello, C. P., *Tax Management International Journal* 1998, 11.

[255] See Hoke, W. D., *Tax Notes International* 1992, 845; Abrams, H. E. and Doernberg, R. L., *Essentials of United States Taxation*, 1999, 4-41.

[256] See McDaniel, P. R. and Ault, H. J., *Introduction to United States International Taxation*, 1998, 39; Isenbergh, J., *International Taxation*, 2000, 28; Doernberg, R. L., *International Taxation In a Nutshell*, 2001, 68.

[257] Certain deductions include interest expense and R&D expenses. Business expenses include, e.g., overhead, general and administrative, and supervisory costs. See Benson, D. M., *The Tax Adviser* 1996, 630; Middleton, C. I., *Journal of Partnership Taxation* 1999, 330; Bittker, B. I. and Eustice, J. S., *Federal Income Taxation of Corporations and Shareholders*, 2002, paragraph 15.02[1][a].

[258] IRC § 861(a) defines income from U.S.-sources with respect to eight specific classes of gross income (dividends, interest, personal services, rentals and royalties, disposition of real estate, sales of inventory property, insurance income, and social security benefits). IRC § 862(a) defines foreign-source income rules for the same classes of income by stating

55

and foreign-source taxable income, expenses that are **definitely** related to one or several classes of income must be allocated to U.S. and foreign-source income on the basis of their factual relationship.[260] A deduction[261] is definitely related and, thus, attributable, to a class of gross income if it is incurred as a result of, or incidental to, an activity or property, if such an activity or property generates or is reasonably expected to generate gross income.[262]

Expenses related to the generation of all gross income, i.e., **not directly** related to any particular source of income, are allocated and apportioned on a pro rata basis between U.S. and various separate limitation categories of foreign-source income to determine the U.S. taxpayer's net foreign income in each category.[263] Apportionment of a deduction between U.S.- and foreign-source gross income is made by using the apportionment base that reflects to a reasonably close extent, the relationship between the deduction and gross income.[264] The rule of thumb for apportioning the deduction, such as the ratio of foreign to domestic gross income, is determined by the vague formulation of the respective regulations issued under IRC § 861.[265] The regulations prescribe a two-step process of:[266]

- firstly, allocating deductions to classes of gross income[267] to which they are definitely related;[268] and
- secondly, apportioning those deductions between the statutory and residual groupings of gross income.[269]

Classes of income may include, for example, gross income incurred on business activities, dividends,[270] interest,[271] or royalties.[272] The statutory groupings of gross income refer to foreign-

---

that an item is foreign-source income if it is not from U.S.-sources as provided in IRC § 861. See Meldman, R. E. and Schadewald, M. S., *A Practical Guide to U.S. Taxation of International Transactions*, 2000, 32.

[259] IRC §§ 861(b) and 862(b).

[260] IRC § 861(b). Reg. § 1.861-8. An apportionment based on gross income is allowed only if no better method exists. See Johnsen, K. M. and Lipton, J. A., *Tax Management International Journal* 1991, 235; Endres, D. and Spengel, C., *Steuerstrukturen in Deutschland aus Sicht eines US-Investors*, 1997, 92; McDaniel, P. R. and Ault, H. J., *Introduction to United States International Taxation*, 1998, 45.

[261] Collectively, "deductions" include expenses, losses, and other deductions.

[262] See Johnsen, K. M. and Lipton, J. A., *Tax Management International Journal* 1991, 235; Meldman, R. E. and Schadewald, M. S., *A Practical Guide to U.S. Taxation of International Transactions*, 2000, 49; Kuntz, J. D. and Peroni, R. J., *U.S. International Taxation*, 2002, paragraph A2.05[3].

[263] IRC § 861(b). Reg. § 1.861-8(c)(3). See Rodriguez, A. E., *The International Tax Journal* 2001, 84; Kuntz, J. D. and Peroni, R. J., *U.S. International Taxation*, 2002, paragraph A2.05[4].

[264] See Meldman, R. E. and Schadewald, M. S., *A Practical Guide to U.S. Taxation of International Transactions*, 2000, 49.

[265] Temp. Reg. § 1.861-8T(b)(3), "... attribute supportive deductions on some reasonable basis directly to activities or property which generate, have generated, or could be reasonably expected to generate gross income". Thus, this implies that deductions that are supportive in nature, such as general and administrative as well as stewardship expenses may be related to all classes of gross income. See *Young & Rubicam Inc v. The United States*, 410 F. 2nd 1233 (Ct. Cl. 1969); *Columbian Rope Co. v. Commissioner*, 42 T.C. 800 [1964].

[266] See McDaniel, P. R. and Ault, H. J., *Introduction to United States International Taxation*, 1998, 46; Meldman, R. E. and Schadewald, M. S., *A Practical Guide to U.S. Taxation of International Transactions*, 2000, 48; Doernberg, R. L., *International Taxation In a Nutshell*, 2001, 91.

[267] The term "classes of gross income" means the gross-income types enumerated in IRC § 61, such as dividends, interest, and compensations.

[268] See Meldman, R. E. and Schadewald, M. S., *A Practical Guide to U.S. Taxation of International Transactions*, 2000, 49.

[269] See Johnsen, K. M. and Lipton, J. A., *Tax Management International Journal* 1991, 235; Meldman, R. E. and Schadewald, M. S., *A Practical Guide to U.S. Taxation of International Transactions*, 2000, 49.

[270] Dividends are U.S.-source income if paid by a domestic corporation or certain foreign corporations. Dividends paid from a foreign corporation will be at least partially U.S.-source income, unless less than 25 percent of the foreign

source gross income that must first be determined to arrive at foreign-source taxable income for purposes of the FTC limitation.[273] The remaining U.S.-source gross income is referred to as the residual grouping of gross income.[274]

As the regulations do not spell out a specific method of apportionment, the taxpayer may consider any factors which are consistent with the requirements of the regulations under IRC § 861.[275] However, the regulations include some factors, such as:[276]

- comparison of profit contribution;
- comparison of expenses incurred, assets used, salaries paid, space utilized, and time spent, that are attributable to the activities or properties giving raise to the class of gross income; and
- comparison of the amount of gross income.

For certain expenses, in particular, interest and R&D expenses, the regulations contain specific allocation and apportionment rules.[277]

Interest expense is allocated and apportioned based on the theory that money is fungible.[278] Basically, interest expense is attributable to all activities and property of the taxpayer, irrespective of the special purpose for incurring the debt on which interest is paid.[279] IRC § 864(e) generally seeks

---

corporation's gross income is effectively connected with a U.S. trade or business during the three-year period preceding the taxable year in which the dividend is declared. If the 25 percent or more of the foreign corporation's gross income is effectively connected with a U.S. trade or business, the amount that equals the ratio of the corporation's effectively connected gross income to its total gross income from all sources for the three-year period is treated as if from U.S.-sources (IRC § 861(a)(2)(B)). See McDaniel, P. R. and Ault, H. J., *Introduction to United States International Taxation*, 1998, 41; Abrams, H. E. and Doernberg, R. L., *Essentials of United States Taxation*, 1999, 4-43; Isenbergh, J., *International Taxation*, 2000, 34; Meldman, R. E. and Schadewald, M. S., *A Practical Guide to U.S. Taxation of International Transactions*, 2000, 34; Andersen, R. E., *Foreign Tax Credits*, 2002, paragraph 8.04[2]; Lau, P. C. and Soltis, S. L., *Journal of Taxation* 2001, 106; Bittker, B. I. and Eustice, J. S., *Federal Income Taxation of Corporations and Shareholders*, 2002, paragraph 15.02[1][a].

[271] IRC § 861(a)(1) provides that the gross income that is "interest from the United States or the District of Columbia, and interest on bonds, notes, or other interest-bearing obligations of noncorporate residents or domestic corporations..." is from U.S.-sources, except for certain items specifically excluded. Hence, the source of interest income is basically determined by the residence of the debtor. See McDaniel, P. R. and Ault, H. J., *Introduction to United States International Taxation*, 1998, 40; Abrams, H. E. and Doernberg, R. L., *Essentials of United States Taxation*, 1999, 4-41; Isenbergh, J., *International Taxation*, 2000, 28; Meldman, R. E. and Schadewald, M. S., *A Practical Guide to U.S. Taxation of International Transactions*, 2000, 32; Andersen, R. E., *Foreign Tax Credits*, 2002, paragraph 8.03[2].

[272] IRC § 864(a)(4) provides that "rentals and royalties from property located in the United States" are U.S.-source income. See Isenbergh, J., *International Taxation*, 2000, 41; Doernberg, R. L., *International Taxation In a Nutshell*, 2001, 75.

[273] See Andersen, R. E., *Foreign Tax Credits*, 2002, paragraph 9.04[3].

[274] Regs. §§ 1.861-8T(c), -8(a) and (b). See McDaniel, P. R. and Ault, H. J., *Introduction to United States International Taxation*, 1998, 46; Kuntz, J. D. and Peroni, R. J., *U.S. International Taxation*, 2002, paragraph A2.05[5][c][ii].

[275] Reg. § 1.861-8. One alternative might be activity-based costing as a straightforward approach to operational cost allocations. For details, see Rodriguez, A. E., *The International Tax Journal* 2001, 89.

[276] See Meldman, R. E. and Schadewald, M. S., *A Practical Guide to U.S. Taxation of International Transactions*, 2000, 49; Andersen, R. E., *Foreign Tax Credits*, 2002, paragraph 9.04[3].

[277] Under Reg. § 1.861-17, 50 percent, or 25 percent in case of the gross income method, of R&D expense should be directly allocated to the location where more than 50 percent of R&D activities are performed. The remaining 50 percent should be apportioned to U.S.- and foreign-source income based on gross income or gross sales, with a 50 percent gross sales floor if the gross income method is chosen. See McDaniel, P. R. and Ault, H. J., *Introduction to United States International Taxation*, 1998, 49; Abrams, H. E. and Doernberg, R. L., *Essentials of United States Taxation*, 1999, 4-59; Meldman, R. E. and Schadewald, M. S., *A Practical Guide to U.S. Taxation of International Transactions*, 2000, 51; Andersen, R. E., *Foreign Tax Credits*, 2002, paragraph 9.06[2]; Bittker, B. I. and Eustice, J. S., *Federal Income Taxation of Corporations and Shareholders*, 2002, paragraph 15.02[1][f].

[278] See McDaniel, P. R. and Ault, H. J., *Introduction to United States International Taxation*, 1998, 47; Meldman, R. E. and Schadewald, M. S., *A Practical Guide to U.S. Taxation of International Transactions*, 2000, 51.

[279] Reg. § 1.861-10T(b) describes circumstances in which interest expense can be directly allocated to specific debt. This exception to the fungibility concept is limited to cases in that specific property is purchased or improved with non-recourse

57

to make this allocation solely on the basis of asset values, i.e., by allocating a U.S. taxpayer's consolidated U.S. interest expense pro rata between the U.S. and foreign assets held by the U.S. consolidated group.[280] The allocation and apportionment are based on the view that interest expense is closely linked to the amount of capital used to conduct business, rather than to the gross income earned from the activity.[281]

The IRC provides two alternatives for determing the value of the assets for purposes of apportioning interest expense, the book value method and the fair market value (FMV) method.[282] The book value method applies when the use of the alternative FMV method is not affirmatively elected.[283] U.S. MNCs using the book value method for allocating interest expense incurred must first classify assets as U.S. or foreign, based on the type of income they generate.[284] U.S. corporations in an affiliated group[285] must also consider the assets on the tax basic balance sheet, while ignoring or looking through the stock of U.S. subsidiaries.[286] In other words, the interest expense of a U.S. subsidiary that generates only U.S.-source income must still be allocated and apportioned to the foreign-source income generated by other members of the affiliated group. The tax basis of stock of foreign subsidiaries must then be increased or lowered by each foreign subsidiary's cumulative E&Ps, even if those E&Ps have been financed only by local country loans, as they are intended to reduce the net foreign-source income.[287]

Alternatively, the apportioning of interest expense can be based on the FMV method,[288] which must be explicitly elected and is binding for future years. For this multi-step computation, the U.S. tax law provides little guidance as to the mechanics of each step.[289] The FMVs of all assets of

---

debt. See Doernberg, R. L., *International Taxation In a Nutshell*, 2001, 94; Kuntz, J. D. and Peroni, R. J., *U.S. International Taxation*, 2002, paragraph A2.03[2][b].

[280] Prior to 1986, interest expense was allocated on a separate company basis. See Regs. §§ 1.861-8(a)(2)-(e)(2) [1977]. Taxpayers could, therefore, create a corporate structure that shielded foreign-source income from interest expense by maintaining debt in domestic group members that held only domestic assets. This structure was referred to as a "top hat", meaning that the debt was maintained at the parent company level and the stock of the foreign subsidiaries was held by a domestic special purpose vehicle that had little or no debt. See McDaniel, P. R. and Ault, H. J., *Introduction to United States International Taxation*, 1998, 47; Zschiegner, H., *Internationale Wirtschaftsbriefe*, Fach 8, USA, Gruppe 2, 1998 II, 952; Abrams, H. E. and Doernberg, R. L., *Essentials of United States Taxation*, 1999, 4-57; Hannes, S. P. and Ried, J. A., *Tax Notes* 2001, 1306; Kuntz, J. D. and Peroni, R. J., *U.S. International Taxation*, 2002, paragraph A2.05[5][c][i]. As a result, U.S. Congress recognized that prior law allowed affiliated taxpayers to use interest expense to reduce consolidated tax on U.S.-source income although the interest expense funded non-taxable foreign activities. See Johnsen, K. M. and Lipton, J. A., *Tax Management International Journal* 1991, 235; Meldman, R. E. and Schadewald, M. S., *A Practical Guide to U.S. Taxation of International Transactions*, 2000, 51; Schreiber, C. and Meiisel, P., *Internationales Steuerrecht* 2002, 585.

[281] See Zschiegner, H., *Internationale Wirtschaftsbriefe*, Fach 8, USA, Gruppe 2, 1998 II, 952.

[282] In either case, assets are, in general, valued based on the average value for the year.

[283] Temp. Regs. under IRC § 861 set forth the provisions governing the book value method. See Johnsen, K. M. and Lipton, J. A., *Tax Management International Journal* 1991, 236.

[284] See Meldman, R. E. and Schadewald, M. S., *A Practical Guide to U.S. Taxation of International Transactions*, 2000, 51.

[285] An affiliated group is defined, for purposes of interest expense allocation, as a parent-subsidiary chain connected through at least 80 percent shareholding with a common parent company which is an includible corporation, according to Reg. § 1.861-11T(d)(1), IRC § 1504(a)(1). Includible corporations do not include tax exempt corporations, insurance companies, foreign corporations, DISCs, regulated investment companies, and real estate trusts (Regs. §§ 1.861-11T(d) and 1.861-9T(f)). See Meldman, R. E. and Schadewald, M. S., *A Practical Guide to U.S. Taxation of International Transactions*, 2000, 51; Kuntz, J. D. and Peroni, R. J., *U.S. International Taxation*, 2002, paragraph A2.05[5][h][iii].

[286] See Kuntz, J. D. and Peroni, R. J., *U.S. International Taxation*, 2002, paragraph A2.05[5][h].

[287] See Johnsen, K. M. and Lipton, J. A., *Tax Management International Journal* 1991, 235; Kuntz, J. D. and Peroni, R. J., *U.S. International Taxation*, 2002, paragraph A2.05[5][j][i].

[288] See Meldman, R. E. and Schadewald, M. S., *A Practical Guide to U.S. Taxation of International Transactions*, 2000, 51.

[289] For details on the FMV computations for publicly traded and non-traded companies, see Johnsen, K. M. and Lipton, J. A., *Tax Management International Journal* 1991, 237.

the affiliated U.S. group must be computed and, in line with the book value method, the character of all assets must be determined by taking into account the type of income they generate.

This allocation of interest expense is important because the U.S. law provides that FTCs can be claimed if and only if there is sufficient net foreign-source income in the separate category to which the credits relate.[290] Thus, the U.S. interest allocation rules are a significant component in computing the amount of net foreign-source income in each respective basket.[291] Most interesting is that the mechanism of valuing and allocating intangible assets has an impact on the final proportions of U.S. and foreign assets, provided the FMV of tangible assets remains the same.[292] Due to this interplay of tangible and allocated intangible assets, significantly more interest expense is allocated to U.S.-source income.

To the extent that U.S. expenses are allocated against foreign-source income, a taxpayer will lose the ability to claim FTCs to offset its residual U.S. tax liability.[293] Therefore, it might be preferable to utilize the "check-the-box" election, i.e., to treat a foreign subsidiary as a pass-through entity, which enables the U.S. corporate shareholder to deduct any losses incurred by the foreign subsidiary against the corporation's U.S. taxable income.[294] When a taxpayer cannot use available credits to offset its U.S. tax liability on foreign earnings, international double taxation is created.[295]

2.2.2.1.1. Impact of Foreign-Source Losses

In computing the FTC limitation, losses generated from income arising in foreign countries reduce income from other foreign countries and, thus, lower the amount of foreign taxes that can be used from those countries as a credit.[296] Foreign losses may not be used to offset U.S. income unless all foreign-source income has been offset. Thus, a taxpayer may not offset a category of separate limitation losses solely against the corresponding category of separate limitation income and then apply excess losses against U.S.-source income without first using the excess to offset overall limitation income or another category of separate limitation income.[297] Moreover, foreign losses must be allocated proportionately among the different categories of separate or overall limitation income, and the percentage of foreign losses that may offset a category of income must equal the category's percentage share of foreign-source income. Only in cases where foreign losses exceed foreign-source gross income from all foreign countries for the tax year can foreign losses reduce U.S. tax on U.S.-source income.[298]

---

[290] See Isenbergh, J., *International Taxation*, 2000, 28; Tello, C. P., *Tax Management International Journal* 2001, 161; Wells, B., *Tax Executive* 2001, 369.

[291] See Johnsen, K. M. and Lipton, J. A., *Tax Management International Journal* 1991, 235.

[292] See Johnsen, K. M. and Lipton, J. A., *Tax Management International Journal* 1991, 241.

[293] See Coffill, E. J. and Wilson, P. Jr., *International Tax Review* 1996, 39; Tello, C. P., *Tax Management International Journal* 1998, 19; Meldman, R. E. and Schadewald, M. S., *A Practical Guide to U.S. Taxation of International Transactions*, 2000, 27; CCH, *2002 U.S. Tax Master Guide*, 2001, paragraph 2477.

[294] See *infra* chapter "Achieving Full FTC by Issuing a Hybrid Instrument", page 144.

[295] See Tello, C. P., *Tax Management International Journal* 2001, 162; Wells, B., *Tax Executive* 2001, 369.

[296] See Culbertson, R. E., *Tax Notes International* 1996, 1761; Dilworth, R. H. and Andrus, J. L., *Tax Law and Practice*, 2001, 1099.

[297] See Rosenbloom, H. D., *Brooklyn Journal of International Law* 2001, 1542.

[298] See Abrams, H. E. and Doernberg, R. L., *Essentials of United States Taxation*, 1999, 4-134; Meldman, R. E. and Schadewald, M. S., *A Practical Guide to U.S. Taxation of International Transactions*, 2000, 82.

Reduction of U.S. tax on U.S.-source income if

Foreign-source loss   >   Σ Foreign-source income (all foreign countries)

However, overall foreign losses are subject to recapture in later years for FTC limitation purposes.[299] Under the recapture rule, U.S. tax savings generated by a U.S. corporation that has foreign losses, including expenditures allocated to foreign-source income, in excess of foreign-source income will be recaptured when foreign-source income exceeds foreign-source expenses in a subsequent year. The recapture rule also applies to the credit for tax attributable to possession-source income under IRC § 936.[300] An overall foreign loss is the amount by which foreign-source gross income is exceeded by the sum of expenses, losses and other deductions properly allocable and apportioned to such foreign-source income.[301] In particular, any net operating loss deductions or theft losses are not taken into consideration. The general effect of this provision is to restrict FTCs in a year subsequent to an overall loss year by recharacterizing some future net foreign-source income as U.S.-source income.[302] In general, the amount of foreign-source income that will be recharacterized is limited to the lesser of:[303]

(1) the overall foreign loss for the earlier year; or
(2) 50 percent of the foreign-source taxable income for the current year.[304]

However, a taxpayer may choose to have more than 50 percent of his taxable income recharacterized as U.S.-source income.[305]

2.2.2.1.2. Impact of Gains on a Disposition of Business Property

Unless business property was not a material factor in the recognition of income by the taxpayer, any gain recognized from the disposition of property predominantly used outside the U.S. during the preceding three-year period is subject to the recapture rule of IRC § 904(f). The amount recharacterized is either the total gain or, if less, the overall foreign loss.[306] Both non-recognized gains as well as recognized gains are generally subject to the recapture provision.[307] Foreign-source

---

[299] IRC § 904(f). See Culbertson, R. E., *Tax Notes International* 1996, 1761; McDaniel, P. R. and Ault, H. J., *Introduction to United States International Taxation*, 1998, 104; Abrams, H. E. and Doernberg, R. L., *Essentials of United States Taxation*, 1999, 4-135.

[300] See Kuntz, J. D. and Peroni, R. J., *U.S. International Taxation*, 2002, paragraph B4.17[4][a].

[301] See Andersen, R. E., *Foreign Tax Credits*, 2002, paragraph 8.14[1]; Kuntz, J. D. and Peroni, R. J., *U.S. International Taxation*, 2002, paragraph B4.17[2].

[302] See Joyce, T. B., *Tax Management International Journal* 1992 I, 56; Anonymous, *Tax Executive* 1999 I, 350; Abrams, H. E. and Doernberg, R. L., *Essentials of United States Taxation*, 1999, 4-136.

[303] See Kuntz, J. D. and Peroni, R. J., *U.S. International Taxation*, 2002, paragraph B4.17[4][a].

[304] See Joyce, T. B., *Tax Management International Journal* 1992 I, 62; Meldman, R. E. and Schadewald, M. S., *A Practical Guide to U.S. Taxation of International Transactions*, 2000, 82.

[305] See Kuntz, J. D. and Peroni, R. J., *U.S. International Taxation*, 2002, paragraph B4.17[4][a].

[306] IRC §§ 904(f)(3) and 904(f)(5)(F).

[307] See Joyce, T. B., *Tax Management International Journal* 1992 I, 62.

gains that otherwise would not be recognized are recognized and recharacterized.[308] Therefore, a disposition of foreign business property could result in both an increase in income and a reduction of the limitation on the FTC.

2.2.2.1.3. Impact of Foreign-Source Capital Gains

The extent to which foreign-source capital gains can be used in computing the limitation on the FTC is restricted. The general effect of the limitation is to require U.S.-source net capital losses to be taken into account in determining foreign-source capital gains.[309] Hence, this provision might reduce the numerator, which in turn reduces the resulting limit while IRC 904 (b)(2)(A) has no effect on the denominator of the FTC limitation formula. After doing so, a corporation must make further adjustments under special rules.[310]

2.2.2.2. Exchange Rate for Foreign Taxes

For purposes of the FTC, foreign taxes accrued are to be translated into U.S. dollars at the average exchange rate for the tax year to which the taxes relate.[311] Under exceptions to this rule, foreign taxes must be converted at the exchange rate in effect when the foreign taxes were paid.[312] This exception applies if foreign taxes are paid within two years of accrual, and if they differ from the accrued amount merely because of currency exchange fluctuations.[313] In this case, no redetermination is required, even though the actual dollar value paid and the accrued amount differ.[314] In other cases, such as when taxes paid differ from the amount accrued, a redetermination is required.[315]

---

[308] See Joyce, T. B., *Tax Management International Journal* 1992 I, 62; Joyce, T. B., *Tax Management International Journal* 1992 II, 123.

[309] See Joyce, T. B., *Tax Management International Journal* 1992 II, 117; Meldman, R. E. and Schadewald, M. S., *A Practical Guide to U.S. Taxation of International Transactions*, 2000, 81; Kuntz, J. D. and Peroni, R. J., *U.S. International Taxation*, 2002, paragraph B4.16[3][b].

[310] For example, IRC § 904(b)(2)(B). See Kuntz, J. D. and Peroni, R. J., *U.S. International Taxation*, 2002, paragraph B4.16[3].

[311] IRC §§ 902 and 960. Reg. § 986(a)(1)(A). On January 19, 2000, the IRS issued Rev. Proc. 2000-13 to remind taxpayers to use the average exchange rate for the taxable year. Rev. Proc. 2000-13, 2000-6 I.R.B. 515. See Fischl, A. and Schneider, R. A., *Tax Management International Journal* 1997, 570; Garrett-Nelson, L., *Tax Notes International* 1997, 1289; Jensen, P., Spikes, P. and Carter, D., *The International Tax Journal* 1998, 8; Meldman, R. E. and Schadewald, M. S., *A Practical Guide to U.S. Taxation of International Transactions*, 2000, 108; Swanick, M. F. and Leary, W., *Tax Management International Journal* 2000, 300.

[312] IRC §§ 986(a)(1)(B) and (C). See Jensen, P., Spikes, P. and Carter, D., *The International Tax Journal* 1998, 8; Andersen, R. E., *Foreign Tax Credits*, 2002, paragraph 6.05[4][c][ii].

[313] See Meldman, R. E. and Schadewald, M. S., *A Practical Guide to U.S. Taxation of International Transactions*, 2000, 253; Andersen, R. E., *Foreign Tax Credits*, 2002, paragraph 6.05[4][c][ii].

[314] See Garrett-Nelson, L., *Tax Notes International* 1997, 1289; Jensen, P., Spikes, P. and Carter, D., *The International Tax Journal* 1998, 8.

[315] See Krehbühl, H.-H., *Das Steueranrechnungsverfahren in den USA*, 1997, 159; Jensen, P., Spikes, P. and Carter, D., *The International Tax Journal* 1998, 8.

2.2.3. Excess Foreign Tax Credits

U.S. taxpayers whose foreign taxes exceed the FTC limitation are said to be in an "excess foreign tax credit position" in which the excess FTCs represent the portion of the foreign taxes that exceed the U.S. tax liability triggered by the foreign-source income.[316]

The FTC limit can result in unused, i.e., non-credited, foreign taxes for the tax year.[317] Under IRC § 904(c), a two-year carryback and a five-year carryforward of excess foreign taxes are provided.[318] Such excess taxes must first be carried to the second preceding taxable year, then to the first preceding taxable year, and finally to the first through fifth succeeding taxable years, beginning with the earliest year first.[319] The taxes can be credited in years when the formula limitation for that year exceeds the foreign taxes attributable to the same tax year. The carryback and carryforward provisions are available only within a separate basket. In other words, excess foreign taxes in one basket cannot be carried over unless there is an excess limitation in the same basket for the carryforward year.[320]

2.2.4. Conclusion

The FTC limitation is partially based on the amount of foreign-source taxable income in the numerator of the limitation ratio. Consequently, the sourcing of income is of significant importance.[321] Income that is taxed by a foreign tax jurisdiction benefits from the FTC only to the extent that it is classified as foreign-source income under U.S. tax law. Thus, elements that have an impact on the souring of income, such as the place of title passage, should be taken into consideration before a transaction is undertaken.

One strategy for alleviating excess FTCs is to increase the proportion of worldwide income that is classified as foreign-source for U.S. tax purposes. This might be achieved by arranging the passage of title abroad[322] or through export sales which give rise to foreign-source income to the extent of any marketing profit. Further, recharacterization of deductions might be a beneficial means for eliminating excess FTCs. For example, by using alternative apportionment bases to source selling, general and administrative expenses, a taxpayer might benefit from having a lower amount of these deductions allocated and apportioned to foreign-source income.[323]

A second strategy for eliminating the excess credits is to blend low- and high-tax foreign-source income within a single limitation. The implication of this is that the excess limitation on the low-tax foreign income offsets the excess credits on the high-tax foreign income. Under the current limitation system, a taxpayer must compute a separate limitation for each basket of income.

It may be possible for a U.S. corporation to alleviate the problem of excess foreign taxes by using the following techniques:

---

[316] See Martin, W. J., *Tax Management International Journal* 1998, 449; Hines, J. R. Jr., *National Tax Journal* 1999, 388.

[317] See Benson, D. M., *The Tax Adviser* 1996, 630; Isenbergh, J., *International Taxation*, 2000, 128.

[318] See Endres, D. and Spengel, C., *Steuerstrukturen in Deutschland aus Sicht eines US-Investors*, 1997, 92; Fischl, A. and Schneider, R. A., *Tax Management International Journal* 1997, 572; McDaniel, P. R. and Ault, H. J., *Introduction to United States International Taxation*, 1998, 106; Zschiegner, H., *Internationale Wirtschaftsbriefe*, Fach 8, USA, Gruppe 2, 1998 VI, 1003; Anonymous, *Tax Executive* 1999 I, 349; Hines, J. R. Jr., *National Tax Journal* 1999, 388; Kroschel, J., *Die Federal Income Tax der Vereinigten Staaten von Amerika*, 2000, 259; Meldman, R. E. and Schadewald, M. S., *A Practical Guide to U.S. Taxation of International Transactions*, 2000, 84; CCH, *2002 U.S. Tax Master Guide*, 2001, paragraph 2482.

[319] See Andersen, R. E., *Foreign Tax Credits*, 2002, paragraph 7.13.

[320] IRC § 904(d)(1). See Meldman, R. E. and Schadewald, M. S., *A Practical Guide to U.S. Taxation of International Transactions*, 2000, 84.

[321] See Newberry, K. J. and Dhaliwal, D. S., *Journal of Accounting Research* 2001, 645.

[322] See Isenbergh, J., *International Taxation*, 2000, 45.

[323] For sourcing gross income rules and the source rules for deduction, refer *supra* page 55.

- generating "same basket" foreign-source income which is subject to a tax rate lower than the U.S. rate;
- reducing highly taxed foreign-source income in favor of foreign-source income that is taxed at a lower rate;
- timing of the repatriation of foreign-source earnings to coincide with excess limitation years; and
- choosing IRC § 164 for foreign taxes for years when the deduction benefit would exceed the FTC benefit.

A taxpayer who can control the timing of income and loss recognition will try to avoid recognizing losses in years when the loss is apportioned among the FTC limitation baskets. Otherwise, the foreign taxes for which a credit is allowed for the tax year are reduced.

3. DEDUCTION OF EXPENSES

In general terms, the objective of the tax planner will be the minimization of a corporate group's effective tax rate, thereby maximizing post-tax profits.[324] In terms of financial agreements, this will significantly impact how maximum relief for interest deductions may be taken, preferably against higher taxed profits. An important consideration pertains to the local rules for the deductibility of costs relating to the holding activity, in particular, the ability to deduct interest expenses triggered by refinancing the foreign investments. In the case of a pure holding company solely generating tax-exempt income, the potential interest expense is not efficient in reducing the tax base. Conversely, a holding entity that also earns income from its own activities might *ceteris paribus* be favorable, as the refinancing costs could be used to net against any profits. However, some restrictions might apply to the deductibility of interest payments relating to tax-exempt income, e.g., dividends received from substantial shareholdings and capital gains recognized on such shareholdings. Some jurisdictions totally disallow any deduction of such expenses. Others, irrefutably assign a certain percentage of the tax-exempt income to expenses directly connected with the receipts, or even do not limit the deductibility.

Also, the issue of which company should be the borrower and which should be the lender will be of vital importance in an international group. Consideration of these issues will, however, turn upon the fundamental distinction between debt and equity as well as the extent to which it is permissible to introduce debt into an EU company, the level of withholding tax imposed on dividends and interest, and the tax effects of foreign exchange differences.

The choice as to debt or equity finance will depend upon the jurisdictions in which the group wishes the interest cost to be treated as a deductible expense. The decision will be influenced by tax capacity, comparative tax rates, tax regulations in the jurisdiction of the borrower and special anti-abuse provisions and withholding tax issues. Additionally, the impact of debt and exchange rate movements on the borrower's financial statements in cases where the debt is not borrowed in the local currency may also influence the final decision, as would any form of official or unofficial exchange control.

Anti-abuse provisions, mostly referred to as thin capitalization rules, impose certain debt-to-equity ratio limitations (the so-called *safe havens*) on companies.[325] When exceeding the statutory or informal ratio, interest and similar payments qualify as constructive distributions of profits, i.e.,

[324] See Klöne, H., *Steuerplanung*, 1980, 4; Wagner, F. W. and Dirrigl, H., *Die Steuerplanung der Unternehmung*, 1980, 8; Tinner, H., *Konzernstruktur und Steuerplanung*, 1984, 5; Kratz, P., *Steuerplanung internationaler Unternehmungen*, 1986, 67; Kessler, W., *Die Euro-Holding*, 1996, 74; Hintzen, B., *Die deutsche Zwischenholding als Gegenstand der internationalen Steuerplanung*, 1997, 45; Bolanz, G., *Die EU-Holding als strategisches Gestaltungsinstrument in der Steuerplanung*, 1998, 16; Boos, M., Rehkugler, H. and Tucha, T., *Der Betrieb* 2000, 2389.

[325] For an overview of the different debt-to-equity ratios in Austria, Belgium, Denmark, France, Germany, Ireland, Luxembourg, the Netherlands, Spain, and Switzerland, refer *infra* page 138.

they are treated as dividends rather than as deductible interest expenses for tax purposes. Some of the local thin capitalization rules apply only to substantial foreign shareholders. Again, the meaning of "substantial participation" differs. Safe havens might also vary according to the basis for calculating the interest, e.g., a special debt-to-equity ratio on hybrid financing instruments.

4. IMMEDIATE UTILIZATION OF LOSSES

Under many local tax laws, losses triggered by a domestic taxpayer can be carried back and/or carried forward. However, limitations might apply to the period in which the losses can be offset. The total amount of the carryback and/or carryforward from any one year can also be limited to a certain amount. Further, loss carrybacks might be restricted by limiting their application to those profits that have not previously been distributed by way of dividends. In effect, loss relief would not be completely granted to a foreign operating entity under foreign tax law or, due to restrictions in the period of time or amount, the increase in liquidity and the interest profits are limited.

Thus, another aim of interposing a holding company is to achieve tax consolidation of profits and losses within the group.[326] In most cases, only entities resident in the same jurisdiction as the EU holding company are included in the tax consolidation. A cross-border tax consolidation might also be possible in Denmark and France. However, a final tax cost reduction cannot be achieved by the immediate loss compensation with profits generated by other group entities. Nonetheless, taxes are temporarily postponed, as the interperiodical loss deduction is replaced by the intraperiodical loss consolidation. The loss consolidation leads, however, to an increase in liquidity within the group and, due to lower tax payments in the present, to an interest profit. Various EU member states support different regimes for tax consolidation. The regimes significantly differ in the treatment of single affiliated entities. While, for example, Austria, Denmark, France, Germany,[327] Ireland, and Luxembourg treat affiliated entities as single, separate entities, the Netherlands[328] views the group as an economic unit, negating the effect of separate entities.[329]

Finally, a U.S. MNC can use losses without establishing a local tax consolidation group. Where the foreign entity is classified either as a branch of a domestic corporation under the U.S. check-the-box regulations, a foreign partnership or a hybrid entity having foreign corporate characteristics but U.S. partnership characteristics, the losses of the foreign operation are immediately accessible in the U.S.[330] Conversely, where the foreign entity is classified as a corporation for U.S. tax purposes, foreign losses will not be available to the U.S. MNC. Losses incurred from foreign subsidiaries could ultimately be a reason to write-down the participation in the foreign operating company. It should be noted, that a write-down of participation might be subject to limitations or may even be impossible.

---

[326] See Baumgärtel, M. and Perlet, H., *Standortfragen bei der Bildung von Holdinggesellschaften*, 1994, 711; Jonas, B., *Die Steuerkonsolidierung als Instrument der internationalen Konzernsteuerplanung*, 2000, 217.

[327] See Endres, D. and Ditsch, S., *The International Tax Journal* 1999, 34.

[328] For the Dutch tax consolidation, the so-called *fiscale eenheid*, in detail, see Grotherr, S., *Internationale Wirtschaftsbriefe*, Fach 5, Niederlande, Gruppe 2, 1994; Bremer, S., *Der Holdingstandort Bundesrepublik Deutschland*, 1996, 251.

[329] See Grotherr, S., *Steuer und Wirtschaft* 1996, 359.

[330] See Meldman, R. E. and Schadewald, M. S., *A Practical Guide to U.S. Taxation of International Transactions*, 2000, 333.

SECTION 3: TAX PLANNING TOOLS

Strategies to achieve tax planning goals outlined in the previous sections are based on, in particular, choosing a legal form or structuring a fact pattern of a business in such a way that a taxable event is met either in a tax beneficial manner or not met at all.[331] Such strategies are independent from any moral obligation to pay taxes but rather, they attempt to address the lack of design neutrality in the tax acts.[332] Further, (German) courts have ruled that no person is obligated to structure their investments to trigger tax at a government friendly level.[333] Given that the creativity of international tax planners is so impressive, their planning advice is more often subject to court decisions ruling that these structures are abusive. However, provided that the tax planning idea is not purely tax driven, i.e., evidence of business motivation exists, the tools available to a U.S. MNC are quite numerous. Ideas can, however, only be developed if the tax planner has an in-depth knowledge of statutory international tax law and is, then, able to use the tools efficiently. As the goals of a U.S. MNC were set forth in the prior section, various international tax planning tools from a U.S. tax point of view are examined within this section.

Even though the transactions giving rise to foreign income, the U.S. taxes the worldwide income of U.S. taxpayers.[334] Because foreign countries might also levy tax on some of this income, taxpayers might be subject to double taxation. Special provisions, such as the FTC, can mitigate this problem.[335] For foreign taxpayers, the U.S. generally taxes only income earned within its borders.[336] The U.S. taxation of cross-border transactions can be defined in terms of "inbound" and "outbound" taxation.[337] Inbound taxation refers to the U.S. taxation of U.S.-source income earned by foreign taxpayers. Outbound taxation refers to the U.S. taxation of foreign-source income earned by U.S. taxpayers. In the following sections, the focus is on optimizing foreign-source income.

In order to lower global tax costs, the U.S. MNC may use several techniques to reduce foreign income taxes. Examples of such techniques include realizing income that is taxed at a lower rate - via routing or conversion -, accelerating the recognition of deductions, and deferring the recognition of taxable income.[338] Moreover, the U.S. MNC might take advantage of debt financing, transfer pricing, local tax incentives,[339] checking the box for eligible entities under U.S. federal tax law, and the use of income tax treaties to reduce foreign taxes.

---

[331] See Teufel, T., *Steuerliche Rechtsformoptimierung*, 2002, 1.

[332] See Tipke, K., *Die Steuerrechtsordnung* I, 1993, 180.

[333] BVerfG, resolution dated April 4, 1959, 1 BvL 23, 34/57, BVerfGE 9, 237; BFH, decision dated March 16, 1993, XI R 52/90, BStBl. II 1993, 564.

[334] U.S. international tax provisions are concerned basically with two types of potential taxpayers: U.S. persons earning foreign-source income and foreign persons earning U.S.-source income. The term "person" is defined in IRC § 7701(a)(1) and includes an individual, corporation, partnership, trust, estate, or association. See Yoder, L. D., *Tax Management International Journal* 1997 I, 204; Martin, W. J., *Tax Management International Journal* 1998, 461. For the criteria of a corporation, partnership, trust, and association, see Boles, E., *Gesellschaften im US-Einkommensteuerrecht*, 1993, 15, 21, 77, and 94.

[335] For the FTC provisions in detail, refer *supra* page 45.

[336] See McDaniel, P. R. and Ault, H. J., *Introduction to United States International Taxation*, 1998, 53.

[337] See Isenbergh, J., *International Taxation*, 2000, 4.

[338] See Kessler, W., *Überlegungen zur Standortwahl einer Euro-Holding aus steuerlicher Sicht*, 1997, 136; Hirschler, K., *Rechtsformplanung im Konzern*, 2000, 106; Kessler, W., *Internationale Holdingstandorte*, 2002, 80.

[339] E.g., companies carrying on manufacturing operations in Ireland are subject to a reduced rate of corporate tax of ten percent on profits arising between January 1, 1981 and December 31, 2010. For the purpose of the relief, certain services are deemed to be manufacturing activities such as financial services for non-residents (IFSC) within the Customs House Dock Area, certain activities conducted at the Shannon Airport, computer services, data processing, shared services, and call centers. Quota restrictions agreed with the EU Commission have limited the number of new manufacturing and new financial services companies that qualify for the ten percent rate, and in the case of activities approved after August 1, 1998 the reduced rate applies only up to December 31, 2002. See Grotherr, S., *Internationale Wirtschaftsbriefe*, Fach 5, Irland, Gruppe 2, 1989, 51; Fischer-Zernin, M. and Schwarz, H., *Internationale Wirtschaftsbriefe*, Fach 5, Irland, Gruppe 2, 1996, 63; Rädler, A. J., Lausterer, M. and Blumenberg, J., *Der Betrieb* 1996, Beilage 3, 2; Gundel, G., *Der Einsatz von ausländischen Finanzierungsgesellschaften im Rahmen der Konzernfinanzierung*, 2000, 294; O'Mahony, G., *International Tax Review* 2001, 37; Ward, J., *Ireland*, 2001, 54; Hollingsworth, G. and Fuller, C., *Tax Planning International mergers &*

1. ROUTING OF INCOME

When routing income, the income is transferred through - one or more - interposed entities (tiers) until it is received by the ultimate parent company.[340] Instead of using a direct transfer route, a holding company is interposed for the following reasons:

- In many cases, a tax optimized routing of income satisfies the sub goal of receiving payments of foreign dividends without triggering any withholding taxes.[341] Utilizing such structures is referred to as "Treaty Shopping" or "Directive Shopping".[342]
- The routing of income might also be used for reducing or eliminating excess FTCs by blending low- and high-tax foreign-source income.[343] This is achievable only if the jurisdiction in which the ultimate parent is located grants a direct and indirect credit on the basis of the overall average tax burden, which applies in the U.S.[344]
- Another purpose of routing income is the potential to claim cross-border imputation credits.[345] This goal can be achieved if a double tax treaty exists under which the imputation credit can be transferred with no or low tax.[346]

2. CONVERSION OF INCOME

In contrast to the routing of income, when converting income, the type of income changes.[347] It may be advantageous to finance high-tax foreign subsidiaries in a way that maximizes interest deductions and minimizes dividend payments. The potential advantages of debt financing provided by a U.S.

---

acquisitions 2002, 5. On January 19, 2000, the German Supreme Tax Court (the so-called *Bundesfinanzhof (BFH)*) ruled in the so-called *Irland I* (I R 94/97), and *Irland II* (I R 117/97) decisions that interposing an Irish subsidiary that is located in the Dublin Docks IFSC cannot be considered *ceteris paribus* an abuse of legal forms, hence, denying the application of § 42 of the *Abgabenordnung* (Tax Management Act). See Anonymous, *Internationale Wirtschaftsbriefe*, Fach 3a, Rechtsprechung, Gruppe 1, 2000, 901; Bogenschütz, E. and Wright, K., *Tax Notes International* 2000, 1513. In the Ministry of Finance (the so-called *BMF*) Circular of March 19, 2001 (IV B4 - S 1300 - 65/01, BStBl. I 2001, 243), the German tax authorities confirmed their view that the decisions made by the BFH will not apply to similar cases, in particular, the denial of the application of § 42 of the *Abgabenordnung*. See Förster, H., *Praxis Internationale Steuerberatung* 2001, 127; Weerth, J. de, *Internationales Steuerrecht* 2001, 228; Rose, G. and Glorius-Rose, C., *Steuerplanung und Gestaltunsgmissbrauch*, 2002, 92.

[340] See Hintzen, B., *Die deutsche Zwischenholding als Gegenstand der internationalen Steuerplanung*, 1997, 47; Hoffmann, W.-D., *Steueroptimales Ausschüttungsverhalten und Repatriierungsstrategien*, 2000, 520.

[341] See Baumgärtel, M. and Perlet, H., *Standortfragen bei der Bildung von Holdinggesellschaften*, 1994, 699; Bader, A., *Steuergestaltung mit Holdinggesellschaften*, 1998, 126; Hoffmann, W.-D., *Steueroptimales Ausschüttungsverhalten und Repatriierungsstrategien*, 2000, 522.

[342] See Bader, A., *Steuergestaltung mit Holdinggesellschaften*, 1998, 130; Hoffmann, W.-D., *Steueroptimales Ausschüttungsverhalten und Repatriierungsstrategien*, 2000, 523; Meldman, R. E. and Schadewald, M. S., *A Practical Guide to U.S. Taxation of International Transactions*, 2000, 345; Kessler, W., Dorfmueller, P., Schmidt, W. and Teufel, T., *Tax Notes International* 2001, 1218.

[343] See Meldman, R. E. and Schadewald, M. S., *A Practical Guide to U.S. Taxation of International Transactions*, 2000, 341; Newberry, K. J. and Dhaliwal, D. S., *Journal of Accounting Research* 2001, 644.

[344] See Kessler, W., *Grundlagen der Steuerplanung mit Holdinggesellschaften*, 2000, 194.

[345] See Kessler, W., *Grundlagen der Steuerplanung mit Holdinggesellschaften*, 2000, 194.

[346] However, this strategy has lost its importance due to the abolishment of both the German imputation credit system and the British advance corporate tax (ACT). See Howlett, K., Rudd, A. and Sylvester, C., *Journal of International Taxation* 1999 (July), 40; Ruchelman, S. C., Asbeck, E. van, Canalejo, G. and et. al., *Journal of International Taxation* 2001 (March), 25; Tardivy, P., Schiessl, M., Haelterman, A. and et. al., *International Tax Review* 2002 (March), 12.

[347] See Hoffmann, W.-D., *Steueroptimales Ausschüttungsverhalten und Repatriierungsstrategien*, 2000, 526.

parent company include a deduction in the high-tax foreign jurisdiction for interest paid to the U.S. parent, as well as the possibility of a reduction in foreign withholding taxes on interest payments, as opposed to dividend distributions. Commonly, an interposed holding company grants an interest-bearing loan to the operating entity.[348] In effect, profit distributions will be converted into interest expenditures at the level of the operating company.[349] The transfer of income from the interposed holding corporation to the parent company can be made simply by paying dividends. To secure the benefits of debt financing, the U.S. parent corporation must ensure that any intercompany payments meant to be interest qualify as such under the host country's tax laws. The rules for determining whether an investment in a local subsidiary is treated as debt and not equity vary from country to country. Some countries employ relatively objective standards, e.g., a maximum debt-to-equity ratio of 3:1,[350] while other jurisdictions employ more subjective standards based on facts and circumstances.[351]

The aims of converting income are diverse and include:

- reducing or eliminating any withholding taxes while interposing a holding company in a jurisdiction with no or low withholding taxes on interest;[352]
- generating taxable income in low-tax jurisdictions; and
- claiming any available FTCs.[353]

However, income conversion is only recommended, i.e., leads to a lower overall tax burden, if the foreign operating company is located in a country with generally high tax rates and the interest income created is subject to no or low statutory corporation/withholding tax.[354] Moreover, the transfer of the interest income earned by the interposed holding company and paid to the parent entity should be tax exempt[355] or not taxed at a higher rate.[356]

A classical example of the conversion of income is the transformation of non-privileged into privileged shareholdings by interposing a country holding entity. The country holding company should be established in a jurisdiction that provides a liberal participation exemption under local law and structures its income tax treaty policies based on the OECD model, i.e., participation exemption.[357] However, in the case of a U.S. MNC, deferral of intermediate corporate level capital gains will not violate the FPHC anti-deferral regime but could result in the loss of FTCs.

Finally, the transformation of income can be used to create an income qualification conflict in order to avoid any withholding taxes and/or to utilize existing excess FTCs.[358]

---

[348] See Hirschler, K., *Rechtsformplanung im Konzern*, 2000, 107; Hoffmann, W.-D., *Steueroptimales Ausschüttungsverhalten und Repatriierungsstrategien*, 2000, 520.

[349] See Schaumburg, H. and Jesse, L., *Die internationale Holding aus steuerrechtlicher Sicht*, 1995, paragraph L 22; Kessler, W., *Grundlagen der Steuerplanung mit Holdinggesellschaften*, 2000, 194.

[350] The debt-to-equity ratio of 3 : 1 can be viewed as an international common safe haven standard. See Bundestag-Drucksache, 14/2683, 2000, 124; PwC Deutsche Revision, *Unternehmenssteuerreform 2001*, 2000, 169.

[351] For example, Austria. For the different thin capitalization provisions, refer to the country-by-country synopsis *infra* page 111.

[352] See Hoffmann, W.-D., *Steueroptimales Ausschüttungsverhalten und Repatriierungsstrategien*, 2000, 527.

[353] See Newberry, K. J. and Dhaliwal, D. S., *Journal of Accounting Research* 2001, 644.

[354] See Newberry, K. J. and Dhaliwal, D. S., *Journal of Accounting Research* 2001, 645.

[355] In the case of an income tax treaty with exemption method.

[356] In the case of an income tax treaty with credit method. See Kessler, W., *Grundlagen der Steuerplanung mit Holdinggesellschaften*, 2000, 195.

[357] See Kessler, W., *Grundlagen der Steuerplanung mit Holdinggesellschaften*, 2000, 196.

[358] See Kessler, W. and Dorfmueller, P., *Praxis Internationale Steuerberatung* 2001, 182.

3. CLASSIFICATION OF ENTITIES (CHECK-THE-BOX REGULATIONS)

On December 17, 1996, the IRS and the Department of the Treasury issued final regulations relating to the classification of U.S. domestic and foreign business organizations.[359] The introduction of the check-the-box regulations (effective since January 1, 1997), has added a great deal of flexibility and created many new alternatives for structuring multinational operations.[360] Corporations are able to organize their branches and subsidiaries around the world in ways that optimize both foreign and U.S. taxation.[361] Although the impact of the check-the-box regulations on U.S. domestic corporations is great, the most significant aspect of the regulations pertains to the rules concerning foreign entities.[362] For example, a U.S. corporation may choose to treat its subsidiary in the U.K. as a partnership or unincorporated branch for U.S. federal tax purposes, hence, taking advantage of loss flow-throughs, while at the same time, treating it as a corporation under U.K. tax law, where certain tax and liability advantages may exist.

In fact, based on the flurry of multinational restructurings after issuance of the check-the-box regulations, the IRS and the Department of the Treasury have already determined that they are concerned with potential abuse.[363] They are currently in the process of exploring ways to curb some of these perceived abuses.[364]

The regulations allow taxpayers to elect to treat business entities, including foreign entities, as corporations, partnerships, or disregarded entities for U.S. federal income tax purposes.[365] U.S.

---

[359] Reg. § 301.7701-1; T.D. 8697, 1996-61 Fed. Reg. 66584. See Benson, D. M., Rollinson, M. A., O'Connor, M. M. and Baik, S. A., *Tax Management International Journal* 1997, 364; Carson, S., Cinnamon, A. and Kronbergs, Z., *International Tax Review* 1998 I, 33; Davis, B. N., *Tax Management International Journal* 1997 I, 3; Anonymous, *Tax Executive* 1999 II, 568; Middleton, C. I., *Journal of Partnership Taxation* 1999, 308; Carson, S. and Santa Maria, J., *The Tax Adviser* 2000, 322.

[360] See Mogenson, H. and Benson, D. M., *Tax Notes International* 1996, 2160; Lipton, R. M. and Thomas, J. T., *Journal of Partnership Taxation* 1997, 98; Marcus, D., *The CPA Journal* 1997, 61; Anson, T. F., Culbertson, R. E. and Dubert, C. A., *International Tax Review* 1998, 77; Barrett, J. H. and Ewing, W. P., *Florida Bar Journal* 1998, 34; Carson, S., Cinnamon, A. and Kronbergs, Z., *International Tax Review* 1998 II, 29; Yoder, L. D., *Tax Management International Journal* 1998 I, 222; May, T. R., *Tax Notes International* 1999, 2357; Martin, K., *International Tax Review* 2000, 27; Yoder, L. D. and Everson, S. L., *Tax Management International Journal* 2000 II, 303; Herrmann, H., *Die Einordnung ausländischer Gesellschaften*, 2001, 141; Schuth, M. R., *The Tax Adviser* 2001, 593.

[361] See Anderson, T., *The CPA Journal* 1997, 86; Davis, B. N., *Tax Management International Journal* 1997, 3; Endres, D. and Spengel, C., *Steuerstrukturen in Deutschland aus Sicht eines US-Investors*, 1997, 98; Boyle, M. P., *Tax Executive* 2000, 250; Marantelli, A., *Steuer Revue* 2000 I, 17.

[362] In Notice 95-14, 1995-1 C.B. 297, the IRS promised to essentially revise the way business organizations are classified under IRC § 7701. Further, the IRS indicated it was considering how a simplified scheme of entity classification could be applied to foreign organizations. See Bergquist, P. H., *Tax Executive* 1995, 323; Davis, B. N., *Tax Management International Journal* 1995, 593.

[363] See Zschiegner, H., *Internationale Wirtschaftsbriefe*, Fach 8, USA, Gruppe 2, 1997 II, 897; Yoder, L. D. and Everson, S. L., *Tax Management International Journal* 2000 II, 306.

[364] Notices 98-11, 1998-6 I.R.B. 18, and 98-35, 1998-27 I.R.B. 25.

[365] Before the check-the-box regulations were enacted, the IRS used four factors to determine if an entity was to be treated as a corporation for federal tax purposes, the so-called *four-factor test* under former Reg. § 301-7701-2: (1) limited liability, (2) centralized management, (3) continuity of life, and (4) free transferability of interests. If a business entity had a majority, i.e., at least three, of the four corporate characteristics, it was treated as a corporation for U.S. tax purposes. Conversely, if it lacked at least two factors, the entity was classified as a partnership. Reg. § 301.7701-2 with its roots in *Morrissey v. Commissioner*, 296 U.S. 344 [1935]. See Hayden, J. R. and Mogenson, H., *Tax Management International Journal* 1991, 507; Hey, F. E. F., *Recht der Internationalen Wirtschaft* 1992, 918; Sieker, K., *Internationale Wirtschaftsbriefe*, Fach 8, USA, Gruppe 2, 1993, 722; Ball, G. T. and Siegel, M. A., *Tax Notes International* 1995, 315; Martin, K., *International Corporate Law* 1995, 44; Andersen, R. E., *International Tax Review* 1996, 3; Conlon, R., *Tax Notes International* 1996, 1380; Lipton, R. M. and Thomas, J. T., *Journal of Partnership Taxation* 1996, 196; Dougan, H. M., *Tax Notes International* 1997, 1925; Kloot, N. van der, Subramaniam, A. I. S. and Ganz, M., *International Tax Review* 1997, 91; Krehbühl, H.-H., *Das Steueranrechnungsverfahren in den USA*, 1997, 161; Ryder, D. R. and Yoder, L. D., *International Tax Review* 1997, 35; Zschiegner, H., *Internationale Wirtschaftsbriefe*, Fach 8, USA, Gruppe 2, 1997 II, 896; Bentley, P. E., *The CPA Journal* 1998, 64; Yoder, L. D., *Tax Management International Journal* 1998 I, 220; Anonymous, *Tax Executive* 1999 II, 568; McDaniel, P. R., McMahon, M. J. Jr. and Simmons, D. L., *Federal Income*

taxation of a foreign entity depends on whether the local entity is classified as a corporation or partnership under the entity classification rule of Reg. § 7701.[366]

Under the check-the-box regulations, a two-step approach for classification has been established for entities. In the first step, it must be determined whether the entity under review is a *per se* corporation, as defined in the list of the regulations. The second step applies to all other entities.[367] These non-*per se* corporations are subject to an elective regime under Reg. § 301.7701.

3.1. Eligible Entities

Eligible entities can choose their desired tax status, either by filing an election or choosing to accept the default status under the regulations.[368] Only separate business entities can be classified as eligible entities, i.e., entities not automatically treated as corporations may elect their classification under Reg. § 301.7701-3.[369] Specified corporations are always treated as corporations, the so-called *per se corporations*.[370] In other words, *per se* corporations are excluded from utilizing the election.[371] *Per se* corporations represent eight categories of U.S. and foreign entities that are not entitled to elect their tax status.

Under the check-the-box regime, **U.S.** ineligible entities - the so-called *per se corporations* - are domestic statutory corporations, associations, statutory joint stock companies, insurance companies taxable under Subchapter L, state chartered banking businesses if insured under the Federal Deposit Insurance Act (FDIA) or similar federal statue, business entities wholly owned by a state or a political subdivision, and corporations under another provision of the IRC.[372]

Reg. § 301.7701-2(b)(8) contains a list of all **foreign** business entities that are treated *per se* as corporations.[373] Basically, all publicly traded foreign entities,[374] for example, Dutch N.V.s,

---

Taxation of Business Organizations, 1999, 10; Stark, K. J. and Zolt, E. M., *European Taxation* 2000, 328; Herrmann, H., *Die Einordnung ausländischer Gesellschaften*, 2001, 123; Willis, A. B., Pennell, J., Postlewaite, P. F. and Lipton, R., *Partnership Taxation*, 2002, paragraph 1.06[1]. A classification as disregarded entity is possible for an entity that has a single owner. See Benson, D. M., Rollinson, M. A., O'Connor, M. M. and Baik, S. A., *Tax Management International Journal* 1997, 365; Fink, E. H., *Intertax* 1997, 106; Flick, H. F. W., *Internationales Steuerrecht* 1998, 110; Kuhlmann, C., *Steuerplanung bei Direktinvestitionen in der Bundesrepublik Deutschland*, 1998, 20; Yoder, L. D. and Everson, S. L., *Tax Management International Journal* 2000 II, 303. Whether an organization is treated as an entity for federal tax purposes does not affect the rights and obligations of its owner under local law. See Davis, B. N., *Tax Management International Journal* 1997 I, 16; Boucher, K. J., *The Tax Adviser* 1998, 167.

[366] See Dougan, H. M., *Tax Notes International* 1997, 1935.

[367] See Conlon, R., *Tax Notes International* 1996, 1377.

[368] Refer *infra* chapter "Automatic Hybridization v. Election of Eligible Entities", page 73.

[369] See Al-Tabatabaie, N., *Tax Notes International* 1998, 1809; Abrams, H. E. and Doernberg, R. L., *Essentials of United States Taxation*, 1999, 4-233; Eckberg, D., *Tax Planning International Review* 2000, 27; Dilworth, R. H. and Andrus, J. L., *Tax Law and Practice*, 2001, 1112; Brown, K. B. and Rothschild, D. P., *Mertens Law of Federal Income Taxation*, 2002, 45:08; Willis, A. B., Pennell, J., Postlewaite, P. F. and Lipton, R., *Partnership Taxation*, 2002, paragraph 1.06[3][e].

[370] See Davis, B. N., *Tax Management International Journal* 1997 II, 603; Ryder, D. R. and Yoder, L. D., *International Tax Review* 1997, 36; Dougan, H. M., *Tax Notes International* 1997, 1926; Yoder, L. D., *Tax Management International Journal* 1998 I, 221; Yoder, L. D. and Everson, S. L., *Tax Management International Journal* 2000 II, 304; Yoder, L. D. and Everson, S. L., *Tax Management International Journal* 2001, 14; Ernst & Young, *International Tax Digest* 2002 (United States), 3.

[371] Reg. § 301.7701-2(b). See Small, D. G., *Internationales Steuerrecht* 1996, 280; Zschiegner, H., *Internationale Wirtschaftsbriefe*, Fach 8, USA, Gruppe 2, 1997 I, 887; Immerman, L. A., *Tax Notes International* 2002, 1006.

[372] U.S. *per se* corporations represent seven out of eight categories of ineligible entities. See Lipton, R. M. and Thomas, J. T., *Journal of Partnership Taxation* 1996, 201; Lipton, R. M. and Thomas, J. T., *Journal of Partnership Taxation* 1997, 92; Cuff, T. F., *Journal of Partnership Taxation* 1998, 106; Abrams, H. E. and Doernberg, R. L., *Essentials of United States Taxation*, 1999, 2-51; Herrmann, H., *Die Einordnung ausländischer Gesellschaften*, 2001, 141.

[373] See Levey, M. M. and Teigen, R. D., *Journal of Taxation* 1996, 261; Cuff, T. F., *Journal of Partnership Taxation* 1998, 108; McDaniel, P. R., McMahon, M. J. Jr. and Simmons, D. L., *Federal Income Taxation of Business Organizations*, 1999, 15.

French SAs, German AGs,[375] Spanish SAs, Swiss AGs,[376] and U.K. PLCs,[377] appear on the list.[378]

3.1.1. U.S. Domestic Entities

Under the check-the-box regulations, an unincorporated business entity with two or more owners, such as a partnership, limited partnership (LP), limited liability company (LLC),[379] limited liability limited partnership (LLLP), or limited liability partnership (LLP), is referred to as an eligible entity.[380] An unincorporated business with a single owner can also elect its tax status.[381]

3.1.2. Foreign Entities

Generally, all foreign entities are eligible entities if they are not domesticated as corporations in the U.S. and if they are not publicly traded entities, i.e., do not appear on the regulation's list of *per se* foreign corporations.[382] Such entities include, for example, Dutch B.V.s, French SARLs and SASs,[383] German GmbHs,[384] Spanish SRLs, and U.K. LLCs.[385]

---

[374] See Mogenson, H. and Benson, D. M., *Tax Notes International* 1996, 2160; Abrams, H. E. and Doernberg, R. L., *Essentials of United States Taxation*, 1999, 2-52; Herrmann, H., *Die Einordnung ausländischer Gesellschaften*, 2001, 141.

[375] For a detailed analysis of the treatment of several German business entities, see Al-Tabatabaie, N., *Tax Notes International* 1998, 1801.

[376] Different linguistic renderings of the name of an entity on the *per se* list are disregarded. For example, Swiss SAs are treated as *per se* corporations like Swiss AGs which are specifically named in the list.

[377] See Lipton, R. M. and Thomas, J. T., *Journal of Partnership Taxation* 1996, 196.

[378] See Andersen, R. E., *International Tax Review* 1996, 3; Conlon, R., *Tax Notes International* 1996, 1377; Kral, K. H. and Serota, J., *Journal of Accountancy* 1996, 35; Anderson, T., *The CPA Journal* 1997, 86; Zschiegner, H., *Internationale Wirtschaftsbriefe*, Fach 8, USA, Gruppe 2, 1997 I, 888; Carson, S., Cinnamon, A. and Kronbergs, Z., *International Tax Review* 1998 I, 34; Yoder, L. D., *Tax Management International Journal* 1998 I, 221; Zschiegner, H., *Internationale Wirtschaftsbriefe*, Fach 8, USA, Gruppe 2, 1998 III, 982; Marantelli, A., *Steuer Revue* 2000 I, 13; Meldman, R. E. and Schadewald, M. S., *A Practical Guide to U.S. Taxation of International Transactions*, 2000, 335; Yoder, L. D. and Everson, S. L., *Tax Management International Journal* 2000 II, 304; Cusí, J. M., *Tax Notes International* 2001, 1494.

[379] For the LLC in detail, see Bishop, C. G. and Kleinberger, D. S., *Limited Liability Companies*, 2002; Willis, A. B., Pennell, J., Postlewaite, P. F. and Lipton, R., *Partnership Taxation*, 2002, paragraph 3.01.

[380] See Lipton, R. M. and Thomas, J. T., *Journal of Partnership Taxation* 1996, 203; Lipton, R. M. and Thomas, J. T., *Journal of Partnership Taxation* 1997, 93; Zschiegner, H., *Internationale Wirtschaftsbriefe*, Fach 8, USA, Gruppe 2, 1997 I, 891; Burton, E., *The Tax Adviser* 1999, 96; Stark, K. J. and Zolt, E. M., *European Taxation* 2000, 328.

[381] See Cuff, T. F., *Journal of Partnership Taxation* 1998, 108.

[382] See Lipton, R. M. and Thomas, J. T., *Journal of Partnership Taxation* 1997, 93; McLaughlin, M., *The CPA Journal* 1998, 60; Middleton, C. I., *Journal of Partnership Taxation* 1999, 309.

[383] See Charriau, J.-Y., Donsimoni, P. and Poli, F., *Journal of International Taxation* 1999, 15.

[384] For a detailed analysis of the treatment of several German business entities, see Al-Tabatabaie, N., *Tax Notes International* 1998, 1801.

[385] See Conlon, R., *Tax Notes International* 1996, 1377; Yoder, L. D., *Tax Management International Journal* 1998 I, 221; Anonymous, *Tax Executive* 1999 II, 568; Yoder, L. D. and Everson, S. L., *Tax Management International Journal* 2000 II, 304; Cusí, J. M., *Tax Notes International* 2001, 1494.

3.2. Automatic Hybridization v. Election of Eligible Entities

All eligible entities are classified in accordance with the default provisions or by election.[386] In many cases, an election may not be necessary.

If an eligible **U.S. domestic** entity makes no election, flow-through status, i.e., partnership treatment, is automatic for U.S. federal tax purposes under the default clause of Reg. § 301.7701-3(b)(1) if it has more than one owner. The entity is disregarded if it has only a single owner.[387] Hence, most types of U.S. domestic entities - other than corporations and joint-stock companies - will be treated by default as pass-through entities.[388] Conversely, a classification as a corporation applies if all owners have limited liability.[389]

As was previously discussed, **foreign** business entities on the *per se* list are automatically treated as corporations for U.S. federal tax purposes. Under the default clause provision of Reg. § 301.7701-3(b)(2), the classification of an eligible entity that fails to make an election is determined.[390] In the absence of an election, foreign eligible entities are classified as corporations, provided that all members have limited liability.[391] Pursuant to Reg. § 301.7701-3(b)(2)(ii), the determination of limited liability must be made under local law.[392] Conversely, flow-through status, i.e., default status, is automatic if at least one of the entity's owners lacks limited liability.[393] Moreover, foreign eligible entities are treated as disregarded as an entity separate from its owner, i.e., a branch or division, if there is a corporate owner.[394]

---

[386] Reg. § 301.7701-3(a). No foreign entities are treated *per se* as partnerships or branches. See McDaniel, P. R., McMahon, M. J. Jr. and Simmons, D. L., *Federal Income Taxation of Business Organizations*, 1999, 11.

[387] See Lipton, R. M. and Thomas, J. T., *Journal of Partnership Taxation* 1996, 204; Hollingsworth, T., *Journal of Accountancy* 1997, 24; Zschiegner, H., *Internationale Wirtschaftsbriefe*, Fach 8, USA, Gruppe 2, 1997 II, 897; Cuff, T. F., *Journal of Partnership Taxation* 1998, 109; Zschiegner, H., *Internationale Wirtschaftsbriefe*, Fach 8, USA, Gruppe 2, 1998 III, 982; McDaniel, P. R., McMahon, M. J. Jr. and Simmons, D. L., *Federal Income Taxation of Business Organizations*, 1999, 11; Stark, K. J. and Zolt, E. M., *European Taxation* 2000, 328; Herrmann, H., *Die Einordnung ausländischer Gesellschaften*, 2001, 142.

[388] See Lipton, R. M. and Thomas, J. T., *Journal of Partnership Taxation* 1996, 195; Lipton, R. M. and Thomas, J. T., *Journal of Partnership Taxation* 1997, 91.

[389] See Lee, P. T. and Kowallik, A., *Internationale Wirtschaftsbriefe*, Fach 8, USA, Gruppe 2, 2001, 1086.

[390] See Cuff, T. F., *Journal of Partnership Taxation* 1998, 110.

[391] See Levenson, A., Shapiro, A. and Reynolds, B., *Tax Notes International* 1996, 2097; Mogenson, H. and Benson, D. M., *Tax Notes International* 1996, 2159; Marcus, D., *The CPA Journal* 1997, 61; Zschiegner, H., *Internationale Wirtschaftsbriefe*, Fach 8, USA, Gruppe 2, 1997 I, 889; Boucher, K. J., *The Tax Adviser* 1998, 167; Cuff, T. F., *Journal of Partnership Taxation* 1998, 110; Yoder, L. D., *Tax Management International Journal* 1998 I, 221; Zschiegner, H., *Internationale Wirtschaftsbriefe*, Fach 8, USA, Gruppe 2, 1998 III, 983; Anonymous, *Tax Executive* 1999 II, 569; McDaniel, P. R., McMahon, M. J. Jr. and Simmons, D. L., *Federal Income Taxation of Business Organizations*, 1999, 11; Yoder, L. D. and Everson, S. L., *Tax Management International Journal* 2000 II, 304; Lee, P. T. and Kowallik, A., *Internationale Wirtschaftsbriefe*, Fach 8, USA, Gruppe 2, 2001, 1086; Yoder, L. D. and Everson, S. L., *Tax Management International Journal* 2001, 15.

[392] See Lipton, R. M. and Thomas, J. T., *Journal of Partnership Taxation* 1996, 207; Cuff, T. F., *Journal of Partnership Taxation* 1998, 111; Zschiegner, H., *Internationale Wirtschaftsbriefe*, Fach 8, USA, Gruppe 2, 1998 III, 983; Meldman, R. E. and Schadewald, M. S., *A Practical Guide to U.S. Taxation of International Transactions*, 2000, 337.

[393] See Levenson, A., Shapiro, A. and Reynolds, B., *Tax Notes International* 1996, 2098; Mogenson, H. and Benson, D. M., *Tax Notes International* 1996, 2159; Bentley, P. E., *The CPA Journal* 1998, 64; Cuff, T. F., *Journal of Partnership Taxation* 1998, 110; Yoder, L. D., *Tax Management International Journal* 1998 I, 221; Zschiegner, H., *Internationale Wirtschaftsbriefe*, Fach 8, USA, Gruppe 2, 1998 III, 983; Anonymous, *Tax Executive* 1999 II, 569; McDaniel, P. R., McMahon, M. J. Jr. and Simmons, D. L., *Federal Income Taxation of Business Organizations*, 1999, 11; Meldman, R. E. and Schadewald, M. S., *A Practical Guide to U.S. Taxation of International Transactions*, 2000, 337; Yoder, L. D. and Everson, S. L., *Tax Management International Journal* 2000 II, 304; Herrmann, H., *Die Einordnung ausländischer Gesellschaften*, 2001, 142; Yoder, L. D. and Everson, S. L., *Tax Management International Journal* 2001, 15.

[394] See Levenson, A., Shapiro, A. and Reynolds, B., *Tax Notes International* 1996, 2098; Mogenson, H. and Benson, D. M., *Tax Notes International* 1996, 2159; Benson, D. M., Rollinson, M. A., O'Connor, M. M. and Baik, S. A., *Tax Management International Journal* 1997, 365; Bentley, P. E., *The CPA Journal* 1998, 64; Meldman, R. E. and Schadewald,

A foreign entity taxable as a corporation in its country of formation can, therefore, **elect** to be treated as a partnership or branch for U.S. federal tax purposes.[395] In such cases, the default provisions are overridden. Such an entity is referred to as a hybrid.[396] Accordingly, a foreign eligible entity treated as a corporation in its local jurisdiction is a hybrid if at least one of its members does not have limited liability.[397] As a result, the eligible entity can elect for flow-through status for U.S. federal tax purposes. On the other hand, an entity classified as a partnership or other type of flow-through entity in its country of incorporation or residence can elect to be treated as a corporation for U.S. federal income tax purposes; such an entity is referred to as a reverse hybrid.[398]

The (simplest) way to achieve flow-through treatment is to elect it by filing Form 8832 "Entity Classification Election".[399] Although the default provisions can reduce the compliance burden,[400] an affirmative election is recommended if uncertainty exists as to the limited liability test under local law.[401] Existing eligible entities will generally retain whatever classification was claimed before the effective date, i.e., January 1, 1997, unless an election is made to change the classification of the entity.[402]

M. S., *A Practical Guide to U.S. Taxation of International Transactions*, 2000, 337; Kroniger, A. and Thies, A., *Internationales Steuerrecht* 2002, 401.

[395] See Small, D. G., *Internationales Steuerrecht* 1996, 281; Flick, H. F. W., *Internationales Steuerrecht* 1998, 110; Yoder, L. D., *Tax Management International Journal* 1998 I, 221; Meldman, R. E. and Schadewald, M. S., *A Practical Guide to U.S. Taxation of International Transactions*, 2000, 335.

[396] See Benson, D. M., Rollinson, M. A., O'Connor, M. M. and Baik, S. A., *Tax Management International Journal* 1997, 364; Anson, T. F., Culbertson, R. E. and Dubert, C. A., *International Tax Review* 1998, 77; Josephs, S. R., *The Tax Adviser* 1998, 294; Kral, K. H. and Tilevitz, O., *International Tax Review* 1998, 14; Tello, C. P., *Tax Management International Journal* 1998, 17; Anonymous, *Tax Executive* 1999 II, 569; Grube, P., *Journal of Taxation* 2000, 6; Meldman, R. E. and Schadewald, M. S., *A Practical Guide to U.S. Taxation of International Transactions*, 2000, 334; Dilworth, R. H. and Andrus, J. L., *Tax Law and Practice*, 2001, 1112.

[397] See American Chamber of Commerce in Germany e.V. and PricewaterhouseCoopers GmbH, *Steuern in den USA*, 2001, 26; Engel, K., *Texas Law Review* 2001, 1552.

[398] See Benson, D. M., Rollinson, M. A., O'Connor, M. M. and Baik, S. A., *Tax Management International Journal* 1997, 364; Abrams, H. E. and Doernberg, R. L., *Essentials of United States Taxation*, 1999, 4-233; Anonymous, *Tax Executive* 1999 II, 573; Grube, P., *Journal of Taxation* 2000, 6; Meldman, R. E. and Schadewald, M. S., *A Practical Guide to U.S. Taxation of International Transactions*, 2000, 338; Dilworth, R. H. and Andrus, J. L., *Tax Law and Practice*, 2001, 1112.

[399] The election specifies that the effective date cannot be more than 75 days prior to the date on which the election is filed. Reg. § 301.7701-3(c)(1)(iii). See Conlon, R., *Tax Notes International* 1996, 1381; Kral, K. H. and Serota, J., *Journal of Accountancy* 1996, 35; Levenson, A., Shapiro, A. and Reynolds, B., *Tax Notes International* 1996, 2098; Mogenson, H. and Benson, D. M., *Tax Notes International* 1996, 2159; Benson, D. M., Rollinson, M. A., O'Connor, M. M. and Baik, S. A., *Tax Management International Journal* 1997, 367; Lipton, R. M. and Thomas, J. T., *Journal of Partnership Taxation* 1997, 94; Marcus, D., *The CPA Journal* 1997, 61; Shapiro, A. and Mantegani, B., *Tax Notes International* 1997, 516; Yu, A. and McClellan, E., *Tax Management International Journal* 1997, 328; Bentley, P. E., *The CPA Journal* 1998, 64; Phillips, B., *The National Public Accountant* 1998, 8; McDaniel, P. R., McMahon, M. J. Jr. and Simmons, D. L., *Federal Income Taxation of Business Organizations*, 1999, 12; Hamill, J. R. and White, C. G., *Taxes* 2001, 36; Lee, P. T. and Kowallik, A., *Internationale Wirtschaftsbriefe*, Fach 8, USA, Gruppe 2, 2001, 1086.

[400] See Mogenson, H. and Benson, D. M., *Tax Notes International* 1996, 2159.

[401] See Lipton, R. M. and Thomas, J. T., *Journal of Partnership Taxation* 1996, 208; Yoder, L. D., *Tax Management International Journal* 1998 I, 221; Yoder, L. D. and Everson, S. L., *Tax Management International Journal* 2000 II, 304.

[402] See Mogenson, H. and Benson, D. M., *Tax Notes International* 1996, 2162; Shapiro, A. and Mantegani, B., *Tax Notes International* 1997, 513; Cuff, T. F., *Journal of Partnership Taxation* 1998, 112.

3.3. Tax Treatment of Different Classifications

3.3.1. Hybrid Entity

As previously discussed, an eligible - domestic or foreign - entity can be classified as a branch for U.S federal tax purposes. Under the default provision, an eligible entity will be a disregarded entity if there is only one owner and that owner does not have limited liability.[403] An eligible entity with a sole owner with limited liability that is classified as a corporation under the default provision will be a branch if an election is made for such treatment.[404] In the case of two or more owners, an eligible entity, presuming an election was made, will be viewed as a partnership.[405] The tax treatment of an entity classification is expressed in Reg. § 301.7701-2(c)(2)(i) as follows:

"A business entity that has a single owner and is not a corporation ... is disregarded as an entity separate from its owner."[406]

The activities of a disregarded entity are treated in the same way as a branch or division.[407] Therefore, a foreign entity classified as a branch is generally ignored for U.S. federal income tax purposes. While an entity treated as a branch generally provides complete transparency for U.S. tax purposes, partnerships are viewed as pass-through entities for certain purposes, e.g., flow-through of income and expenses,[408] but for other purposes they are treated as separate entities, e.g., loans. This applies regardless of the treatment under foreign tax law. For example, foreign tax law may treat the disregarded entity as an entity separate from its owner.[409]

Some foreign entities may require more than one shareholder, e.g., the French SARL, the German KG, or the Spanish SCpA that *per se* would exclude branch classification by definition because of the statutory requirement for two owners.[410] Nonetheless, branch status might be achieved if one of the two owners is wholly-owned by the other owner and the wholly-owned entity elects to be treated as a branch for U.S. federal income tax purposes, e.g., a U.S. LLC could function as a wholly-owned second owner.[411]

Hybrid entities offer the tax advantages of the transparent entity form, i.e., a branch or partnership, while still providing the U.S. MNC with limited liability and a "corporate" presence in the host country. An entity that is classified as a branch or a partnership for U.S. tax purposes allows the pass-through of foreign losses and the immediate deduction of these losses by the U.S. parent. Conversely, losses incurred by a foreign subsidiary are not tax-deductible by the U.S. MNC. Additionally, whereas non-corporate shareholders are not eligible for claiming an indirect FTC for foreign income taxes incurred by a foreign subsidiary,[412] they can claim a direct tax credit for the

---

[403] Reg. § 301.7701-3(b)(2)(i)(C). See Lipton, R. M. and Thomas, J. T., *Journal of Partnership Taxation* 1997, 114; Kral, K. H. and Tilevitz, O., *International Tax Review* 1998, 14.

[404] Regs. §§ 301.7701-1(a)(4), -3(a), (c)(1). See Bentley, P. E., *The CPA Journal* 1998, 64; Yoder, L. D., *Tax Management International Journal* 1998 I, 220.

[405] See Bentley, P. E., *The CPA Journal* 1998, 64; Yoder, L. D., *Tax Management International Journal* 1998 I, 220.

[406] See also Regs. §§ 301.7701-1(a)(4), -2(c)(2), -3(b)(2)(i)(C); Internal Revenue Service & The Department of the Treasury, PS-43-95, 1996-24 I.R.B. 20. Yoder, L. D., *Tax Management International Journal* 1998 I, 222.

[407] Reg. § 301.7701-2(a). See McLaughlin, M., *The CPA Journal* 1998, 60.

[408] For the U.S. partnership taxation refer *supra* page 33.

[409] For example, Belgium, Japan, and Spain. See Al-Tabatabaie, N., *Tax Notes International* 1998, 1810; Jacobs, O. H., *Internationale Unternehmensbesteuerung*, 2002, 583.

[410] See Yoder, L. D., *Tax Management International Journal* 1998 I, 222 ; Raventós Calvo, S. and Cueva González-Cotera, A. de la, *Spain*, 2001, 27; Valat, A. and Bouzidi, C., *France*, 2002, 9.

[411] See Yoder, L. D., *Tax Management International Journal* 1998 I, 222.

[412] IRC §§ 902(a) and 1373(a).

foreign taxes incurred by a foreign branch or partnership under IRC § 901(b)(5).[413] Flow-through classification also provides certain non-controlling U.S. shareholders with the benefit of applying a look-through rule in computing its foreign tax credit limitation, in particular, that the foreign entity's active business is allotted to the general limitation rather than a separate non-controlled IRC § 902 corporation limitation.[414] Finally, hybrid entities allow U.S. MNCs to avoid Subpart F treatment of transfers between CFCs. Under Subpart F (IRC §§ 951-964), interest and dividend payments between commonly controlled CFCs incorporated in different jurisdictions trigger Subpart F income.

One solution for avoiding the constitution of currently taxed income is the use of hybrid entities below a first-tier CFC holding company. Hence, the effective consolidation of U.S. MNC's foreign operations with the first-tier CFC, along with all the lower-tier hybrid entities which are treated as a single taxable entity for U.S. purposes, is achieved. In this structure, the single corporate entity can move cash in and out of each country without triggering any U.S. tax consequences.[415] This structure and similar ones will be analyzed in Section 5 "Specific Tax Planning Techniques".[416]

Although hybrid entities provide several substantial advantages, by the same token, there are significant tax costs associated with converting an existing foreign subsidiary into a foreign branch or partnership.[417] In particular, hybridizing an already existing foreign subsidiary is a two-step transaction, including the inbound liquidation of the foreign corporation, followed by a contribution of all the distributed assets to the foreign branch or partnership.[418] Since inbound repatriating liquidations are subject to a special toll charge tax,[419] and outbound expatriating transfers to a foreign partnership might be trigger special excise taxes under IRC § 721(c), taxpayers must carefully examine such transactions.

Further, hybrid entity status in the international context gives rise to various other potential issues, such as dual-consolidated losses, compliance, transfer pricing, and treaty withholding.

3.3.2. Reverse Hybrid Entity

A reverse hybrid entity is an entity that is treated as not transparent for U.S. tax purposes and as fiscally transparent under foreign tax laws. For U.S. federal tax purposes, an entity is not treated as a pass-through if it is classified as a corporation or if it is an eligible entity and elects to be considered as a corporation.[420] As was discussed under the default provisions, an eligible entity is classified as a corporation if all owners have limited liability.

Reverse hybrids are less common in international tax planning practice compared to hybrid entities, as hybrids permit a pass-through of foreign losses and the immediate deduction of these losses by the U.S. MNC. Nonetheless, the treatment of an entity as a corporation for U.S. tax purposes but as fiscally transparent for foreign tax purposes might also reduce the amount of tax

---

[413] For details on the direct FTC, refer *supra* page 47.

[414] Reg. § 1.904-5(h)(1). This advantage will remain in effect only for a limited period of time. For the tax years beginning after December 31, 2002, all non-controlled IRC § 902 corporations will be treated as one for this purposes. See *supra* note 248.

[415] See Lipton, R. M. and Thomas, J. T., *Journal of Partnership Taxation* 1997, 114.

[416] Refer *infra* page 109.

[417] For details on the elective change, refer *infra* page 77.

[418] Regs. §§ 301.7701.3(g)(1)(ii) and (iii).

[419] IRC §§ 367(b) and 1248(a).

[420] See McKee, W. S., Nelson, W. F. and Whitmire, R. L., *Federal Taxation of Partnerships and Partners*, 2002, paragraph 2.02 [1]-[2]; Bittker, B. I. and Eustice, J. S., *Federal Income Taxation of Corporations and Shareholders*, 2002, paragraph 1.07[2].

imposed.[421] A reverse hybrid entity mainly allows U.S. MNCs to shift income out of high corporate tax rate jurisdictions without triggering any negative Subpart F consequences.[422] Income generated by a corporation in a high-tax country can easily be shifted to a jurisdiction with a low corporate tax rate. For example, assume a partnership is treated as a separate entity for loan purposes and lends funds to a high-taxed affiliated company. The interest incurred on the funds will be deductible by the borrower in computing its profits subject to tax at a high rate. The high-tax jurisdiction considers the lending entity as a partnership and, thus, the foreign partnership generally would not be liable for income tax there. Further, it views the interest payments as a flow-through via the low-tax country to the U.S. and withholds no or low tax, according to an applicable double tax treaty enacted within the U.S. or local tax law.

Overall, foreign income taxes have been reduced. This benefit will not be subject to Subpart F provisions as the U.S. treats the partnership located in a jurisdiction with a low tax rate as a corporation of the high-tax country. This allows the application of the same country exception of IRC § 954(c)(3). Moreover, U.S. domestic reverse hybrid entities could be used as a leveraged holding company when filing a consolidated U.S. tax return.[423]

3.4. Anti-Abusive Type Rules

3.4.1. Elective Change

An eligible entity may subsequently change classification by election.[424] An eligible entity may choose to change its classification from that of a corporation to a partnership or branch or from that of a branch or partnership to a corporation only by election, whether it was initially classified under the default clause rule or by election. On November 29, 1999, the IRS issued final supplements to the check-the-box regulations dealing with the tax neutral change in classification.[425]

These supplementary regulations specify the treatment of such elective changes as follows:[426]

- *Association to Partnership*
  The association distributes all of its assets and liabilities to its shareholders in liquidation of the association and, immediately thereafter, the shareholders contribute all of the distributed assets and liabilities to a newly formed partnership.[427]

---

[421] For example, a foreign partnership that elects to be treated as a corporation for U.S. federal tax purposes can avoid 31 percent backup withholding. See Halphen, C. and Schneider, R. A., *The Tax Adviser* 1998, 221.

[422] For the Subpart F provisions in detail, refer *infra* page 83.

[423] This benefit was targeted as potentially abusive by the IRS under the proposed regulations (IRC § 894) regarding domestic hybrid entities, issued on February 27, 2001 (66 Fed. Reg. 12445). The proposed regulations deal with the eligibility of treaty benefits for U.S.-source payments to U.S. domestic reverse hybrid entities. These proposed regulations should fill the gap in prior issued regulations regarding the treaty benefits of hybrid entity payments (T.D. 8889, 2000-30 I.R.B. 124). The regulations discussed whether the Department of the Treasury has the authority to override double tax conventions through the creation of inconsistent regulations. See Doernberg, R. L., *Florida Tax Report* 1995, 533; Gordon, R. A. and Klein, C. D., *The Tax Adviser* 1997, 688; Guenther, T. S., *Virginia Tax Review* 1997, 664; Klein, C. D. and Renfroe, D. L., *Tax Management International Journal* 1997, 547; Infanti, A. C., *Tax Management International Journal* 2001, 307; Lemein, G. D. and McDonald, J. D., *Taxes* 2001, 7; Yu, A. and Lisecki, C., *Tax Notes International* 2002, 945.

[424] A limitation applies to certain elective changes. Refer *infra* page 78.

[425] See Laffie, L. S., *The Tax Adviser* 1997, 749; Klein, S. I. and Looney, S. R., *Business Entities* 2000, 48; Herrmann, H., *Die Einordnung ausländischer Gesellschaften*, 2001, 143; Willis, A. B., Pennell, J., Postlewaite, P. F. and Lipton, R., *Partnership Taxation*, 2002, paragraph 1.06[3][g].

[426] T.D. 8844, 1999-50 I.R.B. 661. See Harrington, D. and Frediani, M., *Tax Management Memorandum* 2000, 121; Pillow, R. F. and Rooney, J. J., *Journal of Taxation* 2000, 197.

- *Association to Disregarded Entity*
  The association distributes all of its assets and liabilities to its single owner in liquidation of the association.[428]
- *Partnership to Association*
  The partnership contributes all of its assets and liabilities to the association and, immediately thereafter, the partnership liquidates by distributing the stock of the association to its partners.[429]
- *Disregarded Entity to Association*
  The owner of the eligible entity contributes all of the assets and liabilities of the entity to the association in exchange for stock of the association.[430]

However, the change of a partnership to a disregarded entity and *vice versa* was not covered by the regulations.[431] For federal tax purposes, the tax treatment of the change in classification of an entity by election is determined under all relevant provisions of the IRC and general principles of tax law, including the step transaction doctrine.[432]

The check-the-box regulations impose a limitation for changing classification at will.[433] Under Reg. § 301.7701-3(c)(1)(iv), an entity that elected to change its classification cannot again change classification for a 60-month period.[434] In other words, the limitation is not applicable after the initial classification election by a new entity.[435] Also, an entity initially classified under the default clause provisions may elect to change its status at any time.[436] Finally, the IRS may permit

---

[427] Reg. § 301.7701-3(g)(1)(ii). See Davis, B. N., *Tax Management International Journal* 1997 II, 604; Cuff, T. F., *Journal of Partnership Taxation* 1998, 103; Zschiegner, H., *Internationale Wirtschaftsbriefe*, Fach 8, USA, Gruppe 2, 1998 V, 999; McDaniel, P. R., McMahon, M. J. Jr. and Simmons, D. L., *Federal Income Taxation of Business Organizations*, 1999, 12; Klein, S. I. and Looney, S. R., *Business Entities* 2000, 48; Pillow, R. F. and Rooney, J. J., *Journal of Taxation* 2000, 198; Herrmann, H., *Die Einordnung ausländischer Gesellschaften*, 2001, 143.

[428] Reg. § 301.7701-3(g)(1)(iii). See Davis, B. N., *Tax Management International Journal* 1997 II, 612; Cuff, T. F., *Journal of Partnership Taxation* 1998, 103; Zschiegner, H., *Internationale Wirtschaftsbriefe*, Fach 8, USA, Gruppe 2, 1998 V, 999; Grube, P., *Journal of Taxation* 2000, 6; Klein, S. I. and Looney, S. R., *Business Entities* 2000, 48; Pillow, R. F. and Rooney, J. J., *Journal of Taxation* 2000, 198.

[429] Reg. § 301.7701-3(g)(1)(i). See Davis, B. N., *Tax Management International Journal* 1997 II, 608; Cuff, T. F., *Journal of Partnership Taxation* 1998, 103; Zschiegner, H., *Internationale Wirtschaftsbriefe*, Fach 8, USA, Gruppe 2, 1998 V, 998; Klein, S. I. and Looney, S. R., *Business Entities* 2000, 48; Pillow, R. F. and Rooney, J. J., *Journal of Taxation* 2000, 198; Herrmann, H., *Die Einordnung ausländischer Gesellschaften*, 2001, 143.

[430] Reg. § 301.7701-3(g)(1)(iv). See Davis, B. N., *Tax Management International Journal* 1997 II, 613; Cuff, T. F., *Journal of Partnership Taxation* 1998, 103; Zschiegner, H., *Internationale Wirtschaftsbriefe*, Fach 8, USA, Gruppe 2, 1998 V, 999; Klein, S. I. and Looney, S. R., *Business Entities* 2000, 49; Pillow, R. F. and Rooney, J. J., *Journal of Taxation* 2000, 198.

[431] See Jackel, M. A. and Dance, G. E., *Tax Notes* 1998, 595.

[432] Reg. § 301.7701-3(g)(2). See Klein, S. I. and Looney, S. R., *Business Entities* 2000, 49; Herrmann, H., *Die Einordnung ausländischer Gesellschaften*, 2001, 143.

[433] See Benson, D. M., Rollinson, M. A., O'Connor, M. M. and Baik, S. A., *Tax Management International Journal* 1997, 367.

[434] See Levey, M. M. and Teigen, R. D., *Journal of Taxation* 1996, 264; Al-Tabatabaie, N., *Tax Notes International* 1998, 1810; Anonymous, *Tax Executive* 1999 II, 570; McDaniel, P. R., McMahon, M. J. Jr. and Simmons, D. L., *Federal Income Taxation of Business Organizations*, 1999, 12; Yoder, L. D. and Everson, S. L., *Tax Management International Journal* 2000 II, 305.

[435] Such initial classification is not a change for purposes of Reg. § 301.7701-3(c)(1)(iv). See Zschiegner, H., *Internationale Wirtschaftsbriefe*, Fach 8, USA, Gruppe 2, 1998 V, 998; Yoder, L. D. and Everson, S. L., *Tax Management International Journal* 2000 II, 305.

[436] The preamble to the final regulations states that the 60-month restriction applies only if the change in classification occurs by election, and not if the organization's business is transferred or merged with another entity with the desired classification. T.D. 8697, 1996-61 Fed. Reg. 66584. See Zschiegner, H., *Internationale Wirtschaftsbriefe*, Fach 8, USA, Gruppe 2, 1998 V, 997.

an entity to change its classification following a change in ownership of more than 50 percent of the entity's ownership interests, presuming that the taxpayer requests a private letter ruling (P.L.R.).[437]

As was discussed, an eligible foreign entity with two owners that is not classified as a corporation is treated as a partnership. If the same entity has only one member, it is classified as a branch.[438] The regulations provide, on the one hand, that an eligible entity considered as a partnership becomes disregarded as an entity separate from its owner as of the date the entity has a sole member.[439] On the other hand, a single member entity disregarded as an entity separate from its owner is treated as a partnership as of date the entity has more than one member.[440] These changes in classification are not subject to the 60-month limitation.[441] In other words, an entity can flip in and out of branch or partnership status without any limitation. Further, the change in the number of members of an entity does not result in the creation of a new entity for purpose of the 60-month limitation on changes by election.[442] The regulations themselves do not govern how such changes are viewed for U.S. federal tax purposes. Nonetheless, the IRS has issued two rulings, Rev. Rul. 99-5 and Rev. Rul. 99-6, providing guidance on these matters.[443]

3.4.2. Subpart F Hybrid Entity Regulations

Some U.S. taxpayers use hybrid entities to circumvent the purposes of Subpart F.[444] These hybrid entities typically make arrangements to use deductible payments to reduce the taxable income of a CFC under foreign tax law, thereby reducing the CFC's foreign tax costs.[445] In other words, low-taxed, passive income of the type to which Subpart F provisions were intended to apply is created in another entity.[446] However, the income generated is not subject to Subpart F taxation as the hybrids and the CFC are considered as a single taxable entity for U.S. federal tax purposes.[447] Consequently, the IRS and the Department of the Treasury are of the opinion that such hybrid branch structures are contrary to the purposes and provisions of Subpart F.[448]

On January 16, 1998, the IRS issued Notice 98-11,[449] announcing that regulations would be revised to reclassify certain branches of CFCs as separate corporations for Subpart F purposes.[450]

---

[437] See Levenson, A., Shapiro, A. and Reynolds, B., *Tax Notes International* 1996, 2098; Benson, D. M., Rollinson, M. A., O'Connor, M. M. and Baik, S. A., *Tax Management International Journal* 1997, 367; McDaniel, P. R., McMahon, M. J. Jr. and Simmons, D. L., *Federal Income Taxation of Business Organizations*, 1999, 13.

[438] Reg. § 301.7701-2(c).

[439] See Al-Tabatabaie, N., *Tax Notes International* 1998, 1810.

[440] Reg. § 301.7701-3(f)(2). If the elective classification change is effective at the time a membership change occurs, the deemed transactions in Reg. § 301.7701-3(g) resulting from the elective change in ownership apply.

[441] See Levenson, A., Shapiro, A. and Reynolds, B., *Tax Notes International* 1996, 2098; Dougan, H. M., *Tax Notes International* 1997, 1930.

[442] Reg. § 301.7701-3(f)(3).

[443] Rev. Rul. 99-5, 1999-6 I.R.B. 8; Rev. Rul. 99-6, 1999-6 I.R.B. 6.

[444] See Birnkrant, H. J. and Croker, J. E. Jr., *Journal of Taxation* 1998, 45; Engel, K., *Texas Law Review* 2001, 1553.

[445] See Josephs, S. R., *The Tax Adviser* 1998, 294; Engel, K., *Texas Law Review* 2001, 1553.

[446] For the purpose of the Subpart F provisions, refer *infra* page 83.

[447] See Josephs, S. R., *The Tax Adviser* 1998, 294; Marantelli, A., *Steuer Revue* 2000 I, 17.

[448] See Josephs, S. R., *The Tax Adviser* 1998, 294; Raedel, J., Cohen, H. and Chan, D., *The Tax Adviser* 1998, 378; Herrmann, H., *Die Einordnung ausländischer Gesellschaften*, 2001, 145.

[449] 1998-6 I.R.B. 18. See Avi-Yonah, R. S., *Tax Notes International* 1998, 1797; Barrett, J. H. and Ewing, W. P., *Florida Bar Journal* 1998, 38; Hariton, D. P., *Tax Notes International* 1998, 1881; Leblang, S. E., *Tax Management International Journal* 1998, 539; Bittker, B. I. and Eustice, J. S., *Federal Income Taxation of Corporations and Shareholders*, 2002, paragraph 15.61[4].

The IRS and the Department of the Treasury later issued temporary regulations under Subpart F curtailing the application of the check-the-box regulations. The temporary regulations were released on March 23, 1998.[450] These new regulations targeted structures using hybrid entities to reduce foreign tax costs while circumventing the application of Subpart F.[451] The regulations effectively denied transparent treatment for foreign entities electing to be considered as branches or partnerships for U.S. tax purposes, but as separate entities for foreign tax purposes.[452] As the temporary regulations extended Subpart F to reach only hybrid structures that reduce effective foreign tax below U.S. federal income tax rates, the focus was on capital export neutrality.[453] The effect of the regulations was to trigger payments that otherwise would be ignored in deriving Subpart F income. For example, interest paid to the sole owner of a foreign entity disregarded as a separate entity for U.S. federal tax purposes would now be recognized in the application of Subpart F and would result in Subpart F income. These anti-hybrid regulations consider the hybrid as a corporation for Subpart F purposes.[455] Thus, the hybrid's receipt of income constitutes Subpart F income that falls outside the same country exception of IRC § 954(c)(3) as the interest is deemed to be received by the hybrid, an entity situated in a different jurisdiction from that of the related payor.[456]

The new anti-hybrid regulations soon faced heavy opposition. Practitioners questioned whether the IRS had the unilateral regulatory authority to prevent the tax-circumvention impact of the hybrid structure.[457] Practitioners further contended that the IRS's interpretation represents "poor" tax policy vis-à-vis the intended scope of Subpart F.[458] They argued that the hybrid structure merely prevents foreign tax liability, which is not a concern to the U.S. Practitioners were also of the opinion that U.S. MNCs need the hybrid status to maintain a level tax planning playing field with their foreign competitors who were likewise using tax havens to reduce their global tax burdens.[459] U.S. Congress questioned the legislative authority regarding these regulations and recommended legislation placing a moratorium on the Subpart F temporary regulations.[460] As a result, the IRS

---

[450] See Anonymous, *International Tax Review* 1998, 4; Benson, D. M. and Rollinson, M. A., *Tax Management International Journal* 1998 I, 261; Birnkrant, H. J. and Croker, J. E. Jr., *Journal of Taxation* 1998, 45; DeCarlo, J., Granwell, A. and Suringa, D., *International Tax Review* 1998, 19; Engle, H. S., *Journal of Corporate Taxation* 1998, 300; Hariton, D. P., *Tax Notes International* 1998, 1089; Sheppard, L. A., *Tax Notes International* 1998, 580; Yoder, L. D., *Tax Management International Journal* 1998 I, 220; Zschiegner, H., *Internationale Wirtschaftsbriefe*, Fach 8, USA, Gruppe 2, 1998 V, 1000; Doernberg, R. L. and Raad, K. van, *Tax Notes* 1999, 1651; Middleton, C. I., *Journal of Partnership Taxation* 1999, 326; Marantelli, A., *Steuer Revue* 2000 I, 18; Herrmann, H., *Die Einordnung ausländischer Gesellschaften*, 2001, 146.

[451] T.D. 8767, 63 Fed. Reg. 14613. See Anonymous, *Tax Executive* I, 89; Birnkrant, H. J. and Croker, J. E. Jr., *Journal of Taxation* 1998, 45; Gannon, J. M., Calianese, T. J. and Layden, M. P., *Tax Notes* 1998, 473; Ganz, M. D. and Strange, T. E., *Tax Notes* 1998, 487; Yu, A. and Chan, D. F, *International Tax Review* 1999, 43.

[452] See New York State Bar Association Tax Section, *Tax Notes International* 1998, 1669; Zschiegner, H., *Internationale Wirtschaftsbriefe*, Fach 8, USA, Gruppe 2, 1998 V, 1000; Chew, J., *The International Tax Journal* 2002, 54.

[453] See Gannon, J. M., Calianese, T. J., Layden, M. P., Moreland, K. and Seo, S. S., *Tax Notes International* 1998, 1467; New York State Bar Association Tax Section, *Tax Notes International* 1998, 1670; Tello, C. P., *Tax Management International Journal* 1998, 17.

[454] See Birnkrant, H. J. and Croker, J. E. Jr., *Journal of Taxation* 1998, 51.

[455] Temp. Reg. § 1.954-9 T(a)(4) [1998]. See Birnkrant, H. J. and Croker, J. E. Jr., *Journal of Taxation* 1998, 46.

[456] Temp. Reg. § 1.954-9 T(a)(1) [1998]. See Birnkrant, H. J. and Croker, J. E. Jr., *Journal of Taxation* 1998, 48; Gannon, J. M., Calianese, T. J., Layden, M. P., Moreland, K. and Seo, S. S., *Tax Notes International* 1998, 1472.

[457] See Cooper, M., Meicher, G. and Stretch, C., *Tax Notes* 1998, 885; Engle, H. S., *Journal of Corporate Taxation* 1998, 303; Sheppard, L. A., *Tax Notes* 1998, 145; Tillinghast, D. R., *Tax Notes* 1998, 1739; Marantelli, A., *Steuer Revue* 2000 I, 18; Rosenbloom, H. D., *Tax Law Review* 2000, 137.

[458] See Birnkrant, H. J. and Croker, J. E. Jr., *Journal of Taxation* 1998, 53; New York State Bar Association Tax Section, *Tax Notes International* 1998, 1673. For the scope of the Subpart F provisions in detail, refer *infra* page 83.

[459] See New York State Bar Association Tax Section, *Tax Notes International* 1998, 1674.

[460] See Birnkrant, H. J. and Croker, J. E. Jr., *Journal of Taxation* 1998, 53; New York State Bar Association Tax Section, *Tax Notes International* 1998, 1670; Engel, K., *Texas Law Review* 2001, 1556; Marantelli, A., *Steuer Revue* 2000 I, 18; Bittker, B. I. and Eustice, J. S., *Federal Income Taxation of Corporations and Shareholders*, 2002, paragraph 15.61[4].

reissued them as proposed regulations - as announced in Notice 98-35[461] - and delayed the effective date until July 1, 2005.[462] The IRS also indicated that it would issue a Subpart F study of its own that would examine the original intended policy of Subpart F as well as whether the policy is still appropriate in today's global economy.[463] Nonetheless, the withdrawal was more of a strategic retreat, rather than a complete capitulation and the IRS continues to express its view that the regulations are mandatory to carry out the objectives of Subpart F and to maintain its tax policing role.[464]

---

[461] 1998-27 I.R.B. 35. On June 19, 1998, the Department of the Treasury yielded to intense pressure from U.S. Congress and the business community and issued Notice 98-35. It withdrew the highly controversial Notice 98-11, and promised to withdraw the related temporary regulations issued on March 23, 1998. See Granberg, M. W., *The Tax Adviser* 1999, 630; Sheppard, L. A., *Tax Notes* 1999, 1671; Middleton, C. I., *Journal of Partnership Taxation* 1999, 306; Zois, A., *Cardozo Journal of International and Comparative Law* 1999, 197; Marantelli, A., *Steuer Revue* 2000 I, 18; Herrmann, H., *Die Einordnung ausländischer Gesellschaften*, 2001, 146.

[462] T.D. 8827, 1999-30 I.R.B. 120. For calendar year taxpayers the effective date will be January 1, 2006. See Benson, D. M. and O'Connor, P., *Tax Notes* 1999, 769; Grube, P., *Journal of Taxation* 2000, 7; Marantelli, A., *Steuer Revue* 2000 I, 18; Sparagna, G. T. and Chase, R., *Tax Management International Journal* 2000, 132; Engel, K., *Texas Law Review* 2001, 1556; Shields, C. C., *Tax Notes International* 2002, 1114.

[463] The Study was issued on December 29, 2000 and is analyzed in Section 6 "Further Developments and Conclusions".

[464] See Kingson, C. I., *Brooklyn Journal of International Law* 2001, 1570.

SECTION 4: TAX PLANNING BARRIERS (SUBPART F PROVISIONS)

Cross-border transactions create the need for special tax considerations for both the U.S. and its trading partners. From a U.S. perspective, international tax laws should promote the global competitiveness of U.S. enterprises and at the same time protect the tax revenue base for the U.S.[465] These two objectives sometimes conflict, however. The need to deal with each contributes to the complexity of provisions governing U.S. taxation of cross-border transactions.

Taxpayers may be tempted to manipulate the source of income and the allocation of deductions to minimize taxation.[466] This manipulation is more easily accomplished among or between related parties.[467] The IRS uses IRC § 482 to counter such attempts.[468] The provision gives the IRS the power to reallocate gross income, deductions, credits, and allowances among and between organizations, trades, or businesses owned and controlled directly or indirectly by the same interests.[469] This can be done whenever the IRS determines that reallocation is necessary to prevent the evasion of taxes or to reflect income generated more clearly.[470] IRC § 482 is a "one-edge sword" available only to the IRS.[471] Thus, the taxpayer cannot invoke it to reallocate any income and expenses.[472] In applying IRC § 482, an arm's length price must be determined to assign the correct profits to related entities.[473] It is possible that a hybrid entity might be of some value in limited circumstances where foreign losses are anticipated because the foreign losses would offset other worldwide income. The application of IRC § 482 generally requires two separate entities.[474] Thus, if an entity is treated as a disregarded entity for U.S. tax purposes, IRC § 482 might not apply.[475]

Several alternative methods can be used in determining an arm's length price on the sale of tangible and intangible property. The major issue with most pricing methods is that uncontrolled comparable transactions are needed as a benchmark.[476] As an aid to reducing pricing disputes, the

---

[465] See Leblang, S. E., *Tax Management International Journal* 1998, 542.

[466] Refer *supra* page 39.

[467] See McDaniel, P. R. and Ault, H. J., *Introduction to United States International Taxation*, 1998, 137; Meldman, R. E. and Schadewald, M. S., *A Practical Guide to U.S. Taxation of International Transactions*, 2000, 121.

[468] See Abrams, H. E. and Doernberg, R. L., *Essentials of United States Taxation*, 1999, 4-141; Isenbergh, J., *International Taxation*, 2000, 59; Meldman, R. E. and Schadewald, M. S., *A Practical Guide to U.S. Taxation of International Transactions*, 2000, 340. IRC § 482 also applies to partnerships according to the Field Service Advisory (FSA) 200149019, issued on August 31, 2001 and, therefore, the FSA fails to give due consideration to partnership tax provisions (e.g., IRC § 704(c)). Under IRC § 704(c), if property is distributed to the partnership, the resulting income, gains, losses and deductions regarding the property must be shared among the partners, "so as to take account of the variation between the basis of the property to the partnership and its fair market value at the time of the contribution" (IRC § 704(c)(1)(A)). See Immerman, L. A., *Tax Notes International* 2002, 1005; McKee, W. S., Nelson, W. F. and Whitmire, R. L., *Federal Taxation of Partnerships and Partners*, 2002, paragraph 4.01[1][c].

[469] See Tello, C. P., *Tax Management International Journal* 1998, 18; O'Connor, W. F. and Toyoda, Y., *The International Tax Journal* 2000, 83; Newberry, K. J. and Dhaliwal, D. S., *Journal of Accounting Research* 2001, 647; Findeis, B. C. and Bremer, S. C., *Tax Notes International* 2002, 1237.

[470] See Zschiegner, H., *Internationale Wirtschaftsbriefe*, Fach 8, USA, Gruppe 2, 1998 II, 953; Immerman, L. A., *Tax Notes International* 2002, 1011; Lowell, C. H. and Governale, J. P., *US International Taxation*, 2002, paragraph 9.05[3][b].

[471] See Zschiegner, H., *Internationale Wirtschaftsbriefe*, Fach 8, USA, Gruppe 2, 1998 II, 953; Lowell, C. H., Burge, M. and Briger, P. L., *US International Transfer Pricing*, 2002, paragraph 3.02[4].

[472] Reg. § 1.482-1(a)(3). See Fuller, J., *Tax Notes International* 1991, 255.

[473] See Ruding, H. O., *Journal of International Taxation* 1994, 6; Eilers, S., *Advance Pricing Agreements (APAs) im US-amerikanischen Steuerrecht und Abkommensrecht*, 1996, 1; Zschiegner, H., *Internationale Wirtschaftsbriefe*, Fach 8, USA, Gruppe 2, 1998 II, 952; Isenbergh, J., *International Taxation*, 2000, 62; Meldman, R. E. and Schadewald, M. S., *A Practical Guide to U.S. Taxation of International Transactions*, 2000, 121; Zschiegner, H., *Internationale Wirtschaftsbriefe*, Fach 8, USA, Gruppe 2, 2000 I, 1024; Warner, J. P., *Tax Management International Forum* 2002, 50.

[474] See Findeis, B. C. and Bremer, S. C., *Tax Notes International* 2002, 1237.

[475] See Herrmann, H., *Die Einordnung ausländischer Gesellschaften*, 2001, 119. For hybrid entities in detail, refer *supra* page 75.

[476] See Zschiegner, H., *Internationale Wirtschaftsbriefe*, Fach 8, USA, Gruppe 2, 1995, 799; Baumhoff, H., *Einkunftsabgrenzung bei international verbundenen Unternehmen*, 1998, paragraph C 315; Jacobs, O. H., *Internationale Unternehmensbesteuerung*, 2002, 873.

IRS initiated the Advance Pricing Agreement (APA) program whereby the taxpayer can propose a transfer pricing method for certain international transactions.[477] The taxpayer provides relevant data, which are then evaluated by the IRS.[478] If accepted, the APA provides a safe-harbor transfer pricing method for the taxpayer.[479]

Two fundamental features of the U.S. tax system include, on the one hand, the treatment of a corporation as a separate entity and, on the other hand, the imposition of tax on a U.S. person's worldwide income. These features are inconsistent and have produced an inherent tension in the U.S. tax system since the treatment of a corporation as a separate person provides taxpayers with an opportunity to avoid worldwide taxation through the use of a foreign corporation.[480] Hence, in a tax system that employs these two features, the possibility of avoiding or deferring tax is made available, unless anti-deferral techniques are implemented.[481]

Given that U.S. international tax policy seeks to maintain a balance with capital export neutrality objectives, it is clear that Subpart F provisions intensely reflect and enforce this balance.[482] Capital exporting countries typically favor anti-deferral provisions, seeing them as a means to retain the artificial loss of homegrown capital.[483] Capital exporting countries claim that anti-deferral mechanisms are appropriate within the context of international law because ultimate economic ownership of the income generated from foreign subsidiaries is preserved by residents of the capital exporting country.[484] Furthermore, the anti-deferral system taxes only the resident

---

[477] The APA program was formally proposed and described in March 1991 with the publication of Rev. Proc. 91-22 (1991-1 C.B. 26). See Anonymous, *Management Today* 1995, 17; Patton, M. F. and Wood, K. W., *Tax Management International Journal* 1997, 81; Schaumburg, H., *Internationales Steuerrecht*, 1998, paragraph 18.155; Abrams, H. E. and Doernberg, R. L., *Essentials of United States Taxation*, 1999, 4-169; Anonymous, *Tax Executive* 1999 I, 351; Zschiegner, H., *Internationale Wirtschaftsbriefe*, Fach 8, USA, Gruppe 2, 2000 I, 1032.

[478] See Kroppen, H.-K., *Internationale Wirtschaftsbriefe*, Fach 8, USA, Gruppe 2, 1994, 795; Zschiegner, H., *Internationale Wirtschaftsbriefe*, Fach 8, USA, Gruppe 2, 2000 II, 1048; American Chamber of Commerce in Germany e.V. and PricewaterhouseCoopers GmbH, *Steuern in den USA*, 2001, 263; PricewaterhouseCoopers, *Transfer Pricing 1999-2000*, 2001, paragraph 835; Lowell, C. H. and Governale, J. P., *US International Taxation*, 2002, paragraph 3.06[9][a].

[479] The first successful APA submission was accomplished by Apple Computer Inc (*Apple Computer v. Commissioner*, No. 2178-90 T.C. [1993]). See O'Grady, J. E., *Tax Notes International* 1992, 519; C&L Deutsche Revision AG, *Besteuerung deutscher Unternehmen in den USA*, 1994, 52; Kroppen, H.-K., *Internationale Wirtschaftsbriefe*, Fach 8, USA, Gruppe 2, 1994, 795; Triplett, C., *International Tax Review* 1994, 37; Eilers, S., *Advance Pricing Agreements (APAs) im US-amerikanischen Steuerrecht und Abkommensrecht*, 1996, 3; Herzig, N., *Resümee*, 1996, 90; Patton, M. F. and Wood, K. W., *Tax Management International Journal* 1997, 80; Wrappe, S. C., *Tax Management International Journal* 1997, 32; Meyer, D. I. and Outman, W. D. II, *Journal of International Taxation* 2002, 26.

[480] See Department of the Treasury, *Subpart F*, 2000, ix. For the taxation of corporations in detail, refer *supra* page 25.

[481] The Department of the Treasury declared in its Study, dated December 29, 2000, that both of these fundamental features of the U.S. tax system are of importance. On the one hand, worldwide taxation ensures equity in the tax system by treating all income the same, ensuring that investments are not made for tax-driven reasons and avoiding the perception of unfairness that would occur if the tax reduction were more easily available to those with the ability to invest abroad. On the other hand, the treatment of a corporation as a separate entity is integral to maintaining the so-called *classical system* of taxation where corporate earnings are subject to two levels of taxation. Hence, there is an ability to defer the second level of taxation until distribution. See Brumbaugh, D. L., *Tax Notes International* 1992, 235; McNulty, J. K., *Limited Liability Companies*, 1995, 684; Yoder, L. D. and Kahn, J. H., *Tax Management International Journal* 1999, 532; Department of the Treasury, *Subpart F*, 2000, vii; Moussallem, S., *Die Besteuerung einer US-corporation*, 2001, 31. For details on the Study, refer *infra* page 159.

[482] See Shepherdson, D. P., *Case Western Reserve Journal of International Law* 1985, 459; Hariton, D. P., *Tax Notes International* 1998, 1089; Josephs, S. R., *The Tax Adviser* 1998, 295; New York State Bar Association Tax Section, *Tax Notes International* 1998, 1670.

[483] On the other hand, capital importing countries basically favor deferral while seeking to retain their right to set the level of tax for businesses carried on within their territory. See Arnold, B. J. and McIntyre, M. J., *International Tax Primer*, 1995, 7.

[484] Conversely, capital importing countries claim that anti-deferral mechanisms indirectly intrude on their sovereignty because the income of the foreign subsidiary at issue arises solely within their taxing territory. The subsidiary is established within the capital importing country and the activity generating the income similarly arises within the capital importing country. See Hariton, D. P., *Tax Notes International* 1998, 1091.

shareholders from capital exporting countries through deemed dividend income.[485] Anti-deferral systems do not directly tax the foreign subsidiaries themselves.[486] Lastly, anti-deferral systems impose tax only after FTCs offset taxes imposed by capital importing countries, thereby leaving capital importing countries with the right to impose tax in the first instance.

With the enactment of Subpart F provisions, foreign holding companies receiving passive income from subsidiaries incorporated in different jurisdictions will now immediately trigger Subpart F income for their U.S. shareholders, as if the income were distributed directly to the U.S shareholders. Subpart F provisions also serve as a backstop to IRC § 482.[487] In an effort to cover every contingency, the provisions of Subpart F share the complexity that typifies virtually all IRC sections dealing with foreign entities and related transactions.[488] In the end, the provisions allocate many tasks to the Department of the Treasury to discharge through regulation.[489] For example, the Taxpayer Relief Act of 1997 adopted a long-proposed amendment in IRC § 961(c) granting authority to issue regulations for making basis adjustments to stock of lower-tier subsidiaries to reflect prior inclusion of CFC income by U.S. shareholders.[490]

1. PURPOSE AND TAX CONSEQUENCES

The U.S. tax law contains provisions designed to prevent U.S. corporations from delaying the repatriation of low-taxed foreign-source income.[491] Subpart F (IRC §§ 951-964) provides that certain types of income generated by CFCs must be included, in whole or in part, in gross income of the U.S. shareholders in the current period, even if the income has not been distributed back to the shareholders, i.e., tax deferral is limited.[492]

---

[485] See Birnkrant, H. J. and Croker, J. E. Jr., *Journal of Taxation* 1998, 50.

[486] Anti-deferral techniques intrude upon a capital importing country's right to set a low tax rate with the capital exporting country soaking up any low tax differential. The intrusion prevents capital importing countries from using low tax rates as a mechanism for attracting foreign investment.

[487] See Culbertson, R. E., *Tax Notes International* 1996, 1760; Meldman, R. E. and Schadewald, M. S., *A Practical Guide to U.S. Taxation of International Transactions*, 2000, 149; Shields, C. C., *Tax Notes International* 2002, 1116.

[488] See Roin, J. A., *Virginia Law Review* 1989, 920; McDonald, J., *Northwestern Journal of International Law and Business* 1995, 249.

[489] See Horwood, R. M. and Hechtman, J. A., *Journal of Corporate Taxation* 1995, 366; Bittker, B. I. and Lokken, L., *Federal Taxation of Income, Estates and Gifts*, 2002, paragraph 68.2; Isenbergh, J., *International Taxation: U.S. Taxation of Foreign Taxpayers and Foreign Income*, 2002, chapters 37-42.

[490] Pub.L. No. 105-34, H.R. 2014 105th Cong., 1st Sess (1997).

[491] See Benson, D. M., *The Tax Adviser* 1996, 630; Hines, J. R. Jr., *National Tax Journal* 1999, 387; Herrmann, H., *Die Einordnung ausländischer Gesellschaften*, 2001, 143. When forming Subpart F provisions, various policies were included, such as those preventing tax haven abuse, causing immediate taxing of passive income, promoting equity and economic efficiency, and further avoiding undue harm to the competitiveness of U.S. MNCs. See Department of the Treasury, *Subpart F*, 2000, 22; Meldman, R. E. and Schadewald, M. S., *A Practical Guide to U.S. Taxation of International Transactions*, 2000, 147; Aud, E. F. Jr., Benson, D. M. and Garrett-Nelson, L., *Tax Executive* 2001, 48; Yoder, L. D., *Tax Management International Journal* 2001, 222.

[492] See Byrnes, L. A., *Tax Notes International* 1989, 26; Doernberg, R. L., *Tax Notes International* 1991, 503; Grant, P., *Global Finance* 1996, 18; Krehbühl, H.-H., *Das Steueranrechnungsverfahren in den USA*, 1997, 150; Yoder, L. D., *Tax Management International Journal* 1997 II, 260; Yoder, L. D. and McGill, S. P., *Tax Management International Journal* 1997, 455; Tello, C. P., *Tax Management International Journal* 1998, 12; Yoder, L. D., *Tax Management International Journal* 1998 I, 222; Larkins, E. R., Oakley, E. F. and Winkle, G. M., *The Tax Adviser* 1999, 419; Middleton, C. I., *Journal of Partnership Taxation* 1999, 325; Yoder, L. D., *Tax Management International Journal* 1999 I, 339; Marantelli, A., *Steuer Revue* 2000 I, 14; McNulty, J. K., *Brief Look at the Early History of the Unintegrated Corporate and Individual Income Taxes in the U.S.A.*, 2000, 884; Yoder, L. D., *Tax Management International Journal* 2000, 668; Yoder, L. D. and Everson, S. L., *Tax Management International Journal* 2000 II, 303; Herrmann, H., *Die Einordnung ausländischer Gesellschaften*, 2001, 143; Yoder, L. D., *Tax Management International Journal* 2001, 222.

These provisions apply to foreign corporations that are CFCs for an uninterrupted period of 30 days or more during a taxable year (the so-called *thirty-consecutive-day provision*).[493] The provisions require that the U.S. shareholders include in gross income their pro rata share of the Subpart F income of the CFC and increase earnings for amounts that the CFC has invested in U.S. property for the taxable year.[494] This rule applies to U.S. shareholders who own stock in the corporation on the last day of the each taxable year or on the last day the foreign corporation is a CFC.[495] The gross income inclusion must be made by U.S. shareholders in the taxable year in which or within which the CFC's taxable year ends.[496] The amount of Subpart F income is limited to the CFC's current E&P, adjusted for specific prior year deficits.[497] Income that has previously been subject to taxation under IRC § 951(a) is not again taxable when actually distributed to the U.S. shareholder.[498] When the CFC actually distributes its E&P to its shareholders, according to IRC § 959(c)(1), the distributions are first treated as attributable to the CFC's previously taxed income.[499]

2. REQUIREMENTS

Irrespective of whether foreign companies with U.S. owners could be taxed at full force on their foreign-source income without violating U.S. international tax law, several difficulties would occur in levying such a tax on companies that have some foreign shareholders. By selecting the company's U.S. shareholders as its targets, Subpart F provisions sidestep that problem.[500]

2.1. Definition: U.S. Shareholder

In determining if a foreign corporation is a CFC, a U.S. shareholder is defined in IRC § 951(b) as a U.S. person - defined by IRC § 7701(a)(30) - who owns, or is considered to own, ten percent or more of the total combined voting power of all classes of the voting stock of the foreign corporation.[501]

---

[493] See Yoder, L. D., *Tax Management International Journal* 1997 I, 208; Yoder, L. D. and Everson, S. L., *Tax Management International Journal* 2000 I, 4; Doernberg, R. L., *International Taxation In a Nutshell*, 2001, 298.

[494] See Tello, C. P., *Tax Management International Journal* 1998, 12. For purposes of IRC § 956, U.S. property includes, among others, tangible property located within the U.S. territory, interests in U.S. corporations, and obligations of U.S. persons. See Yoder, L. D. and McGill, S. P., *Tax Management International Journal* 1997, 456; Dilworth, R. H. and Andrus, J. L., *Tax Law and Practice*, 2001, 1104; Bittker, B. I. and Eustice, J. S., *Federal Income Taxation of Corporations and Shareholders*, 2002, paragraph 15.61[3].

[495] IRC § 951(a)(1); Regs. §§ 1.905-1(a) and (b); Reg. § 1.956-1(d). See Yoder, L. D. and Kahn, J. H., *Tax Management International Journal* 1999, 532; Yoder, L. D. and Everson, S. L., *Tax Management International Journal* 2000 I, 5; Yoder, L. D. and Everson, S. L., *Tax Management International Journal* 2000 II, 303.

[496] See Yoder, L. D., *Tax Management International Journal* 1999 I, 339; Yoder, L. D. and Kahn, J. H., *Tax Management International Journal* 1999, 532; Yoder, L. D. and Everson, S. L., *Tax Management International Journal* 2000 I, 5.

[497] IRC § 952(c)(1)(A). The E&P are calculated according to the U.S. tax law and not in accordance with the provisions of the foreign jurisdiction. This highlights a number of difficulties in the determination of these amounts for companies whose books and records are mostly not consistent with U.S. tax and accounting standards and that have not had to make several elections (e.g., accounting and depreciation methods) that are usually a prerequisite to the computation of E&P. See ABA Task Force on Earnings and Profits, *Tax Lawyer* 1991, 165; Kuntz, J. D. and Peroni, R. J., *U.S. International Taxation*, 2002, paragraph B3.12. For the term and determination of E&P under U.S. law, see *supra* note 212.

[498] See Yoder, L. D. and Everson, S. L., *Tax Management International Journal* 2000 II, 303; Bouma, H. B. and Rosenbloom, H. D., *Tax Management International Journal* 2002, 84.

[499] IRC § 959(a)(1). See Stoffregen, P. A. and Lipeles, S. R., *Tax Notes International* 1994, 1327.

[500] See Bittker, B. I. and Eustice, J. S., *Federal Income Taxation of Corporations and Shareholders*, 2002, paragraph 15.61[1].

[501] IRC §§ 958(b), 318(a)(2). See Krehbühl, H.-H., *Das Steueranrechnungsverfahren in den USA*, 1997, 150; Yoder, L. D., *Tax Management International Journal* 1997 II, 260; Yoder, L. D. and McGill, S. P., *Tax Management International*

The term "U.S. person" for Subpart F purposes includes a U.S. citizen or resident, a domestic partnership, a domestic corporation, and any estate or trust other than a foreign estate or trust (IRC § 957(c)).[502] Pursuant to IRC §§ 958(a) and (b), stock owned directly, indirectly, and/or constructively is counted.[503]

Indirect ownership applies for ownership of stock held through a foreign entity, such as a foreign corporation, foreign partnership, or foreign trust. This stock is regarded as actually owned proportionately by the shareholders, partners, or beneficiaries.

Constructive ownership rules, with certain modifications, apply for purposes of determining whether a U.S. person is a U.S. shareholder, in determining if a foreign corporation is a CFC, and for specific related-party provisions of Subpart F.

U.S. shareholders must include their pro rata share of the applicable Subpart F income in their gross income only to the extent of their actual ownership.[504] Stock held indirectly is considered actually owned for this purpose.[505]

2.2. Definition: Controlled Foreign Corporation

According to IRC § 957(a), a CFC is any foreign corporation in which more than 50 percent of either the total combined voting power of all classes of stock entitled to vote or the total value of all classes of the corporation's stock is owned, directly or indirectly, by U.S. shareholders on any day during the taxable year of the foreign corporation.[506] The reality of voting control, i.e., effective control, rather than the appearance thereof, must be examined when determining if a foreign corporation is a

---

Journal 1997, 455; Zschiegner, H., *Internationale Wirtschaftsbriefe*, Fach 8, USA, Gruppe 2, 1998 III, 972; Hines, J. R. Jr., *National Tax Journal* 1999, 387; Yoder, L. D. and Kahn, J. H., *Tax Management International Journal* 1999, 531; Yoder, L. D., *Tax Management International Journal* 2000, 668; Yoder, L. D. and Everson, S. L., *Tax Management International Journal* 2000 I, 4; Yoder, L. D. and Everson, S. L., *Tax Management International Journal* 2000 II, 302; CCH, *2002 U.S. Tax Master Guide*, 2001, paragraph 2465; Engel, K., *Texas Law Review* 2001, 1531; Bittker, B. I. and Eustice, J. S., *Federal Income Taxation of Corporations and Shareholders*, 2002, paragraph 15.61[2].

[502] See Zschiegner, H., *Internationale Wirtschaftsbriefe*, Fach 8, USA, Gruppe 2, 1998 III, 972. Special provisions exclude from the definition of "U.S. person" bona-fide residents of Puerto Rico, Guam, American Samoa, and the Northern Marianna Islands with respect to certain corporations organized under the laws of such jurisdictions (IRC §§ 957(c)(1) and (2)).

[503] See *Textron Inc v. U.S.*, 561 F.2d 1023 (1st Cir. 1977) and 117 T.C. 67 [2001]. Yoder, L. D., *Tax Management International Journal* 1997 I, 204; Yoder, L. D., *Tax Management International Journal* 1999 I, 339; Yoder, L. D. and Kahn, J. H., *Tax Management International Journal* 1999, 531; Yoder, L. D., *Tax Management International Journal* 2000, 668; Sinclair, B. and Kopstein, R., *Guaranteed to Enlighten: The Impact of Guarantees on Financing Arrangements*, 2001, 22:18; Yoder, L. D., *Tax Management International Journal* 2001, 222; Yoder, L. D. and Waimon, R. L., *Journal of International Taxation* 2001, 42; Bittker, B. I. and Eustice, J. S., *Federal Income Taxation of Corporations and Shareholders*, 2002, paragraph 15.61[2].

[504] IRC § 951(a)(1). See Shepherdson, D. P., *Case Western Reserve Journal of International Law* 1985, 459; Isenbergh, J., *International Taxation*, 2000, 172; Sinclair, B. and Kopstein, R., *Guaranteed to Enlighten: The Impact of Guarantees on Financing Arrangements*, 2001, 22:18.

[505] IRC § 958(a)(2).

[506] See Eigenbrode, R., *The Tax Adviser* 1993, 444; Yoder, L. D., *Tax Management International Journal* 1997 I, 204; Yoder, L. D., *Tax Management International Journal* 1997 II, 260; Yoder, L. D. and McGill, S. P., *Tax Management International Journal* 1997, 455; McDaniel, P. R. and Ault, H. J., *Introduction to United States International Taxation*, 1998, 111; Tello, C. P., *Tax Management International Journal* 1998, 12; Zschiegner, H., *Internationale Wirtschaftsbriefe*, Fach 8, USA, Gruppe 2, 1998 III, 972; Hines, J. R. Jr., *National Tax Journal* 1999, 387; Larkins, E. R., Oakley, E. F. and Winkle, G. M., *The Tax Adviser* 1999, 419; Yoder, L. D. and Kahn, J. H., *Tax Management International Journal* 1999, 532; Golbert, A. S., *World Trade* 2000 II, 43; Marantelli, A., *Steuer Revue* 2000 I, 14; O'Connor, W. F. and Toyoda, Y., *The International Tax Journal* 2000, 83; Yoder, L. D., *Tax Management International Journal* 2000, 668; Yoder, L. D. and Everson, S. L., *Tax Management International Journal* 2000 I, 4; Yoder, L. D. and Everson, S. L., *Tax Management International Journal* 2000 II, 302; CCH, *2002 U.S. Tax Master Guide*, 2001, paragraph 2465; Engel, K., *Texas Law Review* 2001, 1531; Sinclair, B. and Kopstein, R., *Guaranteed to Enlighten: The Impact of Guarantees on Financing Arrangements*, 2001, 22:18; Bittker, B. I. and Eustice, J. S., *Federal Income Taxation of Corporations and Shareholders*, 2002, paragraph 15.61[2].

CFC.[507] For example, a foreign subsidiary that is wholly owned by a U.S. MNC is a CFC.[508] Conversely, a true 50-50 joint venture by a U.S. corporation and an unrelated foreign company does not result in CFC status for the subsidiary located abroad, as IRC § 957 requires more than 50 percent of voting control or share value to be held by the U.S. shareholders.

2.3. Definition: Subpart F Income

A U.S. shareholder of a CFC does not necessarily lose the ability to defer U.S. taxation of income earned by the CFC. In determining the amount of income currently taxable under the Subpart F provisions, the gross income generated by the CFC must be analyzed.[509] When each item compromising gross income has been specified, expenses are allocated and apportioned among the gross income items.[510] The net income attributable to Subpart F income is included in U.S. gross income unless one of the specific relief provisions applies. However, only certain types of income earned by the CFC triggers immediate U.S. taxation as a constructive dividend.[511] This tainted income, referred to as Subpart F income, can be characterized as income with little or no economic connection to the CFC's country of incorporation.[512] According to IRC § 952(a), Subpart F income consists of the following:[513]

- insurance income (IRC § 953);
- foreign base company income (IRC § 954);
- international boycott factor income (IRC §§ 999 and 952(a)(4));
- illegal bribes, kickbacks, or other payments within the meaning of IRC § 162(c); and
- income derived from a foreign country during a time in which a FTC is denied for foreign taxes paid to the foreign country.

If the ownership of a CFC changes during its taxable year, the U.S. shareholders subject to a Subpart F income inclusion are those owning stock of the CFC on the last day of the taxable year.[514] Such U.S. shareholders are required to include in gross income their pro rata share of Subpart F income based on the proportion of the CFC's stock owned and the number of days during the year that the foreign corporation was a CFC. Subpart F income is included in income before actual dividends received from the CFC. However, the pro rata share of Subpart F income is reduced in certain cases by dividends paid with respect to the shares held by shareholders not required to include the Subpart

---

[507] See Levey, M. M. and Pollack, L. A., *Journal of International Taxation* 1990, 208.

[508] See Bittker, B. I. and Eustice, J. S., *Federal Income Taxation of Corporations and Shareholders*, 2002, paragraph 15.61[2].

[509] The amounts with respect to a CFC included in the gross income of the U.S. shareholder, other than actual dividends received and Subpart F income, are the shareholder's pro rata share of the CFC's: (1) already excluded Subpart F income withdrawn from investments in less developed countries; (2) already excluded Subpart F income withdrawn from foreign base company shipping operations; and (3) increases in earnings invested in U.S. property. IRC §§ 951(a)(1)(B), 956 and 959(a)(2).

[510] Regs. §§ 1.861-10 and 1.861-9T(a). See Tello, C. P., *Tax Management International Journal* 1998, 19.

[511] Also referred to as imputed or deemed dividends.

[512] See Yoder, L. D., *Tax Management International Journal* 1998 I, 222; Abrams, H. E. and Doernberg, R. L., *Essentials of United States Taxation*, 1999, 4-178; Engel, K., *Texas Law Review* 2001, 1534.

[513] See Tello, C. P., *Tax Management International Journal* 1998, 12; Larkins, E. R., Oakley, E. F. and Winkle, G. M., *The Tax Adviser* 1999, 419; Meldman, R. E. and Schadewald, M. S., *A Practical Guide to U.S. Taxation of International Transactions*, 2000, 151; CCH, *2002 U.S. Tax Master Guide*, 2001, paragraph 2465; Bittker, B. I. and Eustice, J. S., *Federal Income Taxation of Corporations and Shareholders*, 2002, paragraph 15.61[1].

[514] Reg. § 1.951-1(a)(2).

F income in gross income. IRC § 1248[515] allows an acquiring U.S. shareholder to reduce any Subpart F inclusion by the lesser of:

(1) the amount of dividend deemed received by the selling U.S. shareholder under IRC § 1248; or
(2) the amount determined by multiplying the Subpart F income by the proportion of the year during which acquiring shareholder did not own the stock.

The Subpart F income inclusion is generally limited to the CFC's E&P of the current taxable year.[516] In certain cases, the E&P for the current taxable year are reduced by qualified deficits in E&P from previous taxable years.[517]

2.3.1. Stock Ownership

As previously discussed, in determining whether a foreign corporation is a CFC and whether a U.S. person is a U.S. shareholder, the stock ownership provisions of IRC § 958 must be evaluated. IRC § 958 requires that direct, indirect, and/or constructive ownership must be considered in making these determinations.[518]

Direct ownership does not require additional explanation. The indirect ownership provision (IRC § 958(a)(2)) requires that stock owned directly or indirectly by a foreign corporation, partnership, trust or estate be considered as owned proportionately by the respective shareholders, partners, and beneficiaries.[519] The provision treats stock that is indirectly owned as if were actually owned. The indirect ownership provisions apply most frequently when a U.S. corporation owns stock of a foreign corporation through an interposed foreign corporation. Under such a chain of ownership, the indirect ownership provisions apply, irrespective of the number of foreign corporations owned indirectly by another foreign corporation. The indirect ownership rule is generally applicable for all purposes of Subpart F. This includes the determination of stock owned for purposes of the income inclusion requirements of IRC § 951(a). Thus, if any foreign corporation which is a CFC through a chain of ownership has Subpart F income, the U.S. shareholder, not the interposed foreign corporation, is required to include the pro rata share of Subpart F income from the CFC in its U.S. income tax return.

Constructive ownership applies only for the four purposes specified in IRC § 958(b).[520] In defining constructive ownership, IRC § 958(b) relies on IRC § 318(a), which defines constructive ownership for purposes of Subchapter C of the IRC.[521]

---

[515] For an analysis of IRC § 1248, see *infra* page 103.

[516] IRC § 952(c)(1)(A). See Fischl, A. L., *Journal of Taxation* 1996, 109; Meldman, R. E. and Schadewald, M. S., *A Practical Guide to U.S. Taxation of International Transactions*, 2000, 151; Yoder, L. D. and Everson, S. L., *Tax Management International Journal* 2000 I, 5; Giannattasio, B. and Suarez-Lasa, D., *Journal of International Taxation* 2002, 48.

[517] IRC § 952(c)(1)(B). See Levey, M. M. and Teigen, R. D., *Journal of Taxation* 1996, 262; Giannattasio, B. and Suarez-Lasa, D., *Journal of International Taxation* 2002, 48.

[518] See Fischl. A. L., *Journal of Taxation* 1996, 106; Abrams, H. E. and Doernberg, R. L., *Essentials of United States Taxation*, 1999, 4-176; Meldman, R. E. and Schadewald, M. S., *A Practical Guide to U.S. Taxation of International Transactions*, 2000, 150; Yoder, L. D. and Everson, S. L., *Tax Management International Journal* 2000 I, 4; Bittker, B. I. and Eustice, J. S., *Federal Income Taxation of Corporations and Shareholders*, 2002, paragraph 15.61[3].

[519] See Levey, M. M. and Pollack, L. A., *Journal of International Taxation* 1990, 207; Yoder, L. D., *Tax Management International Journal* 1998 III, 607.

[520] The four purposes specified are (1) determining if a U.S. person is a U.S. shareholder under IRC § 951(b); (2) determining if a person is related to a CFC under IRC § 954(d)(3) determining whether a CFC generates foreign base company sales income; (3) determining whether an investment is excluded from the definition of an investment in U.S. property under IRC § 956(b); and (4) determining if a foreign corporation is a CFC under IRC § 957(a).

It is important to distinguish between the indirect and constructive ownership provisions. Only direct and indirect ownership is taken into consideration when determining the amount of a CFC's Subpart F income that is included in a U.S. shareholder's income tax return under IRC § 951(a). A U.S. shareholder does not include the CFC's Subpart F income with respect to stock that is only constructively owned. Direct, indirect, and constructive ownership are all considered, however, in determining if a person is a U.S. shareholder, or whether a foreign corporation is a CFC.

2.3.2. Foreign Base Company Income

In general, a foreign base company is formed through an arrangement whereby a U.S. MNC establishes a foreign subsidiary or another limited liability entity in a base country, i.e., a tax haven, while carrying on business in a third country.[522] U.S. MNCs use foreign base companies to route income from foreign jurisdictions with high corporate tax rates to tax havens.[523] These arrangements typically result in the same outcome as the diversionary techniques used to shift income from U.S. shores, i.e., through profit extraction or profit shifting.[524]

In a typical holding structure, a U.S. MNC would hold the stock of a foreign holding company located in a tax haven, i.e., the base country. The foreign holding company would in turn own one or more second-tier foreign subsidiaries, all of which would be established and carry on active business outside the tax haven. The foreign holding company would, therefore, receive dividends and/or other passive income, such as interest and royalties, from the second-tier foreign subsidiaries without a significant worldwide tax burden. The foreign holding company could reinvest this passive income in additional foreign operations without triggering any U.S. tax because the foreign holding company bypassed the need for repatriation back to the ultimate parent, U.S. MNC. Hence, the creation of provisions which apply to foreign base company income implies that tax authorities wish to restrict the common practice of using a foreign base corporation in cross-border business operations to shelter foreign-source income from both foreign and U.S. taxes.

2.3.2.1. Definition

The principal category of Subpart F income is foreign base company income (FBCI) which generally includes passive income, such as foreign personal holding company (FPHC) income, i.e., dividends, interest, rents and royalties, as well as certain items of active income.[525] FBCI provisions target

---

[521] Subchapter C - Corporate Distributions and Adjustments (IRC §§ 301-385). See Hoffman, W. H. Jr. and Gately, M. S., *Journal of Taxation* 1986, 93; Levey, M. M. and Pollack, L. A., *Journal of International Taxation* 1990, 207; Yoder, L. D., *Tax Management International Journal* 1998 III, 607.

[522] The primary example of the application of Subpart F, which was introduced during the Kennedy Administration, involved a U.S.-owned subsidiary in Germany that was subject to a 50 percent tax rate. The German company diverted income to a related entity in Switzerland, with an eight percent tax rate. The Administration regarded this shifting of income to the lower taxed Swiss company as an implicit tax incentive for business investors to operate abroad. One argument against the Administration claimed that the routing of income from German- to Swiss-sources had no U.S. tax consequences because this diversion merely allowed U.S.-owned businesses to avoid German tax costs. Further, the argument concluded that, if anything, this diversion was a favorable development for the U.S. tax system since any German taxes saved would possibly result in more net earnings being repatriated to the U.S. See President's 1961 Tax Recommendations: Hearings before the House Comm. on Ways and Means on the Recommendations of the President Contained in his message transmitted to the Congress, April 20, 1961, 87th Cong., 1st Sess. (Vol. I) 303, 343 (1961); Anonymous, *Tax Executive* 1998 II, 145; Department of the Treasury, *Subpart F*, 2000, 9; Engel, K., *Texas Law Review* 2001, 1540; Bittker, B. I. and Eustice, J. S., *Federal Income Taxation of Corporations and Shareholders*, 2002, paragraph 15.62[1].

[523] See Abrams, H. E. and Doernberg, R. L., *Essentials of United States Taxation*, 1999, 4-175.

[524] For the tax planning goals of a U.S. MNC, refer *supra* page 39.

[525] See Krehbühl, H.-H., *Das Steueranrechnungsverfahren in den USA*, 1997, 150; Tello, C. P., *Tax Management International Journal* 1998, 12; Yoder, L. D., *Tax Management International Journal* 1998 I, 222; Yoder, L. D., *Tax*

certain transactions, such as sales and services income from activities involving related persons[526] in which a CFC earns income that lacks any economic connection to its country of incorporation.[527] FBCI is defined in IRC § 954(a) and includes the following five categories:[528]

- foreign personal holding company income;
- foreign base company sales income;
- foreign base company services income;
- foreign base company shipping income; and
- foreign base company oil related income.

2.3.2.2. Determination

While FBCI is firstly determined with reference to the CFC's gross income, IRC § 954(b)(5) reduces such gross income by deducting expenses properly attributable to such income.[529] The net amount is the amount that is included in the gross income of the U.S. shareholders.[530] IRC § 954(b)(5) contains a special rule with respect to interest paid or accrued by any U.S. shareholder or related CFC.[531] Such interest is allocated first to FPHC income that is passive income as defined under IRC § 904(d)(2).[532]

Losses in the FBCI categories are treated restrictively, i.e., losses in any one category of FBCI cannot be used to offset income in other categories.[533] Further, losses that occurred within the FPHC income subcategories of commodities, exchange, and other property transactions cannot be offset against positive amounts in other FPHC income categories.[534]

Management International Journal 1998 III, 611; Yoder, L. D. and Kahn, J. H., *Tax Management International Journal* 1999, 532; Yoder, L. D., *Tax Management International Journal* 2000, 673; Yoder, L. D. and Everson, S. L., *Tax Management International Journal* 2000 II, 303; Calianno, J. M. and Gregoire, B. J., *Journal of International Taxation* 2001, 44; Yoder, L. D. and Waimon, R. L., *Journal of International Taxation* 2001, 43.

[526] See Kral, K. H. and Tilevitz, O., *International Tax Review* 1998, 15. For details on related persons, see *infra* page 94.

[527] IRC §§ 954(d)(1)(A), (B), (2) and (e)(B). See Yoder, L. D., *Tax Management International Journal* 1998 I, 222; Engel, K., *Texas Law Review* 2001, 1534.

[528] See Flick, H. F. W. and Janka, W., *Deutsches Steuerrecht* 1991 II, 1073; Fischl, A. L., *Journal of Taxation* 1996, 106; Engle, H. S., *Journal of Corporate Taxation* 1998, 299; McDaniel, P. R. and Ault, H. J., *Introduction to United States International Taxation*, 1998, 113; Tello, C. P., *Tax Management International Journal* 1998, 12; Yoder, L. D., *Tax Management International Journal* 1998 III, 610; Zschiegner, H., *Internationale Wirtschaftsbriefe*, Fach 8, USA, Gruppe 2, 1998 III, 972; Zois, A., *Cardozo Journal of International and Comparative Law* 1999, 196; Meldman, R. E. and Schadewald, M. S., *A Practical Guide to U.S. Taxation of International Transactions*, 2000, 153; Calianno, J. M. and Gregoire, B. J., *Journal of International Taxation* 2001, 44; Sinclair, B. and Kopstein, R., *Guaranteed to Enlighten: The Impact of Guarantees on Financing Arrangements*, 2001, 22:18. For Subpart F and source of income issues in e-commerce, refer Maguire, N. and Anolik, S., *Tax Notes* 2000, 1767. In the following sections, only foreign personal holding company income is analyzed, as it applies to income accrued by any U.S. MNC holding stocks overseas.

[529] See Reynolds, B. W. and Melcer, G. J., *Journal of International Taxation* 1995, 532; Meldman, R. E. and Schadewald, M. S., *A Practical Guide to U.S. Taxation of International Transactions*, 2000, 153.

[530] See Reynolds, B. W. and Melcer, G. J., *Journal of International Taxation* 1995, 535; Yoder, L. D., *Tax Management International Journal* 2000, 673; Bittker, B. I. and Eustice, J. S., *Federal Income Taxation of Corporations and Shareholders*, 2002, paragraph 15.62[3].

[531] See Daub, P. M., *Journal of International Taxation* 1990, 72; Cooper, M. J. and Torgersen, S., *International Tax Review* 1998, 67; Meldman, R. E. and Schadewald, M. S., *A Practical Guide to U.S. Taxation of International Transactions*, 2000, 153.

[532] See Windholtz, T. F. and Bernot, J. E., *Journal of International Taxation* 1991 II, 153.

[533] Reg. § 1.954-1(c)(1)(ii).

[534] See Reynolds, B. W. and Melcer, G. J., *Journal of International Taxation* 1995, 538.

2.3.2.3. Related Persons

A number of the FBCI definitional provisions depend on whether a transaction involves a person related to the CFC as defined under IRC § 954(c)(3). In applying the FBCI rules, a person is a related person with respect to a CFC if such a person controls the CFC or is controlled by the CFC or by the same persons that control the CFC. For this purpose, the control threshold is more than 50 percent ownership;[535] in the control test direct, indirect, and/or constructive ownership is considered.[536]

2.3.2.4. Country of Incorporation

Certain FBCI definitional provisions also depend on the country in which the activities giving rise to the income occur. Examples of such provisions are included in IRC § 954(b)(4), the so-called *high-tax kick-out exception* and IRC § 954(c)(3)(A)(i)(II), the definition of related persons.

2.3.2.5. Foreign Personal Holding Company Income

U.S. MNCs owning stock overseas must be aware of FPHC income, which is the principal category of FBCI. FPHC income might impede upon the local tax efficiency of an EU holding company controlled by a U.S. MNC as it is defined as income that is "passive in character".[537] Hence, dividends received from lower-tier subsidiaries will necessitate a full inclusion in U.S. income under IRC § 954(c). FPHC income under IRC § 954(c) must be distinguished from the FPHC of IRC §§ 551-558,[538] although the two anti-deferral regimes are quite similar.

2.3.2.5.1. Categories of Income

According to IRC §§ 954(c)(1)(A)-(G), FPHC income includes:[539]

- dividends and payments in lieu of dividends;
- interest and income equivalent to interest;
- royalties;
- rents and annuities;
- gains or losses from the disposal or exchange of property that constitute FPHC income;

---

[535] IRC § 954(d)(3).

[536] IRC § 958. See Anonymous, *Journal of International Taxation* 2001, 4.

[537] S. Rep. No. 1881, 87th Cong., 2d Sess. 84 (1962), 1962 WL 4862. See Gillmarten, M., *Tax Management International Journal* 1998, 493.

[538] Under IRC § 552(a) FPHC is defined as any foreign corporation in which (1) at least 50 percent [60 percent for the first year] of its gross income from all sources is FPHC income as defined in IRC § 553; and (2) more than 50 percent of the value of the total combined voting power of all classes of stock or outstanding stock of the corporation is owned, directly or indirectly, at any time during the taxable year by five or fewer individuals who are citizens or residents of the U.S. Therefore, this regime does not apply to foreign subsidiaries owned by publicly held U.S. MNCs. If the two rules overlap, CFC provisions takes precedence, pursuant to IRC § 951(d). See Hoffman, W. H. Jr. and Gately, M. S., *Journal of Taxation* 1986, 92; Tello, C. P., *Tax Management International Journal* 1998, 12; Meldman, R. E. and Schadewald, M. S., *A Practical Guide to U.S. Taxation of International Transactions*, 2000, 166; Engel, K., *Texas Law Review* 2001, 1533.

[539] Reg. § 1.954-2(e). See Yoder, L. D., *Tax Management International Journal* 1996 I, 3; Yoder, L. D., *Tax Management International Journal* 1997 I, 209; Yoder, L. D., *Tax Management International Journal* 1998 I, 220; Yoder, L. D., *Tax Management International Journal* 1998 III, 612; Zois, A., *Cardozo Journal of International and Comparative Law* 1999, 196; Yoder, L. D., *Tax Management International Journal* 2000, 674; Engel, K., *Texas Law Review* 2001, 1542; Sinclair, B. and Kopstein, R., *Guaranteed to Enlighten: The Impact of Guarantees on Financing Arrangements*, 2001, 22:18; Yoder, L. D., *Tax Management International Journal* 2001, 222; Bittker, B. I. and Eustice, J. S., *Federal Income Taxation of Corporations and Shareholders*, 2002, paragraph 15.62[2][a].

- certain gains from commodities and commodities futures transactions;
- gains from the disposition of foreign currency;[540] and
- income from notional principal contracts.

This category of Subpart F income provisions effectively prevents a U.S. person from forming an offshore holding entity to hold stock, other investments in foreign affiliates or intangible assets such as patents and trademarks in order to achieve U.S. tax deferral of such income. In the following sections, only FPHC income items that commonly occur at the level of a U.S. MNC, using a holding structure for doing business in Europe, are subject to examination.

2.3.2.5.1.1. Dividends

A portion of the gain on the disposition of stock in a lower-tier CFC is treated as a dividend for inclusion in Subpart F income, pursuant to IRC § 954(c)(1)(A).[541] Under this IRC section, dividends within the general definition of FPHC income are also included.[542] Additionally, the U.S. tax law rules that the constructive dividend portion of the gain under IRC § 1248 does not qualify for the same country exception.[543] In contrast thereto, the dividend portion of the gain may qualify for the high-tax exception under IRC § 954(b)(4).[544]

2.3.2.5.1.2. Interest

The term "interest" means all amounts that are treated as interest income under the IRC, regulations, or any other provisions of U.S. law.[545] This includes income from promissory notes, bonds or savings and other bank deposits, whether interest is stated or implicit, e.g., original issue discount (OID).[546]

2.3.2.5.1.3. Capital Gains

Gains recognized by a CFC from the disposition of stock of another CFC is part of FPHC income, pursuant to IRC § 954(c)(1)(B).[547] This category of FPHC income includes gains from the disposal of stock whether or not the foreign corporation is a subsidiary whose dividends would be excluded from FPHC income under the same country exception (IRC § 954(c)(3)(A)(i)).[548] The IRC does not contain any exceptions with regard to this requirement and the regulations expressly uphold this result.[549] Nevertheless, if the gain on the disposition of stock is taxed under foreign law, the high-tax

---

[540] The term "foreign currency gain" is defined as any gain from an IRC § 988 transaction to the extent such a gain does not exceed the gain realized by reason of changes in exchange rates on or after the booking date and before the payment date (IRC § 954(c)(1)(D)).

[541] Reg. § 1.954-2(b)(1).

[542] See Levey, M. M. and Teigen, R. D., *Journal of Taxation* 1996, 262.

[543] IRC § 964(e)(2). For the same country exception in detail, refer *infra* page 96.

[544] For the high-tax exception in detail, refer *infra* page 102.

[545] Reg. § 1.954-2(a)(4)(i). See Yoder, L. D., *Tax Management International Journal* 1997 I, 209.

[546] Reg. § 1.61-7(a). For the OID in detail, see Levy, D. F., *Florida Tax Review* 1997, 528; Polito, A. P., *Virginia Tax Review* 1998, 528; Beer, Y., *Virginia Tax Review* 2000, 464.

[547] See Yoder, L. D. and Waimon, R. L., *Journal of International Taxation* 2001, 43.

[548] For the same country exception in detail, refer *infra* page 96.

[549] Reg. § 1.954-2(e)(2)(i)(B).

exception under IRC § 954(b)(4) may apply, thereby permitting such gains to be excluded from Subpart F income.[550]

2.3.2.5.2. Exceptions

2.3.2.5.2.1. Related Persons Exception

Under IRC § 954(c)(3)(A), an exception to FPHC income inclusion is provided for dividends, interest, rents and royalties received from a related person if certain prerequisites are satisfied.[551] Particularly, FPHC income does not include dividend and interest income derived from a CFC[552] if the payor meets the following three requirements:[553]

- the payor is a corporation that is a related person;
- the payor is created or organized under the laws of the same foreign jurisdiction as the CFC; and
- a substantial part of the payor's assets are used in a trade or business located in the payor's country of incorporation.[554]

A paying corporation qualifies as a related party if the payor controls the stock of the CFC, or a third party controls both the stock of the CFC **and** the stock of the paying corporation. Control in this case means more than 50 percent of the vote or value of the stock at issue.

Pursuant to IRC § 954(c)(3)(B), the exception only applies to the extent that these payments do not reduce the Subpart F income of the payor corporation.

2.3.2.5.2.2. Same Country Exception

Tax deferral is available for related-party payments that satisfy the same country exception provisions.[555] For dividends and interest to benefit from the same country exception under IRC § 954(c)(3)(A)(i), the distributed earnings must have been accumulated during a period in which the CFC held the stock through a chain of one or more subsidiaries that satisfy the requirements of

---

[550] For the high-tax exception in detail, refer *infra* page 102.

[551] See Tello, C. P., *Tax Management International Journal* 1998, 12; Yoder, L. D., *Tax Management International Journal* 1998 I, 223; Yoder, L. D., *Tax Management International Journal* 2000, 673; Yoder, L. D., *Tax Management International Journal* 2001, 222.

[552] According to IRC § 954(c)(3)(A)(ii), rents and royalties are not FPHC income if received from a corporation that is a related person for the use of, or the privilege of using, property in the same country under the laws of which the CFC is created or organized. For the exception to apply, the rents and royalties (1) must be received from a related person that is a corporation, and (2) must be for the use of property in the same country under which the laws of the CFC are organized. See Engel, K., *Texas Law Review* 2001, 1543.

[553] See Engel, K., *Texas Law Review* 2001, 1543.

[554] IRC § 954(c)(3)(A)(i); Reg. § 1.954-2(b)(4)(i)(A).

[555] See Reynolds, B. W., Denovio, N. J. and Mundstock, G., *Journal of International Taxation* 1994, 58; Doernberg, R. L., *International Taxation In a Nutshell*, 2001, 303; Engel, K., *Texas Law Review* 2001, 1542. The member states of the EU that created a Single Market in 1992 are treated as single countries for purposes of the same country exception. However, it was proposed under Sec. 102 of H.R. 2018 (The International Tax Simplification for American Competitiveness Act of 1999) to treat all member states as one country. See Ruding, H. O., *Journal of International Taxation* 1994, 9; Culbertson, R. E., *Tax Notes International* 1996, 1759; Yoder, L. D., *Tax Management International Journal* 1997 II, 266; Anonymous, *Tax Executive* 1999 I, 348.

the exception.[556] The provisions require that the payor be incorporated or organized in the same foreign country as the recipient and that it uses more than half of its assets in a trade or business in that country.[557]

2.3.2.5.2.3. Active Trade or Business Exception

Rents and royalties received from unrelated persons by a CFC in the active conduct of its trade or business do not constitute FPHC income.[558] Moreover, income that is derived in the active conduct of a banking, financing or similar business,[559] or in the conduct of an insurance business is exempt from Subpart F provisions.[560] However, in order to qualify for the exemption, it is necessary for the CFC to conduct substantial activities with respect to its business.[561]

2.3.2.5.3. Hybrid Structures for Avoiding Foreign Personal Holding Company Income

2.3.2.5.3.1. Deferral

U.S. MNCs may conclude that, for the moment, Subpart F provisions do not apply to partnerships. They could rely on the favorable decision in *Brown Group*,[562] vacating and remanding 104 T.C. 105 [1995],[563] and on the effective date of the proposed "Brown Group" IRC § 702 and Subpart F regulations (REG-112502-00).[564] The issue addressed on appeal in the Brown Group case was whether distributive shares of a foreign partnership's earnings should be taxed to Brown Group under Subpart F of the IRC. The decision in this case impacts the taxable years of a CFC beginning on or after the date the final regulations are published in the Federal Register.[565]

The Brown Group Inc was a publicly traded parent of an affiliated group of domestic corporations (filing a consolidated income tax return). Brown Group International Inc, a Delaware corporation, was a wholly owned subsidiary of Brown Group Inc. Brown Group International Inc, in turn, was the parent of a 100 percent subsidiary, Brown Group Cayman Ltd. Brown Group Cayman Ltd. was an 88 percent partner in Brinco P/S, a Cayman Islands partnership.[566] The remaining twelve percent interest in that partnership was held by two unrelated individuals who had previously performed importing services on behalf of Brown Group.[567] The parties in the court appeal agreed

---

[556] IRC § 954(c)(2)(C). Certain sales and services income that is not earned within a CFC's home country is taxable, while income earned within the home country territory is exempt from taxation under the same country exception (IRC §§ 954(d) and (e)).

[557] IRC § 954(b)(5) and Reg. § 1.954-1(c)(1)(i). See Dilworth, R. H. and Andrus, J. L., *Tax Law and Practice*, 2001, 1104.

[558] IRC § 954(c)(2)(A); Regs. §§ 1.954-2(c)(1)(iv) and -2(d)(1)(ii). See Yoder, L. D., *Tax Management International Journal* 1998 I, 223; Doernberg, R. L., *International Taxation In a Nutshell*, 2001, 302; Yoder, L. D., *Tax Management International Journal* 2001, 222.

[559] IRC § 954(h). See Benson, D. M., O'Connor, P. and Rollinson, M. A., *Tax Management International Journal* 1998 II, 662; Doernberg, R. L., *International Taxation In a Nutshell*, 2001, 301.

[560] IRC § 954(i). See Stevens, M. G., *The Practical Accountant* 1998, 38.

[561] IRC § 954(h)(2)(A).

[562] *Brown Group Inc v. Commissioner*, 102 T.C. 616 [1994].

[563] *Brown Group Inc v. Commissioner*.

[564] 65 Fed. Reg. 56836, September 20, 2000. See Yoder, L. D., *Tax Management International Journal* 1998 III, 605.

[565] See Yoder, L. D., *Journal of International Taxation* 1998, 44.

[566] See Anonymous, *Journal of International Taxation* 1996, 479; Yoder, L. D., *Tax Management International Journal* 1998 III, 625; Di Fronzo, M. A. and Thomas, J. M., *Tax Notes International* 1999, 759.

[567] See Tuerff, T. T. and Gordon, R. A., *Journal of International Taxation* 1994, 293.

that Brown Group International Inc was a "United States shareholder" of Brown Group Cayman Ltd., and that Brown Group Cayman Ltd. was a "controlled foreign corporation (CFC)" within the meaning of the statutes (IRC §§ 957(a) and 954(d)(1) [1986]).

In 1985, the Brown Group decided to consolidate its buying power in Brazil by using only a single purchasing agent. Brinco P/S, a limited foreign partnership, acted as a purchasing agent for Brown Group International Inc, with a view toward attracting two individuals for purchasing Brazilian goods exclusively for the Brown Group. Brinco P/S received a commission of ten percent on sales.[568] Brinco P/S was established for several of reasons, one of which was that it permitted individuals to have entrepreneurial interests in Brinco P/S's operations.[569]

The court case ultimately focused on a very discrete question of law: whether Brown Group Cayman Ltd.'s distributive shares of Brinco P/S's partnership earnings, i.e., the commissions, constituted Subpart F income under IRC § 954(d)(3), given that the commissions did not constitute Subpart F income when earned by Brinco P/S.[570] It was necessary to determine if the Cayman Islands partnership was a related person of the U.S. parent company, according to IRC § 954(d)(3). If so, the income would constitute Subpart F income of the U.S. parent.

Both the aggregate approach and the entity approach are factors in determining whether or not the partnership is related. According to the aggregate approach, the income generated by the CFC would be tested for Subpart F status at the level of the CFC, as the partnership would be viewed as an aggregate of its partners.[571] Conversely, under the entity theory approach, the CFC's income would be analyzed for Subpart F attributes at the level of the partnership.[572]

It was argued that since Brinco P/S earned commission income on behalf of an unrelated person, Brown Group International Inc, that the income was not foreign company sales income for purposes of Subpart F.[573] Given that partnership income is characterized at the partnership level (i.e., the entity theory should prevail), the income earned by Brinco P/S retained its character of being excluded from Subpart F income when distributed to Brown Group Cayman Ltd. The Tax Court initially agreed with the taxpayers and ruled that the commission income received by the Cayman Islands partnership did not constitute Subpart F income, i.e., that the entity approach was applicable.[574] Hence, a controlled partnership was used to change the character of a CFC's income from tainted income into untainted income subject to indefinite tax deferral.

In summary, as partnerships are basically treated as pass through entities with their income taxed in the hands of the partners, the deemed dividend provisions of Subpart F are not necessary. Further, income earned abroad through a foreign partnership would not obtain any deferral benefit,

---

[568] See Tillinghast, D. R., *Tax Law and Practice*, 1994, 644.

[569] See McIntyre, M. J., *Tax Notes International* 1994, 1227; Lam, E. W., *DePaul Business Law Journal* 1996, 92.

[570] See McIntyre, M. J., *Tax Notes International* 1994, 1228.

[571] See Rev. Rul. 89-72, 1989-1 C.B. 257; Rev. Rul. 90-112, 1990-2 C.B. 186; Anonymous, *Journal of International Taxation* 1994, 285; McIntyre, M. J., *Tax Notes International* 1994, 1226; Anonymous, *Journal of International Taxation* 1996, 479; Forst, D. L., *Berkeley Journal of International Law* 1996, 271; Laity, E. T., *Cornell International Law Journal* 1998, 98; Quinn, T. F., Garre, K. and Hangebrauck, W., *The International Tax Journal* 2001, 19.

[572] See Tuerff, T. T. and Gordon, R. A., *Journal of International Taxation* 1994, 295; Lam, E. W., *DePaul Business Law Journal* 1996, 76.

[573] See Tuerff, T. T. and Gordon, R. A., *Journal of International Taxation* 1994, 294; Anonymous, *Journal of International Taxation* 1996, 479; Yoder, L. D., *Tax Management International Journal* 1998 III, 625.

[574] See Anonymous, *Journal of International Taxation* 1994, 285; Tillinghast, D. R., *Tax Law and Practice*, 1994, 643; Tuerff, T. T. and Gordon, R. A., *Journal of International Taxation* 1994, 295; Brown, K. B. and Rothschild, D. P., *Mertens Law of Federal Income Taxation*, 2002, paragraph 45:08; in line with the decision on *U.S. v. Basye*, 410 U.S. 441 [1973]. In 1995, at a motion for reconsideration for the IRS, the respective Tax Court reversed itself and submitted the case to the entire Tax Court. This Court decided in favor of the IRS, i.e., the commission income received by the Cayman Islands partnership was tainted Subpart F income. See Anonymous, *Journal of International Taxation* 1995, 143; Kral, K. H., Serota, J. and Weiss, J., *Journal of Accountancy* 1995, 26; Anonymous, *Journal of International Taxation* 1996, 479; Lam, E. W., *DePaul Business Law Journal* 1996, 93; Di Fronzo, M. A. and Thomas, J. M., *Tax Notes International* 1999, 760; P. M. D., *Journal of International Taxation* 2000, 4; Doernberg, R. L., *International Taxation In a Nutshell*, 2001, 310; Hensley, A. D., *Mertens Law of Federal Income Taxation*, 2002, paragraph 45E:144.

as the U.S. shareholder would be subject to tax in the current year on its share of the income accrued by the foreign partnership.[575] In order to achieve tax deferral on foreign-source income, it would be beneficial to earn income through a foreign partnership controlled by a CFC.[576]

In response to Brown Group ruling, the IRS issued Notice 96-39.[577] In that notice, the IRS announced its disagreement with the 8th Circuit Court decision and clarified its intention to issue regulations under Subpart F for the application of its view of an aggregate theory for partnerships for the purposes of determining Subpart F income.[578]

On March 26, 1998, the Department of the Treasury issued a series of temporary and proposed regulations under IRC § 702 and Subpart F.[579] The regulations affirm the Department of the Treasury and the IRS's intention of issuing regulations to establish the treatment of partnerships in the context of Subpart F following the Brown Group decision. The regulations generally provide for an "aggregate" rather than an entity theory approach for purposes of determining whether a CFC's distributive share of partnership income is Subpart F income.[580] In other words, the determination of whether partnership income is Subpart F income is made as if the CFC partner conducted the partnership's activities itself.[581] If any part of the partnership's income is Subpart F income under this aggregate theory, it must then be separately stated as such. The regulations apply to all items constituting Subpart F income, not only foreign base company sales income, which was at issue in the Brown Group case.[582]

Proposed Reg. § 1.954-1(g)(1) provides that, for the purpose of testing whether a related party transaction has occurred, the determination will be made by reference to the CFC partner rather than the partnership. Related parties, which are necessary for the creation of most types of foreign base company income, are defined under IRC § 954(d)(3). Certain exceptions in the regulations allow for the retention of the entity approach rather than an aggregate treatment for partnerships. The identified exceptions are:[583]

(1) determination of foreign base company sales income (related party status);[584]
(2) determination of foreign base company services income;[585]
(3) determination of foreign personal holding company income;[586] and
(4) the manufacturing exception to foreign base company sales income.[587]

With regard to foreign personal holding company income, the regulations provide that exceptions for active rents and royalties, export financing, and dealer activities in IRC § 954(c)(2) and the regulations thereunder will not be satisfied with respect to a CFC's distributive share of partnership income unless those exceptions would have applied if the CFC had earned the income directly

---

[575] See McIntyre, M. J., *Tax Notes International* 1994, 1229.

[576] See Yoder, L. D., *Tax Management International Journal* 1998 III, 605.

[577] 1996-32 I.R.B. 8. See Yoder, L. D., *Tax Management International Journal* 1998 III, 625.

[578] See Anonymous, *Journal of International Taxation* 1996, 479; Sams, J., *The Tax Adviser* 1998, 374.

[579] T.D. 8767, 63 Fed. Reg. 14813. See Yoder, L. D., *Journal of International Taxation* 1998, 12.

[580] See Anonymous, *Journal of International Taxation* 1996, 479.

[581] See Yoder, L. D., *Journal of International Taxation* 1998, 12.

[582] See Anonymous, *Journal of International Taxation* 1996, 479.

[583] See Yoder, L. D., *Journal of International Taxation* 1998, 12.

[584] Prop. Reg. § 1.954-3(a)(6).

[585] Prop. Reg. § 1.954-4(b)(2)(iii).

[586] Prop. Reg. § 1.954-2(a)(5)(ii).

[587] Prop. Reg. § 1.954-3(a)(4). See Yoder, L. D., *Journal of International Taxation* 1998, 14; Yoder, L. D., *Tax Management International Journal* 1998 III, 628. For the level of activity necessary to qualify for the manufacturing exception, see *Bausch & Lomb Inc v. Commissioner*, 71 T.C. M. 2031 [1996]. For an in-depth analysis of the decision, see Yoder, L. D., *Tax Management International Journal* 1996 II, 427; Willens, R., *Journal of Taxation* 1999, 69.

(aggregate treatment).[588] However, in applying this aggregate theory, the regulations take into account only the activities of, and property owned by, the partnership and not the CFC partner (entity treatment). The regulations treat certain hybrid entity payments that reduce foreign taxes as Subpart F income and deny application of the same country exception for FPHC income of certain types of hybrid entity income.[589]

As indicated in Notice 98-35,[590] the Department of the Treasury held true on its promise to withdraw the regulations under IRC § 702 and Subpart F.[591] However, final regulations have not yet been published. Some taxpayers may conclude that without being able to rely upon final IRC § 702(a)(7) and related Subpart F regulations, the IRS is unlikely to succeed in relitigating the Brown Group Subpart F issue, and may not even try. The aggregate entity regulations, §§ 1.701-2(e) and (f), mentioned in the proposed Brown Group regulations pending finalization of the proposed regulations, act as authority for IRS challenges to Brown Group arrangements. These regulations may not be regarded as binding on the issue, but they may create substantial uncertainties for taxpayers.[592] In particular, the aggregate entity interpretative regulations proposed under IRC § 702(a)(7) may be of no help to the IRS in explaining how and why a court should reach the same decision in future periods as they did in the Brown Group case.

2.3.2.5.3.2. Shifting of Income

The purpose of the hybrid branch is to utilize an intragroup note to shift income from a high-tax jurisdiction to a jurisdiction with a low corporate tax rate.

A typical hybrid branch structure involves three U.S.-owned foreign entities:

(1) a foreign holding company,
(2) a foreign active company, and
(3) a foreign hybrid entity.

The foreign holding company and the active company - as well as the active company's business - are located in the same jurisdiction with a high corporate tax rate, e.g., Germany. The foreign holding company sets up a hybrid branch in a lower tax jurisdiction and elects to check the box so that the hybrid is treated as a corporation for foreign tax purposes but as a branch for U.S. federal tax purposes.

---

[588] Temp. Reg. § 1.954-2T(a)(5).

[589] Temp. Reg. § 1.954-2T(a)(6). See Barrett, J. H. and Ewing, W. P., *Florida Bar Journal* 1998, 38.

[590] 1998-27 I.R.B. 25.

[591] See Laffie, L. S., *The Tax Adviser* 1998, 517; Di Fronzo, M. A. and Thomas, J. M., *Tax Notes International* 1999, 759.

[592] See Tuerff, T. T. and Gordon, R. A., *Journal of International Taxation* 1994, 299.

Fig. 7: Typical Hybrid Branch Structure

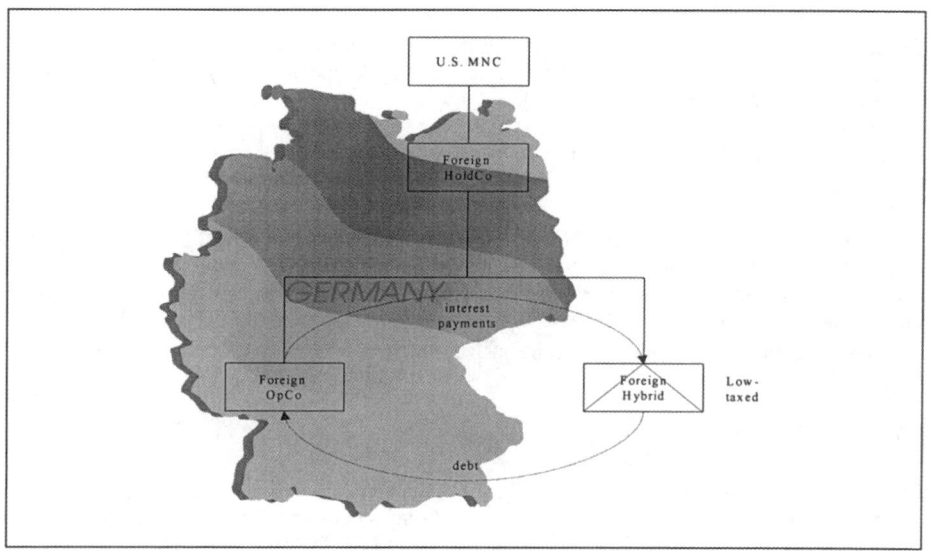

The parties then enter into a loan arrangement whereby the foreign active company pays interest on the intragroup note to the hybrid branch. If the structure works as designed, the hybrid branch structure has a twofold impact. First, the interest payments siphon foreign taxable income from the active (high-taxed) company to the low-taxed hybrid entity because the hybrid is considered as a separate corporation for foreign tax purposes. Second, the transaction avoids Subpart F income inclusion by virtue of the same country exception for related parties under IRC § 954(c)(3)(A)(i). Because the hybrid entity is generally disregarded for U.S. federal tax purposes, the transaction is deemed to be a direct payment between the foreign holding company and active companies located within the same jurisdiction.[593]

2.3.2.6. Special Foreign Base Company Income Rules and Exceptions

2.3.2.6.1. Full Inclusion Rule

If a foreign corporation's FBCI and gross income exceeds 70 percent of the total gross income, according to IRC § 954(b)(3)(B), all the corporation's gross income for the taxable year will be treated as FBCI/Subpart F income.[594]

---

[593] See IRS, Notice 98-11, 1998-6 I.R.B. 18.

[594] Reg. § 1.954-1(b)(1)(ii). See Kral, K. H., Serota, J. and Mandell, J., *International Tax Review* 1995, 42; Yoder, L. D., *Tax Management International Journal* 1998 I, 223; Yoder, L. D. and Kahn, J. H., *Tax Management International Journal* 1999, 532; Meldman, R. E. and Schadewald, M. S., *A Practical Guide to U.S. Taxation of International Transactions*, 2000, 157; Yoder, L. D., *Tax Management International Journal* 2000, 687; Yoder, L. D. and Everson, S. L., *Tax Management International Journal* 2000 I, 4; Yoder, L. D. and Everson, S. L., *Tax Management International Journal* 2000 II, 303; Doernberg, R. L., *International Taxation In a Nutshell*, 2001, 314.
Therefore, if the income is between five percent and 70 percent, the actual amount is treated as FBCI under IRC § 954(b)(3).

2.3.2.6.2. *De minimis* Rule

At the other extreme, a *de minimis* rule provides that none of the CFC's gross income will be treated as FBCI for the taxable year if the total amount of a foreign corporation's FBCI and gross insurance income for the taxable year is less than the lesser of:

(1) five percent of its gross income; or
(2) U.S. $1,000,000.[595]

This provision recognizes that most businesses will typically generate some FBCI, such as interest income on invested working capital, even though the company exists primarily for business reasons. Conversely, if the FBCI or insurance income constitutes a significant percentage of the CFC's gross income, then the corporation would seem to have been formed to defer U.S. taxation. The Subpart F provisions were designed to deal with such abusive situations.[596]

2.3.2.6.3. High Rate of Foreign Tax

IRC § 954(b)(4) provides that FBCI[597] subject to high foreign taxes is not included in Subpart F income if the taxpayer establishes that the income was subject to an effective tax rate, imposed by a foreign country, of more than 90 percent of the maximum U.S. federal corporate tax rate under IRC § 11, the so-called *high-tax kick-out exception*.[598] For example, the rate must be greater than 31.5 percent, where 35 percent represents the highest U.S. corporate tax rate.[599] The use of the high tax exception is elective, but it is binding on all U.S. shareholders.[600] Only foreign taxes subject to FTCs are considered in determining whether the more than 90 percent test is satisfied. Additionally,

---

[595] IRC § 954(b)(3)(A); Reg. § 1.954-1(b)(1)(i). See Yoder, L. D., *Tax Management International Journal* 1998 III, 635. In Sec. 103 of the H.R. 2018 (The International Tax Simplification for American Competitiveness Act of 1999) it was proposed that the *de minimis* income level be increased to ten percent of gross income and that the ceiling be increased to U.S. $2,000,000. However, these proposals have not been enacted, although they were included in previous tax acts, e.g., "The International Tax Simplification for American Competitiveness Act of 1998" (the so-called *Houghton/Levin Bill*), Sec. 104, H.R. 4173. See Benson, D. M., O'Connor, P. and Rollinson, M. A., *Tax Management International Journal* 1998 I, 586; Benson, D. M. and Rollinson, M. A., *Tax Management International Journal* 1998 II, 476; Rollinson, M., *Tax Management International Journal* 1998, 520; Yoder, L. D., *Tax Management International Journal* 1998 I, 223; Zschiegner, H., *Internationale Wirtschaftsbriefe*, Fach 8, USA, Gruppe 2, 1998 III, 972; Anonymous, *Tax Executive* 1999 I, 348; Yoder, L. D. and Kahn, J. H., *Tax Management International Journal* 1999, 532; Meldman, R. E. and Schadewald, M. S., *A Practical Guide to U.S. Taxation of International Transactions*, 2000, 156; Yoder, L. D., *Tax Management International Journal* 2000, 687; Yoder, L. D. and Everson, S. L., *Tax Management International Journal* 2000 I, 4; Yoder, L. D. and Everson, S. L., *Tax Management International Journal* 2000 II, 303; Bittker, B. I. and Eustice, J. S., *Federal Income Taxation of Corporations and Shareholders*, 2002, paragraph 15.62[3].

[596] Small amounts of passive income are not considered abusive.

[597] Other than specific oil related income. See Yoder, L. D. and Everson, S. L., *Tax Management International Journal* 2000 II, 303.

[598] Reg. § 1.954-1(d). See Joyce, T. B. and Parks, S. M., *Tax Management International Journal* 1990 II, 424; Ginty, J. A., *The Tax Adviser* 1991, 433; Ruding, H. O., *Journal of International Taxation* 1994, 6; Yoder, L. D., *Tax Management International Journal* 1997 I, 205; Pollack, L. A., Porter, D. and Corrie, F., *International Tax Review* 1998 I, 76; Yoder, L. D., *Tax Management International Journal* 1998 I, 223; Zschiegner, H., *Internationale Wirtschaftsbriefe*, Fach 8, USA, Gruppe 2, 1998 III, 972; Yoder, L. D. and Kahn, J. H., *Tax Management International Journal* 1999, 532; Yoder, L. D., *Tax Management International Journal* 2000, 687; Yoder, L. D. and Everson, S. L., *Tax Management International Journal* 2000 I, 5; Yoder, L. D. and Everson, S. L., *Tax Management International Journal* 2000 II, 303; Sinclair, B. and Kopstein, R., *Guaranteed to Enlighten: The Impact of Guarantees on Financing Arrangements*, 2001, 22:19; Yoder, L. D., *Tax Management International Journal* 2001, 222.

[599] (90% * 35%) = 31.5%.

[600] Regs. §§ 1.954-1(d)(1) and (5). See Meldman, R. E. and Schadewald, M. S., *A Practical Guide to U.S. Taxation of International Transactions*, 2000, 157; Yoder, L. D., *Tax Management International Journal* 2000, 687.

income is grouped into categories based on both the type of income and the separate FTC limitation basket in determining whether the income is high taxed.[601]

2.4. Computational Rules with Mid-Year Change of Ownership

A U.S. shareholder who sells all of the shares to another U.S. shareholder before the last day a foreign corporation is a CFC during its taxable year would not be required to include in income the foreign corporation's Subpart F income for the entire year.[602] Because the IRC § 951(a) items of income are subject to tax for U.S. shareholders who own shares in a foreign corporation on the last day of the foreign corporation's taxable year during which it was a CFC, such items would be taxable to the acquiring U.S. owner for the entire year.[603] Conversely, Subpart F provisions would apply to a selling U.S. shareholder for the year if the foreign corporation's status as a CFC terminated as a result of the disposition. This would occur, for example, if the increase in ownership by non-U.S. shareholders caused the aggregate U.S. shareholder ownership to fall below the more than 50 percent threshold.[604] In this case, the selling U.S. shareholder would be subject to tax on its share of the CFC's Subpart F income accrued during the year of disposal and allocated to its holding period based on a pro rata portion of the CFC's Subpart F income for the entire year.[605]

Also, a U.S. shareholder who sells stock in a CFC in which CFC status ceases on the date of sale can have Subpart F income as a result of transactions occurring after the sale. For example, a subsequent owner could accrue Subpart F income after the transaction by having the CFC dispose of passive assets or receive dividends from a subsidiary. A pro rata share of such Subpart F income would be allocated to the U.S. shareholder's ownership period. To prevent such adverse tax results at the level of the seller, the sale/purchase agreement should address these issues (e.g., prohibit Subpart F transactions until the following year, or provide an adjustment to the sale price).

2.5. Taxation of a Disposition of CFC Stock

IRC § 1248 provides special rules for taxing U.S. shareholders upon the sale of shares in a CFC.[606] These rules are designed to ensure that any gain recognized on the disposal of CFC stock is taxed to the U.S. shareholders as ordinary income, rather than as capital gains, to the extent of E&P of the CFC that have not already been taxed under Subpart F.[607] To the extent IRC § 1248 is not applicable, the general rules applying to the sale of stock in a foreign corporation apply.[608]

---

[601] See Kuntz, J. D. and Peroni, R. J., *U.S. International Taxation*, 2002, paragraph B3.05[8].

[602] Reg. § 1.951-1(a)(2). Such a disposal may result in the selling shareholder effectively being taxed on a portion of the CFC's earnings for the year under IRC § 1248.

[603] Under IRC § 951(a)(2), the acquiring U.S. shareholder reduces the Subpart F income for the year of sale by all or a portion of (1) dividends paid to the seller during the year of sale, and (2) the sellers IRC § 1248 amount.

[604] IRC § 957(a).

[605] For purposes of determining CFC status at the time stock is acquired or sold, the day stock is purchased is excluded, and the day stock is sold is included. Reg. § 1.951-1(f); Rev. Rul. 75-341, 1975-2 C.B. 308.

[606] See McDaniel, P. R. and Ault, H. J., *Introduction to United States International Taxation*, 1998, 125; Yoder, L. D., *Tax Management International Journal* 1998 III, 637; Yoder, L. D. and Everson, S. L., *Tax Management International Journal* 2000 I, 5.

[607] See Kingson, C. I., *Columbia Law Review* 1981, 1180; Yoder, L. D., *Tax Management International Journal* 1996 III, 491; Yoder, L. D., *Tax Management International Journal* 1996 IV, 590; Abrams, H. E. and Doernberg, R. L., *Essentials of United States Taxation*, 1999, 4-196; Bittker, B. I. and Eustice, J. S., *Federal Income Taxation of Corporations and Shareholders*, 2002, paragraph 15.63[1].
IRC § 1248 was enacted in 1962. Prior to 1962, the shareholder's gain recognized from the disposition of stock in a foreign corporation, on some redemptions of stock, and on a partial/complete liquidation constituted, in general, capital gains. Rather than repatriate a foreign company's foreign earnings in the form of dividends taxable as ordinary income, the U.S.

The special rule contained in IRC § 1248(a) provides that gains recognized by a U.S. shareholder on the taxable sale of stock in a CFC are treated as dividends to the extent of certain E&P attributable to the disposed stock.[609] Only undistributed E&P accumulated in taxable years beginning after December 31, 1962, and during the period while the corporation was a CFC, are taken into account.[610] The E&P of lower-tier CFCs are also considered for this purpose.[611] The amount of a CFC's E&P taken into consideration for purposes of IRC § 1248 are reduced by the amount of E&P that have previously been subject to taxation under Subpart F at the level of the U.S. shareholder.[612]

The deemed dividend is treated as distributed on the day of disposition of the shares. The remaining portion of such gains are classified as capital gains under the general rule. In the case of a corporate shareholder, the amount treated as a dividend by IRC § 1248 may qualify for the indirect FTC of IRC § 902.[613] IRC § 1248 does not apply if there is a loss.[614]

If stock in a CFC is sold during a taxable year, only a pro rata portion of the current year's E&P are taken into account, based on the number of days the selling U.S. shareholder owned the stock.[615] The IRS issued a ruling stating that E&P are reduced by any dividend distributions to the buyer during the year of disposition.[616] If the (sale) transaction closes within the CFC's taxable year, only pre-acquisition earnings and dividends are considered when computing the seller's IRC § 1248 amount.[617] If the foreign target is owned by any U.S. shareholders, or if U.S. connected business assets effectively belong to the foreign corporation, U.S. tax consequences might arise on either the

---

shareholders might allow the earnings to accumulate and then sell their participation or liquidate the foreign company, reporting any profits as long-term capital gains.

[608] Under the general rules, a U.S. shareholder recognizes a gain or loss on the disposition or exchange of stock in a CFC equal to the difference between the sale price or the value received and the shareholder's tax basis in the stock, according to IRC §§ 61(a)(3) and 1001. The gain or loss recognized is generally characterized as a capital gain or loss (IRC § 1221). Capital gains are subject to taxation at the U.S. corporate tax rates that apply to ordinary income. Under IRC § 1211(a), capital losses can be used to reduce only capital gains. See Bittker, B. I. and Eustice, J. S., *Federal Income Taxation of Corporations and Shareholders*, 2002, paragraph 4.20.

[609] Reg. § 1.1248-1(a)(1). IRC § 1248 has a five-year look-back rule, i.e., it applies to U.S. persons who have satisfied the ten percent ownership test at any point during the prior five years and to the stock of any foreign corporation that was a CFC within the five-year period ending on the date of disposition or exchange (IRC § 1248(a)(2)). See Byrnes, L. A., *Tax Notes International* 1989, 26; Levey, M. M. and Pollack, L. A., *Journal of International Taxation* 1990, 204; Fischl, A. and Schneider, R. A., *Tax Management International Journal* 1997, 568; Yoder, L. D. and Kahn, J. H., *Tax Management International Journal* 1999, 531; Yoder, L. D. and Everson, S. L., *Tax Management International Journal* 2000 I, 5; Calianno, J. M. and Gregoire, B. J., *Journal of International Taxation* 2001, 36; Kuntz, J. D. and Peroni, R. J., *U.S. International Taxation*, 2002, paragraph A2.03[4].

[610] See Hoke, W. D., *Tax Notes International* 1992, 840; McDaniel, P. R. and Ault, H. J., *Introduction to United States International Taxation*, 1998, 126; Bittker, B. I. and Eustice, J. S., *Federal Income Taxation of Corporations and Shareholders*, 2002, paragraph 15.63[1].

[611] IRC §§ 1248(a)(2) and (c)(2). See Fischl, A. and Schneider, R. A., *Tax Management International Journal* 1997, 568; Yoder, L. D., *Tax Management International Journal* 1997 II, 269; Yoder, L. D., *Tax Management International Journal* 1998 III, 638; Friedel, D. B., *Journal of Taxation* 2000, 363; Yoder, L. D. and Everson, S. L., *Tax Management International Journal* 2000 I, 6.

[612] IRC § 1248(d)(1). See Friedel, D. B., *Journal of Taxation* 2000, 363; Bittker, B. I. and Eustice, J. S., *Federal Income Taxation of Corporations and Shareholders*, 2002, paragraph 15.63[1].

[613] Regs. §§ 1.1248-1(d) and 902-1(a)(12). See Yoder, L. D., *Tax Management International Journal* 1998 III, 638.

[614] See Belanger, P. and Taylor, G., *Journal of International Taxation* 2002, 28.

[615] Reg. § 1.1248-2(e)(1).

[616] Rev. Rul. 71-388, 1971-2 C.B. 314.

[617] A closing of the taxable year can be achieved with an IRC § 338 election. Pursuant to IRC § 338, U.S. taxpayers who have acquired a U.S. corporation can elect to step up the tax basis in their assets. For the election under IRC § 338 in detail, see Yoder, L. D. and Kahn, J. H., *Tax Management International Journal* 1999, 536; Bittker, B. I. and Eustice, J. S., *Federal Income Taxation of Corporations and Shareholders*, 2002, paragraph 10.42; Eustice, J. S. and Kuntz, J. D., *Federal Income Taxation of S Corporations*, 2002, paragraph 13.05[8]; Giannattasio, B. and Suarez-Lasa, D., *Journal of International Taxation* 2002, 51.

sale of stock or the target's deemed asset sale transaction.[618] Furthermore, if the foreign target is a CFC, Subpart F income for IRC § 1248 dividends might be constituted due to the IRC § 338 election.[619] In summary, IRC § 1248 serves as a backstop to Subpart F.[620]

3. IMPACTS ON FTCS

A U.S. shareholder's tax basis in CFC stock is increased by constructive dividends and decreased by subsequent distributions of previously taxed income.[621] Basically, Subpart F income is treated as foreign-source income, and therefore, U.S. taxes on Subpart F income can be reduced with FTCs.[622] U.S. corporate shareholders who own at least ten percent of the voting stock of a foreign corporation are allowed an indirect FTC for foreign taxes deemed paid on constructive dividends under IRC § 951(a).[623] Pursuant to IRC § 78, the Subpart F income must be grossed up by the FTC granted.[624] According to IRC § 902(b)(2), the indirect credit also is available for Subpart F income attributable to certain lower-tier foreign corporations up to the sixth-tier subsidiaries.[625]

The following amounts derived from U.S.-owned foreign corporations may be treated as U.S.-source income for purposes of the FTC limitation:[626]

(1) interest;
(2) dividends;
(3) Subpart F inclusions; and
(4) FPHC income.

Generally, Subpart F income, FPHC income, and interest are treated as U.S.-source income to the extent such amounts are attributable to the U.S.-source income of the U.S.-owned foreign corporation. Dividends are generally treated as U.S.-source income in proportion to the U.S.-source

---

[618] See Bittker, B. I. and Eustice, J. S., *Federal Income Taxation of Corporations and Shareholders*, 2002, paragraph 15.04.

[619] See Hoke, W. D. and Dablain, D. A., *Tax Notes* 1998, 1169.

[620] See Bittker, B. I. and Eustice, J. S., *Federal Income Taxation of Corporations and Shareholders*, 2002, paragraph 15.63[3].

[621] IRC §§ 961(a) and 951(a). See Meldman, R. E. and Schadewald, M. S., *A Practical Guide to U.S. Taxation of International Transactions*, 2000, 163; Sinclair, B. and Kopstein, R., *Guaranteed to Enlighten: The Impact of Guarantees on Financing Arrangements*, 2001, 22:18.

[622] See Abrams, H. E. and Doernberg, R. L., *Essentials of United States Taxation*, 1999, 4-190; Meldman, R. E. and Schadewald, M. S., *A Practical Guide to U.S. Taxation of International Transactions*, 2000, 160; Yoder, L. D. and Everson, S. L., *Tax Management International Journal* 2000 II, 303.

[623] IRC § 960. See Pugh, E. O. T., *Tax Notes International* 1993, 1430; McDaniel, P. R. and Ault, H. J., *Introduction to United States International Taxation*, 1998, 116; Yoder, L. D. and Kahn, J. H., *Tax Management International Journal* 1999, 533; Yoder, L. D. and Everson, S. L., *Tax Management International Journal* 2000 I, 5; Doernberg, R. L., *International Taxation In a Nutshell*, 2001, 321.

[624] Regs. §§ 1.960-1(a) and 1.960-3. See Ginty, J. A., *The Tax Adviser* 1991, 433; Yoder, L. D. and McGill, S. P., *Tax Management International Journal* 1997, 455; Larkins, E. R., Oakley, E. F. and Winkle, G. M., *The Tax Adviser* 1999, 420; Yoder, L. D. and Everson, S. L., *Tax Management International Journal* 2000 I, 5; Doernberg, R. L., *International Taxation In a Nutshell*, 2001, 322; Bouma, H. B. and Rosenbloom, H. D., *Tax Management International Journal* 2002, 83.

[625] See Larkins, E. R., Oakley, E. F. and Winkle, G. M., *The Tax Adviser* 1999, 420; Bouma, H. B. and Rosenbloom, H. D., *Tax Management International Journal* 2002, 85; Kuntz, J. D. and Peroni, R. J., *U.S. International Taxation*, 2002, paragraph 15.21[2]. See chapter "Ownership", page 44.

[626] IRC § 904(g); Reg. § 1 904-5(c). The term "U.S.-owned foreign corporation" means any foreign corporation in which 50 percent or more of the total combined voting power of all classes of stock of the corporation is held by U.S. persons (IRC § 904(g)(6) and Reg. § 1.904-5(m)).

E&P of the U.S.-owned foreign corporation. A *de minimis* exception applies to interest and dividends.[627]

Interest, Subpart F inclusions, rents or royalties and dividends received or accrued by a U.S. shareholder from a CFC must be treated as separate limitation income if these items were separate limitation income of the corporation before they were passed on to the U.S. shareholder (the so-called *look-though rule*).[628] The look-through approach to interest, which is subject to a five percent or greater gross basis tax that is paid to a U.S. shareholder by a CFC, would apply only to that portion of the interest payment that exceeds the payor's interest income - or its equivalent - and that would be treated as financial services income.

According to IRC § 960(a)(2), if an actual distribution of value attributable to the amount included in income under IRC § 951(a) is made to a shareholder, any taxes that were deemed to be paid under IRC § 960(a)(1) at the time of the inclusion cannot again be deemed paid under IRC § 902 at the time of the actual distribution.[629] According to IRC § 960(a)(3), however, when value treated as previously taxed income is distributed to a domestic corporate shareholder, indirect credits are allowed for certain taxes imposed with respect to that value, provided that the taxes were not previously deemed paid under IRC § 960(a)(1).[630]

3.1. Capital Gains

Pursuant to IRC § 865(a)(1), capital gains from a U.S. person's disposition of stock in a CFC are generally classified as from U.S.-sources, i.e., based on the residence of the U.S. seller.[631] Under IRC § 865(f), an exception to U.S.-source gains is provided for the disposal of interests in a foreign affiliate if the sale occurs in the foreign country in which the affiliate is engaged in the active conduct of a trade or business and certain other conditions are satisfied.[632] In general, losses on the disposal of stock are sourced under the residency rule, although regulations provide certain exceptions.[633] Hence, losses recognized from the disposition of stock of a foreign subsidiary should be allocated and apportioned to the same class of income that would have resulted if a capital gain had been recognized from the disposition of stock.[634]

Generally, a CFC's gain from the disposition of stock would be considered as passive income and potentially included as Subpart F income in the U.S. shareholder's taxable income and included in the passive FTC limitation basket.[635] But IRC § 964(e) treats such gains as dividends to

---

[627] See Abrams, H. E. and Doernberg, R. L., *Essentials of United States Taxation*, 1999, 4-191.

[628] A *de minimis* exception provides that these rules will not be applied against FBCI and gross insurance income received from a CFC if the total income is less than the lesser of (1) five percent of gross income or (2) U.S. $1,000,000, provided that none of the income is financial services income (IRC §§ 904(d)(3), 904(d)(3)(E), and 954(b)(3)(A); Reg. § 1.904-5). Then none of the income is ascribed to a separate FTC limitation basket; instead, it is assigned to the overall limitation basket. In accordance with the *de minimis* rule, passive income that is subject to a high rate of foreign tax will not be treated as income in a separate basket. See Fischl, A. and Schneider, R. A., *Tax Management International Journal* 1997, 571; Abrams, H. E. and Doernberg, R. L., *Essentials of United States Taxation*, 1999, 4-191; Dilworth, R. H. and Andrus, J. L., *Tax Law and Practice*, 2001, 1097.

[629] See Bouma, H. B. and Rosenbloom, H. D., *Tax Management International Journal* 2002, 84.

[630] See Bouma, H. B. and Rosenbloom, H. D., *Tax Management International Journal* 2002, 84.

[631] See Yoder, L. D. and Kahn, J. H., *Tax Management International Journal* 1999, 534.

[632] See Yoder, L. D. and Kahn, J. H., *Tax Management International Journal* 1999, 534.

[633] Reg. § 1.865-2; *International Multifoods Co. v. Commissioner*, 108 T.C. 25 [1997]. See Kral, M. E., *The Tax Adviser* 1999, 222.

[634] See Anonymous, *Tax Executive* 1996, 246.

[635] Regs. §§ 1.904-4(b)(1)(i)(A) and 1.904-5(c)(4)(iii). The proposed five-year period during which the foreign-source capital gains should have been recognized and allocated to the passive basket, under Prop. Reg. § 1.865-2(b)(2) has not been included in the final regs. See Kral, M. E., *The Tax Adviser* 1999, 224; Yoder, L. D. and Kahn, J. H., *Tax Management International Journal* 1999, 534. See for the FTC limitation, *supra* page 51.

the extent they would have been dividends under IRC § 1248 if the CFC had been a U.S. person selling stock in a foreign corporation. If the effective rate of foreign tax equals at least the highest marginal U.S. tax rate, it will be placed in the overall basket.[636] Only if foreign taxes are paid on the gain is it generally beneficial to treat capital gains as foreign-source income. In such cases, a credit will be obtained for the foreign taxes paid which can be offset against U.S. taxes on the gain. Otherwise, even if the capital gain is from a foreign source, it would likely be fully taxable as a result of its inclusion in the passive FTC limitation basket, since most taxpayers do not have excess credit in that basket.

3.2. Ordinary Income

A portion of the gain recharacterized as ordinary income under IRC § 1248 is treated as a dividend deemed distributed by the CFC immediately before the disposition. The deemed dividend is treated as an actual dividend for purposes of applying the FTC rules.[637] As a result, the dividend sourcing rules apply, which generally treat dividends received from foreign corporations as foreign-source income.[638] Therefore, the portion of the gain treated as an IRC § 1248 dividend would be foreign-source income. The IRC § 904 basket to which the deemed dividend applies is determined by looking through the CFC's underlying earnings. As a result, the IRC § 1248 dividend is generally categorized in the IRC § 904 overall limitation basket.[639] If a CFC has earnings in other categories, the deemed dividend is allocated to each category on a pro rata basis.[640] Because the earnings taxable under IRC § 1248 are not typically considered to be Subpart F income, they generally will not be included in the passive basket.

In addition, because the IRC § 1248 amount is treated as a dividend, a corporate shareholder who disposes of stock in a CFC in which it owns ten percent of the voting stock may claim a FTC for any taxes paid by the CFC that are attributable to the earnings deemed distributed as a dividend under IRC § 1248.[641] This applies only if the U.S. shareholder's dividend income is grossed up by the amount of the indirect FTCs.[642]

The application of IRC § 1248, therefore, can be beneficial to corporate shareholders because U.S. taxes on recharacterized gains may be reduced by FTCs.[643] Foreign taxes taken into account for FTC purposes include deemed paid taxes with respect to the IRC § 1248 dividend, any foreign taxes actually paid on that portion of the gain and any excess FTCs in the U.S. shareholder's overall basket. Also, any excess deemed paid taxes associated with the IRC § 1248 dividend can be used to offset U.S. taxes on the seller's other general basket income. E&P deemed distributed as dividends under IRC § 1248 are recharacterized as previously taxed income, and, thus, generally will not be taxed when distributed to the purchasing shareholder.[644] In addition, such amounts are treated as dividends for purposes of determining a subsequent U.S. shareholder's Subpart F income inclusion for the year of sale under IRC § 951(a)(2)(B).

---

[636] IRC § 904(d)(2)(A). See Kral, M. E., *The Tax Adviser* 1999, 224; Yoder, L. D. and Kahn, J. H., *Tax Management International Journal* 1999, 534.

[637] Regs. §§ 1.1248-1(d), 1.902-1(a)(12).

[638] IRC §§ 861(a)(2) and 862(a)(2); Reg. § 1.861-3(a)(3).

[639] IRC §§ 904(d)(1)(I) and (3)(A); Regs. §§ 1.904-5(c)(4)(i) and (iii).

[640] IRC § 904(d)(3)(D). Another category may be financial services income that qualifies for a Subpart F exception. §§ 904(d)(1)(C), 954(c)(2)(B), and 954(h).

[641] See Fischl, A. and Schneider, R. A., *Tax Management International Journal* 1997, 569.

[642] Reg. § 1.1248-1(d)(2).

[643] See Bittker, B. I. and Eustice, J. S., *Federal Income Taxation of Corporations and Shareholders*, 2002, paragraph 15.63[1].

[644] IRC §§ 959(e) and 1248(j). Rev. Rul. 90-31, 1990-1 C.B. 147.

4. CONCLUSION

In the preceding examination, the limited, but expanding, nature of the Subpart F rules is obvious. The treatment as a CFC will not affect a foreign company if the company's shareholding is widely dispersed, if it is organized in the country in which its business activities are performed, or if its business is not conducted with a related U.S. enterprise controlled by U.S. shareholders. Even when they apply, Subpart F provisions are of limited importance due to the high-tax kick-out exception. This exception allows for U.S. tax accrued to the ultimate parent from the attribution of Subpart F income to be partly or wholly offset with the allowable indirect FTCs from the foreign subsidiary's tax liability. Furthermore, various sections of the IRC act to mitigate the full force of Subpart F.[645] Despite the fact that the CFC provisions seem to be a "toothless tiger", the interaction of IRC §§ 951-964 and 1248 basically combine to produce an important check on tax deferral and conversion of ordinary income to capital gains. The ongoing effort by international tax practitioners to avoid this outcome might expose additional tax deferral techniques over time.

The *de minimis* rule allows a CFC to avoid the classification of income as FBCI and prevents the U.S. shareholder from having to include it in gross income as a constructive dividend. Thus, a CFC with total FBCI in an amount close to the five percent or U.S. $1,000,000 level should monitor income realization to assure that the *de minimis* rule applies for the tax year. At least as important is avoiding the classification of all gross income of the CFC as FBCI. This happens when the sum of the FBCI for the taxable year exceeds 70 percent of total gross income.

Careful timing of increases in investment in U.S. property can reduce the potential for constructive dividend income to U.S. shareholders. The gross income of U.S. shareholders attributable to increases in investment in U.S. property is limited to the E&P of the CFC.[646] E&P that are attributable to amounts that have been included in gross income as Subpart F income in either the current year or a prior tax year are not taxed again when invested in U.S. property.

Overall, the treatment of a CFC under Subpart F seems to preclude far more tax evasion and deferral than an initial review of the rules might suggest, assuming that the numerous attempts at tax planning can be viewed as a measure for the effectiveness of these provisions.[647]

---

[645] For example, IRC §§ 954(b)(3), (b)(4), and 951(a)(1) (the so-called *thirty-consecutive-day provision*).

[646] IRC §§ 959(a)(1) and (2). See Yoder, L. D. and McGill, S. P., *Tax Management International Journal* 1997, 456.

[647] See Bittker, B. I. and Eustice, J. S., *Federal Income Taxation of Corporations and Shareholders*, 2002, paragraph 15.64[2].

SECTION 5: SPECIFIC TAX PLANNING TECHNIQUES

Double or multiple taxation might occur when at least two jurisdictions view that they have the primary right to levy taxes on the same income without providing for any tax relief for foreign taxes paid on that income. On the other hand, the intersection of different local tax systems might also provide opportunities to either minimize or even avoid any tax liabilities. Stated more clearly, tax arbitrage is the counterpart to double taxation and results from differences in the local tax provisions regarding taxpayer, residence, source, type of income, and transfer pricing.[648]

When designing cross-border transactions that offer opportunities for a U.S. MNC to minimize or avoid overall tax costs, it is essential to firstly analyze the foreign tax regimes for holding companies. Structures which give rise to tax arbitrage advantages as a result of conflicting tax treatments must then be examined.

1. COUNTRY-BY-COUNTRY SYNOPSIS

In the following paragraphs, some of the most interesting holding company regimes in Europe will be examined, focusing on the typical holding company tax criteria outlined above. The discussions are based on the local rules, applicable as of January 1, 2002.

1.1. Austria

Tax Rate

Corporation tax is imposed on corporate profits at a flat rate of 34 percent.[649] There are no other Austrian business profit taxes or surcharges.[650]

Dividends Received

A tax exemption applies to dividends received from EU companies if the Austrian parent company directly owns at least 25 percent of the share capital of the subsidiary for an uninterrupted period of at least 24 months.[651] These provisions also extend to dividends received from non-EU subsidiaries if the legal form of the foreign corporation is comparable to an Austrian corporation.[652] Any domestic dividends received by an Austrian parent company are tax exempt, irrespective of any holding period or level of shareholding.[653]

Dividends Paid

Austrian withholding tax is imposed on dividends and other corporate distributions made to non-resident recipients. The tax rate amounts to 25 percent unless reduced or eliminated under a double

---

[648] See Abrams, H. E. and Doernberg, R. L., *Essentials of United States Taxation*, 1999, 4-232; Doernberg, R. L., *International Taxation In a Nutshell*, 2001, 397.

[649] See Gahleitner, G. and Moritz, H., *Internationale Wirtschaftsbriefe*, Fach 5, Österreich, Gruppe 2, 1999, 476; Romano, C., *European Taxation* 1999, 257; Jann, M., Schuch, J. and Toifl, G., *Austria*, 2001, 55; Müller, K., *Verwirklichung von Gerechtigkeit und Entscheidungsneutralität*, 2001, 105.

[650] See Romano, C., *European Taxation* 1999, 257.

[651] See Hirschler, K. and Sulz, G., *Steuer & Wirtschaft International* 1997, 216; Jann, M., Schuch, J. and Toifl, G., *Austria*, 2001, 117.

[652] See Doralt, W. and Ruppe, H. G., *Grundriß des österreichischen Steuerrechts*, 2000, 336.

[653] See Doralt, W. and Ruppe, H. G., *Grundriß des österreichischen Steuerrechts*, 2000, 335; Jann, M., Schuch, J. and Toifl, G., *Austria*, 2001, 107.

tax treaty.[654] According to the EU Parent-Subsidiary Directive, dividend distributions made to EU-resident companies are not subject to withholding tax, provided that the EU parent company holds a minimum 25 percent interest in the Austrian subsidiary for an uninterrupted period of two years.[655] A five percent tax is due on dividend payments to a U.S. parent company that holds at least ten percent of the voting stock.[656]

Capital Gains

Capital gains recognized from the disposal of shares in foreign corporations are exempt from taxation if at least 25 percent of the share capital is owned prior to the disposal.[657] The exemption is conditional on the same 24-month holding period that applies to dividends.[658] Capital gains realized on the sale of domestic shares are subject to the regular Austrian tax rate of 34 percent.[659]

Capital Losses

Capital losses arising from the disposal of shares in foreign corporations cannot be deducted for tax purposes if they relate to tax exempt shareholdings.[660]

Capital Taxes

Capital tax of one percent is levied on incorporation as well as on subsequent capital increases by direct shareholders.[661] Capital tax is not imposed on share contributions if the shares in the foreign corporation have been held for at least two years prior to the contribution.[662]

Interest Deductibility

Interest expenses are not tax deductible if they relate to acquisitions of qualifying shareholdings (i.e., those subject to the 24-month holding privilege).[663] Under Austrian law, no specific provisions

---

[654] See Romano, C., *European Taxation* 1999, 258; Jann, M., Schuch, J. and Toifl, G., *Austria*, 2001, 56.

[655] § 94a of the *Einkommensteuergesetz*. See Kleemann, F., *Österreichische Steuer-Zeitung* 1997, 114; Gahleitner, G. and Moritz, H., *Internationale Wirtschaftsbriefe*, Fach 5, Österreich, Gruppe 2, 1999, 480.

[656] Art. 10(2)(a) of the Double Tax Treaty between Austria/U.S. See Djanani, C., *Internationales Steuerrecht*, 1998, 486; Loukota, H., *Internationales Steuerrecht*, 2000, 91.

[657] See Pernegger, R., *Österreichische Steuer-Zeitung* 1999, 430; Gröhs, B. and Schuch, J., *Internationale Wirtschaftsbriefe*, Fach 5, Österreich, Gruppe 2, 2001, 532.

[658] See Pernegger, R., *Österreichische Steuer-Zeitung* 1999, 430; Romano, C., *European Taxation* 1999, 258.

[659] See Gröhs, B. and Schuch, J., *Internationale Wirtschaftsbriefe*, Fach 5, Österreich, Gruppe 2, 2001, 532; Jann, M., Schuch, J. and Toifl, G., *Austria*, 2001, 109.

[660] See Romano, C., *European Taxation* 1999, 258.

[661] §§ 2(2) and 8 of the *Kapitalverkehrsteuergesetz*. See Gahleitner, G. and Moritz, H., *Internationale Wirtschaftsbriefe*, Fach 5, Österreich, Gruppe 2, 1999, 481; Romano, C., *European Taxation* 1999, 258; Schneider, H., *Internationale Wirtschaftsbriefe*, Fach 5, Österreich, Gruppe 2, 2000, 485; Gröhs, B. and Schuch, J., *Internationale Wirtschaftsbriefe*, Fach 5, Österreich, Gruppe 2, 2001, 542. In order to avoid the capital tax burden, equity can be injected by an indirect shareholder, e.g., grandparent company (the so-called *Großmutterzuschuß*). VwGH dated July 6, 1967, ZI 1278/66, ÖStZB 1967, 170. See Baumann, W., *Steueroasen und internationale Holdingkonstruktionen*, 1996, 80; Schneider, H., *Internationale Wirtschaftsbriefe*, Fach 5, Österreich, Gruppe 2, 2000, 486.

[662] See Jann, M., Schuch, J. and Toifl, G., *Austria*, 2001, 121.

[663] VwGH dated June 8, 1988, 87/13/0068, ÖStZB 1989, 15; VwGH dated December 10, 1991, 89/14/0064, ÖStZB 1992, 662; VwGH dated October 10, 1996, 94/15/0187, *Österreichische Steuer-Zeitung* 1997, 404; VwGH dated November 20, 1996, 96/15/0188, *Österreichische Steuer-Zeitung* 1999, 623. See Kaupa, A., *Österreichische Steuer-Zeitung* 1998, 315; Scheucher, R., *Österreichische Steuer-Zeitung* 1998, 158; Pernegger, R., *Österreichische Steuer-Zeitung* 1999, 433;

regarding thin capitalization exist.[664] Under general principles, an arm's length test has to be met.[665]

1.2. Belgium

Tax Rate

Corporation tax is levied at a rate of 40.17 percent (including crisis tax) in Belgium.[666] It has been proposed that the rate be lowered to 33.99 percent, although a tax bill has not yet been drafted.[667]

Dividends Received

Under domestic law, a 95 percent tax exemption for domestic and foreign dividends received is granted provided that:[668]

- the parent company directly owns at least five percent of the share capital or the participation reflects an acquisition value of at least Belgian Franc 50,000,000 (€ 1,239,467); and
- the subsidiary is subject to a tax on profits similar to Belgium's tax (the so-called *taxation condition*) if the subsidiary is located abroad.

The two conditions apply to both dividend distributions made by an EU subsidiary as well as to subsidiaries resident outside the EU.

Dividends Paid

Under Belgian domestic law, withholding tax on dividends is generally levied at a rate of 25 percent.[669] Withholding tax is not imposed on dividend distributions made by a Belgian subsidiary to its parent company situated within the EU that has owned or commits to hold at least 25 percent of the share capital for an uninterrupted period of at least one year.[670] Under the Belgium/U.S. double tax treaty, the withholding tax rate is reduced to five percent for qualifying shareholdings.[671]

Romano, C., *European Taxation* 1999, 258; Doralt, W. and Ruppe, H. G., *Grundriß des österreichischen Steuerrechts*, 2000, 341.

[664] See Gröhs, B. and Schuch, J., *Internationale Wirtschaftsbriefe*, Fach 5, Österreich, Gruppe 2, 2001, 543.

[665] See Doralt, W. and Ruppe, H. G., *Grundriß des österreichischen Steuerrechts*, 2000, 323.

[666] See Ruchelman, S. C., Asbeck, E. van, Canalejo, G. and et. al., *Journal of International Taxation* 2001 I, 24.

[667] See Ernst & Young, *International Tax Digest* 2002 (Belgium), 10; Huyghe, A. and Meeus, L., *Tax Notes International* 2002, 1257; IBFD, *Annual Report 2001-2002*, 2002, 103; O'Grady, E., *Tax Notes International* 2002, 1064.

[668] See Baumann, W., *Steueroasen und internationale Holdingkonstruktionen*, 1996, 97; Romano, C., *European Taxation* 1999, 258; Ruchelman, S. C., Asbeck, E. van, Canalejo, G. and et. al., *Journal of International Taxation* 2001 I, 24; Malherbe, J. and Pauw, B. de, *Tax Management International Forum* 2002, 3.
Under the 2002 draft bill, a proposal was made to increase the participation requirement to ten percent, while leaving the alternative acquisition value unchanged. See Huyghe, A. and Meeus, L., *Tax Notes International* 2002, 1258.

[669] Art. 174 of the *Code des impôts sur les revenus.*

[670] See Offermanns, R., *Belgium*, 2001, 119.

[671] Art. 10(2)(a) of the Double Tax Treaty between Belgium/U.S.

Capital Gains

Capital gains recognized from the disposal of shares in both domestic and foreign corporations are tax exempt in Belgium, provided that dividends received from such shareholdings would not be subject to taxation according to the dividend received deduction regime.[672]

Capital Losses

Irrespective of whether the participation exemption regime applies, capital losses and write-downs of investments are not deductible for Belgian tax purposes.[673] Capital losses recognized from the liquidation of a company are, however, deductible for tax purposes up to the paid-in share capital.[674]

Capital Tax

In Belgium, a registration duty amounting to 0.5 percent of the share capital is levied on incorporation as well as on subsequent capital increases.[675] A contribution of shares of a qualifying EU company to a Belgian holding company is tax exempt under certain conditions.[676]

Interest Deductibility

No specific debt-to-equity ratio is prescribed by Belgian legislation. However, a 7:1 ratio applies to debt from a creditor - resident or non-resident - who is exempt from taxation or who is taxed at a reduced tax rate with respect to the interest paid. Furthermore, interest charges become non-tax-deductible up to 95 percent of dividends received (qualifying for the dividends received deduction) if the corresponding shares are held for less than an uninterrupted period of one year.[677] However, this provision does not apply to shareholdings in affiliated entities.

1.3. Denmark

Tax Rate

Corporations are subject to Danish tax at a rate of 30 percent.[678]

---

[672] See Baumann, W., *Steueroasen und internationale Holdingkonstruktionen*, 1996, 97; Ruchelman, S. C., Asbeck, E. van, Canalejo, G. and et. al., *Journal of International Taxation* 2001 I, 26; Malherbe, J. and Pauw, B. de, *Tax Management International Forum* 2002, 3.

[673] See Romano, C., *European Taxation* 1999, 259; Ruchelman, S. C., Asbeck, E. van, Canalejo, G. and et. al., *Journal of International Taxation* 2001 I, 27.

[674] See Ruchelman, S. C., Asbeck, E. van, Canalejo, G. and et. al., *Journal of International Taxation* 2001 I, 27.

[675] Art. 11 of the *Wetboek der Registratierechten*. See Cinnamon, A., *International Tax Review* 1999, 11; Ruchelman, S. C., Asbeck, E. van, Canalejo, G. and et. al., *Journal of International Taxation* 2001 I, 27; Malherbe, J. and Pauw, B. de, *Tax Management International Forum* 2002, 3.

[676] See Ruchelman, S. C., Asbeck, E. van, Canalejo, G. and et. al., *Journal of International Taxation* 2001 I, 28.

[677] See Romano, C., *European Taxation* 1999, 259.

[678] See Steenholdt, S. and Josephsen, N., *European Taxation* 1999, 153; Kischel, D., *Internationale Wirtschaftsbriefe*, Fach 5, Dänemark, Gruppe 2, 2000, 143; Kriegbaum, K. E., *Tax Planning International Review* 2000, 25; Anonymous, *International Tax Report* 2001, 11; Kriegbaum, K. E. and Petersen, C. M., *Internationale Wirtschaftsbriefe*, Fach 5, Dänemark, Gruppe 2, 2001, 147; Winther-Sørensen, N., *Danish National Report*, 2002, 1.

Dividends Received

Provided that a Danish company holds at least 20 percent of the share capital in a domestic or foreign company for an uninterrupted period of at least 12 months and the activities of the foreign company do not qualify as a financial activity in a low-tax jurisdiction, dividends can be received tax free.[679]

Dividends Paid

Generally, Denmark withholds a tax of 28 percent on dividend distributions[680] made to foreign shareholders unless the tax is reduced or eliminated under an applicable double tax treaty.[681] According to Danish tax provisions, no withholding tax on dividends is imposed provided that:[682]

- the parent company owns at least 20 percent of the share capital in the Danish subsidiary;[683] and
- the parent company has held the qualifying shares for an uninterrupted period of at least 12 months at the time when the dividend distribution is made.

Since 1999, the exemption from withholding taxation also applies to parent companies residing outside the EU if the prerequisites of the EU Parent-Subsidiary Directive are met.[684]

As of July 1, 2001, a legislative amendment to the Danish holding company provisions was enacted. Following this change, dividends distributed to foreign parents of Danish holding companies that are resident in non-treaty countries are excluded from the exemption from withholding taxation.[685] A zero percent withholding tax continues to apply to dividend distributions to a U.S. parent company.[686]

---

[679] § 13 of the *Selskabsskatteloven*. The minimum shareholding percentage was reduced from 25 percent to 20 percent by the "Bill L99" (the so-called *L99 (som vedtaget): Forslag til lov om ændring af afskrivningsloven, aktieavancebeskatningsloven, ligningsloven, personskatteloven, selskabsskatteloven, virksomhedsskatteloven og andre love. (Strukturtilpasninger m.v. og lempelse af tabs- og underskudsregler)*, dated May 17, 2002, which generally takes retroactive effect from January 1, 2002. See Balle, C. H., *European Taxation* 2002, 255; PricewaterhouseCoopers, *Tax Notes International* 2002, 1041; Shelton, N., *Tax Planning International Review* 2002, 22; Shelton, N., *International Tax Report* 2002, 10.

[680] The so-called *udbytteskat*.

[681] Prior to January 1, 2001, withholding tax was imposed at a rate of 25 percent. See Kischel, D., *Internationale Wirtschaftsbriefe*, Fach 5, Dänemark, Gruppe 2, 2000, 144; Andersen, P. S., *Denmark*, 2001, 73; Anonymous, *International Tax Report* 2001, 11; Shelton, N., *International Tax Report* 2001, 4.

[682] See Doran, E. and Vlot, P., *Journal of International Taxation* 1999, 36; Hjortshøj, J. and Bjørnholm, N., *The International Tax Journal* 2000, 69; Kischel, D., *Internationale Wirtschaftsbriefe*, Fach 5, Dänemark, Gruppe 2, 2000, 144; Kriegbaum, K. E. and Petersen, C. M., *Internationale Wirtschaftsbriefe*, Fach 5, Dänemark, Gruppe 2, 2001, 147.

[683] Prior to January 1, 2002, a minimum holding percentage of 25 percent was required. Under Bill L99, the required level of ownership was lowered to 20 percent. See PricewaterhouseCoopers, *Tax Notes International* 2002, 1041.

[684] See Doran, E. and Vlot, P., *Journal of International Taxation* 1999, 34; Shelton, N., *European Taxation* 1999, 33; Hjortshøj, J. and Bjørnholm, N., *The International Tax Journal* 2000, 69; Ruchelman, S. C., Asbeck, E. van, Canalejo, G. and et. al., *Journal of International Taxation* 2000, 47.

[685] See Andersen, P. S., *Denmark*, 2001, 149; Ernst & Young, *International Tax Digest* 2001 (Denmark), 10; Shelton, N., *International Tax Report* 2001, 4; Wittendorff, J. and Graff, T., *Tax Notes International* 2001, 1893; IBFD, *Annual Report 2001-2002*, 2002, 107; O'Grady, E., *Tax Notes International* 2002, 1064; Ottosen, A. M. and Hansen, L. C., *Journal of International Taxation* 2002, 44.

[686] See Hjortshøj, J. and Bjørnholm, N., *The International Tax Journal* 2000, 78; Marantelli, A., *Steuer Revue* 2000 II, 94.

Capital Gains

Capital gains recognized from the sale of stock in a foreign company are not subject to tax if:[687]

- the shares have been owned for at least three years;
- the subsidiary's activity was not mainly of a financial nature; and
- the subsidiary is not taxed at a low rate.

Capital gains realized on the disposal of Danish domestic stock are tax-exempt under the sole prerequisite that the stock has been held for at least three years.[688] Thus, in both cases, there are no threshold ownership requirements.[689]

Capital Losses

Capital losses realized from the disposition of stock in a foreign company within three years of ownership can only be offset against capital gains recognized from shares also held for less than three years.[690] For excess capital losses, a five year loss carry forward period applies.[691] Capital losses realized from the sale of shares in a foreign company that have been held for three years or more are not deductible for tax purposes.[692]

Capital Tax

There is no Danish capital tax (the so-called *kapitaltilførselsafgift*).[693]

Interest Deductibility

Interest expenses are tax deductible even if they relate to acquisitions of qualifying shareholdings.[694] A debt-to-equity limitation of 4:1 applies to Danish holding companies.[695]

---

[687] See Doran, E. and Vlot, P., *Journal of International Taxation* 1999, 34; Laursen, J., *Internationales Steuerrecht* 1999, 718; Hjortshøj, J. and Bjørnholm, N., *The International Tax Journal* 2000, 70; Ruchelman, S. C., Asbeck, E. van, Canalejo, G. and et. al., *Journal of International Taxation* 2000, 46; Kriegbaum, K. E. and Petersen, C. M., *Internationale Wirtschaftsbriefe*, Fach 5, Dänemark, Gruppe 2, 2001, 148.

[688] See Laursen, J., *Internationales Steuerrecht* 1999, 717; Shelton, N., European Taxation 1999, 33.

[689] See Meldgaard, H., *International Tax Report* 1993, 7; Steenholdt, S. and Josephsen, N., *European Taxation* 1999, 147.

[690] See Romano, C., *European Taxation* 1999, 260; Ruchelman, S. C., Asbeck, E. van, Canalejo, G. and et. al., *Journal of International Taxation* 2000, 46.

[691] See Kriegbaum, K. E. and Petersen, C. M., *Internationale Wirtschaftsbriefe*, Fach 5, Dänemark, Gruppe 2, 2001, 148; Balle, C. H., *European Taxation* 2002, 255; PricewaterhouseCoopers, *Tax Notes International* 2002, 1041.

[692] See Ruchelman, S. C., Asbeck, E. van, Canalejo, G. and et. al., *Journal of International Taxation* 2000, 46; Kriegbaum, K. E. and Petersen, C. M., *Internationale Wirtschaftsbriefe*, Fach 5, Dänemark, Gruppe 2, 2001, 148.

[693] See Romano, C., *European Taxation* 1999, 260; Shelton, N., *European Taxation* 1999, 33; Steenholdt, S. and Josephsen, N., *European Taxation* 1999, 154; Andersen, P. S., *Denmark*, 2001, 101; Hansen, A. O., *European Taxation* 2001, 230; Kriegbaum, K. E. and Petersen, C. M., *Internationale Wirtschaftsbriefe*, Fach 5, Dänemark, Gruppe 2, 2001, 151.

[694] See Steenholdt, S. and Josephsen, N., *European Taxation* 1999, 153; Kriegbaum, K. E. and Petersen, C. M., *Internationale Wirtschaftsbriefe*, Fach 5, Dänemark, Gruppe 2, 2001, 153.

[695] § 11 of the *Selskabsskatteloven*. See Doran, E. and Vlot, P., *Journal of International Taxation* 1999, 35; Romano, C., *European Taxation* 1999, 260; Hjortshøj, J. and Bjørnholm, N., *The International Tax Journal* 2000, 75; Ruchelman, S. C., Asbeck, E. van, Canalejo, G. and et. al., *Journal of International Taxation* 2000, 46; Kriegbaum, K. E. and Petersen, C. M., *Internationale Wirtschaftsbriefe*, Fach 5, Dänemark, Gruppe 2, 2001, 153; Emmeluth, C., *Tax Management International Forum* 2002, 12.

Miscellaneous

Danish tax law provides for cross-border tax consolidation, a practice which is essentially unique to Denmark. This practice generates tax planning opportunities for corporations.[696] The goal of the tax consolidation is to pool the taxable incomes and losses of the companies involved, resulting in a (cross-border) offset of profits of one group member against losses of another, thus, achieving immediate loss utilization.[697] According to § 31 of the *Selskabsskatteloven*, earnings of both Danish domestic as well as foreign subsidiaries can be subject to tax consolidation at the level of a Danish parent company.[698]

In order to qualify for tax consolidation privileges, several statutory requirements must be met: First, only certain entities can act as the parent of a cross-border tax consolidation group including, in particular, the Danish *Aktieselskab* (A/S) or *Anpartsselskab* (ApS).[699] It is not required that the Danish controlling company be the ultimate parent. Thus, an interposed Danish holding company can act as a controlling corporation for the purposes of consolidating the (domestic and foreign) profits and losses.[700] Second, the allowance for tax consolidation depends on the legal form of the controlled entity. A domestic entity can act as a controlled entity only if it is specifically incorporated as an A/S or ApS.[701] In the case of a foreign entity, it is necessary that its legal form be comparable from a Danish point of view.

Further, the formation of a tax consolidation group requires the permission of the local tax authorities; however, approval must be given if the following statutory prerequisite is fulfilled:[702] the Danish corporate shareholder can act as a parent for cross-border consolidation if it has directly or indirectly held a participation of 100 percent of the share capital since the beginning of the business year.[703] An exception to the requirement of sole ownership applies if a 100 percent shareholding by a foreign entity is prohibited under local law.[704] In such cases, it is sufficient for cross-border tax consolidation purposes if the Danish entity owns, directly or indirectly, the highest level of shareholding permitted under local law.[705]

There is no statutory need to include all group entities into the tax consolidation.[706] In some cases, not all subsidiaries qualify for inclusion, and in particular, a second-tier subsidiary can only be

---

[696] See Qvist, H., *Area Development Sites & Facility Planning* 1998, 88. Similar provisions exist in France (the so-called *régime de bénéfice consolidé*). However, it is of less practical importance as the French cross-border tax consolidation requires ministerial approval. See Kessler, W., *Internationales Steuerrecht* 1993, 303; Scheuchzer, M., *Recht der Internationalen Wirtschaft* 1995, 43; Bolanz, G., *Die EU-Holding als strategisches Gestaltungsinstrument in der Steuerplanung*, 1998, 129; EU Commission, *Study*, 2001, 340; Endres, D. and Thies, A., *Recht der Internationalen Wirtschaft* 2002, 276.

[697] See Kischel, D., *Internationale Wirtschaftsbriefe*, Fach 5, Dänemark, Gruppe 2, 2000, 145; Andersen, P. S., *Denmark*, 2001, 168. For the sub goal "immediate loss utilization" of a U.S. MNC, refer *supra* page 64.

[698] See Kessler, W., *Internationales Steuerrecht* 1993, 303; Fleischer-Michaelsen, U., *Journal of International Taxation* 1995, 160; Grotherr, S., *Internationale Wirtschaftsbriefe*, Fach 5, Dänemark, Gruppe 2, 1995, 113.

[699] See Grotherr, S., *Internationale Wirtschaftsbriefe*, Fach 5, Dänemark, Gruppe 2, 1995, 114; Böhme, C. A., *Internationales Steuerrecht* 1998, 166.

[700] See Kessler, W., *Internationales Steuerrecht* 1993, 303; Grotherr, S., *Internationale Wirtschaftsbriefe*, Fach 5, Dänemark, Gruppe 2, 1995, 114.

[701] See Böhme, C. A., *Internationales Steuerrecht* 1998, 166.

[702] See Meldgaard, H., *International Tax Report* 1993, 9.

[703] Assuming the subsidiary was founded during a business year, it can be included in the tax consolidation in the current year, provided that the Danish parent was the sole owner since its incorporation. See Kessler, W., *Internationales Steuerrecht* 1993, 304; Grotherr, S., *Internationale Wirtschaftsbriefe*, Fach 5, Dänemark, Gruppe 2, 1995, 115.

[704] See Andersen, P. S., *Denmark*, 2001, 168.

[705] See Kessler, W., *Internationales Steuerrecht* 1993, 304.

[706] See Grotherr, S., *Internationale Wirtschaftsbriefe*, Fach 5, Dänemark, Gruppe 2, 1995, 116; Kischel, D., *Internationale Wirtschaftsbriefe*, Fach 5, Dänemark, Gruppe 2, 2000, 144.

included if its respective first-tier parent is also a controlled company.[707] Finally, in order to benefit from the cross-border tax consolidation group, the following two conditions must be met:[708]

- the business year of all involved entities must correspond; and
- the computation of the taxable income of each of the controlled entities must be made according to Danish tax principles.[709]

1.4. France

Tax Rate

In France, corporation tax is levied at a standard rate of 33 1/3 percent, increased by a three percent surcharge thereon and a social surcharge of 3.3 percent applying to corporations with annual sales of more than € 7,630,000.[710] Hence, the effective tax rate of larger corporations amounts to 35.43 percent.[711]

Dividends Received

Dividends received from both domestic and foreign shareholdings are partially (95 percent) exempt from taxation provided that:[712]

- the French parent owns at least five percent of the share capital; and
- the parent company has owned the qualifying shares for a consecutive period of at least two years or the shares were subscribed when founding the corporation.

French equalization tax is due on distributions of profits which are more than five years old, or on distributions of profits that have not been fully subject to French corporation tax (e.g., foreign dividends). While computing the equalization tax burden, the withholding tax paid abroad is deductible. Thus, the net dividends received are taxable unless otherwise excluded by an applicable tax treaty.

Since December 31, 1999, a recapture of five percent of the gross dividend received applies, capped to the overall amount of parent company's expenses linked to the shareholding.[713] Thus, broadly speaking, 95 percent of dividends received are exempt from French taxation.

---

[707] See Meldgaard, H., *International Tax Report* 1993, 9.

[708] See Kessler, W., *Internationales Steuerrecht* 1993, 304.

[709] See Grotherr, S., *Internationale Wirtschaftsbriefe*, Fach 5, Dänemark, Gruppe 2, 1995, 117.

[710] See Blanluet, G., Bouzidi, C. and Bouzoraa, M.-A., *France*, 2001, 103; D'Hont, P. and Souchal, N., *Tax Planning International Review* 2001, 20; Ernst & Young, *International Tax Digest* 2001 (France), 10; Tillmanns, W., *Internationale Wirtschaftsbriefe*, Fach 5, Frankreich, Gruppe 2, 2001, 1259; Ernst & Young, *Unternehmerische Betätigung in Frankreich*, 2002, paragraph 428.

[711] See D'Hont, P. and Souchal, N., *Tax Planning International Review* 2001, 20; Long, Y. and Leffers, I., *Internationale Wirtschaftsbriefe*, Fach 5, Frankreich, Gruppe 2, 2001, 1266; Feydeau, H. de., *Tax Management International Forum* 2002, 17.

[712] Art. 145-1 of the *Code général des impôts*. See Jouanjan, A., *Tax Notes International* 2000, 1299; Lefebvre, F., *Fiscal*, 2000, paragraph 3671; Tillmanns, W., *Internationale Wirtschaftsbriefe*, Fach 5, Frankreich, Gruppe 2, 2000, 1239; Blanluet, G., Bouzidi, C. and Bouzoraa, M.-A., *France*, 2001, 159; D'Hont, P. and Souchal, N., *Tax Planning International Review* 2001, 20; Ernst & Young, *International Tax Digest* 2001 (France), 11; Tillmanns, W., *Internationale Wirtschaftsbriefe*, Fach 5, Frankreich, Gruppe 2, 2001, 1259; Ernst & Young, *Unternehmerische Betätigung in Frankreich*, 2002, paragraph 434; Vlaanderen, P., *Tax Notes International* 2002, 1101.

[713] Art. 216-1 of the *Code général des impôts*. See Milhac, E., Bayle, P. and Gerner, F., *Journal of International Taxation* 1999, 22.

Dividends Paid

Withholding tax of 25 percent is imposed on dividend distributions to foreign shareholders, unless reduced either under the EU Parent-Subsidiary Directive or an applicable double tax treaty.[714]

Under French law, dividend distributions made to an EU parent do not trigger French withholding tax provided that:[715]

- the parent company owns at least 25 percent of the share capital in the French subsidiary;
- the parent company is not entitled by virtue of a tax treaty to a refund equal to the *avoir fiscal*[716] which is in excess of the withholding tax at the applicable tax treaty rate; and
- the parent company is not directly or indirectly controlled by non-EU residents, unless the structure is not meant to avoid withholding tax.

Dividend distributions made to U.S. parent companies are subject to a five percent withholding tax in France.[717]

Capital Gains

France does not support a capital gains exemption regime.[718] Capital gains realized from long-term domestic and foreign investments[719], e.g., from the disposal of assets owned for longer than two years, trigger taxation at a reduced rate of 19 percent (plus surcharges of three percent and 3.3 percent) provided that:[720]

- the capital gain is retained in a specific reserve account; and
- the French parent owns at least five percent of the share capital.[721]

Capital gains on short-term investments, i.e., those held for less than two years, are subject to taxation at the ordinary corporation tax rate.[722]

---

[714] Art. 187-1 of the *Code général des impôts*. See Romano, C., *European Taxation* 1999, 261; Blanluet, G., Bouzidi, C. and Bouzoraa, M.-A., *France*, 2001, 169; Long, Y. and Leffers, I., *Internationale Wirtschaftsbriefe*, Fach 5, Frankreich, Gruppe 2, 2001, 1277; Feydeau, H. de., *Tax Management International Forum* 2002, 17.

[715] Art. 119 ter of the *Code général des impôts*. See Blanluet, G., Bouzidi, C. and Bouzoraa, M.-A., *France*, 2001, 169; Jaeger, C., *Die Körperschaftsteuersysteme in Europa*, 2001, 151; Long, Y. and Leffers, I., *Internationale Wirtschaftsbriefe*, Fach 5, Frankreich, Gruppe 2, 2001, 1277.

[716] *Avoir fiscal* is a tax credit attached to French-source dividends received by corporate portfolio shareholders. It was reduced to 25 percent in 2001 and amounts to 15 percent for credits claimed on or after January 1, 2002. Art. 158 bis of the *Code général des impôts*. See Ernst & Young, *International Tax Digest* 2002 (France), 10.

[717] Art. 9(2)(b) of the Double Tax Treaty between France/U.S. See Feydeau, H. de., *Tax Management International Forum* 2002, 17.

[718] See Spengel, C., *Europäische Steuerbelastungsvergleiche*, 1995, 280.

[719] The so-called *titres de participation*.

[720] Art. 219(1) a bis and Art. 39 duodecies (3) of the *Code général des impôts*. See Huber, M. F., Kapalle, U. and Koch, M., *Steuer Revue* 2001, 396.

[721] See Tillmanns, W., *Internationale Wirtschaftsbriefe*, Fach 5, Frankreich, Gruppe 2, 1999, 1204; Blanluet, G., Bouzidi, C. and Bouzoraa, M.-A., *France*, 2001, 103; D'Hont, P. and Souchal, N., *Tax Planning International Review* 2001, 22; Long, Y. and Leffers, I., *Internationale Wirtschaftsbriefe*, Fach 5, Frankreich, Gruppe 2, 2001, 1266; Ernst & Young, *Unternehmerische Betätigung in Frankreich*, 2002, paragraph 429.

[722] See Ernst & Young, *Unternehmerische Betätigung in Frankreich*, 2002, paragraph 429.

Capital Losses

In accordance with the treatment of capital gains, capital losses may be deducted for tax purposes. However, capital losses recognized from short-term investments can only be offset against capital gains realized on short-term investments and ordinary business income arising in the same year.[723] Capital losses arising from long-term investments can be offset either against long-term capital gains from the same year or against otherwise taxable releases from the capital gain reserve, otherwise they can be carried forward for up to ten years.[724]

Capital Tax

No capital duty is imposed on incorporation. A fixed registration fee of € 230 is due on subsequent equity injections.[725] A contribution of shares of a foreign company to a French holding company is tax exempt under certain conditions.

Interest Deductibility

Interest paid on funds borrowed in order to finance the acquisition of a foreign participation is deductible for French tax purposes.[726] A pure holding company will not be able to use the interest expense deduction due to a lack of income, other than exempt dividends. In order to prevent negative French tax consequences, a debt-to-equity ratio of 1.5:1 should be maintained.[727] However, this limitation applies to direct shareholders only.[728]

1.5. Germany

Tax Rate

Effective January 1, 2001, German corporation tax is imposed at a flat rate of 25 percent regardless of whether the taxpayer is a domestic or a foreign corporation (with German branch income) and irrespective of the corporation's dividend distribution policy.[729] A local trade tax is levied on taxable income as determined for corporation tax purposes, adjusted for various items.[730] A

---

[723] See Romano, C., *European Taxation* 1999, 261.

[724] See Bärtels, H.-C., *Internationale Wirtschaftsbriefe*, Fach 5, Frankreich, Gruppe 2, 2000, 1253; Blanluet, G., Bouzidi, C. and Bouzoraa, M.-A., *France*, 2001, 101; Long, Y. and Leffers, I., *Internationale Wirtschaftsbriefe*, Fach 5, Frankreich, Gruppe 2, 2001, 1267; Ernst & Young, *Unternehmerische Betätigung in Frankreich*, 2002, paragraph 427.

[725] See Bayle, P. and Mariano, F., *Journal of International Taxation* 2002, 23; Ernst & Young, *Unternehmerische Betätigung in Frankreich*, 2002, paragraph 496.

[726] See Romano, C., *European Taxation* 1999, 261; Blanluet, G., Bouzidi, C. and Bouzoraa, M.-A., *France*, 2001, 66.

[727] Art. 212 of the *Code général des impôts*. See Blanluet, G., Bouzidi, C. and Bouzoraa, M.-A., *France*, 2001, 66; Long, Y. and Leffers, I., *Internationale Wirtschaftsbriefe*, Fach 5, Frankreich, Gruppe 2, 2001, 1273; Newberry, K. J. and Dhaliwal, D. S., *Journal of Accounting Research* 2001, 646; Not, N., *Tax Planning International Review* 2001, 16; Ernst & Young, *Unternehmerische Betätigung in Frankreich*, 2002, paragraph 435; Gouthière, B., *European Taxation* 2002, 159.

[728] Art 39, 1-3 ° and 212 of the *Code général des impôts*. See Baumann, W., *Steueroasen und internationale Holdingkonstruktionen*, 1996, 107; Ernst & Young, *Unternehmerische Betätigung in Frankreich*, 2002, paragraph 435; Feydeau, H. de., *Tax Management International Forum* 2002, 20.

[729] See Dötsch, E. and Pung, A., *Der Betrieb* 2000, Beilage 10, 4; Hartmann, J., *International Tax Review* 2000, 10; Jaeger, C., *Die Körperschaftsteuersysteme in Europa*, 2001, 124.

[730] See Dehnen, P. H., Heinlein, A. and Dubert, C. A., *Journal of International Taxation* 1994, 454; Endres, D. and Ditsch, S., *The International Tax Journal* 1999, 37; Kessler, W., Dorfmueller, P., Schmidt, W. and Teufel, T., *Tax Notes International* 2001, 1220.

solidarity surcharge of 5.5 percent on the regular corporation tax is also charged.[731] In summary, a corporation's total tax burden will be between 37 percent and 41 percent, depending on its location in Germany.[732]

Dividends Received

German corporate shareholders qualify for a 100 percent deduction with respect to dividends received from both foreign companies as well as from German domestic companies, irrespective of the amount of their shareholding and regardless of any holding period.[733] However, five percent of dividends received from foreign subsidiaries are deemed to be non-deductible business expenditures directly connected to tax exempt income.[734] Hence, only 95 percent of the dividends received from foreign subsidiaries will effectively be exempt from German taxation.

Dividends Paid

Dividend distributions made by a domestic subsidiary to its foreign parent company are subject to withholding taxation at a rate of 20 percent, unless eliminated or reduced under either the EU Parent-Subsidiary Directive or an applicable double tax treaty.[735] Under German law, no withholding tax is imposed on dividends paid to parent companies resident within the EU provided that:[736]

- the parent company owns at least 25 percent of the share capital in the German subsidiary; and
- the parent company has owned the qualifying shares for an uninterrupted period of at least 12 months. Withholding tax on dividend payments made before the expiry of the 12-month period is also reduced to zero provided that the holding period prerequisite is subsequently met.

The threshold of 25 percent ownership is reduced to ten percent if the country in which the recipient is located also grants a reciprocal participation exemption to shareholdings of at least ten percent.[737] Under the Germany/U.S. double tax treaty, the withholding tax rate for dividends paid to a qualifying U.S. parent company is limited to five percent.[738]

Capital Gains

While gains realized from the disposal of qualifying foreign investments have already been exempt from German taxation, effective January 1, 2002, the scope of corporate capital gains exemption will be extended to the sale of stock in a resident company.[739] The exemption applies irrespective of the

---

[731] See Endres, D. and Möller, M., *Corporate Taxation*, 2001, E 23.

[732] See Schreiber, C. and Dorfmueller, P., *CTF*, 2001, 13:11.

[733] § 8b(1) of the *Körperschaftsteuergesetz*. See Endres, D., *International Finance & Treasury* 2000, 2; Grotherr, S., *Internationale Wirtschaftsbriefe*, Fach 3, Deutschland, Gruppe 1, 2000, 1725; Hartmann, J., *International Tax Report* 2000, 11; Berger, H. and Quack, J. S., *Intertax* 2001, 78.

[734] § 8b(5) of the *Körperschaftsteuergesetz*. See Dötsch, E. and Pung, A., *Der Betrieb* 2000, Beilage 10, 6; Berger, H. and Quack, J. S., *Intertax* 2001, 82; Kessler, W., Dorfmueller, P., Schmidt, W. and Teufel, T., *Tax Notes International* 2001, 1219; Menger, J. and Kahl, I., *Journal of International Taxation* 2001, 31.

[735] See Endres, D. and Möller, M., *Corporate Taxation*, 2001, E 53.

[736] See Jaeger, C., *Die Körperschaftsteuersysteme in Europa*, 2001, 132.

[737] § 43b(3) of the *Einkommensteuergesetz*. E.g., France, Luxembourg, the Netherlands, and the U.K. See Romano, C., *European Taxation* 1999, 265; IBFD, *European Tax Handbook*, 2000, 221; Leffers, I., *Germany*, 2000, 151.

[738] Art. 10(2)(a) of the Double Tax Treaty between Germany/U.S. See Debatin, H. and Endres, D., *The new US-German double tax treaty*, 1990, Art. 10, paragraph 6; Endres, D., *International Finance & Treasury* 2000, 2; Grotherr, S., *Internationale Wirtschaftsbriefe*, Fach 3, Deutschland, Gruppe 1, 2000 II, 1723.

[739] § 8b(2) of the *Körperschaftsteuergesetz*. See Hartmann, J., *International Tax Review* 2000, 11.

level of shareholding.[740] However, if an unincorporated business is contributed to a corporation on a tax-free basis, the capital gains exemption applies only on a subsequent sale of the shares in the corporation after a seven-year holding period.[741]

Capital Losses

As a consequence of the generous exemption for capital gains, capital losses, write-downs and write-offs of investments in German and foreign companies are no longer deductible for German tax purposes.[742]

Capital Tax

The establishment of a German holding company does not trigger any tax charges and there is no capital tax when injecting capital into a German company.[743]

Interest Deductibility

There is a fictitious five percent interest disallowance based on the amount of any foreign dividends received.[744] Any other interest expenses linked to foreign shareholdings are tax deductible. Hence, a foreign subsidiary can retain its earnings for several years, allowing its German parent company a full deduction for all directly related interest charges in the interim. Debt-to-equity ratios applicable to interest on related-party debt are 3:1 for holding companies[745] and 1.5:1 for operating companies.[746] There is no deduction at all for related-party interest on hybrid debt or any other form of loan where the interest is not defined as a percentage of the outstanding principal.[747] On December 12, 2002, the European Court of Justice decided in the case of *"Lankhorst-Hohorst GmbH v. Finanzamt Steinfurt"* that the German thin capitalization provision (§ 8a of the *Körperschaftsteuergesetz*) violates the freedom of establishment.[748] So far, no statement from the German tax authority has been issued to clarify how the thin capitalization provision will be adjusted in order to comply with this decision and, therefore, EU law.

---

[740] See Grotherr, S., *Internationale Wirtschaftsbriefe*, Fach 3, Deutschland, Gruppe 1, 2000 I, 1713.

[741] § 8b(4) of the *Körperschaftsteuergesetz*.

[742] § 8b(3) of the *Körperschaftsteuergesetz*. See Dötsch, E. and Pung, A., *Der Betrieb* 2000, Beilage 10, 11; Hartmann, J., *International Tax Review* 2000, 11; Hey, J., *German Perspective*, 2002, 14.

[743] See Hammer, M., *Journal of International Taxation* 2002, 38.

[744] See Hartmann, J., *International Tax Review* 2000, 11.

[745] § 8a(4) of the *Körperschaftsteuergesetz*, provides a definition of holding companies that are eligible for the extended safe haven. A holding company means "a company whose main business activity is to hold investments in other companies and to finance these companies, or who have invested more than 75 percent of their gross assets in investments in companies…". See Bodenschütz, E. and Dorfler, O., *International Tax Review* 1997/1998, 40.

[746] See Endres, D. and Oestreicher, A., *Intertax* 2000, 419; Hartmann, J., *International Tax Review* 2000, 12; Kramer, J.-D., *Tax Management International Forum* 2002, 26.

[747] See Endres, D., *International Finance & Treasury* 2000, 10; Freiling, C. and Schmucker, Y., *Internationales Steuerrecht* 2001, 98.

[748] European Court of Justice, Lankhorst-Hohorst GmbH v. Finanzamt Steinfurt, C-324/00.

1.6. Ireland

Tax Rate

Effective January 1, 2002, profits arising from the trading activities of an Irish company are liable for Irish corporation tax at an effective rate of 16 percent.[749] The rate of corporation tax on trading profits will be reduced to 12.5 percent from January 1, 2003, onward.[750] The rate of corporation tax on investment income and non-trading income is 25 percent.[751]

Dividends Received

Dividend distributions made by foreign subsidiaries to an Irish parent company are subject to corporation tax in Ireland.[752] However, a foreign tax credit is granted such that the level of the foreign tax is irrelevant.[753] An exemption applies to dividend distributions by foreign subsidiaries provided that the Irish parent company holds, directly or indirectly, at least 25 percent of the shares in the foreign subsidiary.[754] In such cases, both the foreign withholding tax and the foreign taxes paid by the foreign subsidiary can be credited against the Irish tax.[755] The direct and indirect foreign tax credits are also granted for shareholdings of less than 25 percent provided that a respective double tax treaty with a tax credit method is in place. Such treaties have been signed with Belgium,[756] France,[757] Germany,[758] Italy,[759] and Luxembourg.[760] Conversely, dividends paid by an Irish subsidiary to its Irish parent company are tax-exempt (the so-called *franked investment income*).[761] Moreover, no withholding tax is due on these dividend distributions.[762]

---

[749] See Ernst & Young, *International Tax Digest* 2002 (Ireland) II, 12; Gara, M., *Tax Planning International Review* 2002, 11; Hollingsworth, G. and Fuller, C., *Tax Planning International mergers & acquisitions* 2002, 5.

[750] See Kischel, D., *Internationale Wirtschaftsbriefe*, Fach 5, Irland, Gruppe 2, 2000, 83; Saunders, G., *Tolley's Taxation in the Republic of Ireland 2000-01*, 2000, 130; McLoughlin, K., *Tax Notes International* 2001, 1140; O'Mahony, G., *International Tax Review* 2001, 36; Vrouwenvelder, M., *Tax Management International Journal* 2001, 405; Ernst & Young, *International Tax Digest* 2002 (Ireland) I, 14.

[751] See O'Brien, C., *International Tax Review* 1999, 24; Kischel, D., *Internationale Wirtschaftsbriefe*, Fach 5, Irland, Gruppe 2, 2000, 83; Ward, J., *Ireland*, 2001, 96; Vrouwenvelder, M., *Tax Management International Journal* 2001, 405; Ernst & Young's Foreign Desk, *Journal of International Taxation* 2002, 9; Gara, M., *Tax Planning International Review* 2002, 11; Hollingsworth, G. and Fuller, C., *Tax Planning International mergers & acquisitions* 2002, 6; PricewaterhouseCoopers, *Tax Data*, 2002.

[752] See Kischel, D., *Internationale Wirtschaftsbriefe*, Fach 5, Irland, Gruppe 2, 2000, 84.

[753] See Quirke, L. and Walsh, A., *International Tax Review* 1999, 46; Jaeger, C., *Die Körperschaftsteuersysteme in Europa*, 2001, 124.

[754] See Kischel, D., *Internationale Wirtschaftsbriefe*, Fach 5, Irland, Gruppe 2, 2000, 84; O'Mahony, G., *International Tax Review* 2001, 39.

[755] See Jacobs, O. H., *Internationale Unternehmensbesteuerung*, 2002, 165; IBFD, *European Tax Handbook*, 2000, 302.

[756] Art. 23(2) of the Double Tax Treaty between Belgium/Ireland.

[757] Art. 21(B) of the Double Tax Treaty between France/Ireland.

[758] Art. 22(1) of the Double Tax Treaty between Germany/Ireland.

[759] Art. 21(a) of the Double Tax Treaty between Ireland/Italy.

[760] Art. 23(2) of the Double Tax Treaty between Ireland/Luxembourg. See Ward, J., *Ireland*, 2001, 101.

[761] See Kischel, D., *Internationale Wirtschaftsbriefe*, Fach 5, Irland, Gruppe 2, 2000, 84

[762] See Jaeger, C., *Die Körperschaftsteuersysteme in Europa*, 2001, 124.

Dividends Paid

Withholding tax at the standard rate of income tax (currently 20 percent) applies to dividend payments and other distributions made by an Irish tax resident company.[763] However, exemptions from withholding taxation apply to the following categories of shareholders (among others):[764]

- an Irish resident company;
- a company resident outside Ireland and ultimately controlled by shareholders resident in another EU member state or in a treaty country;
- a company, or a 75 percent subsidiary of a company, the principal class of shares of which are substantially and regularly traded on a recognized stock exchange located in an EU member state (other than Ireland), in a country with which Ireland has a double tax treaty, or another approved stock exchange;
- a company resident in another EU member state or in a treaty country that is not controlled by Irish residents; or
- a company resident in another EU member state and holding 25 percent of the share capital of the dividend paying Irish company.[765]

Hence, no dividend withholding tax will normally arise in an inbound holding company scenario.

Capital Gains

Capital gains arising on the sale of shares in domestic as well as foreign subsidiaries are subject to tax at regular rates (20 percent).[766]

Capital Losses

Capital losses can only be offset against capital gains. Loss carry backs are limited to one year whereas loss carry forwards are available for an unlimited period.

Capital Tax

Capital tax is payable on the issue or increase of a resident company's share capital. The imposed rate of the duty is one percent of the actual value of the assets contributed to a company in consideration for the issuance of shares, or the nominal value of the shares allocated (if higher).[767] A contribution of shares of a foreign company to an Irish holding company is subject to Irish capital tax provided that the contributing company receives shares in the Irish entity in return for its contribution.

---

[763] See Ward, J., *Ireland*, 2001, 102; McLoughlin, K., *Tax Notes International* 2001, 1141; O'Mahony, G., *International Tax Review* 2001, 36.

[764] See O'Brien, C., *International Tax Review* 1999, 25; Kischel, D., *Internationale Wirtschaftsbriefe*, Fach 5, Irland, Gruppe 2, 2000, 85; Ward, J., *Ireland*, 2001, 181.

[765] See Jacobs, O. H., *Internationale Unternehmensbesteuerung*, 2002, 165; IBFD, *European Tax Handbook*, 2000, 303; Kischel, D., *Internationale Wirtschaftsbriefe*, Fach 5, Irland, Gruppe 2, 2000, 85; Saunders, G., *Tolley's Taxation in the Republic of Ireland 2000-01*, 2000, 200.

[766] See O'Brien, C., *International Tax Review* 1999, 26; Quirke, L. and Walsh, A., *International Tax Review* 1999, 46; Kischel, D., *Internationale Wirtschaftsbriefe*, 2000, Fach 5, Irland, Gruppe 2, 86.

[767] See Albrecht, A., *Internationale Wirtschaftsbriefe*, 1998, Fach 5, Irland, Gruppe 3, 37; Hollingsworth, G. and Fuller, C., *Tax Planning International mergers & acquisitions* 2002, 3.

Interest Deductibility

Financing costs are tax deductible if they relate to a shareholding of at least five percent in a foreign entity.[768] No specific debt-to-equity ratio requirement is in force.[769]

1.7. Luxembourg

This section outlines the tax attributes of the typical taxable holding company, the so-called SOPARFI (Société de Participations Financières). The special tax regime of the so-called 1929 holding companies does not qualify for the benefits of either the EU directives or the applicable double tax treaties and, hence, is not discussed herein.[770]

Tax Rate

Profits are subject to corporation tax at a rate of 30.38 percent in Luxembourg.[771] The rate is a conglomeration of a 22 percent corporation tax,[772] a 0.88 percent surcharge, and a 7.5 percent non-deductible municipal business tax.[773]

Dividends Received

Under Luxembourg law, a dividend participation exemption[774] applies to domestic and foreign dividends received provided that:[775]

- the parent company owns at least ten percent of the share capital in the subsidiary or the participation reflects an acquisition value of at least € 1,200,000;
- the parent company has held the qualifying shares for an uninterrupted period of at least 12 months; and
- the subsidiary is subject to tax on profits.

---

[768] See Ward, J., *Ireland*, 2001, 73.

[769] See Baumann, W., *Steueroasen und internationale Holdingkonstruktionen*, 1996, 115; Hollingsworth, G. and Fuller, C., *Tax Planning International mergers & acquisitions* 2002, 6.

[770] See Kessler, W., *Internationales Steuerrecht* 1995, 11; Bremer, S., *Der Holdingstandort Bundesrepublik Deutschland*, 1996, 281; Könen, R., *Internationale Wirtschaftsbriefe*, Fach 5, Luxemburg, Gruppe 2, 1998, 149; Zois, A., *Cardozo Journal of International and Comparative Law* 1999, 199; Ruchelman, S. C., Asbeck, E. van, Canalejo, G. and et. al., *Journal of International Taxation* 2000, 42; Offermanns, R., *Luxembourg*, 2001, 119; Bogaerts, R., *European Taxation* 2002, 381.

[771] See KPMG, 2001 *WTD* 164-2; KPMG, 2001 *WTD* 206-7; Anonymous, *International Tax Review* 2002, 3; Bogaerts, R., *European Taxation* 2002, 380; IBFD, *Annual Report 2001-2002*, 2002, 124; Mayor, J., *International Tax Report* 2002, 10; Mayor, J. and Davezac, C., *International Tax Report* 2002, 2; Neffati, S. and Gutknecht, M., *Internationale Wirtschaftsbriefe*, Fach 5, Luxemburg, Gruppe 2, 2002, 162.

[772] *Impôt sur le revenu des collectivités* or *Körperschaftsteuer*.

[773] *Impôt commercial communal*. See Ministére des Finance, *Reforme*, 2001, 3; Beltjens, R. and Saussoy, S., *Tax Planning International Review* 2002, 8; Heyvaert, W. and Springael, B., *Intertax* 2002, 327; PricewaterhouseCoopers, *Holding Companies*, 2002, Addendum 1; Springael, B., *Tax Notes International* 2002, 1245.

[774] The so-called *Privlége d'affiliation*.

[775] Art. 147 of the *Loi impôt sur le revenu des collectivités*. See Steichen, A., *Internationale Wirtschaftsbriefe*, Fach 5, Luxemburg, Gruppe 2, 1999, 153; Ruchelman, S. C., Asbeck, E. van, Canalejo, G. and et. al., *Journal of International Taxation* 2000, 42; Beltjens, R. and Saussoy, S., *Tax Planning International Review* 2002, 9; Bogaerts, R., *European Taxation* 2002, 384; Heyvaert, W. and Springael, B., *Intertax* 2002, 328; Mayor, J., *International Tax Report* 2002, 10.

Dividends Paid

Dividend distributions made by a Luxembourg SOPARFI are subject to withholding tax at a rate of 20 percent[776] unless eliminated under the EU Parent-Subsidiary Directive or reduced due to a double tax treaty.[777]

Under Luxembourg law, no withholding tax is imposed on dividends paid to parent companies resident within the EU provided that:[778]

- the parent company owns at least ten percent of the share capital in the Luxembourg subsidiary or the participation reflects an acquisition value of at least € 1,200,000; and
- the parent company has owned the qualifying shares for an uninterrupted period of at least 12 months.

Luxembourg withholds no tax on dividend distributions made to U.S. companies that have a direct shareholding of at least 25 percent of the voting stock in a Luxembourg company during an uninterrupted period of at least two years preceding the date of distribution.[779] If the U.S. company directly owns at least ten percent but less than 25 percent of the voting stock of the Luxembourg company, a withholding tax rate of five percent applies.[780]

Capital Gains

The participation exemption applies not only to dividends but also to capital gains recognized from the disposal of shares in both domestic and foreign companies. However, the prerequisites for capital gains exemptions are more restrictive. Capital gains are exempt from Luxembourg taxation provided that:[781]

- the parent company owns at least ten percent of the voting shares in a foreign subsidiary or the participation reflects an acquisition value of at least € 6,000,000; and
- the parent company has held the qualifying shares for an uninterrupted period of at least 12 months.

In the case of a foreign participation, the exception additionally requires that the foreign subsidiary is subject to tax at an effective rate of at least 15 percent.[782]

---

[776] Art. 148(1) of the *Loi impôt sur le revenu des collectivités*. See Bogaerts, R., *European Taxation* 2002, 385; Heyvaert, W. and Springael, B., *Intertax* 2002, 327.

[777] See KPMG, 2001 *WTD* 206-7; Beltjens, R. and Saussoy, S., *Tax Planning International Review* 2002, 10; Mayor, J. and Davezac, C., *International Tax Report* 2002, 2; O'Grady, E., *Tax Notes International* 2002, 1065; PricewaterhouseCoopers, *Holding Companies*, 2002, Addendum 4; Springael, B., *Tax Notes International* 2002, 1245.

[778] Art. 147 of the *Loi impôt sur le revenu des collectivités*. See Romano, C., *European Taxation* 1999, 264; Steichen, A., *Internationale Wirtschaftsbriefe*, Fach 5, Luxemburg, Gruppe 2, 1999, 156; PricewaterhouseCoopers, *Tax Guide*, 2000, 13; Offermanns, R., *Luxembourg*, 2001, 107; Bogaerts, R., *European Taxation* 2002, 385; Springael, B., *Tax Notes International* 2002, 1246.

[779] Art. 10(2)(b) of the Double Tax Treaty between Luxembourg/U.S. See Warner, P. and Allgaier, D., *International Tax Review* 2001, 13.

[780] Art. 10(2)(a)(i) of the Double Tax Treaty between Luxembourg/U.S.

[781] See Ruchelman, S. C., Asbeck, E. van, Canalejo, G. and et. al., *Journal of International Taxation* 2000, 42; KPMG, 2001 *WTD* 206-7; Ministére des Finances, *Reforme*, 2001, 9; Beltjens, R. and Saussoy, S., *Tax Planning International Review* 2002, 9; Bogaerts, R., *European Taxation* 2002, 386; Heyvaert, W. and Springael, B., *Intertax* 2002, 328; Mayor, J., *International Tax Report* 2002, 10; Mayor, J. and Davezac, C., *International Tax Report* 2002, 2; Neffati, S. and Gutknecht, M., *Internationale Wirtschaftsbriefe*, Fach 5, Luxemburg, Gruppe 2, 2002, 162; Springael, B., *Tax Notes International* 2002, 1247.

[782] See Kessler, W., *Die Euro-Holding*, 1996, 117.

Capital Losses

Capital losses recognized from the disposal of shares in foreign corporations are only deductible to the extent they exceed the dividends or capital gains that are exempt from Luxembourg taxation.[783]

Capital Tax

Capital tax amounting to one percent is levied on any capital contributions.[784] A contribution of shares of a foreign company to a Luxembourg holding company is tax exempt under certain conditions.[785]

Interest Deductibility

Interest expenses are tax deductible insofar as they exceed the tax exempt income.[786] A debt-to-equity ratio of 85:15 is required to counteract excessive shareholder debt financing.[787]

1.8. The Netherlands

Tax Rate

Dutch corporation tax is levied at a rate of 34.5 percent.[788]

Dividends Received

Dutch law provides for a participation exemption applying to dividend payments from domestic and foreign subsidiaries if:[789]

- the parent company owns at least five percent of the nominal and paid-in share capital of the Dutch subsidiary;[790]

---

[783] See Romano, C., *European Taxation* 1999, 264; Zois, A., *Cardozo Journal of International and Comparative Law* 1999, 201.

[784] See Steichen, A., *Internationale Wirtschaftsbriefe*, Fach 5, Luxemburg, Gruppe 2, 1997, 142; Romano, C., *European Taxation* 1999, 264; Ruchelman, S. C., Asbeck, E. van, Canalejo, G. and et. al., *Journal of International Taxation* 2000, 45; Bogaerts, R., *European Taxation* 2002, 383; Heyvaert, W. and Springael, B., *Intertax* 2002, 331.

[785] See Ruchelman, S. C., Asbeck, E. van, Canalejo, G. and et. al., *Journal of International Taxation* 2000, 45; Beltjens, R. and Saussoy, S., *Tax Planning International Review* 2002, 11.

[786] See Bogaerts, R., *European Taxation* 2002, 385; PricewaterhouseCoopers, *Holding Companies*, 2002, 21.

[787] See Cinnamon, A., *International Tax Review* 1999, 11; Ruchelman, S. C., Asbeck, E. van, Canalejo, G. and et. al., *Journal of International Taxation* 2000, 45; Bogaerts, R., *European Taxation* 2002, 385.

[788] See Lindonk, C. van, *Tax Planning International Review* 2001, 9; Lohuis, H. and Rubbens, B., *Internationale Wirtschaftsbriefe*, Fach 5, Niederlande, Gruppe 2, 2001, 328; Stok, E. van der, *International Tax Review* 2001, 38; Ernst & Young, *International Tax Digest* 2002 (Netherlands) I, 15; IBFD, *Annual Report 2001-2002*, 2002, 126; Müssener, I., *Internationale Wirtschaftsbriefe*, Fach 5, Niederlande, Gruppe 2, 2002, 345; O'Grady, E., *Tax Notes International* 2002, 1064.

[789] Art. 13(2) of the *Wet op de vennootschapsbelasting*. See Kam, F. de, *Tax Notes International* 1994, 910; Doornbosch, H. and Engelman, M., *CTF*, 2001, 13:7; Ruchelman, S. C., Asbeck, E. van, Canalejo, G. and et. al., *Journal of International Taxation* 2001 I, 28; Bongers, E. and Visser, K.-J., *Journal of International Taxation* 2003, 36.

[790] A less than five percent shareholding may also be sufficient to benefit from the participation exemption under Art. 13(3) of the *Wet op de vennootschapsbelasting*, provided that the shares are held in the line of business conducted by the Dutch parent company and the shares are not held as a mere portfolio investment. Based on a decision of the *Hoge*

- the subsidiary's capital is divided into shares;
- the investment is not held as a current asset;[791] and
- neither the parent corporation nor the subsidiary retains the tax status of an investment institution (the so-called *fiscale beleggingsinstelling*).

If the subsidiary is situated abroad, the following prerequisites also have to be met:[792]

- the participation must not be in the nature of a portfolio investment (the so-called *portfolio test*); and
- the subsidiary resident outside the Netherlands must be subject to tax on profits in the jurisdiction where it is located. In clear settings, the level of foreign taxes imposed is irrelevant under Dutch law.[793]

Within the EU, the non-portfolio investment requirement is not applicable to shareholdings of at least 25 percent under the EU Parent-Subsidiary Directive.[794] As of January 1, 2002, this exception to the non-portfolio investment, however, does not apply to EU subsidiaries that are held as portfolio investments or that own one or more non-EU subsidiaries which would not qualify for the exception if owned directly by the Dutch parent company.[795] More specifically, Art. 13g (3) of the *Wet op de vennootschapsbelasting* provides that the participation exemption will not apply to a shareholding in an EU subsidiary that is held as a portfolio investment if:[796]

the assets of such an EU subsidiary consist largely, i.e., 70 percent or more, of shareholdings held, directly or indirectly, in one or more non-EU subsidiaries (the so-called *70% of assets test*); and
- where such non-EU shareholdings would not have qualified for the participation exemption if held directly by the Dutch parent company.

With respect to the 70 percent of assets test, the Under-Minister of Finance explained that if the interposed EU subsidiary is also engaged in other activities of a certain scope[797] in addition to its shareholdings in passive non-EU subsidiaries, anti-abuse provisions will not apply because in such cases, it has not been sufficiently demonstrated that the EU corporation has been interposed for tax avoidance purposes.

Raad in 2001 (BNB 2001/210), it is deemed that the participation is in line with the business conduct if the shares in the subsidiary are not held as portfolio investments. See Molenaars, M. L. and Bongers, E., *The Netherlands*, 2002, 10.

[791] Based on three decisions by the *Hoge Raad* (BNB 2000/215; BNB 2000/216; BNB 2000/217), it would appear that stock is held as inventory if (1) the parent company intends to dispose of the shares and the respective shares can be allocated to the Dutch parent's assets; (2) the subsidiary does not carry on business; and (3) the subsidiary consists mostly of cash and other liquid assets. See Molenaars, M. L. and Bongers, E., *The Netherlands*, 2002, 10.

[792] See Doornbosch, H. and Engelman, M., *CTF*, 2001, 13:7; Jong, C. E. de, *Internationale Wirtschaftsbriefe*, Fach 5, Niederlande, Gruppe 2, 2001, 312; Ruchelman, S. C., Asbeck, E. van, Canalejo, G. and et. al., *Journal of International Taxation* 2001 I, 28; Vlaanderen, P., *Tax Notes International* 2002, 1096.

[793] See Vlaanderen, P., *Tax Notes International* 2002, 1096.

[794] Art 13g of the *Wet op de vennootschapsbelasting*.

[795] In its report of June 11, 2001, the Dutch International Corporate Income Tax Study Group (the so-called *Studiegroep vennootschapsbelasting in internationaal perspectief*) stated both their desire and the feasibility of changing the Dutch corporate tax burden. In particular, the Tax Study Group recommended that income be legally excluded from the participation exemption if it was generated directly or indirectly from non-EU companies that have a certain passive portfolio investment character. See Ernst & Young, *International Tax Digest* 2002 (Netherlands) II, 14; Molenaars, M. L. and Bongers, E., *The Netherlands*, 2002, 11; Vlaanderen, P., *Tax Notes International* 2002, 1096.

[796] See Ernst & Young, *International Tax Digest* 2002 (Netherlands) II, 14.

[797] In other words, at least 30 percent.

Dividends Paid

Withholding tax is imposed on dividend distributions at a rate of 25 percent if not reduced by a tax treaty or eliminated under the EU Parent-Subsidiary Directive.[798] In order to distribute dividends without withholding tax to an EU parent, it is required that:[799]

- the shares in the Dutch company be held for at least one year straddling the date of the distribution; and
- the parent company owns at least 25 percent of the nominal paid-up capital of the EU subsidiary (or 25 percent of the voting rights under specific tax treaties). A ten percent shareholding is sufficient in cases in which the receiving company is located in a member state that adheres to the EU Parent-Subsidiary Directive, which also applies an ownership threshold of ten percent.[800]

Under the Dutch/U.S. Double Tax Treaty, the Netherlands has the right to withhold taxes on dividends at a maximum rate of five percent provided that the U.S. MNC holds at least ten percent of the shares of the Dutch company.[801]

Capital Gains

Capital gains recognized from the disposal of shares in domestic as well as foreign subsidiaries are exempt from Dutch taxation if the dividends received from such participations would be also tax free, i.e., the above-mentioned requirements are fulfilled.

Capital Losses

Capital losses realized on the sale of shares are not deductible for tax purposes.[802]

Capital Tax

Under Dutch law, the rate of capital tax amounts to 0.55 percent of the amount (market value) of the cash contribution.[803] No stamp duties are imposed on contributions of shares in foreign subsidiaries to Dutch corporations.[804]

---

[798] See Baumann, W., *Steueroasen und internationale Holdingkonstruktionen*, 1996, 138; Jong, C. E. de, *Internationale Wirtschaftsbriefe*, Fach 5, Niederlande, Gruppe 2, 2001, 319.

[799] See Obluda, S., *Internationale Wirtschaftsbriefe*, Fach 5, Niederlande, Gruppe 2, 1998, 288.

[800] For example, France, Germany, Luxembourg, and the U.K.

[801] Art. 10(2)(a) of the Double Tax Treaty between The Netherlands/U.S. See Ruchelman, S. C., Asbeck, E. van, Canalejo, G. and et. al., *Journal of International Taxation* 2001 I, 29.
   On February 21, 2002, the Dutch Finance Minister proposed that the U.S. and the Netherlands consider revising their current income tax treaty. The negotiations would relate to the elimination of any withholding taxes on dividends received from substantial shareholdings. See Huber, M. F., Kapalle, U. and Kubaile, H., *Steuer Revue* 2002, 379.

[802] See Obluda, S., *Internationale Wirtschaftsbriefe*, Fach 5, Niederlande, Gruppe 2, 1998, 284; Ruchelman, S. C., Asbeck, E. van, Canalejo, G. and et. al., *Journal of International Taxation* 2001 I, 29.

[803] See Doornbosch, H. and Berings, S., *Journal of International Taxation* 2001, 4; Jong, C. E. de, *Internationale Wirtschaftsbriefe*, Fach 5, Niederlande, Gruppe 2, 2001, 316; Lier, P. and Paardekooper, W. J., *Tax Management International Forum* 2002, 35.

[804] See Molenaars, M. and Bongers, E., *Journal of International Taxation* 2001, 44.

Interest Deductibility

Interest expenses incurred on acquisitions of foreign subsidiaries are non-deductible items for Dutch tax purposes.[805] The maximum allowable debt-to-equity ratio is 85:15.[806]

1.9. Spain

Tax Rate

The corporation income is taxed at a rate of 35 percent in Spain.[807]

Dividends Received

Under Spanish law,[808] dividends received from non-resident subsidiaries are exempt from taxation provided that:[809]

- the parent company owns, directly or indirectly, at least five percent of the shares in the non-resident subsidiary for an uninterrupted period of one year prior to the dividend distribution or acquisition costs exceed € 6,000,000;
- the subsidiary is subject to taxation comparable to the Spanish tax system, regardless of the tax rate.[810] However, the subsidiary must not be a resident of a country considered by the Spanish tax authorities to be a tax haven[811] or which has not signed a tax treaty with Spain with an exchange of information clause; and
- the subsidiary's income must be derived from business activities outside Spain, or for certain passive income, derived in the jurisdiction where the subsidiary is located. The foreign subsidiary is deemed to have business activities when at least 85 percent of its total income stems from entrepreneurial activities.

---

[805] Art. 13 of the *Wet op de vennootschapsbelasting*. See Baumann, W., *Steueroasen und internationale Holdingkonstruktionen*, 1996, 137; Obluda, S., *Internationale Wirtschaftsbriefe*, Fach 5, Niederlande, Gruppe 2, 1998, 285; Ruchelman, S. C., Asbeck, E. van, Canalejo, G. and et. al., *Journal of International Taxation* 2001 I, 29.

[806] See Ruchelman, S. C., Asbeck, E. van, Canalejo, G. and et. al., *Journal of International Taxation* 2001 I, 29; Vrouwenvelder, M., *Tax Management International Journal* 2001, 414; Müssener, I., *Internationale Wirtschaftsbriefe*, Fach 5, Niederlande, Gruppe 2, 2002, 345.

[807] See Baumann, W., *Steueroasen und internationale Holdingkonstruktionen*, 1996, 147; Schnieder, E.-A., *Internationales Steuerrecht* 1997, 69; Lüdemann, P., Echevarria, A. and Hruschka, F., *Steuerfolgen gewerblicher Unternehmen in Spanien*, 1999, paragraph 184; Courage, C., *Körperschaftsteuer*, 2000, 88; Ernst & Young, *Spain*, 2001, 24; Müller, K., *Verwirklichung von Gerechtigkeit und Entscheidungsneutralität*, 2001, 116; Raventós Calvo, S. and Cueva González-Cotera, A. de la, *Spain*, 2001, 191; Rodríguez, P. and Briones, L., *Tax Management International Forum* 2002, 39.

[808] Art. 20bis of the *Ley del Impuesto sobre Sociedades*. The Spanish holding company regime is referred to as *Entidad de Tenencia de Valores Extranjeros (ETVE)* which can be translated as "entities holding foreign securities". Special provisions are implemented in Art. 129-132 of the *Ley del Impuesto sobre Sociedades*. For the ETVE definition, see Zois, A., *Cardozo Journal of International and Comparative Law* 1999, 183; Raventós Calvo, S. and Cueva González-Cotera, A. de la, *Spain*, 2001, 191.

[809] See Romano, C., *European Taxation* 1999, 266; Ernst & Young's Foreign Desk, *Journal of International Taxation* 2000, 13; Mullerat, R. and Rodriguez, R., *Tax Notes International* 2000, 682; Cusí, J. M., *Tax Notes International* 2001, 1494; Ernst & Young, *Spain*, 2001, 25; Martín Jiménez, A. J., *Tax Notes International* 2001, 93; Ruchelman, S. C., Asbeck, E. van, Canalejo, G. and et. al., *Journal of International Taxation* 2001 I, 31.

[810] For a discussion of the comparability, see Cueva González-Cotera, A. de la, *European Taxation* 2000, 153.

[811] See Courage, C., *Recht der Internationalen Wirtschaft* 1996, 667. Royal Decree 1080/1991, dated July 5, 1991, mentioned 48 jurisdictions or territories considered to be tax havens. See Agencia Tributaria, Taxation.

Domestic dividends received by a Spanish ETVE do not qualify for the participation exemption. The dividends are subject to Spanish corporate tax at the level of the ETVE; however, a full tax credit is granted if certain requirements are met.

Dividends Paid

Withholding tax on dividend distributions is levied at a rate of 25 percent or, in the case of a non-resident entity operating without a p.e. in Spain, 18 percent,[812] unless reduced under a double tax treaty or eliminated under the EU Parent-Subsidiary Directive.[813]

Under Spanish domestic law, no Spanish tax is withheld on dividend distributions to an EU parent provided that the dividends distributed are from income which has been exempt from income tax at the level of the Spanish holding company, e.g., dividends received from foreign shareholdings.[814] This exemption also applies to profit distributions to parent companies resident outside the EU provided that they are not residents of tax havens.[815] Hence, no dividend withholding tax will normally arise in an inbound holding company scenario.[816] If the dividends distributed consist of non-exempt income, vis-à-vis a U.S. parent, a ten percent withholding tax will apply.[817]

Capital Gains

Capital gains arising from the disposal of stock in foreign subsidiaries are not subject to Spanish taxation if the dividend distributions received from such participations are tax exempt.[818] Conversely, in line with the (potential) taxation of dividends received from Spanish domestic subsidiaries, respective capital gains are also taxable.

Capital Losses

As no Spanish tax provisions specifically deal with the utilization of capital losses recognized from the sale of foreign shareholdings, the deductibility of such losses appears possible.[819]

Capital Tax

In Spain, capital tax of one percent is triggered by the issuance of share capital.[820] Spanish capital tax is generally not imposed if shares in foreign entities are contributed to the Spanish holding company.[821]

---

[812] See Sanders, T. and Clancy, F., *International Tax Review* 2002, 25.

[813] See Morris, A., *Tax Notes International* 1992, 323; Lüdemann, P., Echevarria, A. and Hruschka, F., *Steuerfolgen gewerblicher Unternehmen in Spanien*, 1999, paragraph 24; Romano, C., *European Taxation* 1999, 266; Ruchelman, S. C., Asbeck, E. van, Canalejo, G. and et. al., *Journal of International Taxation* 2001 I, 33. The EU Parent-Subsidiary Directive is implemented in Art. 13(1)(b) of the *Ley del Impuesto sobre la Renta de no residentes*.

[814] See Ruchelman, S. C., Asbeck, E. van, Canalejo, G. and et. al., *Journal of International Taxation* 2001 I, 33.

[815] Art. 130(1)(b) of the *Ley del Impuesto sobre Sociedades*. See Schnieder, E.-A., *Internationales Steuerrecht* 1997, 72; Zois, A., *Cardozo Journal of International and Comparative Law* 1999, 193; Mullerat, R. and Rodriguez, R., *Tax Notes International* 2000, 682; Cusí, J. M., *Tax Notes International* 2001, 1496.

[816] See Marantelli, A., *Steuer Revue* 2000 II, 94; Sanders, T. and Clancy, F., *International Tax Review* 2002, 25.

[817] Art. 10(2)(a) of the Double Tax Treaty between Spain/U.S. See Mullerat, R. and Rodriguez, R., *Tax Notes International* 2000, 682.

[818] See Mullerat, R. and Rodriguez, R., *Tax Notes International* 2000, 683; Cusí, J. M., *Tax Notes International* 2001, 1494; Ernst & Young, *Spain*, 2001, 25; Martín Jiménez, A. J., *Tax Notes International* 2001, 94; Ruchelman, S. C., Asbeck, E. van, Canalejo, G. and et. al., *Journal of International Taxation* 2001 I, 33.

[819] See Romano, C., *European Taxation* 1999, 267; Barrenechea, S., Ogea, R. and Mullerat, R., *Tax Notes International* 2000, 586.

Interest Deductibility

Interest expenses in connection with an acquisition of an interest in a foreign company are tax deductible.[822] Under the Spanish thin capitalization provision, a maximum debt-to-equity ratio of 3:1 is acceptable.[823]

1.10. Switzerland

Tax Rate

Swiss corporations are subject to corporation tax at the federal, cantonal and communal levels.[824] At the federal level, corporation tax is levied at a flat rate of 8.5 percent.[825] At cantonal and communal levels, the rates vary substantially and can be progressive. The overall effective tax burden is between 17 percent and 30 percent. A company qualifies for the holding company privilege if:[826]

- its main purpose is to hold shares;
- no business activities are carried out in Switzerland; and
- the investment amounts to at least 2/3rd of its total assets or earnings from the shareholdings are at least 2/3rd of the annual earnings.

Assuming a pure holding company structure, a company can be fully exempt from income taxation at cantonal/communal levels.[827]

Dividends Received

At both the federal level and cantonal/communal levels, a holding company carrying out its own business activities can claim a participation deduction for both domestic and foreign shareholdings if it owns at least 20 percent of the shares in the subsidiary or the fair market value of the investment

---

[820] See Cinnamon, A., *International Tax Review* 1999, 11; Lampreave, P., Verkehrsteuer, 2000, 66; Cusí, J. M., *Tax Notes International* 2001, 1496; Raventós Calvo, S. and Cueva González-Cotera, A. de la, *Spain*, 2001, 171; Rodríguez, P. and Briones, L., *Tax Management International Forum* 2002, 40.

[821] See Romano, C., *European Taxation* 1999, 267; Barrenechea, S., Ogea, R. and Mullerat, R., *Tax Notes International* 2000, 586; Ruchelman, S. C., Asbeck, E. van, Canalejo, G. and et. al., *Journal of International Taxation* 2001 I, 59.

[822] See Raventós Calvo, S. and Cueva González-Cotera, A. de la, *Spain*, 2001, 191.

[823] Art. 20 of the *Ley del Impuesto sobre Sociedades*. See Courage, C., *Internationale Wirtschaftsbriefe*, Fach 5, Spanien, Gruppe 2, 1996, 217; Schnieder, E.-A., *Internationales Steuerrecht* 1997, 73; Courage, C., *Körperschaftsteuer*, 2000, 86; López-Muñoz, G. de Arce, *International Tax Report* 2000, 5; Cusí, J. M., *Tax Notes International* 2001, 1496; Martín Jiménez, A. J., *Tax Notes International* 2001, 94; Calderón, J., *Tax Notes International* 2002, 633; Palacios, J. and Bootello, V., *Journal of International Taxation* 2002, 41; Rodríguez, P. and Briones, L., *Tax Management International Forum* 2002, 41.

[824] See Ruchelman, S. C., Asbeck, E. van, Canalejo, G. and et. al., *Journal of International Taxation* 2000, 47.

[825] See Ruchelman, S. C., Asbeck, E. van, Canalejo, G. and et. al., *Journal of International Taxation* 2000, 47; Altenburger, P., *Tax Management International Forum* 2002, 43. Under the 2001 Tax Package (the so-called *Steuerpaket 2001*), it is proposed to lower the federal tax rate to eight percent. See WAK-N, *Unternehmensbesteuerung*, 2001; Anonymous, *Steuer Revue* 2001 II, 447; Beilstein, W. and Ah, J. von, *Internationale Wirtschaftsbriefe*, Fach 5, Schweiz, Gruppe 2, 2002, 504.

[826] See Höhn, E., *Internationale Steuerplanung*, 1996, 345; Riedweg, P., *Internationales Steuerrecht* 1998, 586.

[827] See Beilstein, W., *Internationale Wirtschaftsbriefe*, Fach 5, Schweiz, Gruppe 2, 1995, 453; Ruchelman, S. C., Asbeck, E. van, Canalejo, G. and et. al., *Journal of International Taxation* 2000, 49.

amounts to at least Swiss Franc 2,000,000 (the so-called *qualifizierende Beteiligung*).[828] In the case of a pure holding company, a dividend exemption will apply at cantonal/communal levels.

The participation deduction reduces the tax otherwise payable by the proportion of the net investment income to the total net profit. The net investment income is 95 percent (to reflect a five percent charge for general expenses) of the gross investment income less the financing costs for the investment. Thus, depending on the relationship between net investment income and total net profit, the participation deduction might lead to a full exemption of the dividends received.

Dividends Paid

Withholding tax at a rate of 35 percent is imposed on dividend distributions made by a Swiss corporation unless reduced or eliminated under a tax treaty (e.g., the withholding tax will be refunded to a Dutch qualifying dividend recipient).[829] In the case of a U.S. parent company, Swiss withholding tax on dividends from substantial shareholdings (at least ten percent of the voting stock) will be reduced at source to five percent.[830]

Capital Gains

At both the federal and cantonal/communal levels - if the holding company carries out its own business activities - gains from the sale of investments to third parties rank as investment income qualifying for the participation deduction. The participation deduction applies provided that:[831]

- the capital gain exceeds the acquisition value;
- the parent company owns at least 20 percent of the shares in the subsidiary (*only at cantonal/communal levels alternatively: or* the fair market value of such an investment amounts to at least Swiss Franc 2,000,000); and
- the parent company has held the investment for at least one year.

At cantonal/communal levels, capital gains recognized by a pure holding company that does not carry out any business activities are exempt from taxation.[832]

Capital Losses

At the federal level, in accordance with the ordinary taxation of capital gains, losses are tax deductible as they relate to investments in foreign companies if the corresponding dividends or capital gains are not exempt. Otherwise, losses are not tax deductible.

---

[828] Art. 69 and 70 of the *Bundesgesetz über die direkte Bundessteuer*. See Höhn, E., *Internationale Steuerplanung*, 1996, 334; Bremer, S. and Staudt Vontobel, H., *Internationale Wirtschaftsbriefe*, Fach 5, Schweiz, Gruppe 2, 1999, 483; Ruchelman, S. C., Asbeck, E. van, Canalejo, G. and et. al., *Journal of International Taxation* 2000, 47; Graf, T., *International Tax Review* 2001, 77; Reich, M., *Steuer & Wirtschaft International* 2001, 486; Beilstein, W. and Ah, J. von, *Internationale Wirtschaftsbriefe*, Fach 5, Schweiz, Gruppe 2, 2002, 514. For the canton of Zurich, see Anonymous, *Steuer Revue* 2001 I, 235.

[829] See Baumann, W., *Steueroasen und internationale Holdingkonstruktionen*, 1996, 145; Ruchelman, S. C., Asbeck, E. van, Canalejo, G. and et. al., *Journal of International Taxation* 2000, 48; Ernst & Young, *International Tax Digest* 2001 (Switzerland), 15.

[830] Art. 10(2)(a) of the Double Tax Treaty between Switzerland/U.S. See Marantelli, A., *Steuer Revue* 2000 II, 94; Ruchelman, S. C., Asbeck, E. van, Canalejo, G. and et. al., *Journal of International Taxation* 2000, 48; Ernst & Young, *International Tax Digest* 2001 (Switzerland), 15.

[831] See Graf, T., *International Tax Review* 2001, 77; Beilstein, W. and Ah, J. von, *Internationale Wirtschaftsbriefe*, Fach 5, Schweiz, Gruppe 2, 2002, 514.

[832] See Ruchelman, S. C., Asbeck, E. van, Canalejo, G. and et. al., *Journal of International Taxation* 2000, 49.

Capital Tax

There is a federal capital tax of one percent on the issued share capital of a Swiss corporation.[833] There is also a similar cantonal tax at local rates varying between 0.005 percent and 0.1 percent. Swiss securities transfer tax is not levied on the transfer of shares in a Swiss corporation if the holding company holds less than Swiss Franc 10,000,000 of securities. Securities tax is due at a rate of 0.15 percent for the contribution of national shareholdings and at a rate of 0.3 percent for the contribution of shares in a foreign company.[834]

Interest Deductibility

Interest payments on loans drawn to finance an investment are deductible for tax purposes if there is a business justification. However, a pure holding company will not be able to use the deduction unless it has income other than exempt dividends. The required debt-to-equity ratios vary from canton to canton, but are generally in the order of 6:1.[835]

1.11. Summary Table

There is of course no right or wrong answer for a U.S. MNCs in devising a European group structure. Although the table below provides a basis for comparison of the most significant tax factors for each contender and, thus, enables an initial short list of possible locations for holding companies to be drawn up, the final decision will require a detailed analysis, taking into account the particular needs of each group.[836] Some of the tax factors, such as loss utilization, might not be important in some specific cases, whereas other criteria, e.g., capital gains taxation or taxation of dividends received, might be essential factors for a certain jurisdiction.[837]

If the emphasis is on tax-free treatment of dividends and capital gains, the Netherlands, Luxembourg, Spain, and Switzerland may be short-listed. If nil withholding on dividends paid to the U.S. is a main objective, Denmark, Ireland, Luxembourg, and Spain would seem to be attractive. If maximum deductibility of interest is important, countries like Germany, Belgium, Denmark, Ireland, and Spain seem to offer the best conditions. The treaty network is best in Germany, France, the Netherlands, and Denmark,[838] while the Netherlands, Luxembourg, and Switzerland show the most commitment in their endeavors to attract holding companies.[839]

Needless to say, the more points a country can score in this regard, the better chance it has of being selected by the parent company as the location of the EU holding company. It must also be emphasized that contender countries are not restricted to traditional low-tax countries. Often the opposite is true, and the ideal holding company location is situated in a higher tax country that offers special tax breaks for the planned holding activities.

---

[833] See Ruchelman, S. C., Asbeck, E. van, Canalejo, G. and et. al., *Journal of International Taxation* 2000, 47.

[834] Art. 16(1) of the *Bundesgesetz über die Stempelabgaben*. See Wuermli, R. J., *Internationale Wirtschaftsbriefe*, Fach 5, Schweiz, Gruppe 2, 1993, 397; Möller, M. A., *Der Holdingstandort Schweiz*, 1998, 71.

[835] See Baumann, W., *Steueroasen und internationale Holdingkonstruktionen*, 1996, 70.

[836] See Kessler, W., *Holdinggesellschaften und Kooperationen in Europa*, 1998, 189; Endres, D. and Eckstein, H.-M., *Steuerrecht International*, 2001, 30; Kessler, W., *Steuer Revue* 2001, 771.

[837] See Endres, D. and Eckstein, H.-M., *Steuerrecht International*, 2001, 30.

[838] See Fleischer-Michaelsen, U., *Journal of International Taxation* 1995, 156; Meldman, R. E. and Schadewald, M. S., *A Practical Guide to U.S. Taxation of International Transactions*, 2000, 275.

[839] A similar conclusion was drawn by Baumann, W., *Steueroasen und internationale Holdingkonstruktionen*, 1996, 155.

**********	Austria	Belgium	Denmark	France	Germany	Ireland	Luxembourg	Netherlands	Spain	Switzerland
Tax rate (effective)	34%	39% plus 3% crisis tax (total effective tax burden: 40.17%)	30%	33 1/3% plus surcharges of 3% and 3.3% (total effective tax burden: 35.43%)	25% (2003: 26.5%) plus 5.5% solidarity surcharge thereon 13-20% trade tax (total effective tax burden: 37 - 41%)	2002: 16% 2003: 12.5% Investment income / Non-trading income: 25%	30.38%	34.5%	35%	17% - 30%
Treatment of dividends from										
- domestic shareholdings	Exempt, if	95% Exempt, if - at least 5% of subsidiary's capital or acquisition value Belgian Franc 50,000,000 (€ 1,239,467)	Exempt, if - at least 20% holding for 1 year prior to or the entire tax year of receipt	95% Exempt, if - holding of at least 5% - holding for at least 2 years and - both parent and subsidiary, must be subject to corporate tax	Exempt	Exempt	Exempt, if - holding of at least 10% or € 1,200,000 and - for 12 month	Exempt, if - holding of at least 5%	Taxable but tax credit relief	Exempt if holding of at least 20% of the foreign corporation's equity or fair market value of the participation is at least Swiss Franc 2,000,000 At cantonal level pure holding companies are often fully exempt from income taxes
- foreign shareholdings	Exempt, if - at least 25% holding for 24 months	95% Exempt, if - at least 5% of subsidiary's capital or acquisition value Belgian Franc 50,000,000 (€ 1,239,467) and - subsidiary's income tax similar to Belgium's tax	Exempt, if - at least 20% holding for 1 year prior to or the entire tax year of receipt and - subsidiary's activity is not mainly finance and it is not taxed at a low rate	95% Exempt, if - holding of at least 5% - holding for at least 2 years and - both parent and subsidiary, must be subject to corporate tax	95% Exempt	Taxable but foreign tax credit relief, if - holding of at least 25% of the voting rights (reduced to 10% under most treaties)	Exempt, if - holding of at least 10% or € 1,200,000 and - for 12 month and - subsidiary is subject to tax	Exempt, if - holding of at least 5% and - income subject to tax in subsidiary's country of residence and - shares not held as a current asset or portfolio investment	Exempt, if - at least 5% holding for 1 year prior to or after receipt, and - subsidiary's income tax system similar to Spain's tax system or located in treaty country and - subsidiary's business income equals at least 85% of total income	Exempt if holding of at least 20% of the foreign corporation's equity or fair market value of the participation is at least Swiss Franc 2,000,000 At cantonal level pure holding companies are often fully exempt from income taxes

135

	Austria	Belgium	Denmark	France	Germany	Ireland	Luxembourg	Netherlands	Spain	Switzerland
Treatment of capital gains resulting from the disposal of **- domestic shareholding**	Taxable	Exempt if dividend received deduction applies	Exempt if - held for at least 3 years and - subsidiary's activity is not mainly finance	Taxable, however, reduced rate of 19% (plus 2 surcharges of 3% and 3.3%), if - 5% for 2 years	Exempt, unless unincorporated businesses have been contributed tax neutral prior to sale and disposal of shares within 7 years after contributions	Taxable	Exempt if - held for 12 months before year of sale and 25% of capital or € 6,000,000	Exempt if - holding of at least 5% and - shares not held as a current asset or portfolio investment	Taxable	Exempt if - holding of at least 20% of the domestic corporation's equity or fair market value of the participation is at least Swiss Franc 2,000,000. At cantonal level pure holding companies are often fully exempt from income taxes
- foreign shareholding	Exempt if - at least 25% holding for 24 months	Exempt if dividend received deduction applies	Exempt if - held for at least 3 years and - subsidiary's activity is not mainly finance and - it is not simultaneously taxed at a low rate	Taxable, however, if held 2 years, reduced rate of 19% (plus 2 surcharges of 3% and 3.3%)	Exempt	Taxable	Exempt if - held for 12 months before year of sale and 25% of capital or € 6,000,000 subsidiary is subject to tax of at least 15% on a basis similar to Luxembourg's tax	Exempt if - holding of at least 5% and - income subject to tax in subsidiary's country of residence and - shares not held as a current asset or portfolio investment	Exempt if - at least 5% holding for 1 year prior to or after receipt, or acquisition cost exceeds € 6,000,000 and - subsidiary's income tax system similar to Spain's tax system or located in treaty country and - subsidiary's business income equals at least 85% of total income	Exempt if - holding of at least 20% of the foreign corporation's equity or fair market value of the participation of at least Swiss Franc 2,000,000. At cantonal level pure holding companies are often fully exempt from income taxes

*********	Austria	Belgium	Denmark	France	Germany	Ireland	Luxembourg	Netherlands	Spain	Switzerland
Withholding tax on dividends paid to EU parent company	- Zero if at least 25% holding for 24 months	- Zero if holding more than 1 year and at least 25%	- Zero if holding for at least 1 year and at least 20%	- Zero if holding at least 2 years and at least 25% of share capital	- Zero if holding for at least 1 year and at least 25% / 10% of nominal capital	Nil (Generally)	- Zero if holding of at least 10% or € 1,200,000 and for 12 months	- Zero if holding of at least 25% share capital for at least year	- Zero if distributed out of exempt income; applies to any non-resident shareholders	- 35% which may be reduced to nil under double tax treaties
Withholding taxes on dividends paid to U.S. parent company	- 5%	- 5%	Nil	- 5%	- 5%	Nil (Generally)	- 5%	- 5%	Nil (in case of exempt income); 10% if distributed out of non-exempt income	- 5%
Deductibility of capital losses resulting from the disposal of: - domestic shareholding	Deductible (over 7 years)	Not deductible	Not deductible	Seems possible	Not deductible	Only against capital gains	Limited	Not deductible	Seems possible	Seems possible
- foreign shareholding	Not deductible	Not deductible	Capital losses within 3 years of ownership can be offset with respective capital gains	Capital losses on short-term investments can be offset with capital gains on short-term investments or ordinary business income; Capital losses on long-term investments only with respective capital gains	Not deductible	Only against capital gains	Only insofar as exceeding the tax exempt dividends / capital gains	Not deductible	Seems possible	At federal level only if relating to tax exempt foreign investments. At cantonal level no deduction
Capital Duty - on cash contributions	- 1% (with exemptions)	- 0.5% of new capital	- Nil	- Nil	- Nil	- 1%	- 1%	- 0.55%	- 1%	- 1% (at federal level); 0.005 - 0.1% (at cantonal level)
- on contributions of shares in a foreign subsidiary	- Nil if holding exists at least 24 months prior to contribution	- Nil under certain conditions	- Nil	- Nil under certain conditions	- Nil	- Nil under certain conditions	- Nil under certain conditions	- Nil under certain conditions	- Nil	- Nil if less than Swiss Franc 10,000,000 securities among assets

137

**********	Austria	Belgium	Denmark	France	Germany	Ireland	Luxembourg	Netherlands	Spain	Switzerland
Deductibility of interest expenses linked to foreign shareholdings	Not deductible	Not deductible up to 95% of foreign dividends received if held for less than 1 year	Deductible	Deductible if other income than exempt foreign dividends	Deductible	Deductible	Deductible if exceeding tax exempt dividends	Not deductible	Deductible	Deductible
Debt-to-equity limitations	No specific thin capitalization rules (arm's length principle)	No specific debt-to-equity ratio rules (practice: 7:1, if tax haven based/taxed)	4:1 debt-to-equity ratio	1.5:1 debt-to-equity ratio, applies to direct shareholders only	3:1 debt-to-equity ratio	No thin capitalization rules, but interest paid to non treaty resident affiliate generally non-deductible	85:15 debt-to-equity ratio	No specific debt-to-equity ratio rules (practice: 85:15)	3:1 debt-to-equity ratio	Varies from canton to canton (mostly: 6:1)
EU member state	Yes	Yes	Yes	Yes	Yes	Yes	Yes	Yes	Yes	No
(Max.) Individual income tax rate (without any church taxes)	50%	55% plus 7% communal tax plus 3% crisis tax	59%	52.5%	48.5% 2003-2004; 47% 2005, onward 43% plus 5.5% solidarity surcharge thereon	42%	38% plus 2.5% solidarity surcharge thereon	52%	48%	11.5% at federal level plus ca. 20% local tax
Double tax treaties	47	46	78	91	75	30	33	68	40	62
CFC/subpart F provisions	Draft	No	Yes	Yes	Yes	No	No	No	Yes	No

138

2. NEW LUXEMBOURG/U.S. INCOME TAX TREATY

As was discussed, U.S. MNCs seek to minimize their total tax costs. Hence, one sub goal is to reduce/avoid foreign withholding taxes on any type of foreign income.[840] From a tax planning point of view, attention should be drawn to the new Luxembourg/U.S. tax convention, which took effect January 1, 2001, and might lead - together with the significant reduction in the Luxembourg corporate tax rate from 30 percent to 22 percent in 2002 - to a renaissance of the Luxembourg SOPARFI regime which was introduced in 1990.[841]

In the current assortment of existing U.S. tax treaties, only Luxembourg[842] withholds no taxes on dividend distributions made to a U.S. company which has a direct shareholding of at least 25 percent of the voting stock in a Luxembourg company during an uninterrupted period of at least two years preceding the date of distribution.[843] In cases where a U.S. company directly owns less than 25 percent but at least ten percent of the voting stock of a Luxembourg company, a withholding tax rate of five percent applies (Art. 10(2)(a)(i) of the Luxembourg/U.S. tax convention). Thus, the recent completed income tax treaty provides for a new kind of "substantial shareholding", i.e., a double privilege for "substantial shareholdings". Surpassing the advantages of the 1990 German/U.S. tax treaty, the new Luxembourg/U.S. income tax convention might represent the new U.S. treaty policy.

The interposition of a Luxembourg holding company might not only be recommended to a U.S. investor for bundling its EU operations, but Luxembourg might also serve as a gateway to Asia, e.g., Japan. Under the income tax treaty in place between the U.S. and Japan, a ten percent withholding tax on dividends received through a shareholding of at least ten percent has been agreed,[844] so a Luxembourg holding company might be beneficial in reducing these taxes. According to the tax convention in effect between Japan and Luxembourg, Japan has the right to withhold only five percent on dividend payments to Luxembourg. Hence, when interposing a Luxembourg SOPARFI, the tax costs would *ceteris paribus* be reduced by 50 percent.

Furthermore, interposing a Luxembourg holding company might also result in a favorable outcome for a Swiss operation of a U.S. MNC, as any withholding taxes could completely be avoided. i.e., no withholding taxes are due on either the dividend payments made by the Swiss operation to the interposed Luxembourg holding entity[845] or the transfer of these dividends received by the Luxembourg holding company to the ultimate U.S. parent company. Compared to a direct investment into Switzerland where withholding taxes would be triggered at a rate of five percent, the tax cost reduction would *ceteris paribus* amount to 100 percent.

---

[840] For details on the goals of a U.S. MNC, see *supra* page 39.

[841] See Rosenbach, G., *Steuerliche Parameter für die Internationale Standortwahl*, 1995, paragraph M 103; Zois, A., *Cardozo Journal of International and Comparative Law* 1999, 199; BDO, *SOPARFI*, 2001, introduction.

[842] Art. 10(2)(b) of the Double Tax Treaty between Luxembourg/U.S. See Gordon, R., Venuti, J. and Renfroe, D., *Tax Management International Journal* 2002 II, 180.

[843] See Warner, P. and Allgaier, D., *International Tax Review* 2001, 13.

[844] Art. 12(2)(b)(i) of the Double Tax Treaty between Japan/U.S.

[845] See Kessler, W., Dorfmueller, P., Schmidt, W. and Teufel, T., *Tax Notes International* 2001, 1219.

Fig. 8: Treaty Shopping by Using the New Double Tax Treaty between Luxembourg/U.S.

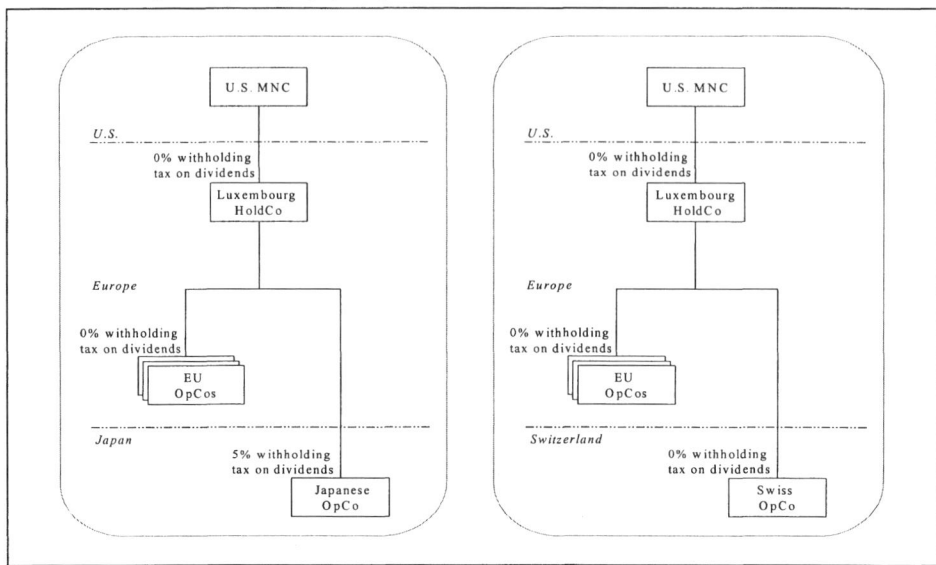

However, prior to implementing these structures, it must ultimately be determined whether the so-called *anti-treaty shopping provisions* will apply abroad, i.e., in Japan[846] and Switzerland.[847]

This Luxembourg/Swiss structure provides the U.S. MNC with a high level of flexibility as the Luxembourg holding company would not necessarily be required to directly own the (potential) stock in an Austrian, Danish, Dutch, Luxembourg, and Swedish, and maybe in the future, a German OpCo.[848] Rather, the Swiss operating company can hold the stock in the respective operating companies, as under each applicable tax treaty no withholding taxes on dividend income are levied.[849] Hence, a Swiss OpCo could own EU investments if business purposes would require such a structure.

---

[846] In Japan, no specific anti-treaty shopping provision exists. However, careful tax arbitrage planning is necessary. See Kawada, G., *Intertax* 1989, 361.

[847] In 1962, a decree was issued to prevent the use of any benefits granted under tax treaties, especially the reduction of or the exemption from withholding taxes on dividends, interest, and royalties. However, the decree applies only to structures where payments have been routed through Switzerland by non-residents who would otherwise not qualify for such a tax relief, i.e., Swiss interposed holding companies. Hence, the decree has no impact on a Swiss operating company. See Ryser, W., *Intertax* 1975, 60; Lüthi, D., *Intertax* 1989, 338; Baumann, S., *Steuersensitive Finanzierung der Holdinggesellschaft*, 1994, 147; Höhn, E., *Internationale Steuerplanung*, 1996, 383.

[848] The EU Parent-Subsidiary Directive would apply such that any withholding taxes on dividends within the Community would be avoided. The favorable tax treaty existing between the Netherlands and Switzerland is very well known and was used for the so-called *Swiss-Dutch Sandwiches*. Switzerland has actually negotiated a (revised) income tax treaty with Germany under which withholding taxes on dividends received on substantial shareholdings will be reduced to zero percent. The new tax treaty should take retroactive effect from January 1, 2002. See Bundesrat, Drucksache 324/02, 1; Bundestag, Drucksache 14/9201, 1; Huber, M. F., Kapalle, U. and Kubaile, H., *Steuer Revue* 2002, 371.

[849] See O'Grady, E., *Tax Notes International* 2002, 1065. The following table summarizes the details regarding the withholding taxes on dividends realized on substantial shareholdings under the respective double tax treaties:

Payor's Country of Residence	Art. of Respective Double Tax Treaty with Switzerland	Minimum Percentage Required
Austria	10(2)	20% of the capital
Denmark	10(1)	none
Luxembourg	10(2)(b)	25% of the capital during an uninterrupted period of two years preceding the date of payment of the dividends
The Netherlands	9(2)(a)(i)	25% of the capital
Sweden	10(2)	25% of the capital

3. DOUBLE DIP

3.1. Financing in a Luxembourg Holding Company Structure

A Luxembourg holding company structure might not only be beneficial for withholding tax purposes, but might further achieve a double dip of interest expenses and may convert taxable types of income into tax-free receipts. Hence, it would reduce the overall tax burden of a U.S. MNC. For example, presume the U.S. investor company borrows debt from a (third-party) bank in the U.S. and then lends those funds to the Luxembourg corporation. In turn, the Luxembourg company itself extends loans to several EU operating corporations.

Fig. 9: Double Dip in a Luxembourg Holding Company Structure

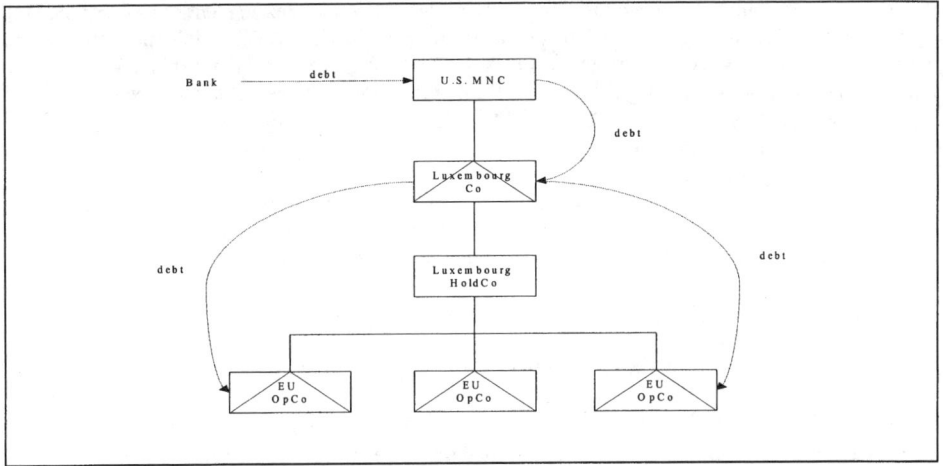

All dividend payments made by the EU operating companies to the Luxembourg SOPARFI (HoldCo) will benefit from the EU Parent-Subsidiary Directive, i.e., local withholding taxes will be avoided.[850] Interest paid to the Luxembourg company is generally deductible for tax purposes in all member states, presuming that the companies are not related for the purpose of financing any investments and respective thin capitalization provisions do not apply. Due to this intra-group loan, profits are converted from (potential) dividend income into interest income. As a result, profits will be shifted from a European jurisdiction with a high effective corporate tax rate, such as Austria (34 percent), France (35.43 percent), or Germany (about 40 percent) to Luxembourg, which levies tax at a comparable low effective rate of 30.38 percent. The dividends received by the Luxembourg holding company can be transferred to its Luxembourg parent on a tax-exempt basis under the domestic participation exemption.[851] Under Luxembourg law, the interest expenses incurred on the loan from the U.S. parent are deductible by the Luxembourg company in computing its profits, subject to tax. The respective interest payments are not subject to any Luxembourg withholding taxes, according to the Luxembourg/U.S. income tax convention.[852]

For U.S. tax purposes, the U.S. MNC checks the box for the Luxembourg corporation to make the Luxembourg corporation a Luxembourg branch for the U.S. investor corporation. Thus, for U.S. federal tax purposes, the interest payments made to U.S. MNC are incurred by a branch of the ultimate

---

[850] See PricewaterhouseCoopers, *Holding Companies*, 2002, 6.

[851] For details on the Luxembourg domestic participation exemption, refer *supra* page 125. The double Luxembourg entity structure is necessary to avoid any U.S. tax consequences. See *infra* page 142.

[852] Art. 12(1) of the Double Tax Treaty between Luxembourg/U.S.

U.S. parent and are tax-deductible, i.e., lower the tax base and, hence, the total tax costs. Any dividends received by the ultimate U.S. parent from the branch are free of any withholding taxes.[853] Further, for U.S. federal tax purposes, the U.S. parent company checks the box for the European OpCos to receive flow-through status and, hence, avoid the constitution of Subpart F income, i.e., the same country exception (IRC § 954(c)(3)(A)(i)) would apply.[854]

The double Luxembourg entity structure is necessary to avoid any flow-through of EU OpCos' profits to the U.S. MNC which would be included in U.S. taxable income. Put another way, the tax planning goal of tax deferral would not have been achieved without the double entity structure. Depending on the tax status of the two Luxembourg entities, it might be recommended that a tax consolidation group be established in Luxembourg. In the simplified structure discussed, the tax consolidation group is *ceteris paribus* not necessary from a tax point of view, as Luxembourg Co receives interest income which is offset by related interest expenses. Hence, no unutilized losses would be triggered.

The significance of this structure is that the interest paid to the U.S. MNC by the Luxembourg company is not recognized as a taxable receipt since it is paid within the same entity as far as the U.S. tax authorities are concerned. Thus, while the interest paid by the U.S. MNC is deductible for U.S. tax purposes, the interest received is not subject to tax. It should be noted that care must be taken to ensure that the interest paid to the U.S. company is at arm's length rates to comply with U.S. and Luxembourg transfer pricing regulations.[855] This effectively results in double relief for the same interest payment, without a matching tax liability, i.e., conversion of taxable dividend income into tax-exempt interest income.

In summary, when setting up this structure, a shift of income within Europe to a low taxation environment is achieved. Furthermore, a double dip of interest expenses as well as recognition of tax-free receipts is accomplished. Hence, this structure provides three different starting points for reducing total tax costs.

3.2. Financing Through a German Double KG Structure

The 2001 German Tax Reform has increased the attractiveness of Germany as a location for holding companies.[856] As a result, it might be recommended that a p.e. be set up as a holding entity, as foreign and domestic dividends received as well as capital gains recognized on shares indirectly held through a partnership which apportions its income by source among the partners, are tax exempt.[857] Moreover, profit repatriations of the p.e. to the foreign headquarters can be made without triggering any taxes, as Germany does not impose any branch profits tax.[858] Further, as the German thin capitalization provisions do not apply to German domestic partnerships,[859] the implementation of a partnership holding structure might be beneficial for a U.S. MNC.[860]

---

[853] See structure under the new Luxembourg/U.S. tax treaty *supra* page 139.

[854] See Zink, W. J., *The Tax Adviser* 1997, 81. For the same country exception in detail, see *supra* page 96.

[855] In the U.S. IRC § 482 must be considered. For details, refer *supra* page 85.

[856] See Endres, D. and Dorfmueller, P., *Praxis Internationale Steuerberatung* 2001, 103; Endres, D. and Möller, M., *Corporate Taxation*, 2001, E 62; Kessler, W., Dorfmueller, P., Schmidt, W. and Teufel, T., *Tax Notes International* 2001, 1217.

[857] See Endres, D. and Möller, M., *Corporate Taxation*, 2001, E 97.

[858] See Endres, D., Dorfmueller, P. and Urse, M., *International Tax Report* 2001 I, 6; Kessler, W., Dorfmueller, P., Schmidt, W. and Teufel, T., *Tax Notes International* 2001, 1221.

[859] In general, German partnerships are transparent for income tax purposes but they are taxable entities for trade tax purposes. Trade tax is a municipal levy aimed at compensating towns, villages, and smaller communities for additional expenses that are indirectly caused by the presence of a business within their regional areas. Trade tax is imposed on taxable income as determined for corporation tax purposes, adjusted for various items. In practical terms, one of the most important adjustments is usually the add-back of long-term interest costs that are fully deductible for corporation tax purposes, but are only deductible up to one-half for trade tax purposes. It should be noted that the German thin capitalization provisions do not apply to trade tax. Further, according to § 9 No. 2a of the *Gewerbesteuergesetz*, the profits from shares in a non tax exempt domestic corporation reduce the total of the profit and the amounts added back, provided that the investment was at least one-tenth of the issued share capital at the beginning of the period of levy and the shares of profits is included in the computation

Creating a p.e. or participating in a partnership generally creates a German tax obligation for the foreign investor. A German partnership is equated with a p.e. as it is also transparent for German tax purposes. The profits accrued at the partnership level are allocated among the partners in whose hands they are taxed at individual rates, as though they had been earned directly. The profits attributed to the foreign corporate owner through the German p.e. or partnership interest will be taxed at the same rates that apply to a German subsidiary.[861]

Assume U.S. MNC establishes a German partnership structure after having recognized the inherent tax benefits. Under German civil law, a KG (limited partnership) requires at least two partners: one with unlimited liability (general partner; the so-called *Komplementär*) and one with liability limited to capital contributions (limited partner; the so-called *Kommanditist*).[862] Hence, it is necessary to set up further entities. First, a German general partner must be established. In order to avoid the risk of unlimited liability of the general partner, the U.S. MNC would usually incorporate a German GmbH whose liability is limited by German commercial law. The potential liability amounts to at least € 25,000, as this is the minimum capital required.[863] Second, the U.S. company, U.S. Co., can function as the limited partner.

Fig. 10: Double Dip in a German Double KG Structure

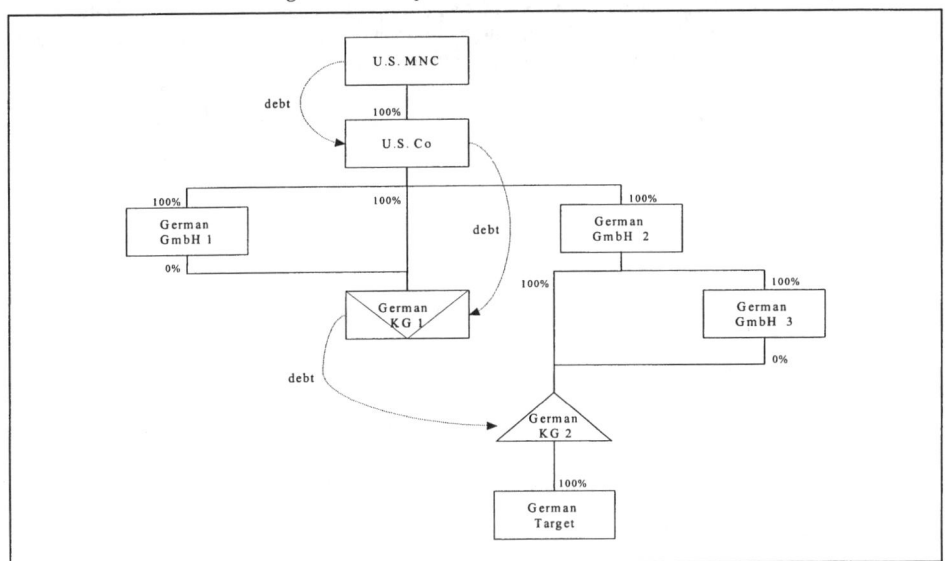

of profit. The adjusted trade income is subject to a five percent trade tax, which is then increased by a local multiplier set by each single municipality. For 2001, local multipliers for municipalities with a population of 100,000 and higher range from 380 percent (e.g., Cottbus and Wolfsburg) to 515 percent (e.g., Frankfurt am Main). However, some trade tax havens exists, i.e., municipalities, where the multiplier amounts to zero percent. For example, Norderfriedrichskoog. Presuming that the business is located within the area of more than one municipality, the tax base must be divided among the local authorities. As the trade tax base is apportioned by wages and salaries, it might be beneficial to relocate business activities, in particular, only the management. The trade tax income is deductible not only from its own base of assessment, but also for corporation tax purposes. See Fleischer, K., *Fusion & Acquisitions Magazine* 2000, 26; Herold, C., *Gestaltende Steuerberatung* 2001, 67. For the taxation of a German partnership in detail, refer Lethaus, H. J. and Mohr, H., *Bulletin for International Fiscal Documentation* 2000, 397.

[860] See Endres, D. and Dorfmueller, P., *Praxis Internationale Steuerberatung* 2001, 103; Kessler, W., Dorfmueller, P., Schmidt, W. and Teufel, T., *Tax Notes International* 2001, 1217.

[861] Corporation tax of 25 percent, solidarity surcharge at a rate of 5.5 percent thereon, and municipal trade tax.

[862] See Endres, D. and Ditsch, S., *The International Tax Journal* 1999, 24.

[863] § 5(1) of the *Gesetz betreffend die Gesellschaften mit beschränkter Haftung (GmbHG)*.

If a U.S. MNC intends to expand its existing German operations via acquisitions, the ultimate parent company should use another German partnership, KG 2, as the acquisition vehicle. The acquisition price of German Target can be fully loaned by KG 1 to KG 2, as no debt-to-equity limitation applies to partnerships. Thus, KG 2 can make a 100 percent debt funded acquisition on behalf of U.S. MNC. But where will KG 1 get the liquidity? For example, U.S. MNC can loan funds to U.S. Co. and U.S. Co. in turn, can lend those funds to German KG 1. This chain of loans might be a tool to decrease the overall tax costs of U.S. MNC. Under German laws, since partnerships are not taxable as such for income tax purposes, any profits and expenses flow-through to the partners. Hence, the interest paid by partnerships (KG 2 and KG 1) are business expenditures at the level of the partners. By using this structure a double dip might be achieved. Interest payments on funds borrowed by U.S. MNC are tax deductible in the U.S. These interest payments also result in tax deductions in Germany as they relate to the investment in the German KG 1 (the so-called *Sonderbetriebsvermögen II*).

KG 1 should be elected to be treated as a corporation for U.S. federal tax purposes in order to defer any U.S taxes. The reverse hybrid is a conduit under German tax law and, hence, the income earned by the partnership will be allocated pro rata among the partners. In order to avoid any negative tax consequences in Germany, KG 1 should be a non-business entity, i.e., its principal activity should be property management. Thus, the purpose of the KG should be very specifically and precisely formulated. German KG 1 receives interest income on the funds loaned to the acquisition vehicle. The interest income, passive income within the meaning of Subpart F, would classify as foreign personal holding company income under Subpart F. As the interest income was earned within Germany, the same country exception (IRC § 954(c)(3)) applies, i.e., U.S. tax deferral is achieved.[864]

To sum up, this acquisition structure achieves a double dip of interest expenses and full U.S. tax deferral.

4. ACHIEVING FULL FTC BY ISSUING A HYBRID INSTRUMENT

4.1 Financing in a Dutch Holding Company Structure

If a U.S. investor company chooses the Netherlands as a more or less "classical" jurisdiction for establishing EU holding companies, a transaction designed to use hybrid entities, including a hybrid instrument, might offer further tax arbitrage opportunities. While a hybrid entity is an entity that is treated as a corporation by one country and as a flow-through entity by another country,[865] a hybrid instrument is a financial obligation that is classified as equity in one country and as debt by another country.

For example, the U.S. MNC issues a hybrid instrument to the Dutch B.V. The U.S. treats the instrument as equity. The Netherlands treats the instrument as debt. The Dutch B.V. then lends funds to several EU operating companies.

---

[864] For details on the same country exception, refer *supra* page 96.

[865] For the definition and the tax treatment of a hybrid entity, see *supra* page 75.

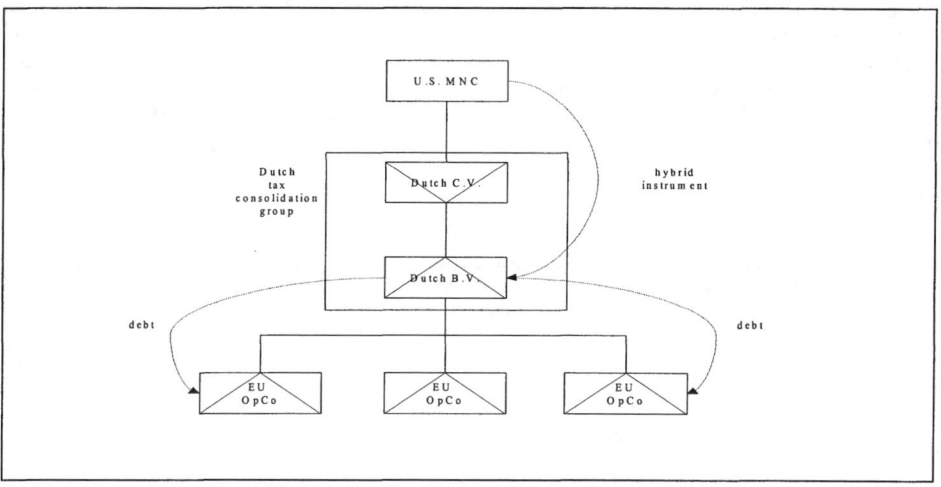

All dividends paid by the EU operating companies to the Dutch B.V. will generally benefit from the EU Parent-Subsidiary Directive, i.e., local withholding taxes will be avoided.[866] The interest payments made by the EU OpCos are generally subject to withholding tax and are typically tax-deductible in each jurisdiction. In cases, where the effective corporate tax rate applied at the level of the European OpCos is higher than the corporate tax rate imposed on interest income in the Netherlands, the conversion of (potential) dividends into interest income would *ceteris paribus* result in a permanent tax saving.

At the level of the Dutch B.V., payments on the hybrid instrument are treated as interest expenses in the Netherlands and, thus, are tax-deductible by the B.V. in computing its profits, subject to Dutch tax. Further, as the Netherlands view the payments on the instrument as interest expenditures, the interest paid to the U.S. MNC is not subject to any withholding taxes in the Netherlands.[867] For Dutch tax purposes, it is necessary to interpose a Dutch C.V. and to enter into a tax consolidation group in order to be able to time the dividend distributions to the U.S. MNC.

The U.S. MNC checks the box for the Dutch C.V. to make the Dutch partnership a Dutch corporation, i.e., a subsidiary of the U.S. MNC, in order to prevent any flow-through of profits. For U.S. federal tax purposes, the U.S. MNC further checks the box for the Dutch B.V and the EU OpCos to avoid any Subpart F income, i.e., the same country exception would apply. As the hybrid instrument is treated as equity in the U.S., any foreign taxes paid qualify for the full amount of FTC under U.S. tax law.

In summary, U.S. MNC is entitled to claim a FTC for taxes paid on amounts loaned to the Dutch B.V. and there is no pick up of taxable dividend income in the Netherlands.

4.2. Financing in a German Holding Company Structure

To fully optimize a holding company structure, a transaction involving a hybrid instrument, that is classified differently from the example above, might offer further tax opportunities, including the entitlement to claim a FTC for the full amount of withholding taxes paid abroad. Assume a German corporation, whose only common stock is owned by U.S. MNC, issues a hybrid instrument to a foreign investor. Also assume that the foreign investor is a resident in Germany, but is an unrelated

---

[866] See PricewaterhouseCoopers, *Holding Companies*, 2002, 6.

[867] Under the tax convention between Germany and the U.S., it has been agreed that a zero percent withholding tax on interest will apply (Art. 11(1)).

person to German Co. The German corporation subsequently purchases preferred stock of a foreign corporation (hereafter "ForCo"). ForCo pays annual dividends which will be subject to a foreign withholding tax at a rate of ten percent. Suppose that Germany treats the instrument as an equity investment in German Co. In contrast thereto, under the laws of the U.S., the hybrid instrument from the German unrelated investor to German Co is treated as debt. Furthermore, the German corporation will be a disregarded entity under the check-the-box regulations, as U.S. MNC elected to have it classified as a single member entity.

Fig. 12: Achieving Full U.S. FTC by Issuing a Hybrid Instrument in Germany

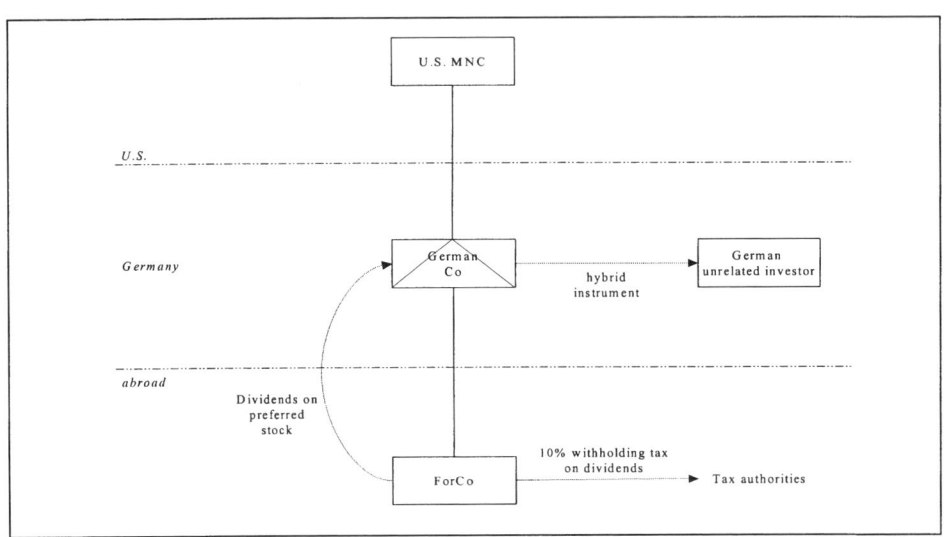

Under foreign law, both the U.S. and foreign investors share the foreign withholding tax pro-rata, each claiming a credit against any foreign country tax due on their share of the German entity's income. Because the loan is respected for U.S tax purposes and the U.S. MNC is regarded as the sole owner of the German entity that is a branch of a U.S. taxpayer for U.S. tax purposes, the U.S. MNC is entitled to claim a FTC for the full amount of the withholding taxes paid to the foreign country.

The significant effect of this structure is that, due to the inconsistent classification of the hybrid instrument by Germany and the U.S., the German unrelated investor and the U.S. MNC can duplicate the benefit of the FTC.

It should be noted that any other country that classifies the hybrid instrument as equity under domestic law would work in place of Germany. An all-inclusive list of countries cannot be provided here, however, as the inconsistent treatment of a hybrid instrument only results if the hybrid instrument lacks more debt than equity characteristics, which must be determined through a complex examination process.[868] Furthermore, many different kinds of hybrid instruments have been created and an examination of each one is beyond the scope of this analysis.

To sum up, under U.S. rules, the distribution to the foreign investor is treated as a deductible interest payment and the distribution of the after-tax earnings to the U.S. investor is treated as a dividend which entitles the U.S. investor to a IRC § 902 credit.

---

[868] For the criteria used in the classification of a hybrid instrument by the IRS and the courts, see Dilworth, R. H. and Andrus, J. L., *Tax Law and Practice*, 2001, 1113; Bittker, B. I., Emory, M. and Streng, W. P., *Federal Income Taxation of Corporations and Shareholders*, 2002, paragraph 4.1; Bittker, B. I. and Eustice, J. S., *Federal Income Taxation of Corporations and Shareholders*, 2002, paragraph 4.02. Notice 94-47, 1994-19 I.R.B. 9.

5. SHIFTING INCOME TO LOW-TAX JURISDICTIONS

As was discussed, another tool which can be utilized to minimize overall tax costs is the shifting of income out of high-tax and into low-tax jurisdictions.[869] Assume U.S. MNC uses an affiliate entity located in a jurisdiction with a low corporate tax rate, e.g., Ireland, to finance an operation in a high-tax jurisdiction, e.g., another business carried on in the U.S. Income generated by the U.S. operating company would be subject to a 35 percent federal corporate tax rate.

Fig. 13: Shifting of Income via a U.S. Hybrid Entity

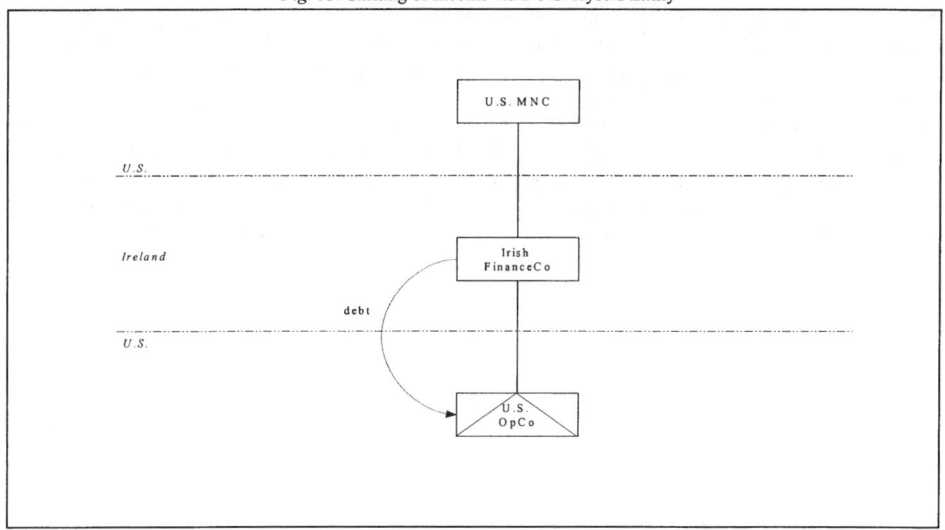

In order to shift income out of this high-tax jurisdiction, Irish FinanceCo issues an interest bearing loan to U.S. OpCo. Under tax law in the U.S., interest expenses are tax deductible and reduce the U.S. tax base. Suppose the interest payment amounts to 100, the U.S. tax liability would be reduced *ceteris paribus* by 35. The interest payments on the loan constitute interest income at the level of Irish FinanceCo. The Irish tax authorities will impose taxes on the income at a rate of ten percent until 2002 or 2010, respectively.[870] From 2003 [2011] onward, when the tax incentives have expired, the ordinary corporate tax rate of 12.5 percent will apply. Hence, up to the 2002 [2010] tax year, the overall tax liability could be reduced *ceteris paribus* by 25. After that the structure would lead to a marginal tax cost saving of 22.5. If the U.S. OpCo is treated as a corporation for U.S. tax purposes, the interest received by Irish FinanceCo would be foreign personal holding company income, taxable to U.S. MNC under the Subpart F provisions, assuming that the *de minimis* rule of IRC § 954(b)(3)(A) does not apply.

As was proven in the examination of the previous structures, hybrid entities are essential to many cross-border tax arbitrage transactions. So, suppose U.S. OpCo is a domestic company that is eligible to choose its classification as a transparent or corporate entity. For example, the domestic business entity is not an entity incorporated in any U.S. state which appears on the *per se* list. If U.S. MNC checks the box for the U.S. operating entity, the entity will be disregarded as a separate entity. The U.S. will classify the loan agreement as a non-event because Irish FinanceCo and U.S. OpCo are treated as one entity and intercompany loans are ignored. Under U.S. tax law there will be no realization of interest income and no constitution of Subpart F income at the level of U.S. MNC. Tax

---

[869] See *supra* page 68.

[870] For details on the Irish IFSC regime and the respective expiration dates, see *supra* note 339.

arbitrage is achieved here through an interest payment, i.e., shifting of income to a jurisdiction with a low corporate tax rate, so that the overall tax liability will be reduced without an immediate increase in the U.S. tax liability.[871]

However, the overall tax saving would only be permanent if the loan agreement meets the arm's length standard, i.e., the agreed interest rate does not exceed the actual market interest rate. Otherwise, the foreign jurisdiction would add-back the excess and tax it. In the above structure, the U.S. would apply IRC § 482.

Another illustration of tax arbitrage involving hybrid entities involves a holding company carrying on business through several European operating companies. Assume U.S. MNC owns a German AG, which is a *per se* corporation under the check-the-box regulations. The AG will be classified as a corporation for both U.S. and German tax purposes. For illustration purposes, suppose that German AG owns all the shares of two entities: another (high-taxed) German operating corporation and a corporation in Ireland, a jurisdiction with a low corporate tax rate. Suppose that Irish OpCo issues an interest-bearing loan to German OpCo. Under the laws of Germany, the interest expenses incurred by German OpCo are tax-deductible and will lower the German tax base. Assume the interest payments would amount to 100, the tax saving in Germany would be 32, i.e., interest expenses multiplied by the German effective tax rate of approximately 40 percent and a 50 percent add-back for trade tax purposes,[872] presuming an effective trade tax rate of 16 percent. Conversely, Irish OpCo will generate interest income of 100 and will result in a tax liability of 16 in 2002 [12.5 from 2003 onward], assuming that Irish OpCo does not qualify for the IFSC regime.

Fig. 14: Shifting of Income via a Foreign Hybrid Entity

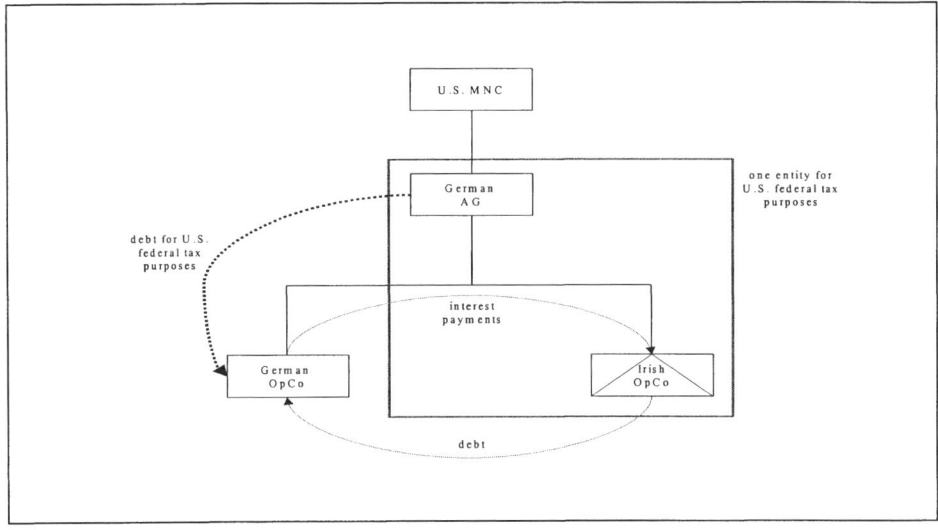

In total, the overall foreign tax savings would amount to 16 [19.5 from 2003 onward]. However, it must be determined whether the tax savings would be permanent or whether Subpart F income would be created for U.S. MNC. Provided that Irish OpCo is classified as a corporation for U.S. tax purposes, U.S. MNC must include *ceteris paribus* the interest income earned by the low-taxed Irish OpCo as Subpart F income (FPHC income as part of FBCI) in its tax base, assuming that the *de minimis* rule of IRC § 954(b)(3)(A) does not apply. Hence, no tax deferral would be achieved.

---

[871] The proposed regulations issued by the Department of the Treasury relating to U.S. domestic hybrid entities must be considered (Prop. Regs. § 1.894-1(d)(2)). Under these regulations, a structure including a domestic hybrid entity might be classified as tax abusive if the structure would result in non-taxed income. See Flick, H. F. W., *Internationales Steuerrecht* 2001 II, 6.

[872] § 8 Nr. 1 of the *Gewerbesteuergesetz*.

Furthermore, assume that U.S. MNC sets-up Irish OpCo as an eligible entity under the U.S. check-the-box regulations and elects that the Irish corporation be a single member entity. Hence, for U.S. federal tax purposes, Irish OpCo will be disregarded and all income and expenses will flow through to German AG, the holding company. The U.S. will treat Irish OpCo and German AG as one entity. The loan made by Irish OpCo will be treated by the U.S. as a loan from German AG to its German subsidiary and, therefore, German AG is deemed to have interest income of 100. Subpart F income would not arise in the case of the hybridization as the interest income is generated by a related party located in the same country as the payor, i.e., the same country exception in IRC § 954(c)(3) applies.

6. ACHIEVING TAX-EXEMPT CAPITAL GAINS

Given that capital gains recognized from the sale of a subsidiary are generally taxed at 35 percent at the U.S. federal level, some might assume that a (potential) capital gain would be better realized by an interposed holding company which is resident in a jurisdiction that grants a liberal exemption for capital gains.

At present, the most preferential jurisdiction for such an endeavor is Germany that provides a tax-exemption for capital gains recognized from the disposal of both German domestic and foreign stock, irrespective of any minimum ownership percentage and holding period.[873] Other EU member states including Belgium, Denmark, Luxembourg, and the Netherlands also exempt domestic and foreign capital gains from taxation. However, in these countries, certain prerequisites regarding the level of shareholding and duration of ownership must be met.[874]

Fig. 15: Inefficient Structure to Achieve Deferral on Tax-Exempt Capital Gains

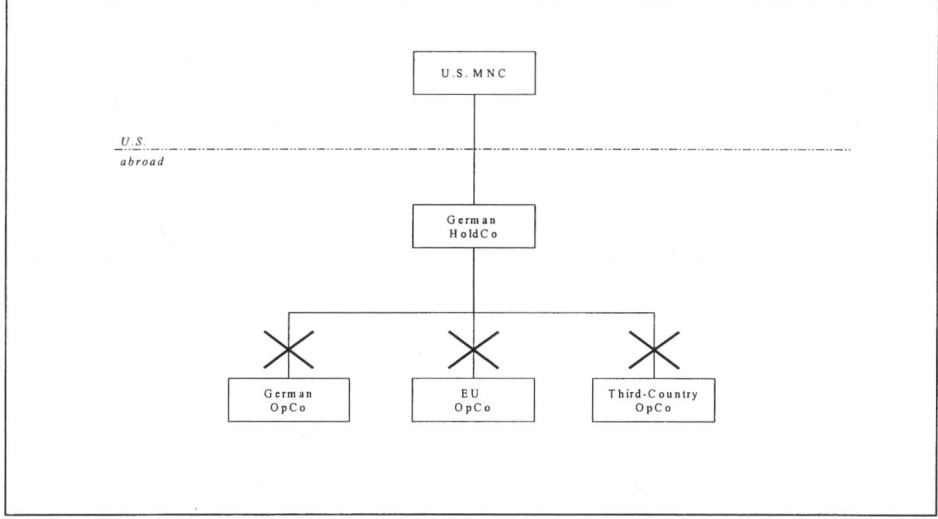

Such a structure might not be efficient in minimizing the overall effective tax burden, as the "capital gain exemption" effect would be counteracted by the Subpart F provisions. As was discussed, capital gains recognized by the interposed holding company would be FPHC income at the level of U.S. MNC. Thus, no tax deferral would be achieved, provided that the *de minimis* rule of

---

[873] See *supra* Chapter "Country-by-Country Synopsis", page 111.

[874] See *supra* Chapter "Country-by-Country Synopsis", page 111.

IRC § 954(b)(3)(A) does not apply. Given that any capital gains are exempt from taxation, the high-tax exception would also not be applicable. Nor would the same-country exception apply on capital gains realized on the disposal of stock in another domestic company, as the exception under IRC § 954(c)(3)(A)(i) is granted only for dividends and interest income.

An international tax practitioner would examine different tax planning tools in order to avoid the application of an anti-deferral regime. Once more, the appropriate tool would be the check-the-box regulations. Assume German HoldCo, which is a 100 percent subsidiary of U.S. MNC, holds stock in another German corporation, an EU OpCo, and an operating company incorporated in an external jurisdiction. If the U.S. MNC checks the box for all of the second-tier companies, they would be treated as disregarded entities for U.S. federal tax purposes. Put another way, the U.S. would treat German OpCo, EU OpCo, Third-Country OpCo, and German HoldCo as one entity.

Fig. 16: Structure to Achieve Deferral on Tax-Exempt Capital Gains

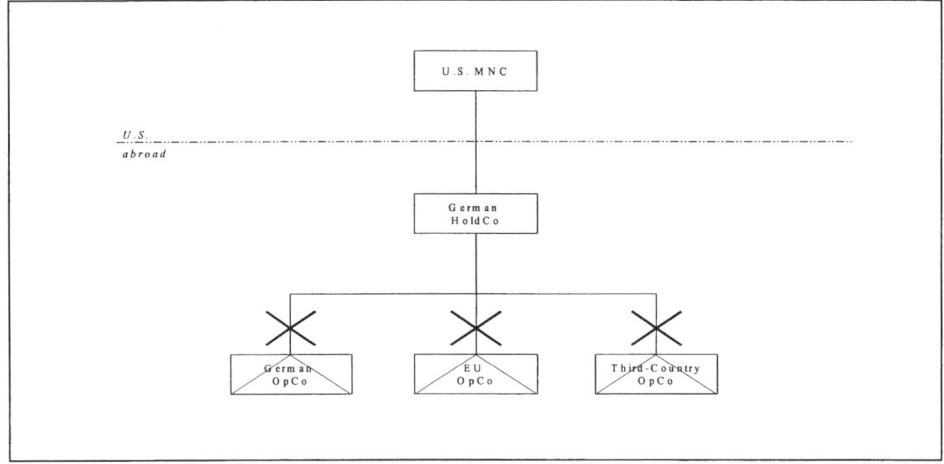

The significance of this structure is that the capital gains realized are not recognized as a taxable receipt since they are incurred within the same entity as far as the U.S. tax authorities are concerned. Hence, due to the interposition of a German holding company, any capital gains taxation would be completely eliminated.

7. NEW U.K. ONSHORE POOLING PROVISION

Prior to March 31, 2001, U.K. holding companies tended to hold non-U.K. operations through a Dutch holding company in order to realize certain tax planning benefits. First, income generated by the Dutch holding company benefited from a liberal participation exemption.[875] Any gross dividend income could be paid between the Dutch corporation and the U.K. company under the EU Parent-Subsidiary Directive. The ultimate U.S. parent company checked the box for the subsidiaries which led to a more tax efficient structure globally than if dividends were paid directly to the ultimate parent by the Dutch company, since they would be subject to a five percent withholding tax in the Netherlands.[876]

---

[875] For the Dutch participation exemption in detail, see *supra* page 127. The U.K. exempts capital gains recognized from substantial shareholdings, if certain prerequisites are met, from July 1, 2002 onward. For details on this new regime, see Kessler, W. and Dorfmueller, P., *Internationales Steuerrecht* 2003, forthcoming.

[876] See Cussons, P., Dorfmueller, P. and Endres, D., *European Holding Companies*, 2002, 6-9.

Another benefit of such a structure was the ability to achieve dividend-mixing. The interposed Dutch holding company mixed income from both non-U.K. high and low-tax sources with the goal of maximizing U.K. double taxation relief. The ideas was that a dividend distribution made by the Dutch mixer company would be a single dividend, i.e., not taxed on a strictly source-by-source basis, creating the largest possible tax credit as a result of blending taxes paid by several foreign operating companies.

Fig. 17: Former U.K. Offshore Mixing

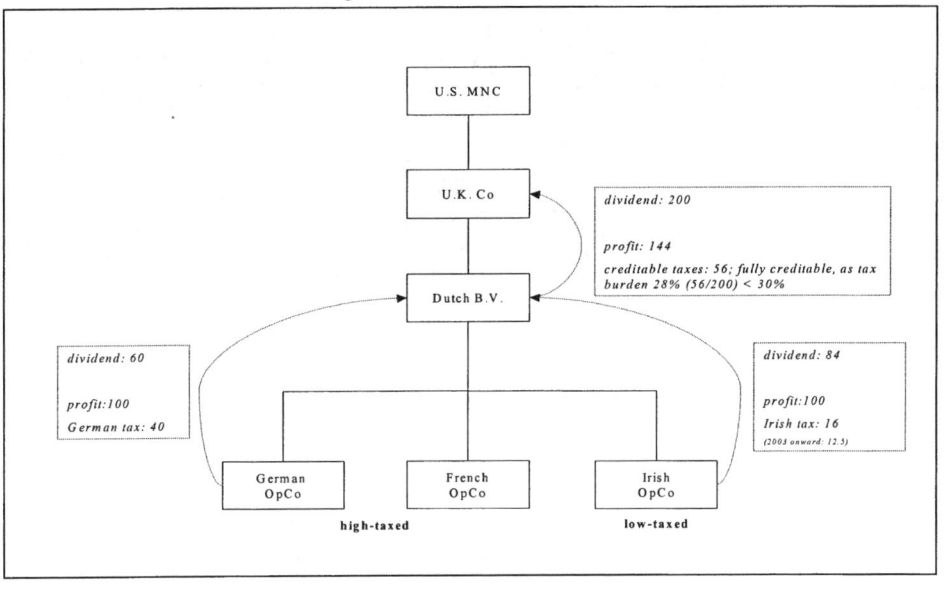

From March 31, 2001, the system of offshore mixing (the so-called *mixer cap*) has been abolished and replaced by a more restrictive form of onshore pooling.[877] Hence, the structure displayed above is no longer tax efficient. The new pooling system will operate by allowing certain low-taxed dividends to be pooled onshore, and by permitting eligible unrelieved foreign tax (EUFT) on high-taxed dividends to be credited against the U.K. tax on the pooled low-taxed income.[878] The U.K. tax liability would be the same as under the mixer company structure in place prior to March 31, 2001.

However, the extent of onshore pooling is subject to two limitations. The first restriction relates to the 30 percent mixer cap, which caps all foreign underlying tax in excess of 30 percent on dividends paid between different jurisdictions by using the formula $(D + U) * M$ percent where D is the dividend received, U the underlying foreign tax and M the U.K. corporate tax rate (currently 30%).[879] EUFT only arises on the highest taxed dividend that is subjected to the 30 percent cap.[880] Hence, if a dividend is distributed to the U.K. through a chain of foreign companies, and on its route the 30 percent mixer cap is applied more than once, EUFT will only arise on the highest taxed dividends subjected to the 30 percent cap, and no relief will be allowed for any capped foreign tax on lower taxed dividends.[881]

---

[877] See Cussons, P., Dorfmueller, P. and Endres, D., *European Holding Companies*, 2002, 6-11.

[878] See Ruchelman, S. C., Asbeck, E. van, Canalejo, G. and et. al., *Journal of International Taxation* 2001 II, 24.

[879] See Howlett, K., Reed, M. and Sylvester, C., *Journal of International Taxation* 2000, 16; Sandison, F. G., *Tax Planning International Forum* 2002, 40.

[880] See Cussons, P., Dorfmueller, P. and Endres, D., *European Holding Companies*, 2002, 6-10.

[881] § 806 B(3)-(5) of the *Income and Corporation Tax Act 1988*. See Sandison, F. G., *Tax Planning International Forum* 2002, 41.

The second limitation applies when an offshore holding company receives high-taxed dividends that are subjected to both a 30 percent mixer cap and low-taxed dividends. When the combined dividends are repatriated to the U.K., they will have been subject to a tax rate that is lower than 30 percent as a result of the 30 percent mixer cap. Therefore, an incremental U.K. tax will arise on the dividends. Given that the EUFT has already applied to them, the dividends are excluded from onshore pooling,[882] even though the FTCs are less than 30 percent. Put another way, the EUFT that was triggered by the lower level of high-taxed dividends cannot be offset against the significant residual U.K. tax imposed on the dividends received in the U.K. Any U.K. tax on other low-taxed pooled dividends can only be sheltered by the EUFT. The new provisions allow a three year carry back of EUFT or a unlimited carry forward period.[883]

Under the new rules, it is recommended that U.K. companies move from the structure displayed above to a structure in which high- and low-tax subsidiaries are held through separate holding companies or directly from the U.K.[884]

Fig. 18: U.K. Onshore Pooling

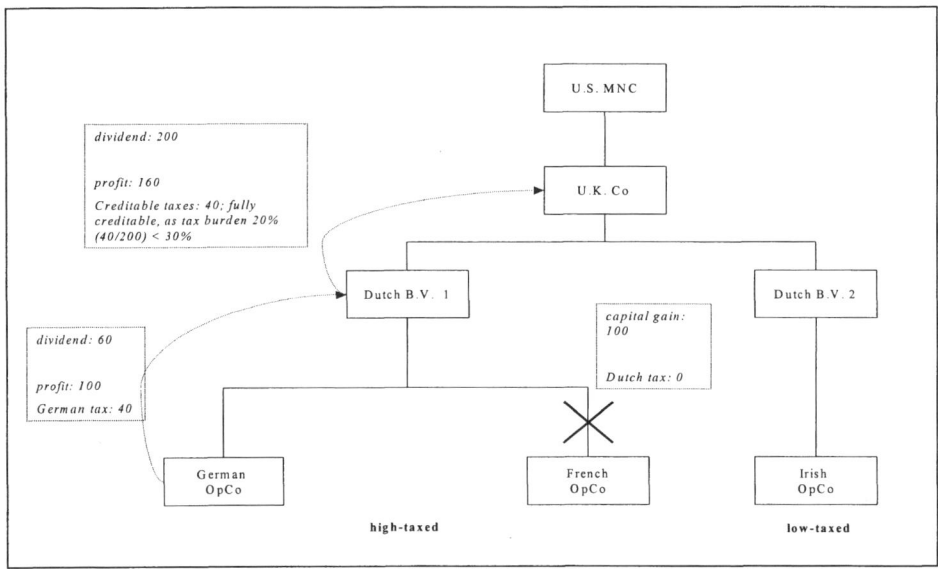

For example, assume a Dutch holding company disposes of its French subsidiary, realizing a tax-free capital gain pursuant to the Dutch participation exemption regime. In the same period, German OpCo pays a dividend to Dutch B.V. 1 which is ultimately paid to the U.K. company. In the event that the Dutch holding company has received no other income apart from the German dividend and the French capital gain, the CFC provisions would not apply in the U.K, as § 13 of the *Taxation of Chargeable Gains Act 1992* applies only where the non-U.K. company is a close company. In general, a company is a close company if it is under control of five or fewer participators. However, it will not be a close company, if it is both:[885]

---

[882] § 806 C(1)(c) of the *Income and Corporation Tax Act 1988.*

[883] See Sandison, F. G., *Tax Planning International Forum* 2002, 41.

[884] See Cussons, P., Dorfmueller, P. and Endres, D., *European Holding Companies*, 2002, 6-11; Sandison, F. G., *Tax Management International Forum* 2002, 40.

[885] § 414 of the *Income and Corporation Tax Act 1988.*

(1) controlled by a company that is not a close company, or by two or more companies none of which is a close company; and

(2) it cannot be treated as a close company except taking as one of the five or fewer owners requite for being so treated a company is not a close company.

Under the new law, it is only possible to determine the period in which a dividend has been paid but it is not possible to explicitly identify highly taxed profits. Given that the German-source dividend and the French-source capital gain arise in the same taxable year, the subsequent dividend distribution made to the U.K. is deemed to arise from a blend of the 30 percent tax-capped German profits and the tax-free capital gain recognized from the sale of the French subsidiary, thereby resulting in an underlying tax rate much lower than 30 percent.

To sum up, any U.K. tax on other low-taxed pooled dividends can only be sheltered by the EUFT. Hence, U.S. MNCs that have chosen the U.K. as the location for their holding company must reconsider their group structure and might adjust it from the offshore mixing structure to the onshore structure displayed above.

8. SPAIN AS A GATEWAY TO ARGENTINA

As of December 31, 2001, the U.S. had income tax treaties in place with 64 countries,[886] however, no tax conventions exist with Argentina.[887] Thus, when a U.S. MNC carries on business through an Argentine subsidiary, the withholding tax rate imposed under local law would apply on dividend payments to the U.S. Under Argentine tax law, a 35 percent withholding tax on dividend payments is levied.

As the South American market might be of high relevance for a U.S. MNC, especially in the textile industry, the interposition of a holding company might be considered.[888] Since it is very well recognized that changes in local tax laws are frequent and abolishment of earlier tax laws are sometimes repealed, a U.S. MNC might consider bundling all of its operations in South America through a Spanish holding entity, not only for tax reasons such as the potential re-introduction of withholding taxes, but also to overcome potential language barriers. Due to their historic relationship, favorable tax treaties exist between Spain and Argentina.

---

[886] See Gordon, R., Venuti, J. and Renfroe, D., *Tax Management International Journal* 2002 I, 114.

[887] Argentina is actively negotiating a tax treaty with the U.S. Argentina and the U.S. had their preliminary talks in 1992 and correspondence relating to the treaty has been sent by the U.S. to Argentina. See Gordon, R., Venuti, J. and Renfroe, D., *Tax Management International Journal* 2002 I, 117.

[888] For example, in 2000, U.S. direct investments in Argentina reached approximately U.S. $18 billion. Due to the 2001 Investment Climate Statement of Argentina, the U.S. and Spain were the largest foreign investors in Argentina, which might prove the discussed structure of an interposed Spanish holding company is of particular relevance. See Embassy of the United States of America, *2001 Statement*, paragraph 36.

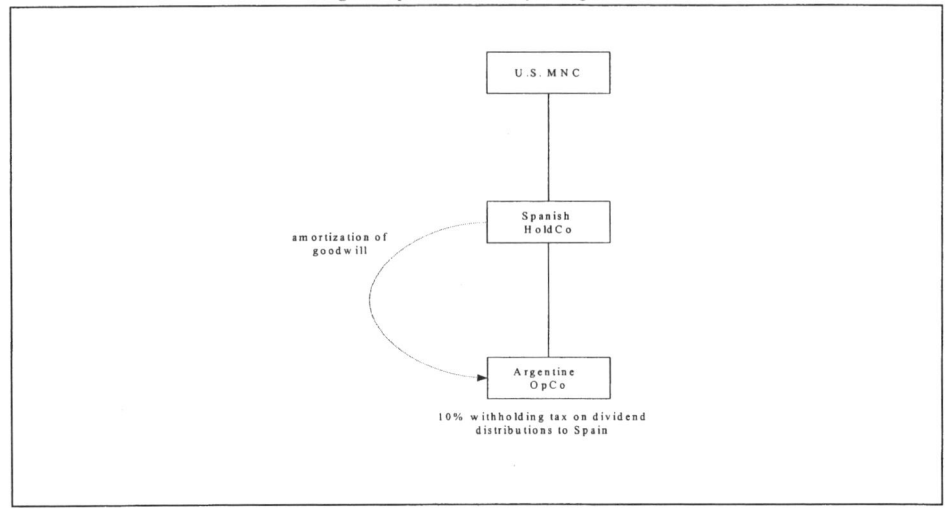

In the case of an Argentine OpCo, the withholding tax liability would be reduced from 35 percent to ten percent in the case of a direct shareholding of ten percent by U.S. MNC.[889] This ten percent tax liability, triggered by the dividend payment from the Argentine OpCo to the Spanish HoldCo, would not be increased when the dividends are transferred to the ultimate parent company, as Spain provides generous exceptions from withholding taxes under local law.[890] In summary, the overall tax saving would amount to 72 percent and would be permanent under the assumption that anti-abuse rules are not applicable.

The interposition of a Spanish holding company might be recommended not only based on its treaty network with South American countries, but also because, since January 1, 2002, Spain has implemented a unique international provision regarding a foreign entity's goodwill depreciation.[891] Under Spanish laws, goodwill relating to a foreign acquisition is computed as the difference between the acquisition price and the net book value of the foreign investment, reduced by inherent gains in the assets of the target.[892] Such goodwill balances can be amortized over 20 years, i.e., a maximum of five percent per annum.[893] This new Spanish amortization provision has increased the attractiveness of Spain as a location for European holding companies as it offers new tax planning opportunities to offset profits and losses under the assumption the Spanish HoldCo is not a pure holding entity. However, if a Spanish holding company is set up properly, there would not be any Spanish taxable income to be offset by the goodwill amortization.

9. EU ENLARGEMENT

The EU enlargement from the current 15 member states to 28 member states is upcoming, as Bulgaria, Cyprus, Czech Republic, Estonia, Hungary, Latvia, Lithuania, Malta, Poland, Romania, Slovak

---

[889] The reduced treaty rate applies to shareholdings of at least 25 percent. Art. 10(2)(a) of the Argentine/Spanish tax treaty.

[890] See *supra* page 131.

[891] See O'Grady, E., *Tax Notes International* 2002, 1065; Palacios, J. and Bootello, V., *Journal of International Taxation* 2002, 39.

[892] See O'Grady, E., *Tax Notes International* 2002, 1065.

[893] See Mullerat, R. and Kolff, A. Q., *Intertax* 2002, 252; O'Grady, E., *Tax Notes International* 2002, 1065; Palacios, J. and Bootello, V., *Journal of International Taxation* 2002, 40.

Republic, Slovenia, and Turkey are candidates for entering the Community.[894] As a result of this impending EU enlargement, new questions will arise for governments, corporations, and international tax practitioners. On the one hand, domestic laws must be amended to incorporate EU law, in particular, the EU Parent-Subsidiary Directive and the EU Merger Directive. On the other hand, the enlargement can provide new opportunities for tax arbitrage.

Tab. 3:   Treaty Withholding Tax Rates on Dividends and Interest Received by U.S. MNCs from Substantial Shareholdings in Candidate Countries

Payor's Country of Residence	Dividends		Interest
	Actual Rate	Minimum Percentage Required	
Bulgaria	n/a	n/a	n/a
Cyprus	0%	none	10%
Czech Republic	5%	10% of the voting shares	0%
Estonia	5%	10% of the voting shares	10%
Hungary	5%	10% of the voting stock	0%
Latvia	5%	10% of the voting shares	10%
Lithuania	5%	10% of the voting shares	10%
Malta[895]	n/a	n/a	n/a
Poland	5%	10% of the outstanding voting stock	0%
Romania	10%	none	10%
Slovak Republic	5%	10% of the voting shares	0%
Slovenia[896]	5%	25% of the voting stock or if there is no voting stock, 25% of the statutory capital	5%
Turkey	15%	10% of the voting stock	15%

As can be seen from the above table, under most respective double tax treaties, tax will be withheld on dividend payments on substantial shareholdings to the U.S. parent company, commonly at a rate of five percent. In order to achieve the major tax planning goal of reducing the overall tax liability to the U.S. parent company, it might be recommended that a holding company be interposed which firstly, benefits from the EU Parent-Subsidiary Directive on dividend distributions from a company carrying on business in one of the new (potential) EU member states. Secondly, the holding company must be incorporated in an EU member state which does not impose any withholding taxes on dividends paid on substantial shareholdings under local law[897] such as Denmark, Ireland, Spain, and the U.K., or in a jurisdiction in which a treaty rate of zero percent was agreed with the U.S., e.g., Luxembourg.[898]

---

[894] See EU, *Enlargement*, 2001, 5.

[895] As of December 31, 2001 no income tax treaty is in force with Malta.

[896] The Slovenia/U.S. Income Tax Treaty entered into force on June 22, 2001. The new treaty is effective for taxes withheld on dividends, interest, and royalties on or after September 1, 2001. For other taxes, the income tax treaty is effective for taxable periods beginning on or after January 1, 2002. See Internal Revenue Service, *International Taxpayer*; Gordon, R., Venuti, J. and Renfroe, D., *Tax Management International Journal* 2002 I, 115.

[897] For details refer *supra* chapter "Country-by-Country Synopsis", page 111.

[898] For the new Luxembourg/U.S. treaty see *supra* page 139.

Fig. 20: New Withholding Tax Arbitrage Opportunities due to EU Enlargement

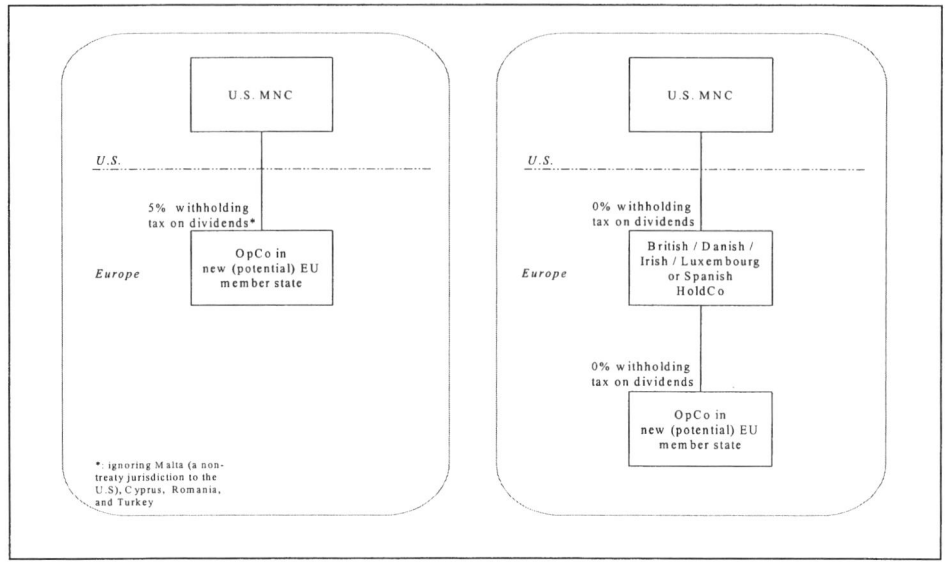

In summary, any withholding taxes on dividends would be completely eliminated. Hence, when interposing certain holding companies between an ultimate U.S. parent and its operating entities, the tax liability would be reduced *ceteris paribus* by 100 percent.

As was discussed when developing the structures noted above, it must be determined whether local provisions exist that will prevent the use of "Treaty Shopping" practices. In such cases, it might be necessary to ensure that there are business or other good reasons for the interposed holding company's existence, unless it conducts its own business activity.

SECTION 6: FUTURE DEVELOPMENTS AND SUMMARY

1. THE DEPARTMENT OF THE TREASURY SUBPART F STUDY

On December 29, 2000, the Department of the Treasury issued the long-awaited, lengthy Subpart F study[899] entitled, "The Deferral of Income Earned Through U.S. Controlled Foreign Corporations, A Policy Study" (hereafter "the Study").[900]

1.1. Intention

The Department of the Treasury embarked on its Study of the Subpart F provisions to determine if such an anti-deferral regime should be retained and, if so, if it required modification.[901] The Study considered different policies for taxing foreign income and the purpose of the Subpart F legislation.[902] Further, it focused on the effectiveness of the Subpart F provisions in the legal and business environment at present, which is mainly influenced by a service-based economy, electronic commerce, and globalization.[903] The Department of the Treasury drew the conclusion that the Subpart F provisions should be retained and modified to enhance their effectiveness.[904] As a result, the opinion expressed in the Study may influence subsequent decisions regarding Subpart F.[905]

1.2. Results

The Study analyzed whether or not the Subpart F provisions are effectively fulfilling their original goals[906] and concluded that this anti-deferral regime is ineffective in some instances.[907] In the Study, the Department of the Treasury provided examples of techniques which may be used to avoid any Subpart F consequences, including hybrid entities,[908] contract manufacturing, and e-business structures.[909] Therefore, the Study recognized that it is possible to shift income to low-tax jurisdictions and earn passive income in these low-tax jurisdictions without giving rise to Subpart F

---

[899] See Aud, E. F. Jr., Benson, D. M. and Garrett-Nelson, L., *Tax Executive* 2001, 48; Benson, D. M., Hicks, H. and O'Connor, M., *International Tax Review* 2001, 6568.

[900] See Department of the Treasury, *Subpart F*, 2000. A significant portion of the Study discussed the history and policies underlying the Subpart F provisions and international taxation, and reviewed various economic analyses relating to the taxation of foreign income. From this review, the Study contended that the policy of capital export neutrality should govern the taxation of income earned by U.S. MNCs outside the U.S. The Study highlighted that developments occurring after Subpart F legislation was enacted in 1962 provide numerous opportunities to earn low-taxed foreign income, and recommended that the Subpart F provisions be expanded to address these circumstances. See Aud, E. F. Jr., Benson, D. M. and Garrett-Nelson, L., *Tax Executive* 2001, 48; Hannes, S. P. and Ries, J. A., *Tax Notes* 2001, 1316; Vlaanderen, P., *Tax Notes International* 2002, 1098.

[901] See Aud, E. F. Jr., Benson, D. M. and Garrett-Nelson, L., *Tax Executive* 2001, 48.

[902] See Aud, E. F. Jr., Benson, D. M. and Garrett-Nelson, L., *Tax Executive* 2001, 48.

[903] See Aud, E. F. Jr., Benson, D. M. and Garrett-Nelson, L., *Tax Executive* 2001, 53; Yoder, L. D., *Tax Management International Journal* 2001, 222.

[904] In order to measure the economic welfare, the Department of the Treasury assessed two base studies conducted by *Peggy B. Musgrave* (Taxation of Foreign Investment Income, An Economic Analysis (1963); United States Taxation of Foreign Investment Income (1969)) and *Gary C. Hufbauer* (Guide to Law and Policy, in: US Taxation of American Businesses Abroad (1975)) while changing some of the assumptions.

[905] However, the Department of the Treasury acknowledged that the conclusions of the Study were neither recommendations nor legislative proposals. See Warco, D. and Nyari, L., *International Tax Review* 2001, 37.

[906] Refer *supra* page 87.

[907] See Department of the Treasury, *Subpart F*, 2000, 67.

[908] For the definition of "hybrid entity", refer *supra* page 75.

[909] See section of the Study entitled "Illustrations of Techniques to Avoid Subpart F", 62; Flick, H. F. W., *Internationales Steuerrecht* 2001 I, 2. For a detailed analysis of the e-business discussion, see Warco, D. and Nyari, L., *International Tax Review* 2001, 37.

income, which the Department of the Treasury asserted is opposite to the intent of the Subpart F legislation.[910]

In the Study, two scenarios outlining hybrid financing structures that reduce foreign taxes but avoid classification as FPHC income and, thus, Subpart F income inclusion, were reviewed.[911] The analysis of the Department of the Treasury did not refer to any specific jurisdictions. However, this paper uses specific jurisdictions for illustration purposes.

In one example, a company in a high-tax jurisdiction (e.g., Germany) is held by a U.S. MNC and makes a deductible payment, e.g., interest, to its subsidiary, a **hybrid entity**, formed in a jurisdiction with a low corporate tax rate (e.g., Bermuda), i.e., the Bermudian subsidiary advances a loan.[912] As the Bermudian entity is treated as a corporation by Germany but is disregarded for U.S. federal tax purposes, the interest paid by the German CFC to the Bermudian hybrid entity would be tax deductible in Germany and, thus, would lower the amount of the German CFC's operating income that otherwise would be subject to tax at an average effective tax rate of about 40 percent. The respective interest income earned by the Bermudian entity would not be subject to tax. Finally, because the U.S. MNC elected to check the box for the Bermudian entity to be classified as disregarded for U.S. tax purposes, the interest payment received by the Bermudian entity is disregarded for U.S. tax purposes and all income and expenses will flow through to the German company, hence, eliminating any FPHC income.

Several features create this favorable result in international tax planning, which is an example of classic entity arbitrage. On the one hand, the U.S. taxes foreign entities qualified as branches or partnerships differently, i.e., as disregarded, than foreign entities treated as corporations. The inconsistent tax treatment of these foreign entities allows for the avoidance of FPHC income.[913] On the other hand, the foreign jurisdiction treats the entity as a separate entity, irrespective of the flow-through treatment for U.S. federal tax purposes. This creates the tax planning opportunity to deduct interest expenses and, consequently, reduce high-taxed income. These two features work together to permit the shifting of operating income from high-tax jurisdictions to low-tax jurisdictions, while avoiding the constitution of Subpart F income.

In the second illustration, an intragroup loan is made to a corporation resident in a high-taxed jurisdiction by a **reverse hybrid entity**[914] that is not subject to foreign taxation.[915] Assume that a U.S. MNC holds an operating CFC organized and carrying on business in a jurisdiction with a high corporate tax rate, e.g., France. U.S. MNC establishes another entity in a low-tax jurisdiction, e.g., the Cayman Islands, that is treated as a partnership for French tax purposes but as a corporation under U.S. federal taxation; the Cayman Islands entity is a reverse hybrid.[916] U.S. MNC contributes cash to the Cayman Islands entity, and the Cayman Islands entity then lends the funds to the French CFC. The French corporation claims a tax-deduction for the interest expenses thereby lowering the amount of French taxable income that otherwise would be subject to French taxation at an effective tax rate of about 36 percent. As the Cayman Islands entity is a disregarded entity for French tax purposes, the Cayman Islands entity is not subject to French income tax on interest received from French CFC in France. France would instead treat the interest paid to the Cayman Islands entity as if paid to U.S. MNC. Under the double tax treaty between France and the U.S., the interest paid to the Cayman Islands entity qualifies for treaty benefits, and, therefore, is subject to zero percent withholding tax in France.[917] Because the Cayman Islands entity is treated by the U.S. as a French corporation, the

---

[910] See Aud, E. F. Jr., Benson, D. M. and Garrett-Nelson, L., *Tax Executive* 2001, 51.

[911] See section of the Study entitled "Impact of the Check-the-Box Entity Classification Rules", 68.

[912] See section of the Study entitled "Use of Hybrids to Deflect Income from High-Tax Jurisdictions to Low-Tax Jurisdictions", 63.

[913] For the different tax treatment of entities in the U.S., see *supra* page 75.

[914] For the definition of "reverse hybrid entity", refer *supra* page 76.

[915] See section of the Study entitled "Use of Hybrids to Shelter Income from Current Tax in All Jurisdictions", 63.

[916] The Cayman Islands entity would be treated as a corporation for U.S. tax purposes under default rules if no owner is liable for the obligations of the entity (Reg. § 301.7701-3(b)(2)), or if a member does not have limited liability, an election may be made to treat the Cayman Islands entity as a corporation (Reg. § 301.7701-3(a)). For details on the default rule, refer *supra* page 73.

[917] Art. 11(1) of the French/U.S. Double Tax Treaty.

interest payments received by the Cayman Islands entity would not constitute FPHC income, as the same country exception of IRC § 954(c)(3)(A)(i) would apply.

The significant feature of this structure is that foreign-source income is sheltered from current tax in any jurisdiction. First, under U.S. tax law, corporations and partnerships (branches) are treated differently, thereby avoiding any taxes on income received by a foreign entity qualified as a corporation. Second, foreign taxes are avoided as the foreign jurisdiction classifies the entity differently than the U.S., i.e., as a flow-through entity rather than as a corporation. Lastly, the interest payments are allowed and avoid the application of the FPHC income provisions under the same country exception.

Although the two techniques outlined above result in reducing high-taxed foreign taxable income, no U.S. taxes are reduced. Nevertheless, while acknowledging that the interest payments do not constitute FPHC income under existing law, the Department of the Treasury asserts that the hybrid structures avoid the application of Subpart F legislation.[918] These structures are not consistent with international tax policies, as income from a high-tax jurisdiction is shifted to a low-tax jurisdiction in the form of passive income. The **hybrid entity structure** illustrated above is the kind of technique targeted by the IRS and the Department of the Treasury in Notice 98-11 and the corresponding, subsequently issued, temporary regulations.[919] However, the Department of the Treasury retreated by withdrawing its Subpart F temporary hybrid entity regulations and by reissuing them as proposed regulations with a significantly delayed effective date.[920] While the proposed regulations would require inclusion of the interest received by the hybrid entity in FPHC income, the Study confirmed that the structure is consistent with U.S. tax law at present.[921] Thus, the hybrid entity structure might be an efficient element in reducing a corporation's overall effective tax rate.[922]

The **reverse hybrid structure** described above, however, was not addressed by previously issued notices or regulations. The Study indicated that the Department of the Treasury is aware of the practice of using reverse hybrids to reduce foreign taxes while avoiding any Subpart F consequences. Further, the Department of the Treasury highlighted that such structures are inconsistent with the objectives of Subpart F legislation. Nonetheless, the Department of the Treasury also acknowledged that the reverse hybrid structures work as an international tax planning tool at the moment. Put another way, such structures work under current law and will work under proposed law. As a result, reverse hybrids are tax planning tools which will continue to increase in importance.

The Study highlighted that the tax arbitrage opportunities arising from hybrid entities under the check-the-box regulations present fundamental challenges to the effectiveness of the Subpart F anti-deferral regime.[923] The Department of the Treasury pointed out that payments of passive income between foreign entities should be included in Subpart F income, irrespective of how the entities are treated for U.S. federal tax purposes. Hence, the Study recommended that any modification to the Subpart F regime provide clearer and more rational provisions with respect to the treatment of flow-through entities.[924]

---

[918] See Aud, E. F. Jr., Benson, D. M. and Garrett-Nelson, L., *Tax Executive* 2001, 51.

[919] T.D. 8767, 63 Fed. Reg. 14613, 1998-16 I.R.B. 4. See Tello, C. P., *Tax Management International Journal* 1998, 17; Yoder, L. D., *Tax Management International Journal* 1998, 219; Aud, E. F. Jr., Benson, D. M. and Garrett-Nelson, L., *Tax Executive* 2001, 48. For details refer *supra* page 80.

[920] Prop. Reg. § 1.954-9, REG-113909-98, 64 Fed. Reg. 37727, July 13, 1999, 1999-30 I.R.B. 125. The effective date of the proposed regulations has been delayed for five years after the date they were finalized (for calendar year taxpayers the effective date will be January 1, 2006), as was announced in Notice 98-35, 1998-27 I.R.B. 35. See Tello, C. P., *Tax Management International Journal* 1998, 17; Yoder, L. D., *Tax Management International Journal* 1998 II, 427; Yoder, L. D., *Tax Management International Journal* 1999 II, 707; Dilworth, R. H. and Andrus, J. L., *Tax Law and Practice*, 2001, 1113.

[921] The Study did not examine the use of pre-sale hybrid branch elections to avoid the recognition of the FPHC income on the gain on the disposition of stock in a lower-tier subsidiary. See Yoder, L. D. and Everson, S. L., *Tax Management International Journal* 2000 II, 301; Yoder, L. D. and Everson, S. L., *Tax Management International Journal* 2001, 14.

[922] For details on this technique, refer *supra* page 100.

[923] See Aud, E. F. Jr., Benson, D. M. and Garrett-Nelson, L., *Tax Executive* 2001, 51.

[924] The Study did not refer to the proposed regulations dealing with the treatment of partnerships for Subpart F purposes. For a discussion of these regulations, see Yoder, L. D., *Tax Management International Journal* 1998 III, 615; Yoder, L. D., *Tax Management International Journal* 2000, 671.

1.3. Options for Modification

The Department of the Treasury highlighted that the Subpart F regime should be retained and expanded to address legal and business developments which have emerged since the Subpart F provisions were enacted in 1962.[925] As was discussed, the Study outlined certain techniques that avoid the application of Subpart F legislation in a manner the Department of the Treasury viewed as contrary to the original purpose of Subpart F.[926]

The Study described three basic options[927] for the reform of Subpart F:[928]

- first, a complete repeal of tax deferral;[929]
- second, a repeal of tax deferral with a reduced U.S. tax rate on foreign active income;[930] and
- finally, an elimination of the foreign-to-foreign related party rules, but with a requirement that active earnings be subject to current taxation unless a minimum tax rate applies.[931]

Variations for implementing each of the options have also been proposed, but the Department of the Treasury recommended none of these approaches.[932] Under all alternatives, passive income received would continue to be taxed at full U.S. tax rates.[933]

1.4. Analysis

In any event, while the Study mainly echoes the Department of the Treasury's oft-stated views, the difference is that proponents of these views now have a comprehensive study to point to for support. Opponents of these views can be grateful that the Department of the Treasury's stated options for reforming Subpart F - ending deferral or most deferral - are so extreme as to make them unlikely candidates for legislative action.[934] In this latter regard, it seems equally unlikely that any major or controversial tax law changes will occur in the near term.[935] There may well be opportunities, however, for modest revisions to the Subpart F provisions, changes that could be focused on updating the provisions to reflect the business realities of the 21st century, rather than dwelling on the supposed

---

[925] See Aud, E. F. Jr., Benson, D. M. and Garrett-Nelson, L., *Tax Executive* 2001, 52.

[926] See Yoder, L. D., *Tax Management International Journal* 2001, 240.

[927] The alternatives were evaluated based on the goals of equity, economic efficiency, simplicity and ease of administration, consistency, and competitiveness. However, multinational competitiveness was not addressed. See Department of the Treasury, *Subpart F*, 2000, 82; Benson, D. M., Hicks, H. and O'Connor, M., *International Tax Review* 2001, 6568; Kral, K. H. and Katz, S. B., *International Tax Review* 2001, 7985.

[928] See Department of the Treasury, *Subpart F*, 2000, 86; Aud, E. F. Jr., Benson, D. M. and Garrett-Nelson, L., *Tax Executive* 2001, 53; Benson, D. M., Hicks, H. and O'Connor, M., *International Tax Review* 2001, 6568; Flick, H. F. W., *Internationales Steuerrecht* 2001 I, 2; Yoder, L. D., *Tax Management International Journal* 2001, 224.

[929] See Department of the Treasury, *Subpart F*, 2000, 88.

[930] See Department of the Treasury, *Subpart F*, 2000, 91.

[931] See Department of the Treasury, *Subpart F*, 2000, 92.

[932] See Department of the Treasury, *Subpart F*, 2000, 94; Peroni. R. J., *Brooklyn Journal of International Law* 2001, 1581.

[933] See Aud, E. F. Jr., Benson, D. M. and Garrett-Nelson, L., *Tax Executive* 2001, 53; Yoder, L. D., *Tax Management International Journal* 2001, 224.

[934] See Aud, E. F. Jr., Benson, D. M. and Garrett-Nelson, L., *Tax Executive* 2001, 54; Shields, C. C., *Tax Notes International* 2002, 1114.

[935] The Study was undertaken during the Clinton Administration and it is questionable whether or not the current Bush Administration will implement any of the options. See Kral, K. H. and Katz, S. B., *International Tax Review* 2001, 7985; Benson, D. M., *Tax Notes International* 2002, 855.

intent of the rules laid out in a bygone era. Surprisingly, the Study is rarely subject to discussion in the literature.[936]

2. HARMFUL TAX COMPETITION

Changes to holding company regimes in Europe have become frequent and varied, such that there is need for periodic review to ensure all possible benefits are claimed and tax pitfalls avoided. Within Europe, various countries have lowered their corporate tax rates or reformed their corporate tax systems.[937] In light of these developments, there may be new changes on the horizon as European countries seeking to establish themselves as preferable holding company regimes will face increasing pressure from both the EU and the OECD to eliminate what is perceived to be harmful tax competition.[938] However, the exact nature of the EU and OECD mandates is uncertain, thereby creating further potential for intrusion.

2.1. Pressure from the EU

A comprehensive approach to taxation policy has been under review within the EU for a number of years. As part of this review, a package of tax measures designed to eliminate harmful tax competition was approved in December 1997 (the so-called *Monti package*).[939] Included in the package was a resolution adopting a Code of Conduct on Business Taxation[940] pursuant to the first aim of the Report of the Ruding Committee ("Conclusions and Recommendations of the Committee of Independent Expert on Company law").[941] In adoption this resolution, the EU singles out:

- tax measures that affect, or may affect, in a significant way, the location of business activity in the EU; and
- tax measures that provide for a significantly lower effective level of taxation than those levels that generally apply in the member state. Such tax measures are to be regarded as potentially harmful.

Subsequently, a working group issued a report in November 1999 on harmful tax competition within the EU and their dependent/associated territories. This report has a binding effect on direct EU members. The Report lists 66 measures with potentially harmful features (the so-called *Primarolo*

---

[936] See Kral, K. H. and Katz, S. B., *International Tax Review* 2001, 7985.

[937] See Baker & McKenzie, *Effective Tax Burden - Summary*, 2001, 3; Lutter, M., *Betriebs-Berater* 2002, 7.

[938] See Endres, D. and Dorfmueller, P., *Praxis Internationale Steuerberatung* 2001, 103.

[939] See Ellis, M. J., *European Taxation* 2000, 414; Hamaekers, H., *European Taxation* 2000, 398; Hendricks, B., *European Taxation* 2000, 413; Malherbe, J., *Tax Notes International* 2000, 151; Lannoo, K. and Levin, M., *EU company*, 2002, 11.

[940] The Code was intended to initially provide for a standstill on certain tax regimes, and later a rollback, over a period of five years (1997-2002).

[941] The Ruding Committee noted that the goals of approximating and coordinating the corporate tax systems of member states require attention to the manner and extent to which tax relief is provided to shareholders with respect to corporate tax levied on profits, as well as the statutory corporate tax rate and tax base. The Committee recommended that the discrimination that exists in taxing dividends distributed from profits earned in another member state should be eliminated. See Commission of the European Community, *Report of the Committee of Indepent Experts on Company Taxation*, 1992; Ruding-Bericht, *Der Betrieb* 1992, Beilage 5; Goldsworth, J. G., *Tax Notes International* 1992, 751; McLure, C. E. Jr., *EC Tax Review* 1992, 13; Vanistendael, F., *EC Tax Review* 1992, 3; Rädler, A., *Vorstellung des EG-Sachverständigenausschusses zur Unternehmensbesteuerung (Ruding Ausschuß)*, 1994, 1; Ruding, H O, *Journal of International Taxation* 1994, 7; Herzig, N., *Besteuerung der Unternehmen in Europa*, 1996, 126; Hey, J., *Harmonisierung der Unternehmensbesteuerung in Europa*, 1997, 72; Lodin, S.-O. and Gammie, M., *European Taxation* 1999, 288; Eden, S., *British Tax Review* 2000, 631; Gerken, L., Märkt, J. and Schick, G., *Internationaler Steuerwettbewerb*, 2000, 196; EU Commission, *Study*, 2001, 17; Lannoo, K. and Levin, M., *EU Company*, 2002, 10; Vlaanderen, P., *Tax Notes International* 2002, 1099.

Report).[942] At present there is no common agreement among the member states as to what framework should be used to identify and eliminate harmful tax practices.

2.2. Pressure from the OECD

The OECD Report on Harmful Tax Competition[943] was prepared in response to a request by the OECD ministers to "develop measures to counter the distorting effects of harmful tax competition on investment and financing decisions and the consequences for national tax bases". The Report identifies so-called *harmful practices* that exist in tax havens[944] and preferential tax regimes.[945]

A more recent OECD Report, issued in June 2000, sets out the progress made in identifying and curtailing harmful tax practices both within and outside the OECD.[946] The OECD Report distinguishes between low-tax legislation in general, and low-tax legislation that is indicative of harmful tax competition. On the one hand, the OECD recognizes that a country has a right to set its own level of taxation. On the other hand, it views legislation as harmful if that legislation is designed to attract capital from other countries by eroding the local tax system. This Report identified 35 jurisdictions as having met the technical criteria for inclusion as a tax haven and 47 preferential tax regimes that were potentially harmful but in which the OECD lacks any direct power of implementation.[947] A series of recommendations are listed in the remainder of the Report. Most relevant, the OECD recommends Controlled Foreign Companies ("CFC")[948] and Passive Foreign Investment Companies ("PFIC") regimes.[949] According to the OECD Report, the CFC regimes should be designed to address passive income, base company income and income and entities covered by tax practices considered to constitute harmful tax competition, based on the factors developed in the Report.

Holding company regimes were not included in the Report because their status as potentially harmful preferential regimes is still under review. However, the Report did state that holding company

---

[942] See Kaye, T. A., *Boston College International and Comparative Law Review* 1996, 142; Bolkestein, F., *European Taxation* 2000, 405; Endres, D., Dorfmueller, P. and Urse, M., *International Tax Report* 2001 II, 8; MacLachlan, J. E., *Tax Planning International Review* 2001, 18; Nijkamp, H., *International Tax Review* 2001, 35.

[943] OECD, *Harmful Tax Competition - An Emerging Global Issue*, dated April 27, 1998.

[944] Tax havens are defined as jurisdictions with (1) no or only nominal taxes; (2) lack of effective exchange of information; (3) lack of transparency; and (4) absence of a requirement for substantial domestic activities. See OECD, *Harmful Tax Competition*, 1998, paragraph 52; OECD, *The OECD Observer* 2000, 88.

[945] For a detailed analysis of the 1998 Report, see Spencer, D. E., *Journal of International Taxation* 1998, 26; Zagaris, B., *Tax Notes International* 1998, 1507; Ault, H., *Tax Competition*, 2000, 1117; Business and Industry Advisory Committee, *European Taxation* 2000, 421; Gerken, L., Märkt, J. and Schick, G., *Internationaler Steuerwettbewerb*, 2000, 200; Malherbe, J., *Tax Competition*, 2000, 1125; Spencer, D. E., *Journal of International Taxation* 2001 I, 29; Hishikawa, A., *Boston College International and Comparative Law Review* 2002, 393.

[946] See Endres, D. and Dorfmueller, P., *Praxis Internationale Steuerberatung* 2001, 103; Spencer, D. E., *Journal of International Taxation* 2002 I, 11.

[947] See Zagaris, B., *Tax Management International Journal* 2000, 521; Endres, D., Dorfmueller, P. and Urse, M., *International Tax Report* 2001 II, 8; Karp, J. J., *The International Tax Journal* 2001, 13; Mens, H. van and Porquet, F. G., *European Taxation* 2001, 336; Scott, C., *Tax Notes International* 2001, 1128; Spencer, D. E., *Journal of International Taxation* 2001 II, 30; Huber, M. F., Kapalle, U. and Kubaile, H., *Steuer Revue* 2002, 367; Owens, J., *Tax Planning International e-commerce* 2002, 11.

[948] Since 1962, when the U.S. introduced the principles of immediate taxation of CFCs, many countries have incorporated these principles including: Australia, Canada, Denmark, Estonia, Finland, France, Germany, Hungary, Indonesia, Italy, Japan, Korea, Mexico, New Zealand, Norway, Portugal, South Africa, Spain, Sweden, and the U.K. In 2001, the Austrian government issued a draft on the introduction of CFC legislation, which was quite similar to the German CFC rules. However, in Austria, CFC legislation has not yet been enacted and has been delayed, as it might violate EU law. See Kaufmann, R., *Steuer & Wirtschaft International* 2001, 17; Lang, M., *Internationales Steuerrecht* 2002, 217. For the German CFC legislation, see Kessler, W., Dorfmueller, P. and Schmitt, C., *International Tax Report* 2001, 2; Kessler, W., Dorfmueller, P. and Schmitt, C., *Praxis Internationale Steuerberatung* 2001, 318.

[949] See Department of the Treasury, *Subpart F*, 2000, 61; Kaufmann, R., *Steuer & Wirtschaft International* 2001, 16; Malherbe, J. and Neirynck, O., *Belgian Measures*, 2002, 14; Schön, W., *General Report*, 2002, 31.

regimes in the following countries were being examined: Austria, Belgium, Denmark, Germany, Greece, Iceland, Ireland, Luxembourg, Netherlands, Portugal, Spain and Switzerland.[950]

In November 2001, the OECD issued its 2001 Progress Report as part of the organization's initiative against harmful tax practices.[951] It is a follow-up to the June 2000 Report and responds to the Ministerial Mandate. The recent Report - originally planned for release in July 2001 - reduces the number of jurisdictions meeting the tax haven criteria from the original 35 to 24, as there are eleven new committed jurisdictions.[952] The OECD has made a number of modifications to the tax haven work to facilitate future commitments by tax havens. Most important, the "no substantial activities" criterion will no longer be used in determining uncooperative tax havens.[953] However, it appears that the focus of the OECD has changed, as transparency and effective exchange of information - in both civil and criminal tax matters - play a more important role in the recent Report.

A list of uncooperative tax havens, as announced in the 2000 Report, was not included. However, after a half-year delay, such a list was issued on April 18, 2002.[954] The OECD identified seven jurisdictions as being uncooperative tax havens, i.e., jurisdictions that have not yet made any commitment to transparency and effective exchange of information. The seven uncooperative non-OECD member states that appear on the list are: Andorra, Liechtenstein, Liberia, Monaco, the Marshall Islands, Nauru, and Vanuatu.[955] Meanwhile, the OECD and the primary eleven committed jurisdictions developed a legal framework that would facilitate the exchange of information for tax purposes between OECD members and committed jurisdictions.[956] The OECD anticipates that the implementation of transparent regimes and effective exchange of information will be completed by January 2006.[957]

2.3. Comparison of the Initiatives

The mosaic of efforts discussed above outlines the intensive scope of international public and private factor cooperation required to develop standardization and multilateral provisions to resolve complex global financial issues, and, thus, to overcome national boundaries. Through the various efforts of the EU and the OECD, tax evasion in the international context will be resolved step by step over time.

The strategies proposed by the EU and the OECD to reduce tax evasion might not be considered complete or fully consistent with one another. However, these proposals could lead to an international tax system which achieves the objectives of the OECD 1998 Report: cross-border, mobile income should not escape taxation.

One of the newest aspects of the anti-deferral debate involves the OECD's and EU's targeting of harmful tax competition.[958] These OECD and EU efforts to eliminate harmful tax competition focus on legislative practices of tax havens. The capital exporting country has the same long-term stake in preventing harmful tax competition as in preventing three-party diversionary transactions. In

---

[950] See Langer, M. J., *Tax Notes International* 2000, 2837.

[951] Switzerland and Luxembourg, both OCED countries, abstained from signing the Report. See Spencer, D. E., *Journal of International Taxation* 2002 I, 11.

[952] A jurisdiction is committed if commitments to transparency and effective exchange of information have been made.

[953] A jurisdiction is uncooperative if no commitments to transparency and effective exchange of information have been made. See Owens, J., *Tax Planning International e-commerce* 2002, 11.

[954] See OECD, *List*, 2002.

[955] See Anonymous, *International Tax Report* 2002, 11; Eimermann, D., *Internationales Steuerrecht* 2002, 1; Goulder, R., *Tax Notes International* 2002, 375; Kondo, S., *Ending*, 2002; Owens, J., *Tax Planning International e-commerce* 2002, 11; Spencer, D. E., *Journal of International Taxation* 2002 II, 16.

[956] The eleven committed jurisdictions are: Aruba, Bermuda, Bahrain, the Cayman Islands, Cyprus, Malta, Mauritius, the Netherlands Antilles, San Marino, and the Seychelles. See Eimermann, D., *Internationales Steuerrecht* 2002, 1; Makhlouf, G., *Exchange*, 2002; Makhlouf, G., *Statement*, 2002; OECD, *Agreement*, 2002, 2; OECD, *Model Agreement*, 2002.

[957] See Huber, M. F., Kapalle, U. and Kubaile, H., *Steuer Revue* 2002, 368; Owens, J., *Tax Planning International e-commerce* 2002, 12; Spencer, D. E., *Journal of International Taxation* 2002 I, 12.

[958] For a comparison of the EU and OECD list, see Malherbe, J., *Tax Notes International* 2000, 2542; Pantaleo, N., *European Holding and Financing Companies*, 2001, 13:35.

both cases, the capital exporting country's MNCs are being lured offshore in favor of lower tax rates. While this concern could apply to all low-tax country rates, the OECD does not view all low-tax regimes as harmful tax competition, only those low-tax regimes that fall outside the standard tax-revenue paradigm. Tax-haven holidays and poaching legislation fall outside this paradigm because this legislation attracts foreign tax dollars that would otherwise not be forthcoming.

Overall, the trend favors capital exporting countries. Capital exporting countries have successfully expanded their jurisdictional claims through anti-deferral legislation, such as Subpart F. Capital exporting countries have further achieved a bilateral waiver of capital importing country taxation through tax treaties. In effect, the creation of tax treaties substantiates the view that the capital importing country's tax is the barrier to international trade, not the capital exporting country's tax.

3. EU INTERNAL MARKET WITHOUT TAX OBSTACLES AND EU COMPANY TAXATION

As can be seen from the country-by-country synopsis above, companies face a tax jungle when working on a cross-border basis in Europe. In October 2001, the EU Commission presented a communication entitled "Towards an Internal Market without tax obstacles - A strategy for providing companies with a consolidated corporate tax base for their EU-wide activities" (hereafter "the Communication") and a study on company taxation, "Company Taxation in the Internal Market" (hereafter "the Study"). These reports might be seen as significant steps toward adopting a new direction for company taxation in the EU.[959]

In the Communication, the EU Commission noted that company tax systems in the EU have failed to keep up with developments such as globalization and economic integration in the Internal Market and the Economic and Monetary Union.[960] In particular, the economic environment has changed significantly in the past ten years since the last comprehensive study (the so-called *Ruding Report*) with a wave of international mergers and acquisitions,[961] the emergence of electronic commerce, the increased variability of factors of production and the consequent difficulties in defining and safeguarding a company's tax base.[962] According to the Communication, for European businesses to remain competitive in the globally integrated economy, they must be able to consolidate their accounts on a Community-wide basis.[963] While enabling member states to continue to collect tax revenue from their local operations, the consolidated tax base would be apportioned to the member states using an agreed common formula. Moreover, the Commission expressed its belief that company tax rates are a matter on which the member states must decide.[964]

According to the Study, the significant variation in effective tax rates within the EU - more than 30 percent[965] - highlights the main element of the existing tax obstacles in the Single Market. The Study noted that, based on numerous simulations of alternative policy choices,[966] the EU could recap potentially significant benefits when reducing the variation in effective taxation. There were no

---

[959] Also Weiner, J. M., *Tax Notes International* 2001, 423; Baron, R., *Tax Planning International transfer pricing* 2002, 14.

[960] See EU Commission, *Communication*, 2001, 4; Wiesner, P. M., *GmbH-Rundschau* 2001, R461.

[961] For example, Daimler-Chrysler, Hoechst-Rhône-Poulenc (Aventis), and Vodafone-Mannesmann.

[962] See EU Commission, *Communication*, 2001, 4; EU Commission, *Memo*, 2001; EU Commission, *Study*, 2001, 20; Mueller, J., *Internationale Wirtschaftsbriefe*, Fach 11, Europäische Gemeinschaften, Gruppe 2, 2001, 475; Weiner, J. M., *Tax Notes International* 2001, 423.

[963] See EU Commission, *Communication*, 2001, 15.

[964] See EU Commission, *Communication*, 2001, 16.

[965] In the case of a profitable investment, the effective corporate taxation rates vary between 10.5 percent in Ireland and 39.7 percent in Belgium. See EU Commission, *Communication*, 2001, 32; EU Commission, *Study*, 2001, 6.

[966] The computations are based on the so-called *King & Fullerton* approach, set out by Michael P. Devereux and Rachel Griffith (1998) and supplemented by the "European Tax Analyzer" developed by the University of Mannheim and Zentrum für Europäische Wirtschaftsforschung (ZEW) (1999). See King, M. A. and Fullerton, D., *The Taxation from Income of Capital*, 1984; Devereux, M. and Griffith, R., *The Taxation of Discrete Investment Choices*, 1999; Jacobs, O. H. and Spengel, C., *European Tax Analyzer*, 1996; Jacobs, O. H. and Spengel, C., *Intertax* 2000, 334; Spengel, C. and Lammersen, L., *Steuer und Wirtschaft* 2001, 226; Jacobs, O. H. and Spengel, C., *Effective Tax Burden in Europe*, 2002, 7.

recommendations for any coordination of member state tax rates in the EU Study.[967] In contrast thereto, the Study stated that the failure to tax EU companies may be the major tax obstacle remaining in the internal market. Hence, the primary goal might be eliminating that obstacle rather than harmonizing tax rates within the EU.

According to the results of the study, EU companies face four key tax obstacles:[968]

(1)   they must use different accounting and arm's length transfer pricing to allocate profits and losses among related parties;

(2)   they cannot offset cross-border losses incurred by related entities;[969]

(3)   they incur tax costs associated with cross-border reorganizations of a group; and

(4)   they face double taxation from conflicting taxation rights.

The study examined four comprehensive solutions[970] that would allow companies to consolidate their EU activities on one basis:[971]

-   **Home State Taxation (HST)** - A MNC can opt for computing its consolidated tax base according to the rules of the member state where the head office is based.

-   **Common Base Taxation (CBT)** - A MNC can opt for computing its consolidated tax base according to a completely new set of restructured EU-wide rules.

-   **European Unity Company Income Tax (EUCIT)** - Company tax would be levied at the European level and revenues would go (at least partly) to the EU budget.

-   **Single Compulsory Harmonized Tax Base** - All companies in the EU would compute their consolidated tax base according to harmonized rules.

The aim is to achieve a consolidated tax base, therefore, the choice of approach is fundamental and should not result in an immediate change. In removing the tax obstacles, the Commission agreed upon a dual track strategy. First, a series of specific short- and mid-term measures which are targeted at defined obstacles, such as improving the EU Merger Directive, have been suggested. Second, a recommendation was made to work toward a common consolidated EU tax base in the long-term. The Commission believes that in the longer term, a single tax base must be established which engenders substantial benefits for companies, e.g., significantly reducing the compliance costs, (nearly) eliminating Community-wide transfer pricing disputes, allowing (cross-border) consolidation of profits and losses, and almost eliminating double taxation.[972]

---

[967] However, on April 29/30, 2002, at the European Conference on Company Taxation in Brussels (hereafter "the Conference", it was proposed that a minimum corporate tax rate be incorporated which would result in a lower rate than the current EU average. See Weiner, J. M., *Tax Notes International* 2002 II, 517.

[968] See EU Commission, *Communication*, 2001, 36; EU Commission, *Study*, 2001, 8. These obstacles have previously been identified by Prof. Sven-Olof Lodin, who was a member of panel II which was composed of experts from among the business community and social partners at the Community level. The task of the second panel was to advise the Commission on the remaining company tax obstacles to the proper functioning of the Single Market and to analyze these obstacles from the perspective of the EU business community and its social partners. See Lodin, S.-O. and Gammie, M., *European Taxation* 1999, 286; Lodin, S.-O., *European Taxation* 2001, 170.

[969] In its Communication, the Commission stated that it is planning to either calculate losses according to the legislation of the state in which the parent company is located, or work on the basis of the Danish joint tax system for taxing a company's worldwide consolidated profit/loss in order to prevent companies from being taxed on profits made in one member state without, at the same time, being able to take into consideration losses in another member state. See EU Commission, *Communication*, 2001, 12; EU Commission, *Study*, 2001, 341. For details on the Danish system, see *supra* page 114.

[970] For the discussion at the European Conference on Company Taxation, April 29/30, 2002, Brussels, see Troup, E., Le Floc'h Louboutin, H., Juchum, G. and Bijl, J. van der, *Choice of Approach*, 2002.

[971] See Kessler, W. and Schmalz, A., *Praxis Internationale Steuerberatung* 2002, 211; Mintz, J. M., *CESinfo Forum* 2002, 3; Mors, M., *CESinfo Forum* 2002, 22; Spahn, P. B., *Reflections*, 2002, 1; Weiner, J. M., *CESinfo Forum* 2002, 11.

[972] See EU Commission, *Communication*, 2001, 16; Anonymous, *International Tax Review* 2001/2002, 3; Bolkestein, F., *Internal Market*, 2002; Haase, F. F., *Tax Notes International* 2002, 713; Mintz, J. M., *CESinfo Forum* 2002, 8; UNICE, *Reaction*, 2002, 3.

An agreement based upon the best long-term approach should be reached.[973] Needless to say, the ideal approach does not yet exist. The study only analyzed in detail the first two approaches, the HST[974] and the CBT, as the EUCIT[975] and Single Compulsory Harmonized Tax Base approach did not appear to be feasible at that point in time, i.e., those approaches were beyond the Community's immediate capacity.[976] Both proposals considered by the Commission would allow MNCs to compute their EU profits under a single set of rules, rather than under 15 different sets of rules as at present, and to apportion EU-wide profits for taxation in the individual member states. A benefit of the HST approach is that no full tax harmonization (tax base and tax rate) in the member states is necessary.[977] By the same token, one jurisdiction has to give up its sovereignty to levy taxes in favor of the home state, which can be a critical issue.[978]

Both HST and CBT require agreement by the member states on the definition of a group of companies and a uniform formula for apportioning profits. These requirements raise a number of complex questions.[979] Further, these approaches would operate alongside, or in parallel to, the existing local corporate tax provisions.[980] Common to all four approaches is the requirement that company income be consolidated on a Community-wide basis and allocated among the participating EU member states using a specific formula.

There are certain disadvantages however, to the introduction of a single tax base. First, there will be less potential for tax planning, and companies may, thus, find it more difficult to minimize their global effective tax costs. It is also uncertain how a single tax base will affect the tax revenues of governments.[981] Even though the Commission's results suggest that the initial outcome of a harmonized tax base may be an increase in the effective tax rates of companies, the impact differs from one country to another. Despite these limitations, a single tax base will be more fair and equitable, more efficient, simple and transparent.[982]

In summary, each approach eliminates the basic problems caused by the existence of 15 different tax systems within the Single Market. Political and economic disadvantages are common among all approaches. The study did not state a preferred approach, as specific proposals must be issued to address each approach. Although the formula apportionment[983] is analyzed, the unitary tax

---

[973] Initially, HST and CTB were options available by the EU enterprises by election. At the Conference, Malcom Gammie QC and H. Onno Ruding both promoted the elective system, providing a greater level of flexibility. Since, on the one hand, HST is the preferred option by small and medium sized enterprises and, on the other hand, CTB is of interest for large enterprises, an option model seems to be reasonable. The EU Commission will work on the possible application of the HST approach for small and medium sized enterprises. See EU Commission, *Study*, 2001, 390; Kirwin, J., *Daily Tax Report* 2001, G-2; EU Commission, *Memorandum*, 2002; Vanden Abbele, M., *Closing Remarks*, 2002, 7.

[974] The HST approach was developed by Prof. Dr. Sven-Olof Lodin and Malcom Gammie QC; for the concept in detail, refer to their monograph "Home State Taxation" (2001). From their point of view, the EU member states would not likely agree upon an EUCIT in the foreseeable future without a political and institutional framework. This concern was also expressed at the Conference. See Lodin, S.-O. and Gammie, M., *European Taxation* 1999, 288; Ruding, H. O., *Remarks*, 2002; Vanden Abbele, M., *Closing Remarks*, 2002, 9.

[975] For an in-depth analysis of the EUCIT, see Lodin, S.-O. and Gammie, M., *European Taxation* 1999, 287.

[976] See EU Commission, *Memorandum*, 2002.

[977] See EU Commission, *Communication*, 2001, 45; EU Commission, *Study*, 2001, 15.

[978] At the Conference, it was determined that HST is not the preferred solution. Further, it was noted that countries with no consolidated tax regimes, like Belgium and Italy, will find it difficult to implement such a system and also that the treatment of non-EU income needs clarification. See Thiel, S. van, *Removal*, 2002, 2; Vanden Abbele, M., *Closing Remarks*, 2002, 7; Weiner, J. M., *Tax Notes International* 2002 II, 516.

[979] See Lodin, S.-O., *European Taxation* 2001, 170; Peter, M., *Fortentwicklung des Betriebsstättenprinzips*, 2002, 279; Sunley, E. M., *CESinfo Forum* 2002, 36. The question of formula apportionment was not explicitly discussed, although it loomed over the discussions throughout the Conference. See Weiner, J. M., *Tax Notes International* 2002 II, 517.

[980] See EU Commission, *Study*, 2001, 14; Giannini, S., *CESinfo Forum* 2002, 26; Kessler, W. and Dorfmueller, P., *Tax Planning International European Union Focus* 2002, 4.

[981] Tax authorities are faced with increasing costs as they have to engage in cross-border enquiries and audits.

[982] See EU Commission, *Memorandum*, 2002. Tax harmonization might also affect the competitiveness of European industry, the legal structures of doing business, the EU labor markets, and the capital markets. For an in-depth analysis, see Lannoo, K. and Levin, M., *EU Company*, 2002, 26.

[983] Under formula apportionment, a taxable profit of a company in a certain state is apportioned by applying a certain formula to the state(s) where the profit was realized. Rather than having to file tax accounts in the different states of a

approach[984] - used by the U.S. states - is not discussed. The EU Commission and the EU Parliament[985] share the opinion that in order to reduce the legal costs of complying with 15 different tax systems and to reconcile their existence with the internal market, it ought to be possible for EU companies with Community-wide operations to have a consolidated corporate tax base, or one calculated on the basis of a single set of rules, as well as a mechanism for distributing the consolidated tax base across the various member states.[986]

4. EUROPEAN COMPANY (THE SO-CALLED *SOCIETAS EUROPAEA*)

The European company (the so-called *Societas Europaea (SE)*) is closely linked to that of a common comprehensive approach to company taxation in the Community. Therefore, the concept will be discussed in the following paragraphs.

In 2001, after almost 40 years of debate,[987] the EU finally adopted the European Company Statute.[988] The agreement came as a surprise, since support from the business community for the very complex system was lacking. The SE provides an optional solution for MNCs, as it will allow single incorporation for firms in the EU, single governance, and single reporting structures.[989] Thus, it is an essential measure to satisfy the objectives of the Single Market and to improve the competitiveness of

---

federation and apply complex transfer pricing rules for intra-company transactions, a company files only one single account and pays a single tax, which is distributed based upon a certain share to the states where the profit was realized.

[984] The unitary theory of taxation provides that separate corporate entities engaged in a single or unitary business may be required to report their income on a combined basis. As a result, a non-resident affiliate, which by itself lacks nexus for state taxation purposes, can effectively be taxed through inclusion in a combined tax filing with an affiliate which has nexus. Whether a business is unitary will depend on the degree of interrelationship and interdependence among the business activities of the affiliated companies. For the unitary taxation approach in the U.S., see McLure, C. E. Jr., *The State Corporation Income Tax*, 1984; Luttermann, C., *Internationales Steuerrecht* 1994, 489; Luttermann, C., *Recht der Internationalen Wirtschaft* 1996, 935; Salzberger, W., *Internationales Steuerrecht* 1999, 97; Oestreicher, A., *Konzern-Gewinnabgrenzung*, 2000, 128; Weiner, J. M., *CESinfo Forum* 2002, 16.

[985] Resolution, dated March 14, 2002. See Weiner, J. M., *Tax Notes International* 2002 I, 252.

[986] See Della Vedova, B., *Choice of Approach*, 2002.

[987] The very first proposal for the introduction of an SE was made in 1970 (*Official Journal of the European Communities*, dated October 10, 1970, C 124, 1). The main hurdle for the adoption of the Statute was the controversy surrounding the type of employee involvement in the management of the SE, in particular, where one or more of the participating companies have a system of employee participation in management. See Kohlhepp, K., *Recht der Internationalen Wirtschaft* 1989, 88; Strub, A., *Internationales Steuerrecht* 1993, 179; Endres, D., *Recht der Internationalen Wirtschaft* 1994, 581; Schulz, A. and Eicker, K., *Intertax* 2001, 336; Blanquet, F., *Zeitschrift für Unternehmens- und Gesellschaftsrecht* 2002, 22; Heinze, M., *Zeitschrift für Unternehmens- und Gesellschaftsrecht* 2002, 66; Lutter, M., *Betriebs-Berater* 2002, 1.

[988] Council Regulation (EC) No. 2157/2001 of October 8, 2001. According to Art. 70 of the *EU SE Statute*, the SE is to be introduced on October 8, 2004. The related directive concerning employee rights became effective immediately on the date of the publication in the Official Journal of the European Communities (Art. 16 of the *SE Statute Supplement*), which was November 10, 2001. According to Art. 249(1) of the *EC Treaty*, the regulation (EU SE Statute) does not require transformation into local law, but does require a direct application to the organization and governance of the SE. In contrast thereto, EU directives need to be transformed into local laws by the EU member states, e.g., the related directive concerning employee rights. However, the EU SE Statute suffers many shortcomings, which must be fulfilled either by existing local laws, e.g., the respective Stock Corporation Acts, or new local provisions. Despite the fact that a statute does not need transformation, Art. 9(1)(c) of the *EU SE Statute* makes quite clear that each EU government must adopt new national laws, regulations and administrative provisions for the introduction of the SE by October 8, 2004. Hence, there will not be uniform European law for the SE; the SE will be stamped by both European and local laws, and, therefore, the SE might not be the universal European business entity. Nonetheless, it must understood that the national laws governing domestic companies were subject to nine directives, dealing with most aspects of the organization and operation of domestic companies (with the notable exceptions including the proposal for a Fifth Directive that would deal with the management of companies, and the proposed Tenth Directive on cross-border mergers). See Bogenschütz, E., *Verletzung materiellen Rechts*, 1997, 36; Jahn, A. and Herfs-Röttgen, E., *Der Betrieb* 2001, 632; Schulz, A. and Eicker, K., *Intertax* 2001, 332; Schulz, A. and Geismar, B., *Deutsches Steuerrecht* 2001, 1079; Herzig, N. and Griemla, S., *Steuer und Wirtschaft* 2002, 50; Joris, J.-L., *International Financial Law Review* 2002, 19; Lutter, M. *Betriebs-Berater* 2002, 3.

[989] See Lodin, S.-O. and Gammie, M., *European Taxation* 1999, 286; Schulz, A. and Eicker, K., *Intertax* 2001, 332; Ebert, S., *Internationale Wirtschaftsbriefe*, Fach 11, Europäische Gemeinschaften, Gruppe 3, 2002, 980; Kessler, W. and Dorfmueller, P., *Journal of International Taxation* 2002, 55.

EU companies.[990] The Statute should permit the creation of companies with European-wide operations, free from the obstacles arising from the disparity and the limited territorial application of national company law.[991] Hence, the main objective of the SE Statute is the creation of a pan-European legal form that can be used throughout the EU, regardless of any national borders. In other words, it should simplify the organizational structure of EU MNCs and, therefore, lead to substantial cost savings and efficiency gains.[992]

The SE Statute will allow, for example, large enterprises[993] to rethink their organizational structure and to re-organize themselves along specific lines of activity, rather than having to incorporate on a country-by-country basis.[994] The formation of an SE[995] is governed by two key principles:

(1) the process to create an SE is derivative, i.e., an SE can only be formed through the restructuring of existing companies;[996] and
(2) as a rule, only companies whose registered and head offices are located within the EU may participate in the creation of an SE.

Therefore, a U.S. MNC could not directly participate in the formation of an SE, but could do so through one or more of its subsidiaries located in the EU.

The question then arises as to whether this SE Statute will contribute to resolving the prevailing impasse in the efforts toward elimination of the obstacles in the area of company taxation. The effect in practice seems questionable, as the SE Statute lacks any tax component such as the EU-wide consolidation of profits and losses.[997, 998] Currently, a significant weakness of the SE Statute is

---

[990] See Joris, J.-L., *International Financial Law Review* 2002, 19.

[991] The SE must have its registered office in the same member state as its headquarters. Under Art. 4 of the *SE Statute*, the minimum capital requirement for an SE amounts to € 120,000. An SE can only be created if there is consensus on the degree of worker involvement, which is defined in a separate directive (EU, SE Statute Supplement, 2001). If it proved impossible to negotiate a mutually satisfactory arrangement, then a set of standard principles as detailed in the annex to the Directive will apply. See Schiffer, K. J. and Wahlers, U., *Steuern und Bilanzen* 2001, 468; Blanquet, F., *Zeitschrift für Unternehmens- und Gesellschaftsrecht* 2002, 47.

[992] See Rödder, T., *Die Wirtschaftsprüfung* 1991, 201; Jahn, A. and Herfs-Röttgen, E., *Der Betrieb* 2001, 631; Schulz, A. and Eicker, K., *Intertax* 2001, 332; Blanquet, F., *Zeitschrift für Unternehmens- und Gesellschaftsrecht* 2002, 64; Förster, G. and Lange, C., *Recht der Internationalen Wirtschaft* 2002, 585.

[993] Even though the minimum capital requirement was lowered to € 120,000 to make the SE also attractive to medium-sized businesses, it seems unlikely that companies of this size, which often will not have work councils or employee participation at management level, will be attracted by the SE, if only because of the cost and length of its formation process. See Ruding, H. O., *Tax Law Review* 2000, 109; Schulz, A. and Eicker, K., *Intertax* 2001, 341; Blanquet, F., *Zeitschrift für Unternehmens- und Gesellschaftsrecht* 2002, 63.

[994] The EU authorities are placing high hopes on the SE, suggesting that at a minimum 8,000 SEs will be created. See Joris, J.-L., *International Financial Law Review* 2002, 19.

[995] The Statute specifies four (primary) forms for creating an SE. According to Art. 2(1) of the *EU SE Statute*, an SE can be established (1) by merging two or more existing public or private limited liability companies (e.g., Dutch N.V., French SA, or German AG) formed under the laws of a member state and having their registered and head offices within the EU; (2) by the set up of a holding company by public limited liability companies or private limited liability companies (e.g., Dutch B.V., French SARL, or German GmbH), formed under the laws of a member state and having their registered and head offices within the EU; (3) as a joint subsidiary of two or more corporate bodies governed by public or private law (e.g., partnership, state-owned companies) from at least two different member states; or (4) by the transformation of a public limited liability company that has operated in two (or more) member states for at least two years, without the prerequisite to dissolve the company. The fifth and secondary form for establishing an SE is the creation by an SE of a wholly-owned single shareholder subsidiary. See Schulz, A. and Eicker, K., *Intertax* 2001, 334; Blanquet, F., *Zeitschrift für Unternehmens- und Gesellschaftsrecht* 2002, 44; Bungert, H. and Beier, C. H., *Europäisches Wirtschafts- und Steuerrecht* 2002, 6; Joris, J.-L., *International Financial Law Review* 2002, 20; Lannoo, K. and Levin, M., *EU Company*, 2002, 14; Lutter, M., *Betriebs-Berater* 2002, 4; O'Grady, E., *Tax Notes International* 2002, 1065; Schulz, A. and Petersen, S., *Deutsches Steuerrecht* 2002, 1509.

[996] Except if created as a wholly-owned subsidiary of an SE.

[997] See Jahn, A. and Herfs-Röttgen, E., *Der Betrieb* 2001, 636; Schulz, A. and Eicker, K., *Intertax* 2001, 337; Schulz, A. and Geismar, B., *Deutsches Steuerrecht* 2001, 1082; Warner, R. and Cussons, P., *International Financial Law Review* 2002, 53.

[998] The EU Commission issued a draft directive on cross-border loss utilization (EU, Proposal, 1990). However, the directive was never finalized. See Schwarz, J. S., *Journal of International Taxation* 1992, 372; Schreiber, U., *Steuer und*

that neither it, nor any related legislative instrument at the EU level, so far addresses the obstacles that exist from a tax perspective for the types of corporate reorganization that the formation of an SE makes possible. If, for example, the SE is created by cross-border amalgamation,[999] existing domestic tax rules in member states would tax capital gains on the assets of the merging entities at the time of the merger or would treat the resulting exchange of shares as a taxable disposition of shares by the shareholders of the participating companies.[1000]

The EU Merger Directive[1001] would address these problems.[1002] It essentially provides a mechanism for tax deferral whereby the existing tax basis in the assets of the merging entities is attributed to the merged entity which is deemed to acquire a p.e. in the jurisdiction in which the assets are located, so as to preserve the taxable substance relating to those assets in those jurisdictions.[1003] The EU Merger Directive is not yet explicitly applicable to SEs,[1004] but the Commission set up a working group to deal with amendments to both the EU Merger Directive and the EU Parent-Subsidiary Directive, which will eliminate double taxation on intragroup dividend payments within the Community.[1005]

As the focus of this paper is on holding companies, only the formation of a holding SE will be analyzed. The creation of an SE is only permitted if it meets cross-border tests. In the case of a formation via establishment of a holding company, at least two of the participating companies must be governed by the laws of different member states or have had a subsidiary or branch within the EU during the preceding two years.[1006] Prior to the creation of the holding SE, the management or administrative organs of the companies involved must agree on the draft terms of creating the holding

---

Wirtschaft 1994, 250; Rosenbach, G., *Steuerliche Parameter für die Internationale Standortwahl*, 1995, paragraph M 63; Dautzenberg, N., *Unternehmensbesteuerung im EG-Binnenmarkt*, 1997, 331.

[999] The complexity and length of the formation process through amalgamations or the formation of a joint holding company may severely complicate such creation, in particular, for listed public companies, given the interaction between the provisions for the formation of an SE and the public offering or takeover provision requirements, often in at least two member states. Thus, it seems very likely that those groups would be created by maintaining existing companies at the first stage, followed at the second stage, by the creation of an SE through conversion or merger, if they wanted to adopt that format.

[1000] For example, assume a scenario where a double tax treaty exits between two jurisdictions. If the parent company disposes of stock in a foreign subsidiary, the capital gain recognized may be taxed in the jurisdiction in which the seller is resident, according to Art. 13(4) of the *2000 OECD model tax convention*. If the participation is part of the business property of a p.e., then the jurisdiction where the business is carried out through the branch may impose tax on the capital gain (Art. 13(2) of the *2000 OECD model tax convention*).

[1001] No. 90/434, dated July 23, 1990, *Official Journal of the European Communities*, No. L 225/1, dated August 20, 1990.

[1002] However, at this point in time, some member states, such as France, Germany, and the U.K., have not completely transformed the EU Merger Directive into local law, disregarding the due date for transformation, which was December 31, 1991 (Art. 12 of the *EU Merger Directive*). For example, these authorities reasoned the partial transformation with the lack of EU company law on cross-border amalgamations and division was insufficient cause to implement the Directive. Thus, due to the adopted EU SE Statute they are forced to adjust their local laws (to comply with the 1990 Directive), as the arguments brought forward by the different authorities will lose their plausibility on the date of the SE Statute. As a result, the direct application of the regulation (see *supra* note 988) and its reference to national laws will require the respective member states to adapt their domestic tax acts, i.e., transform the remaining parts of the Merger Directive, by October 8, 2004. See Herzig, N. and Förster, G., *Der Betrieb* 1992, 962; Thömmes, O. and Tomsett, E., *EC Tax Review* 1992, 230; Bogenschütz, E., *Verletzung materiellen Rechts*, 1997, 40; Jesse, L., *Errichtung internationaler Holdingstrukturen durch Anteilstausch*, 1997, 834; Griemla, S., *Die ertragsteuerliche Behandlung der Europäischen Aktiengesellschaft*, 1999, 49; Schulz, A. and Eicker, K., *Intertax* 2001, 338; Schulz, A. and Geismar, B., *Deutsches Steuerrecht* 2001, 1083; Lutter, M., *Betriebs-Berater* 2002, 6. For a discussion of the need for an European Law Institute, see Ebke, W. F., *Unternehmenstrechtsangleichung in der Europäischen Union*, 1999, 189.

[1003] Art. 4(1) and (2) of the *EU Merger Directive*. See Schulz, A. and Eicker, K., *Intertax* 2001, 337; Schulz, A. and Geismar, B., *Deutsches Steuerrecht* 2001, 1082.

[1004] See Blanquet, F., *Zeitschrift für Unternehmens- und Gesellschaftsrecht* 2002, 55. Discussions have been held as to whether it is necessary for the SE to be explicitly mentioned in the appendix to the EC Merger Directive in order to benefit from it. As Art. 10 of the *EU SE Statute* is linked to the national laws for stock corporations and the respective stock corporations are included, the directive should also apply to the SE without further amendment. See Herzig, N. and Griemla, S., *Steuer und Wirtschaft* 2002, 59.

[1005] It is further proposed that the scope of both directives be extended in order to cover direct taxes on cross-border company restructurings. See EU Commission, *Communication*, 2001, 12; Vanden Abbele, M., *Closing Remarks*, 2002, 3; Warner, R. and Cussons, P., *International Financial Law Review* 2002, 53.

[1006] Art. 2(2) of the *EU SE Statute*.

SE, which must include the minimum proportion of the shares in each of the companies involved which the shareholders must contribute upon formation of the holding SE, the share-exchange ratio and the proposed statute of the SE.[1007]

The minimum proportion of shares in each of the participating companies must include shares conferring more than 50 percent of the permanent voting rights.[1008] The statutory auditor of each company involved, or a single independent auditor must review the draft terms of formation and report, in particular, on any issues arising from the valuation and the proposed share-exchange ratio.[1009] The draft terms must then be approved in a general meeting of shareholders for each of the companies promoting the operation.[1010]

Pursuant to Art. 33(1) of the *EU SE Statute*, the shareholders will have a period of three months to inform the promoting companies whether they intend to contribute their shares to the formation of the holding SE.[1011] The SE shall only be deemed to be formed if the shareholders have assigned the required minimum proportion of shares within the three-month period.[1012] The formation of a holding SE is not restricted to a stock corporation, as Art. 32(7) of the *EU SE Statute* provides the analogous application to private limited liability companies. Moreover, the companies promoting the operation can be residents of the same member state if they own a subsidiary that is incorporated under the laws of another member state or a branch in another member state, adhering to the theory of cross-border relations.[1013]

When considering whether the SE might be a useful vehicle, it is mostly put forward that the SE will allow groups to merge their European subsidiaries into a single legal entity with branches in the several member states in which the business is carried out. This is expected to reduce administrative costs and achieve some form of tax consolidation.[1014] In my view, it is a known fact that corporations have always been able to organize their foreign enterprises as branches rather than subsidiaries, however, it is clear, that for a variety of reasons, only a few groups currently conduct significant business through EU branches.[1015] Why would the SE Statute change the common strategy?

In order to promote the SE, it was resolved at the European Conference on Company Taxation in Brussels on April 29/30, 2002 that the SE, which needs a Community-wide tax regime to be a useful corporate vehicle, would be used as a pilot project to test the CTB approach.[1016] The EU Commission will, in particular, work on the SE and its appropriate tax treatment.[1017] The Commission will further consider other possible options and will issue a communication on progress early in 2003.[1018]

To sum up, the number of companies that need to manage their tax affairs on a pan-European basis will increase, with implications for both tax strategy and financial systems.[1019] This applies to both European companies and inbound investors from external countries, especially the U.S. The SE would enable cross-border mergers between public limited liability companies within the EU under a

---

[1007] Art. 32(2) and Art. 20(1)(a), (b), (c), (f), (g), (h), and (i) of the *EU SE Statute*.

[1008] Art. 32(2) last sentence of the *EU SE Statute*.

[1009] Art. 32(4) and (5) of the *EU SE Statute*.

[1010] Art. 32(6) of the *EU SE Statute*. According to Art. 32(3) of the *EU SE Statute*, the draft terms for the formation of the holding SE shall be publicized at least one month before the date of the general meeting.

[1011] The three-month period begins on the date upon which the terms of formation of the holding SE have been finally determined (Art. 33(1) last sentence of the *EU SE Statute*).

[1012] Art. 33(2) of the *EU SE Statute*.

[1013] See Blanquet, F., *Zeitschrift für Unternehmens- und Gesellschaftsrecht* 2002, 45.

[1014] See Cussons, P., Cooke, D. and Newton, D., *Journal of International Taxation* 2002, 47.

[1015] For the internationalization of operations, refer *supra* page 19.

[1016] See EU Commission, *Memorandum*, 2002.

[1017] See Vanden Abbele, M., *Closing Remarks*, 2002, 10.

[1018] See O'Grady, E., *Tax Notes International* 2002, 1060; Vanden Abbele, M., *Closing Remarks*, 2002, 11; Weiner, J. A., *Tax Notes International* 2002 II, 520.

[1019] There will also be significant impacts on specific corporate functions, such as cross-border electronic commerce. For an analyzis, see Benjamin, W. C. and Nathanson, M. J., *Journal of International Taxation* 1998, 29.

tax-neutral regime, which might be viewed as a clear and important benefit.[1020] In the absence of an appropriate Community-wide legal framework, such mergers are, at present, either impossible or extremely complex. Even then, the SE will be taxed on its income in its home jurisdiction like any domestic corporation, as well as in the jurisdiction of the former merged entities under the rule on branch taxation. This regime is far removed from the concept that an SE should be taxed under a single set of tax rules.[1021] As a result, without appropriate tax treatment, most companies will not likely see advantages in adopting this new legal form. In my opinion, the SE can be a very attractive vehicle for pan-European operations, provided that it receives appropriate tax treatment.

5. SUMMARY

The U.S. is a high-tax jurisdiction that does not provide a special tax regime for holding companies. Hence, typical holding company income, such as dividends and capital gains received from domestic and foreign shareholdings, is generally subject to U.S. tax. Further, given that under U.S. tax law a maximum debt-to-equity ratio of 1.5:1 is prescribed,[1022] an important tax planning tool, which consists of shifting income from high-tax to low-tax jurisdictions, is limited in its effect. Hence, a U.S. enterprise doing business in multiple EU member states must consider establishing an EU holding company, not only for business reasons, but also for tax reasons.

In order to finalize the selection of a specific location for an EU holding company and to impart the most relevant guidance for tax planning purposes, this paper analyzed the primary tax benefits of holding companies as well as the tax planning goals of a U.S. MNC. Based on this analysis, tax planning tools available to a U.S. MNC to achieve the previously specified goals were identified, and their functionality in practice was demonstrated. The traditional debates would have ended here, but this paper went one step further and assessed the tax impacts at the ultimate parent company level and identified tax planning barriers that counteract the functionality of the tax planning tools and, therefore, influence the likely achievement of the stated objectives.

If, and to what extent, various EU member states are suited to tax planning measures was analyzed in a country-by-country synopsis. Using this information, various tax planning techniques were designed that give rise to the maximum available tax benefits and avoid the application of counteracting provisions. When designing tax efficient structures, it was noted that due to the dual nature of hybrid entities, significant tax savings are achieved on an international tax planning basis by U.S. MNCs when such structures are incorporated in the tax planning process. This paper included an analysis at the level of the ultimate parent company, U.S. MNC, and as a result, the tax planning structures designed herein will achieve the highest possible tax benefits.

Moreover, the examination did not end there, but went on to consider potential changes to the U.S. Subpart F provisions that were identified as tax planning barriers, and elaborated on which tax planning structures would function to generate tax savings in the long-term. The paper not only analyzed potential changes to local laws, but also examined international initiatives on harmful tax competition and the European Company. The latter was viewed in detail as it is expected that, due to the recent approval of the European Company Statute, numerous investors will rethink their organizational structure and will reorganize themselves along specific lines of activity in the form of a holding company. This restructuring of operations through a holding company is one of four ways to create an SE.

Proposals for more intensive research relating to tax planning opportunities for EU holding companies derived from this analysis might include, in particular:

- concentrating on international initiatives for holding companies and harmful tax practices;

[1020] See Herzig, N. and Griemla, S., *Steuer und Wirtschaft* 2002, 56; Schulz, A. and Geismar, B., *Deutsches Steuerrecht* 2001, 1086.

[1021] See Ruding, H. O., *Tax Law Review* 2000, 109; Kessler, W. and Dorfmueller, P., *Journal of International Taxation* 2002, 56.

[1022] IRC § 163(j).

- analyzing the developments in the taxation in the internal market and the impact on international tax planning for EU holding companies;
- elaborating on the benefits of establishing an SE holding company for a U.S. MNC; and
- reviewing the frequent changes in tax laws and updating the recommended holding company structures or designing new ones. While undertaking this analysis, it became clear that the catch phrase of "needing to keep up to date" has, for international tax practitioners, taken on a new meaning. Local tax systems continue to compete to attract businesses[1023] with an international trend toward lowering statutory tax rates and broadening the tax base.[1024] These persistent changes will require ongoing research to ensure that all tax planning initiatives are utilized to reduce global tax costs.

[1023] See Jackstein, C.-D., *Das deutsche Steuerrecht im Wettbewerb mit ausländischen Steuersystemen*, 179; Bos, W. J., *European Taxation* 2000, 410.

[1024] See Peroni, R. J., *University of Miami Law Review* 1997, 976.

REFERENCES

Abrams, H. E./Doernberg, R. L. (Essentials of United States Taxation, 1999): Essentials of United States Taxation, The Hague/London/Boston 1999

Albrecht, A. (Internationale Wirtschaftsbriefe, Fach 5, Irland, Gruppe 3, 1998): Recht der Kapitalgesellschaften in Irland, in: Internationale Wirtschaftsbriefe, Fach 5, Irland, Gruppe 3, 1998, 33-52

Al-Tabatabaie, N. (Tax Notes International 1998): Tax Classification of German Business Entities Under the U.S. Check-the-Box Regulations, in: Tax Notes International 1998 (8 June), 1801-1816

Altenburger, P. (Tax Management International Forum 2002): Switzerland, in: Tax Management International Forum 2002, Vol. 23, No. 1, 42-44

Altshuler, R./Fulghieri, P. (National Tax Journal 1994): Incentive Effects of Foreign Tax Credits on Multinational Corporations, in: National Tax Journal 1994, 349-361

Altshuler, R./Grubert, H. (National Tax Journal 2001): Where Will They Go if We Go Territorial? Dividend Exemption and the Location Decisions of U.S. Multinational Corporations, in: National Tax Journal 2001, 787-809

American Bar Association Task Force on Earnings and Profits (Tax Lawyer 1991): Comments On The Current Rules Governing Earnings And Profits Of Foreign Corporations And Suggestions For Change, in: Tax Lawyer 1991, 165-193

American Chamber of Commerce in Germany e.V./PricewaterhouseCoopers GmbH (Hrsg.) (Steuern in den USA, 2001): Steuern in den USA - ein Leitfaden für deutsche Investoren, herausgegeben von American Chamber of Commerce in Germany e.V./PricewaterhouseCoopers GmbH, bearbeitet von Besch, C./Endres, D./Heise, H.-J., u.a., Frankfurt 2001

Andersen, P. S. (Denmark, 2001): Denmark, in: IBFD, The Taxation Of Companies In Europe, Binder *, Last Supplement No. 162, April 2002

Andersen, R. E. (International Tax Review 1996): Check-the-Box: US Entity Classification Proposal May Have Significant International Consequences, in: International Tax Review 1996, Vol. 7, Iss. 6, 3

Andersen, R. E. (Foreign Tax Credits, 2002): Foreign Tax Credits, Boston 1996, Current Through 2002 Supplement No. 1

Anesini, S. (Die Holding als Instrument der Führung in konzernierten Unternehmen, 1991): Die Holding als Instrument der Führung in konzernierten Unternehmen, Bamberg 1991

Angus, B. M./Kies, K. J. (Tax Executive 2000): The United States Responds to the WTO FSC Decision: Round One and Counting, in: Tax Executive 2000, 436-443

Anonymous (Journal of Accountancy 1991): Tax Court Reverses IRS on Foreign Tax Credits, in: Journal of Accountancy 1991, 24

Anonymous (Journal of International Taxation 1994): Income From Foreign Partnership Was Not Subpart F Income, in: Journal of International Taxation 1994 (June), 285

Anonymous (Management Today 1995): On the tax borderline, in: Management Today 1995, November, 17-18

Anonymous (Journal of International Taxation 1995): Tax Court About-Face In Brown Group: Income From Foreign Partnership Was Subpart F Income, in: Journal of International Taxation 1995 (March), 143

Anonymous (Tax Executive 1996): Souring of Capital Losses, in: Tax Executive 1996, 246-247

Anonymous (Journal of International Taxation 1996): IRS Guidance On When CFC Income Earned Through Partnership Is Subpart F Income, in: Journal of International Taxation 1996 (October), 479

Anonymous (Tax Executive 1997): Tax Simplification and Reform - March 25, 1997, in: Tax Executive 1997, 153-159

Anonymous (International Tax Review 1998): US Hybrid Branches - Urgent Review Required, in: International Tax Review 1998, 4

Anonymous (Tax Executive 1998 I): Notice on Hybrid Branch Arrangements: Poor Tax Policy That Should Be Withdrawn, in: Tax Executive 1998, 89

Anonymous (Tax Executive 1998 II): Notice 98-11, Relating to the Treatment of Hybrid Arrangements under Subpart F, in: Tax Executive 1998, 145-146

Anonymous (Tax Executive 1999 I): International complexity and simplification, in: Tax Executive 1999, 347-351

Anonymous (Tax Executive 1999 II): Creating and Using Hybrid Entities, in: Tax Executive 1999, 568-573

Anonymous (Internationale Wirtschaftsbriefe, Fach 3a, Rechtsprechung, Gruppe 1, 2000): Kein Missbrauch bei Zwischenschaltung irischer Finanzanlagegesellschaften ("Irland I"), in: Internationale Wirtschaftsbriefe, Fach 3a, Rechtsprechung, Gruppe 1, 2000, 901-908

Anonymous (Tax Executive 2001): Limitation on Using Foreign Tax Credits to Offset AMT Liability, in: Tax Executive 2001, 308

Anonymous (International Tax Report 2001): Denmark, in: International Tax Report 2001 (June), 11

Anonymous (Steuer Revue 2001 I): Zürich: Weisung der Finanzdirektion über die Besteuerung von Beteiligungs-, Holding-, Domizil- und gemischten Gesellschaften, in: Steuer Revue 2001, 235-244

Anonymous (Steuer Revue 2001 II): Bund: Im Steuerpaket auch etwas für Unternehmen, in: Steuer Revue 2001, 447

Anonymous (Journal of International Taxation 2001): Case Of 1st Impression: Acquiror Had To Include Subpart F Income Of Voting/Grantor Trust, in: Journal of International Taxation 2001 (November), 3-5

Anonymous (International Tax Review 2001/2002): EU Company Taxation Stirs Up Controversy, in: International Tax Review 2001/2002, Vol. 13, Iss. 1, 3

Anonymous (International Tax Review 2002): Luxembourg offers corporates a sweetener, in: International Tax Review 2002, Vol. 13, Iss. 2, 3

Anonymous (International Tax Report 2002): OECD: Offshore centers accede to anti-harmful tax initiative, in: International Tax Report 2002 (June), 11

Anson, T. F./Culbertson, R. E./Dubert, C. A. (International Tax Review 1998): United States, in: International Tax Review 1998, Tax Developments Yearbook, 77-84

Arndt, H.-W./Ringel, E. (Betriebs-Berater 1988): Inländische Holdinggesellschaften und § 42 AO, in: Betriebs-Berater 1988, 2147-2153

Arnold, B. J. (Tax Notes International 2002): Comments on the Proposed Adoption of a Territorial Tax System in the United States, in: Tax Notes International 2002 (11 March), 1091-1094

Arnold, B. J./McIntyre, M. J. (International Tax Primer, 1995): International Tax Primer, Den Haag 1995

Aud, E. F. Jr./Benson, D. M./Garrett-Nelson, L. (Tax Executive 2001): Treasury's Long-Awaited Subpart F Study Breaks No New Ground, Touts Ending Deferral, in: Tax Executive 2001, 48-54

Ault, H. (Tax Competition, 2000): Tax Competition: What (If Anything) To Do About It?, in: Kirchhof, P./Lehner, M./Raupach, A./Rodi, M. (Hrsg.): Staaten und Steuern: Festschrift für Klaus Vogel zum 70. Geburtstag, Heidelberg 2000, 1117-1123

Avi-Yonah, R. S. (Texas Law Review 1996): The Structure of International Taxation: A Proposal for Simplification, in: Texas Law Review 1996, 1301-1359

Avi-Yonah, R. S. (Tax Notes International 1998): U.S. Notice 98-11 and the Logic of Subpart F: a Comparative Perspective, in: Tax Notes International 1998 (8 June), 1797-1800

Bader, A. (Steuergestaltung mit Holdinggesellschaften, 1998): Steuergestaltung mit Holdinggesellschaften, Herne 1998

Bärtels, H.-C. (Internationale Wirtschaftsbriefe, Fach 5, Frankreich, Gruppe 2, 2000): Der Unternehmenskauf im französischen Steuerrecht - unter besonderer Berücksichtigung aktueller Rechtsänderungen, in: Internationale Wirtschaftsbriefe, Fach 5, Frankreich, Gruppe 2, 2000, 1243-1256

Ball, G. T./Siegel, M. A. (Tax Notes International 1995): U.S. Issues Foreign Entity Classification Ruding Procedure Guidelines: The Insanity Continues, in: Tax Notes International 1995 (23 January), 315-325

Balle, C. H. (European Taxation 2002): Denmark - Current Developments in Denmark, in: European Taxation 2002, 255-257*Baron, R.* (Tax Planning International transfer pricing 2002): Tax and the Internal Market, in: Tax Planning International transfer pricing 2002, Vol. 3, No. 1, 14-16

Barrenechea, S./Ogea, R./Mullerat, R. (Tax Notes International 2000): Spain Improves Holding Company Regime, in: Tax Notes International 2000 (7 August), 585-586

Barrett, J. H./Ewing, W. P. (Florida Bar Journal 1998): International Implications Of The Check-The-Box Regulations, in: Florida Bar Journal 1998 (August), 34-39

Bauman, C./Schadewald, M. (Journal of International Accounting, Auditing & Taxation 2001): Impact of foreign operations on reported effective tax rates: interplay of foreign taxes, U.S. taxes and U.S. GAAP, in: Journal of International Accounting, Auditing & Taxation 2001, 177-196

Baumann, S. (Steuersensitive Finanzierung der Holdinggesellschaft, 1994): Steuersensitive Finanzierung der Holdinggesellschaft - Eine Betriebswirtschaftliche Analyse des Standortes Schweiz aus Sicht der Unternehmen, Oberhallau 1994

Baumann, W. (Steueroasen und internationale Holdingkonstruktionen, 1996): Steueroasen und internationale Holdingkonstruktionen: Einführung in das internationale Steuerrecht, Wien 1996

Baumgärtel, M./Perlet, H. (Standortfragen bei der Bildung von Holdinggesellschaften, 1994): Standortfragen bei der Bildung von Holdinggesellschaften, in: Maßbaum, M./Meyer-Scharenberg, D./Perlet, H. (Hrsg.): Die deutsche Unternehmensbesteuerung im europäischen Binnenmarkt - Besteuerungsgrundlagen und grenzüberschreitende Steuerplanung in Deutschland, Köln 1994, 691-781

Baumhoff, H. (Einkunftsabgrenzung bei international verbundenen Unternehmen, 1998): Einkunftsabgrenzung bei international verbundenen Unternehmen, in: Mössner, J. M./u.a., Steuerrecht international tätiger Unternehmen - Handbuch der Besteuerung von Auslandsaktivitäten inländischer Unternehmen und von Inlandsaktivitäten ausländischer Unternehmen, 2. Auflage, Köln 1998

Bayle, P./Mariano, F. (Journal of International Taxation 2002): France 2001/2002: Tax Policy Reflects European Constraints And Economic Challenges, in: Journal of International Taxation 2002 (September), 20-29 and 48

Beer, Y. (Virginia Tax Review 2000): Unpacking The Cancellation Of Indebtedness Income Doctrine: Towards Economic Reality-Based Taxation, in: Virginia Tax Review 2000 (Winter), 457-514

Beilstein, W. (Internationale Wirtschaftsbriefe, Fach 5, Schweiz, Gruppe 2, 1995): Holding-, Domizil-, Hilfs- und Verwaltungsgesellschaften in der Schweiz, in: Internationale Wirtschaftsbriefe, Fach 5, Schweiz, Gruppe 2, 1995, 447-462

Beilstein, W./Ah, J. von (Internationale Wirtschaftsbriefe, Fach 5, Schweiz, Gruppe 2, 2002): Änderungen im Steuerrecht der Schweiz, in: Internationale Wirtschaftsbriefe, Fach 5, Schweiz, Gruppe 2, 2002, 501-514

Belanger, P./Taylor, G. (Journal of International Taxation 2002): Structuring Opportunities To Use CFC Losses, in: Journal of International Taxation 2002 (May), 18-31

Beltjens, R./Saussoy, S. (Tax Planning International Review 2002): The 2002 Luxembourg Tax Reform, in: Tax Planning International Review 2002, Vol. 29, No. 4, 8-15

Benjamin, W. C./Nathanson, M. J. (Journal of International Taxation 1998): Conducting Business Using the Internet: Gauging the Treat of Foreign Taxation, in: Journal of International Taxation 1998 (March), 29-32 and 48

Benson, D. M. (The Tax Adviser 1996): Entering Foreign Markets - One Step at a Time, in: The Tax Adviser 1996, 628-631

Benson, D. M. (Tax Notes International 2002): 2001: A Subpart F Odyssey - From U.S. Treasury to Suggestion of Territoriality, in: Tax Notes International 2002 (25 February), 855-864

Benson, D. M./Hicks, H./O'Connor, M. (International Tax Review 2001): US and WTO Fight On, in: International Tax Review 2001, Vol. 12, Iss. 2, 6568

Benson, D. M./O'Connor, P. (Tax Notes 1999): Treasury's Retreat On Hybrid Branches, in: Tax Notes 1999, 769-771

Benson, D. M./O'Connor, P./Rollinson, M. A. (Tax Management International Journal 1998 I): Current Status of Proposed Legislation Affecting International Tax Rules, in: Tax Management International Journal 1998, 585-597

Benson, D. M./O'Connor, P./Rollinson, M. A. (Tax Management International Journal 1998 II): Current Status of Proposed Legislation Affecting International Tax Rules, in: Tax Management International Journal 1998, 662-676

Benson, D. M./Rollinson, M. A. (Tax Management International Journal 1998 I): Current Status of Proposed Legislation Affecting International Tax Rules, in: Tax Management International Journal 1998, 259-264

Benson, D. M./Rollinson, M. A. (Tax Management International Journal 1998 II): Current Status of Proposed Legislation Affecting International Tax Rules, in: Tax Management International Journal 1998, 476-478

Benson, D. M./Rollinson, M. A./O'Connor, M. M./Baik, S. A.(Tax Management International Journal 1997): "Hybrid" Entities: Practical Application Under the Check-the-Box Regime, in: Tax Management International Journal 1997, 363-385

Bentley, P. E. (The CPA Journal 1998): Foreign Entity Classification - Checking A Pandora's Box?, in: The CPA Journal 1998, 64

Berger, H./Quack, J. S. (Intertax 2001): Aspects of the German Tax Reduction Act with regard to the Treatment of Dividends and Capital Gains, in: Intertax 2001, 76-86

Bergquist, P. J. (Tax Executive 1995): Notice 95-14 - Check-the-Box Procedure for Entity
    Classification, in: Tax Executive 1995, 323-327

Birnkrant, H. J./Croker, J. E. Jr. (Journal of Taxation 1998): Hybrid Regs. Raise Issues About Subpart
    F, Treasury's Regulatory Authority, and Check-the-Box, in: Journal of Taxation 1998,
    45-53

Bishop, C. G./Kleinberger, D. S. (Limited Liability Companies, 2002): Limited Liability Companies -
    Tax and Business Law, Boston 1994, Current Through 2002 Supplement No. 2

Bittker, B. I./Emory, M./Streng, W. P. (Federal Income Taxation of Corporations and Shareholders,
    2002): Federal Income Taxation of Corporations and Shareholders: Forms, 4th ed.,
    Boston 1995, Current Through 2002 Supplement No. 2

Bittker, B. I./Eustice, J. S. (Federal Income Taxation of Corporations and Shareholders, 2002): Federal
    Income Taxation of Corporations and Shareholders, 7th ed., Boston 2000, Current
    Through 2002 Supplement No. 3

Bittker, B. I./Lokken, L. (Federal Taxation of Income, Estates and Gifts, 2002): Federal Taxation of
    Income, Estates and Gifts, 3rd ed. Boston 2000, Current Through 2002 Supplement No. 3

Blanluet, G./Bouzidi, C./Bouzoraa, M.-A. (France, 2001): France, in: IBFD, The Taxation Of
    Companies In Europe, Binder **, Last Supplement No. 162, April 2002

Blanquet, F. (Zeitschrift für Unternehmens- und Gesellschaftsrecht 2002): European Company Law
    Review: Das Statut der Europäischen Aktiengesellschaft (Societas Europaea „SE") - Ein
    Gemeinschaftsinstrument für die grenzüberschreitende Zusammenarbeit im Dienste der
    Unternehmen, in: Zeitschrift für Unternehmens- und Gesellschaftsrecht 2002, 20-65

Böhme, C. A. (Internationales Steuerrecht 1998): Entwicklung der internationalen Organschaft in
    Dänemark, in: Internationales Steuerrecht 1998, 165-171

Bogaerts, R. (European Taxation 2002): Corporate Tax Reform Influences Luxembourg's
    International Competitiveness as Holding Company Location, in: European
    Taxation 2002, 380-393

Bogenschütz, E. (Verletzung materiellen Rechts, 1997): Verletzung materiellen Rechts durch nicht
    richtlinienkonforme Transformationsakte der Fusionsrichtlinie, in: Burmester, G./Endres,
    D. (Hrsg.): Aussensteuerrecht, Doppelbesteuerungsabkommen und EU-Recht im
    Spannungsverhältnis, Festschrift für Helmut Debatin zum 70. Geburtstag, München 1997,
    35-54

Bogenschütz, E./Dorfler, O. (International Tax Review 1997/1998): Combining Objectives - A US
    acquisitions in Germany, in: International Tax Review 1997/1998, Vol. 9, Iss. 1, 38-40

Bogenschütz, E./Wright, K. (Tax Notes International 2000): German Supreme Tax Court Rules on
    Irish Financial Services Companies, in: Tax Notes International 2000 (3 April), 1512-
    1514

Bolanz, G. (Die EU-Holding als strategisches Gestaltungselement in der Steuerplanung, 1998): Die
    EU-Holding als strategisches Gestaltungselement in der Steuerplanung internationaler
    Schweizer Konzerne - Standortwahl und kritische Beurteilung der Besteuerungsfolgen,
    Zürich 1998

Boles, E. (Gesellschaften im US-Einkommensteuerrecht, 1993): Gesellschaften im US-
    Einkommensteuerrecht, München 1993

Bolkestein, F. (European Taxation 2000): Taxation and Competition: The Realization of the Internal
    Market, in: European Taxation 2000, 401-406

Bongers, E./Visser, K.-J. (Journal of International Taxation 2003): New Dutch Hybrid Loan
    Legislation Fills in Some Gaps, in: Journal of International Taxation 2003 (January), 30-
    37 and 64

Boos, M./Rehkugler, H./Tucha, T. (Der Betrieb 2000): Internationale Verrechnungspreise - Ein Überblick, in: Der Betrieb 2000, 2389-2393

Bos, W. J. (European Taxation 2000): Netherlands - The Changing World of European Tax Policy, in: European Taxation 2000, 409-412

Boucher, K. J. (The Tax Adviser 1998): State Conformity to the Check-the-Box Regs., in: The Tax Adviser 1998, 166-167

Bouma, H. B./Rosenbloom, H. D. (Tax Management International Journal 2002): Taxes Covered by §960(a)(3), in: Tax Management International Journal 2002, 83-94

Boyle, M. P. (Tax Executive 2000): Comments on Changes in Entity Classification: Special Rule for Certain Foreign Eligible Entities, in: Tax Executive 2000, 250-252

Bremer, S. (Der Holdingstandort Bundesrepublik Deutschland, 1996): Der Holdingstandort Bundesrepublik Deutschland - Eine vergleichende Analyse der Besteuerung europäischer Holdingstandorte, Frankfurt a.M./Berlin/Bern/u.a. 1996

Bremer, S./Staudt Vontobel, H. (Internationale Wirtschaftsbriefe, Fach 5, Schweiz, Gruppe 2, 1999): Capital Gains nach neuem schweizerischen Bundessteuerrecht, in: Internationale Wirtschaftsbriefe, Fach 5, Schweiz, Gruppe 2, 1999, 481-486

Brewer, K. P./Forouhar, M. N. (Tax Management International Journal 1997): Final and Proposed Passive Foreign Investment Company Regulations, in: Tax Management International Journal 1997, 160-165

Brown, K. B./Rothschild, D. P. (Mertens Law of Federal Income Taxation, 2002): Chapter 45. Nonresident Aliens and Foreign Corporations, in: Mertens Law of Federal Income Taxation, New York 2002

Bruggen, E. van der (Intertax 2001): State Responsibility under Customary International Lay in Matters of Taxation and Tax Competition, in: Intertax 2001, 115-139

Brumbaugh, D. L. (Tax Notes International 1992): Federal Tax and Foreign Investment in the United States: An Assessment, in: Tax Notes International 1992 (3 February), 229-237

Bühner, R. (Management-Holding, 1992): Management-Holding: Unternehmensstruktur der Zukunft, Landsberg/Lech, 1992

Bühner, R. (Der Betrieb 1993): Management-Holding in der Praxis - Eine empirische Untersuchung deutscher Unternehmen, in: Der Betrieb 1993, 285-290

Bühner, R. (Der Betrieb 1994): Aussagefähigkeit des Konzernabschlusses in der Management Holding, in: Der Betrieb 1994, 437-444

Bühner, R./Walter, H. (Der Betrieb 1977): Divisionalisierung in der Bundesrepublik Deutschland - Eine empirische Analyse der Geschäftsberichte von 1965 bis 1975 der größten deutschen Industrie-Aktiengesellschaften, in: Der Betrieb 1977, 1205-1207

Bungert, H./Beier, C. H. (Europäisches Wirtschafts- und Steuerrecht 2002): Die Europäische Aktiengesellschaft - Das Statut und seine Umsetzung in die Praxis, in: Europäisches Wirtschafts- und Steuerrecht 2002, 1-12

Burek, D. (Die Besteuerung der Holdinggesellschaft, 1998): Die Besteuerung der Holdinggesellschaft, Würzburg 1998

Burton, E. (The Tax Adviser 1999): State Tax Pitfalls for LLCs, in: The Tax Adviser 1999, 96

Business and Industry Advisory Committee (European Taxation 2000): A Business View on Tax Competition - Prepared by the Business and Industry Advisory Committee to the OECD (BIAC) June 1999, in: European Taxation 2000, 421-425

Byrnes, L. A. (Tax Notes International 1989): The Effects of a Capital Gain Tax Preference On U.S. International Tax Provisions, in: Tax Notes International 1989 (July), 26

C&L Deutsche Revision AG (Besteuerung deutscher Unternehmen in den USA, 1994): Besteuerung deutscher Unternehmen in den USA, C&L Deutsche Revision (Hrsg.), Herne/Berlin 1994

Calderón, J. (Tax Notes International 2002): Review of Spain's Thin Capitalization Provisions, in: Tax Notes International 2002 (6 May), 633-645

Calianno, J. M./Gregoire, B. J. (Journal of International Taxation 2001): CFC Restructurings And Disposition: How International Provisions Alter the General Rules, in: Journal of International Taxation 2001 (October), 34-46

Carr, J. L. Jr./Moetell, M. C. (Tax Management International Journal 1995): IRS Issues Proposed Regulations Under Section 902, in: Tax Management International Journal 1995, 219-228

Carson, S./Cinnamon, A./Kronbergs, Z. (International Tax Review 1998 I): How to make the most of hybrids, in: International Tax Review 1998, October 1998, Vol. 9, Iss. 9, 33-35

Carson, S./Cinnamon, A./Kronbergs, Z. (International Tax Review 1998 II): US hybrids: The changing landscape, in: International Tax Review 1998, November, Vol. 9, Iss. 10, 25-29

Carson, S./Santa Maria, J. (The Tax Adviser 2000): Entity Classification Simplification Not That Simple, in: The Tax Adviser, 322-323

Casna, R. (International Tax Report 2002): From the Editor, in: International Tax Report 2002 (January/February), 1

CCH (2002 U.S. Tax Master Guide, 2001): 2002 U.S. Tax Master Guide, 85th ed., Chicago 2001

Cecil, W./Ciccotello, C. S./Grant, T. (Journal of Accountancy 1995): The Choice of Organizational Form, in: Journal of Accountancy 1995, 45-52

Charriau, J.-Y./Donsimoni, P./Poli, F. (Journal of International Taxation 1999): France: New SAS is the Perfect Vehicle for U.S. Check-the-Box Planning, in: Journal of International Taxation 1999 (September), 15

Chew, J. (The International Tax Journal 2002): Proposed Subpart F Hybrid Regulations Take Aim at Disregarded Entities, in: The International Tax Journal 2002, Vol. 28, Iss. 1, 54-65

Cinnamon, A. (International Tax Review 1999): Tasty regimes tempt holding companies, in: International Tax Review 1999, Vol. 10, Iss. 5, 9-11

Coffill, E. J./Wilson, P. Jr. (International Tax Review 1996): Federal/state confusion grows, in: International Tax Review 1996, Vol. 7, Iss. 2, 39-41

Commission of the European Community (Report, 1992): Report of the Committee of Independent Experts on Company Taxation, Brussels 1992

Conlon, R. (Tax Notes International 1996): Streamlining the U.S. Check-the-Box Regulations for the Foreign Corporation, in: Tax Notes International 1996 (21 October), 1377-1382

Cooper, M. J./Meicher, G./Stretch, C. (Tax Notes 1998): Suddenly Saving Foreign Taxes Is Abusive? An Untenable Proposal, in: Tax Notes 1998, 885-891

Cooper, M. J./Torgersen, S. (International Tax Review 1998): US Pauses For Breath On Subpart F, in: International Tax Review 1998, Vol. 9, Iss. 8, 67-70

Courage, C. (Recht der Internationalen Wirtschaft 1996): Die Holdingregelung im spanischen Steuerrecht, in: Recht der Internationalen Wirtschaft 1996, 674-678

Courage, C. (Internationale Wirtschaftsbriefe, Fach 5, Spanien, Gruppe 2, 1996): Änderungen des spanischen Körperschaftsteuergesetzes für ausländische Investoren, in: Internationale Wirtschaftsbriefe, Fach 5, Spanien, Gruppe 2, 1996, 213-220

Courage, C. (Körperschaftsteuer, 2000): in: Courage, C./Dechant, R.-M./González, D./u.a.: Steuerfibel Spanien: Erläuterungen zum spanischen Steuerrecht, Deutschsprachige Wiedergabe wichtiger steuerlicher Regelungen, Steuerliche Formulare, Steuerliches Glossarium, 1. Auflage, Frankfurt am Main 2000, 79-99

Coven, G. E. (Florida Tax Review 1999): International Comity And The Foreign Tax Credit: Crediting Nonconforming Taxes, in: Florida Tax Review 1999, 83-127

Crocco, P. Jr. (The Tax Adviser 2000): Effect of NOL carryovers on FTC, in: The Tax Adviser 2000, 480-482

Cueva González-Cotera, A. de la (European Taxation 2000): Spain: Tax Authorities Issue Ruling on "Comparable Income Taxes" for Participation Exemption Purposes, in: European Taxation 2000, 153-155

Cuff, T. F. (Journal of Partnership Taxation 1998): Impact of the New Proposed and Final Check-the-Box Regulations on Partnership Tax Status, in: Journal of Partnership Taxation 1998, 99-119

Culbertson, R. E. (Tax Notes International 1996): U.S. Tax Issues Affecting European Planning Techniques, in: Tax Notes International 1996 (25 November), 1759-1761

Cusí, J. M. (Tax Notes International 2001): ETVE: The Spanish Holding Entity, in: Tax Notes International 2001 (31 December), 1493-1499

Cussons, P./Cooke, D./Newton, D. (Journal of International Taxation 2002): European Direct Tax Policies Impede Single Market, in: Journal of International Taxation 2002 (February), 22-27 and 47

Cussons, P./Dorfmueller, P./Endres, D. (European Holding Companies, 2002): European Holding Companies, in: Dixon, J. (editor), Tolley's International Corporate Tax Planning, Croydon 2002, 6-1-6-49

Dagan, T. (Virginia Tax Review 1998): National Interests in the International Tax Game, in: Virginia Tax Review 1998 (Fall), 363-416

Daub, P. M. (Journal of International Taxation 1990): Foreign Finance Subsidiaries Are Still Useful After TRA'86, in: Journal of International Taxation 1990 (July/August), 69-77

Davis, B. N. (Tax Management International Journal 1995): U.S. Tax Treatment of "Reverse Hybrid" Foreign Entities, in: Tax Management International Journal 1995, 593-596

Davis, B. N. (Tax Management International Journal 1997 I): International Tax Planning under the final Check-the-Box Regulations, in: Tax Management International Journal 1997, 3-17

Davis, B. N. (Tax Management International Journal 1997 II): International Tax Planning Under "Check-the-Box" Remains Viable As New Regulations Explain Conversion Consequences, in: Tax Management International Journal 1997, 603-616

Davis, B. N./Lainoff, S. R. (Tax Law Review 1991): U.S. Taxation Of Foreign Joint Ventures, in: Tax Law Review 1991 (Winter), 165-297

Dautzenberg, N. (Unternehmensbesteuerung im EG-Binnenmarkt, 1997): Unternehmensbesteuerung im EG-Binnenmarkt - Problembereiche und Perspektiven, Lohmar/Köln 1997

Debatin, H./Endres, D. (The new US-German double tax treaty, 1990): Das neue Doppelbesteuerungsabkommen USA/Bundesrepublik Deutschland - The new US-German double tax treaty, München 1990

DeCarlo, J./Granwell, A./Suringa, D. (International Tax Review 1998): Hybrid Branches Face Stern Test, in: International Tax Review 1998, Vol. 9, Iss. 3, 19-21

Dehnen, P. H./Heinlein, A./Dubert, C. A. (Journal of International Taxation 1994): Crossing The Line Into A German Permanent Establishment, in: Journal of International Taxation 1994 (October), 450-455

Devereux, M. P./Griffith, R. (The Taxation of Discrete Investment Choices, 1999): The Taxation of Discrete Investment Choices (Revision 2), The Institute for Fiscal Studies, Working Paper Series No. W98/16, London 1999

D'Hont, P./Souchal, N. (Tax Planning International Review 2001): France's Finance Act for 2001, in: Tax Planning International Review 2001, Vol. 28, No. 3, 19-23

Dickenson, H. (The Practical Tax Lawyer 2001): Nine Practical Things You Should Know About Partnership Taxation, in: The Practical Tax Lawyer 2001 (Fall), 5-21

Dilworth, R. H./Andrus, J. L. (Tax Law and Practice, 2001): Financing International Operations Of U.S. Multinationals, in: Practising Law Institute (editor), Tax Law And Estate Planning Course Handbook Series - Tax Law and Practice, WL 2001, 1089-1125

DiMuzio, D. A./Sheard, T. J. (The Tax Adviser 1998): IRS Targets Multinationals, in: The Tax Adviser 1998, 290-294

Di Fronzo, M. A./Thomas, J. M. (Tax Notes International 1999): Proposed Brown Group Regulations: Heads - Treasury Wins, Tails - Taxpayer Loses, in: Tax Notes International 1999 (23 August), 759-772

Djanani, C. (Internationales Steuerrecht, 1998): Internationales Steuerrecht: österreichisches Außensteuerrecht, OECD-Musterabkommen, österreichische Doppelbesteuerungsabkommen, 2., überarbeitete Auflage, Wien 1998

Djanani, C./Brähler, G./Lösel, C. (Internationale Wirtschaftsbriefe, Fach 10, International, Gruppe 2, 2002): Konzepte der Mindestbesteuerung - Eine vergleichende Darstellung für Deutschland, Österreich und die USA, in: Internationale Wirtschaftsbriefe, Fach 10, International, Gruppe 2, 2002, 1603-1618

Doering, J. A. (Journal of International Taxation 1995): Planning For Direct Foreign Investment Under The PFIC Rules, in: Journal of International Taxation 1995 (May), 209-216

Doernberg, R. L. (Tax Notes International 1991): U.S. Double Corporate Taxation Under Subpart F, in: Tax Notes International 1991 (5 May), 503-506

Doernberg, R. L. (Florida Tax Review 1995): Treaty Override by Administrative Regulation: The Multiparty Financing Regulation, in: Florida Tax Review 1995, 521-551

Doernberg, R. L. (International Taxation In a Nutshell, 2001): International Taxation In a Nutshell, 5th ed., St. Paul 2001

Doernberg, R. L./Raad, K. van (Tax Notes 1999): Hybrid Entities and the U.S. Model Income Tax Treaty, in: Tax Notes 1999, 1651-1662

Dötsch, E./Pung, A. (Der Betrieb 2000, Beilage 10): Steuersenkungsgesetz: Die Änderungen bei der Körperschaftsteuer und bei der Anteilseignerbesteuerung, in: Der Betrieb 2000, Beilage 10, 1-27

Dolan, D. K./DuPuy, C. M./Bower, D. I. (Tax Management Memorandum 1998): Notice 98-5: Shoot Now, Aim Later, in: Tax Management Memorandum 1998, 143-158

Doornbosch, H./Berings, S. (Journal of International Taxation 2001): Netherlands Wrap-Up, in: Journal of International Taxation 2001 (August), 2-7

Doornbosch, H./Engelman, M. (CTF, 2001): The Netherlands (Pantaleo, N., New Developments for European Holding and Financing Companies), in: CTF, Report of Proceedings of the Fifty-Second Tax Conference, 2000 Conference Report, Toronto 2001, 13:6-13:10

Doralt, W./Ruppe, H. G. (Grundriß des österreichischen Steuerrechts, 2000): Grundriß des österreichischen Steuerrechts, Band 1: Einkommensteuer, Körperschaftsteuer, Umgründungssteuergesetz, Umsatzsteuer, Kommunalsteuer, 7. Auflage, Wien 2000

Doran, E./Vlot, P. (Journal of International Taxation 1999): Danish-Dutch Sandwich for EU-Bound Investment: New Tax-Efficient Holding Structure?, in: Journal of International Taxation 1999 (August), 33-36

Dougan, H. M. (Tax Notes International 1997): Check-the-Box - Looking Under the Lid, in: Tax Notes International 1997 (9 June), 1925-1942

Dreßler, G. (Gewinn- und Vermögensverlagerungen in Niedrigsteuerländer und ihre steuerliche Überprüfung, 2000): Gewinn- und Vermögensverlagerungen in Niedrigsteuerländer und ihre steuerliche Überprüfung, 3. Auflage, Neuwied 2000

Ebert, S. (Internationale Wirtschaftsbriefe, Fach 11, Europäische Gemeinschaften, Gruppe 3, 2002): Die Europäische Aktiengesellschaft auf dem level playing field der Gemeinschaft, in: Internationale Wirtschaftsbriefe, Fach 11, Europäische Gemeinschaften, Gruppe 3, 2002, 281-288

Ebke, W. F. (Unternehmensrechtsangleichung in der Europäischen Union, 1999): Unternehmensrechtsangleichung in der Europäischen Union: Brauchen wir ein European Law Institute?, in: Hübner, U./Ebke, W. F. (Hrsg.): Festschrift für Bernhard Großfeld zum 65. Geburtstag, Heidelberg 1999, 189-221

Eckberg, D. (Tax Planning International Review 2000): Proposed Changes to "Check-the-Box", in: Tax Planning International Review 2000, Vol. 27, No. 7, 27-28

Eden, S. (British Tax Review 2000): Corporate Tax Harmonisation in the European Community, in: British Tax Review 2000, 624-652

Eigenbrode, R. (The Tax Adviser 1993): Investing in Europe Through Hybrid Entities Can Ease U.S. FTC Problems, in: The Tax Adviser 1993, 443-446

Eilers, S. (Advance Pricing Agreements (APAs) im US-amerikanischen Steuerrecht und Abkommensrecht, 1996): Advance Pricing Agreements (APAs) im US-amerikanischen Steuerrecht und Abkommensrecht, in: Herzig, N., Advance Pricing Agreements (APAs) - Ein neues Instrument zur Vermeidung von Verrechnungspreiskonflikten?, Köln 1996, 1-12

Eimermann, D. (Internationales Steuerrecht 2002): OECD: Liste der „unkooperativen" Steueroasen, in: Internationales Steuerrecht 2002, Länderbericht 11/2002, 1-2

Ellis, M. J. (European Taxation 2000): The Code of Conduct in 2000: Cracking the Code or Coating the Crack?, in: European Taxation 2000, 414-416

Emmeluth, C. (Tax Management International Forum 2002): Denmark, in: Tax Management International Forum 2002, Vol. 23, No. 1, 10-13

Endres, D. (Recht der Internationalen Wirtschaft 1994): Steuerliche Aspekte der europäischen Integration - Eine Bestandsaufnahme der Steuergrenzen im Binnenmarkt, in: Recht der Internationalen Wirtschaft 1994, 572-584

Endres, D. (International Finance & Treasury 2000): A New Look at German Tax Planning, in: International Finance & Treasury 2000, 1-2 and 10-11

Endres, D./Ditsch, S. (The International Tax Journal 1999): German Corporate Tax Planning, in: The International Tax Journal 1999, Vol. 25, No. 1, 16-99

Endres, D./Dorfmueller, P. (Praxis Internationale Steuerberatung 2001): Holdingstrukturen in Europa, in: Praxis Internationale Steuerberatung 2001, 94-103

Endres, D./Dorfmueller, P./Urse, M. (International Tax Report 2001 I): Holding Companies - Choosing the right location in Europe (Part I), in: International Tax Report 2001 (March), 2-6

Endres, D./Dorfmueller, P./Urse, M. (International Tax Report 2001 II): Holding Companies - Choosing the right location in Europe (Part II), in: International Tax Report 2001 (April), 5-11

Endres, D./Eckstein, H.-M. (Steuerrecht International, 2001): Steuerrecht International - Ein Wegweiser für den Unternehmer beim Schritt über die Grenze, herausgegeben von PricewaterhouseCoopers GmbH, 2. Auflage, Schwäbisch-Hall 2001

Endres, D./Möller, M. (Corporate Taxation, 2001): Unternehmensbesteuerung in Deutschland - Corporate Taxation in Germany, herausgegeben von PricewaterhouseCoopers GmbH, 2. Auflage, Düsseldorf 2001

Endres, D./Oestreicher, A. (Intertax 2000): 2001 Tax Reform in Germany - Planning for a New Era, in: Intertax 2000, 408-422

Endres, D./Spengel, C. (Steuerstrukturen in Deutschland aus Sicht eines US-Investors, 1997): Steuerstrukturen in Deutschland aus Sicht eines US-Investors, in: Burmester, G./Endres, D. (Hrsg.): Aussensteuerrecht, Doppelbesteuerungsabkommen und EU-Recht im Spannungsverhältnis, Festschrift für Helmut Debatin zum 70. Geburtstag, München 1997, 81-106

Endres, D./Thies, A. (Recht der Internationalen Wirtschaft 2002): Bekämpfung doppelter Verlustnutzung im UntStFG - Oder: Wer danebenschießt, muss eine Strafrunde laufen, in: Recht der Internationalen Wirtschaft 2002, 275-280

Engel, K. (Texas Law Review 2001): Tax Neutrality to the Left, International Competitiveness to the Right, Stuck in the Middle With Subpart F, in: Texas Law Review 2001, 1525-1607

Engle, H. S. (Journal of Corporate Taxation 1998): International Developments - Treatment of Hybrid Arrangements Under Subpart F, in: Journal of Corporate Taxation 1998, 299-310

Ernst & Young (Doing Business in the United States, 1999): Doing Business in the United States, New York 1999

Ernst & Young (International Tax Digest 2001 (Denmark)): Denmark, in: International Tax Digest 2001 (April), 9-10

Ernst & Young (International Tax Digest 2001 (France)): France, in: International Tax Digest 2001 (April), 10-12

Ernst & Young (International Tax Digest 2001 (Switzerland)): Switzerland, in: International Tax Digest 2001 (November), 14-15

Ernst & Young (Unternehmerische Betätigung in Frankreich, 2002): Unternehmerische Betätigung in Frankreich, 2002

Ernst & Young (The Ernst & Young Tax Guide 2002, 2002): The Ernst & Young Tax Guide 2002, New York 2002

Ernst & Young (International Tax Digest 2002 (Belgium)): Belgium, in: International Tax Digest 2002 (January), 10

Ernst & Young (International Tax Digest 2002 (France)): France, in: International Tax Digest 2002 (April), 8-11

Ernst & Young (International Tax Digest 2002 (Ireland) I): Ireland, in: International Tax Digest 2002 (January), 14

Ernst & Young (International Tax Digest 2002 (Ireland) II): Ireland, in: International Tax Digest 2002 (April), 11-12

Ernst & Young (International Tax Digest 2002 (Netherlands) I): Netherlands, in: International Tax Digest 2002 (January), 15

Ernst & Young (International Tax Digest 2002 (Netherlands) II): Netherlands, in: International Tax Digest 2002 (April), 14-15

Ernst & Young (International Tax Digest 2002 (United States)): United States, in: International Tax Digest 2002 (April), 1-5

Ernst & Young's Foreign Desk (Journal of International Taxation 2000): Spain Introduces Major Improvements to Holding Company Regime, in: Journal of International Taxation 2000 (December), 13

Ernst & Young's Foreign Desk (Journal of International Taxation 2002)Irish Budget 2002, in: Journal of International Taxation 2002 (June), 5-17

Eustice, J. S./Kuntz, J. D. (Federal Income Taxation of S Corporations, 2002): Federal Income Taxation of S Corporations, 4th ed., Boston 2001, Current Through 2002 Supplement No. 2

Everling, W. (Der Betrieb 1981): Konzernführung durch eine Holdinggesellschaft, in: Der Betrieb 1981, 2549-2554

Feydeau, H. de (Tax Management International Forum 2002): France, in: Tax Management International Forum 2002, Vol. 23, No. 1, 13-23

Findeis, B. C./Bremer, S. C. (Tax Notes International 2002): A German Perspective on Transfer Pricing Documentation Requirements, in: Tax Notes International 2002 (18 March), 1237-1244

Fink, E. H. (Intertax 1997): Final 'Check-the-Box' Regulations Issued, in: Intertax 1997, 106

Fischer-Zernin, M./Schwarz, H. (Internationale Wirtschaftsbriefe, Fach 5, Irland, Gruppe 2, 1996): Besteuerung deutscher Investitionen in Irland, in: Internationale Wirtschaftsbriefe, Fach 5, Irland, Gruppe 2, 1996, 63-76

Fischl, A. L. (Journal of Taxation 1996): New Subpart F Regs. Ease Some Of the Difficulties Created Under Prior Rules, in: Journal of Taxation 1996, 106-114

Fischl, A. L./Schneider, R. A. (Tax Management International Journal 1997): Foreign Tax Credit Changes Made by the Taxpayer Relief Act of 1997, in: Tax Management International Journal 1997, 567-574

Fleischer, K. (Fusions & Acquisitions Magazine 2000): Aspects fiscaux de l'acquisition d'entreprise, in: Fusions & Acquisitions Magazine 2000, 24-30

Fleischer-Michaelsen, U. (Journal of International Taxation 1995): Denmark Makes Tax Avoidance More Difficult for Multinationals, in: Journal of International Taxation 1995 (April), 156-161

Fleming, J. C. Jr./Peroni, R. J./Shay, S. E. (Florida Tax Review 2001): Fairness In International Taxation: The Ability-To-Pay Case For Taxing Worldwide Income, in: Florida Tax Review 2001, 299-354

Flick, H. (Deutsches Steuerrecht 1989): Unternehmensplanung für den europäischen Binnenmarkt - Steuerliche Aspekte, in: Deutsches Steuerrecht 1989, 557-561

Flick, H. F. W. (U.S. steuerliche Konsequenzen bei Umstrukturierungen, 1997): U.S. steuerliche Konsequenzen bei Umstrukturierungen internationaler Konzerne im Rahmen einer Globalisierung und Spezialisierung - Die Taube auf dem Dach oder der Spatz in der Hand, in: Klein, F./Stihl, H. P./Wassermeyer, F. (Hrsg.): Unternehmen Steuern: Festschrift für Hans Flick zum 70. Geburtstag, Köln 1997, 709-719

Flick, H. F. W. (Internationales Steuerrecht 1998): Wer wird zuletzt lachen? Revolutionäre Steuervereinfachung durch die US-Finanzverwaltung: Die „Check the Box" Regeln, in: Internationales Steuerrecht 1998, 110-111

Flick, H. F. W. (Internationales Steuerrecht 2001 I): USA: Steuerreform, Steuerjahr, Quellenregeln, in: Internationales Steuerrecht 2001, Länderbericht 5/2001, 2

Flick, H. F. W. (Internationales Steuerrecht 2001 II): USA: Missbrauch bei inländischen „Reverse Hybrids", und Unternehmenserwerb, in: Internationales Steuerrecht 2001, Länderbericht 7/2001, 6

Flick, H. F. W./Janka, W. (Deutsches Steuerrecht 1991 I): Steuerliche Charakteristika der U.S.-Holdinggesellschaft (Teil I), in: Deutsches Steuerrecht 1991, 1037-1042

Flick, H. F. W./Janka, W. (Deutsches Steuerrecht 1991 II): Steuerliche Charakteristika der U.S.-Holdinggesellschaft (Teil II), in: Deutsches Steuerrecht 1991, 1069-1075

Förster, G./Lange, C. (Recht der Internationalen Wirtschaft 2002): Grenzüberschreitende Sitzverlegung der Europäischen Aktiengesellschaft aus ertragsteuerlicher Sicht, in: Recht der Internationalen Wirtschaft 2002, 585-590

Förster, H. (Praxis Internationale Steuerberatung 2001): Nichtanwendungserlass zu Beteiligungen an irischen „IFSC-Kapitalgesellschaften", in: Praxis Internationale Steuerberatung 2001, 127-129

Fohr, I. (Besteuerungskonzept für Holdinggesellschaften, 2001): Besteuerungskonzept für Holdinggesellschaften - eine systematische Analyse der Anforderungen an die Ertragsbesteuerung internationaler Holdinggesellschaften unter besonderer Berücksichtigung des deutschen Steuerrechts, Frankfurt am Main/Berlin/Bern, u.a. 2001

Forst, D. L. (Berkeley Journal of International Law 1996): The U.S. International Tax Treatment of Partnerships: A Policy-Based Approach, in: Berkeley Journal of International Law 1996, 239-289

Foster, J. D. (Tax Foundation's Tax Features 2000 I): The FSC Conundrum, in: Tax Foundation's Tax Features 2000, Vol. 44, Iss. 3, 7

Foster, J. D. (Tax Foundation's Tax Features 2000 II): Going Bananas Over the FSC, in: Tax Foundation's Tax Features 2000, Vol. 44, Iss. 6, 7

Frankel, A. T./Weichholz, J. (The CPA Journal 1994): The 1993 Tax Act Mandates a Closer Look at S Corporations, in: The CPA Journal 1994, 22-27.

Franz, N. (Chemical Week 2001): Zoellick Appeals WTO Ruling Striking Down FSC Legislation, in: Chemical Week 2001, Vol. 163, Iss. 38, 14

Freiling, C./Schmucker, Y. (Internationales Steuerrecht 2001): Anwendungsprobleme des § 8 a KStG nach dem Steuersenkungsgesetz, in: Internationales Steuerrecht 2001, 97-102

Friedel, D. B. (Journal of Taxation 2000): Intercompany Sales of CFC Stock - Where Does Reality End and Wonderland Begin?, in: Journal of Taxation 2000, 362-377

Fuller, J. (Tax Notes International 1991): Section 482 Transfer Pricing Developments, in: Tax Notes International 1991 (March), 251-256

Fuller, J. P. (Tax Notes International 2002): U.S. Tax Review, in: Tax Notes International 2002 (26 August), 1079-1095

Gahleitner, G./Moritz, H. (Internationale Wirtschaftsbriefe, Fach 5, Österreich, Gruppe 2, 1999): Das Steuerrecht Österreichs, in: Internationale Wirtschaftsbriefe, Fach 5, Österreich, Gruppe 2, 1999, 467-484

Gannon, J. M./Calianese, T. J./Layden, M. P./Moreland, K./Seo, S. S. (Tax Notes 1998): U.S. Subpart F, Hybrid Entities, and Other Little Things, in: Tax Notes 1998, 473-485

Gannon, J. M./Calianese, T. J./Layden, M. P./Moreland, K./Seo, S. S. (Tax Notes International 1998): U.S. Subpart F, Hybrid Entities, and Other Little Things, in: Tax Notes International 1998 (4 May), 1467-1475

Ganz, M. D./Strange, T. E. (Tax Notes 1998): Subpart F Inclusion Income Under Hybrid Branch Regs.: How The Regs Work, in: Tax Notes 1998, 487-489

Gara, M. (Tax Planning International Review 2002): Irish Tax Changes: Finance Act 2002, in: Tax Planning International Review 2002, Vol. 29, No. 8, 10-13

Garrett-Nelson, L. (Tax Notes International 1997): An Updated Survey of Selected International Tax Provisions Affecting U.S. Multinational Corporations in the U.S. Taxpayer Relief Act of 1997, in: Tax Notes International 1997 (20 October), 1287-1294

Gerken, L./Märkt, J./Schick, G. (Internationaler Steuerwettbewerb, 2000): Internationaler Steuerwettbewerb, Untersuchungen zur Ordnungstheorie und Ordnungspolitik, 40, Tübingen 2000

Gerken, L./Märkt, J./Schick, G. (Intereconomics 2001): Double Income Taxation as a Response to Tax Competition in the EU, in: Intereconomics 2001, 244-254

Giannattasio, B./Suarez-Lasa, D. (Journal of International Taxation 2002): Subpart F Recapture Accounts - Caveat Emptor, in: Journal of International Taxation 2002 (January), 47-52

Giannini, S. (CESinfo Forum 2002): Home State Taxation vs. Common Base Taxation, CESinfo Forum 2002 (Spring), 24-30

Gillmarten, M. (Tax Management International Journal 1998): Active Financing Income - Back to the Future, in: Tax Management International Journal 1998, 491-505

Ginty, J. A. (The Tax Adviser 1991): High Tax Exception to Subpart F - Potential Pitfalls, in: The Tax Adviser 1991, 433-434

Giuliani, F. M. (The International Tax Journal 2001): Notes on DISCs, E-Commerce, and Tax Sparing Credit - Part I, in: The International Tax Journal 2001, Vol. 27, Iss. 4, 53-57

Gocke, R./Baumhoff, H. (Internationale Wirtschaftsbriefe, Fach 3, Deutschland, Gruppe 1, 1989): Steuerliche Überlegungen bei der Gründung einer Holdinggesellschaft im Ausland, in: Internationale Wirtschaftsbriefe, Fach 3, Deutschland, Gruppe 1, 1989, 1233-1240

Golbert, A. S. (World Trade 2000 I): Principles of international taxation: Part 1 of 2, in: World Trade 2000 (July), 48-50

Golbert, A. S. (World Trade 2000 II): Principles of international taxation: Part 2 of 2, in: World Trade 2000 (August), 42-45

Goldberg, S. H./Alpert, H. H. (Journal of Taxation 1994): Can Subpart F Income Be Avoided Through The Use Of A Partnership?, in: Journal of Taxation 1994, 4-10

Goldsworth, J. G. (Tax Notes International 1992): Ruding Committee Recommendations Unlikely to Solve U.K Surplus Act Problem, in: Tax Notes International 1992 (13 April), 751-752

Gordon, R./Venuti, J./Renfroe, D. (Tax Management International Journal 2002 I): Current Status of U.S. Tax Treaties, in: Tax Management International Journal 2002, 114-121

Gordon, R./Venuti, J./Renfroe, D. (Tax Management International Journal 2002 II): Current Status of U.S. Tax Treaties, in: Tax Management International Journal 2002, 180-187

Gordon, R. A./Klein, C. D. (The Tax Adviser 1997): New Hybrid Legislation and Regulations Affecting Treaty Planning, in: The Tax Adviser 1997, 688-690

Goulder, R. (Tax Notes International 2002): OECD Updates Tax Haven Blacklist, Claims Progress in Curbing Harmful Tax Competition, in: Tax Notes International 2002 (29 April), 375-380

Gouthière, B. (European Taxation 2002): France - Thin Capitalization Rules and the Non-Discrimination Principle, in: European Taxation 2002, 159-163

Graetz, M. J. (Tax Law Review 2001): The David R. Tillinghast Lecture - Taxing International Income: Inadequate Principles, Outdated Concepts, and Unsatisfactory Policies, in: Tax Law Review 2001 (Spring), 261-336

Graf, T. (International Tax Review 2001): Switzerland, in: International Tax Review 2001, Supplement: Capital Markets, Iss. 2, 73-79

Granberg, M. W. (The Tax Adviser 1999): Subpart F treatment of hybrid branches and partnerships, in: The Tax Adviser 1999, 630-632

Grant, P. (Global Finance 1996): 'The Bottom Line Is You Can Save Millions', in: Global Finance 1996, 18-19

Green, G. L. Jr. (The National Public Accountant 1993): Foreign tax credit, in: The National Public Accountant 1993, 35

Griemla, S. (Die ertragsteuerliche Behandlung der Europäischen Aktiengesellschaft, 1999): Die ertragsteuerliche Behandlung der Europäischen Aktiengesellschaft, Marburg 1999

Gröhs, B./Schuch, J. (Internationale Wirtschaftsbriefe, Fach 5, Österreich, Gruppe 2, 2001): Steuerliche Aspekte des Unternehmenskauf in Österreich, in: Internationale Wirtschaftsbriefe, Fach 5, Österreich, Gruppe 2, 2001, 531-544

Grotherr, S. (Internationale Wirtschaftsbriefe, Fach 5, Irland, Gruppe 2, 1989): Steueranreize für das Internationale Finanzdienstleistungszentrum in Dublin, in: Internationale Wirtschaftsbriefe, Fach 5, Irland, Gruppe 2, 1989, 51-56

Grotherr, S. (Internationale Wirtschaftsbriefe, Fach 5, Niederlande, Gruppe 2, 1994): Einheitsbesteuerung von Konzernen in den Niederlanden, in: Internationale Wirtschaftsbriefe, Fach 5, Niederlande, Gruppe 2, 1994, 225-238

Grotherr, S. (Betriebs-Berater1995): Besteuerungsfragen und -probleme bei der Einschaltung inländischer Holdinggesellschaften im grenzüberschreitenden Konzern (Teil I), in: Betriebs-Berater1995, 1510-1517

Grotherr, S. (Internationale Wirtschaftsbriefe, Fach 5, Dänemark, Gruppe 2, 1995): Konzernbesteuerung in Dänemark, in: Internationale Wirtschaftsbriefe, Fach 5, Dänemark, Gruppe 2, 1995, 113-126

Grotherr, S. (Steuer und Wirtschaft 1996): Die unterschiedlichen Konzernbesteuerungssysteme in den Mitgliedstaaten der Europäischen Union - eine steuersystematische Analyse im Hinblick auf Reformüberlegungen beim steuerlichen Organschaftskonzept, in: Steuer und Wirtschaft 1996, 356-378

Grotherr, S. (Grundlagen der internationalen Steuerplanung, 2000): Grundlagen der internationalen Steuerplanung, in: Grotherr, S. (Hrsg.), Handbuch der internationalen Steuerplanung, herausgegeben von Grotherr, S., Herne 2000, 3-28

Grotherr, S. (Internationale Wirtschaftsbriefe, Fach 3, Deutschland, Gruppe 1, 2000 I): Änderungen bei der Besteuerung von Einkünften aus ausländischen Beteiligungen durch das Steuersenkungsgesetz, in: Internationale Wirtschaftsbriefe, Fach 3, Deutschland, Gruppe 1, 2000, 1709-1720

Grotherr, S. (Internationale Wirtschaftsbriefe, Fach 3, Deutschland, Gruppe 1, 2000 II): Änderungen bei der Besteuerung der Inlandsbeziehungen von Steuerausländern durch das Steuersenkungsgesetz, in: Internationale Wirtschaftsbriefe, Fach 3, Deutschland, Gruppe 1, 2000, 1721-1736

Grube, P. (Journal of Taxation 2001): Putting Tiered Entities into a Foreign Holding Company Structure Using Check-the-Box, in: Journal of Taxation 2001, 5-12

Guenther, T. S. (Virginia Tax Review 1997): Tax Treaties and Overrides: The Multiple-Party Financing Dilemma, in: Virginia Tax Review 1997 (Spring), 645-680

Gundel, G. (Finanzierungsgesellschaften, 2000): Der Einsatz von ausländischen Finanzierungsgesellschaften im Rahmen der Konzernfinanzierung, in: Grotherr, S. (Hrsg.), Handbuch der internationalen Steuerplanung, herausgegeben von Grotherr, S., Herne 2000, 283-313

Haase, F. F. (Tax Notes International 2002): EU to Scrutinize Taxation of Societas Europaea in Germany, in: Tax Notes International 2002 (5 August), 713-717

Haidorfer Nikolenkov, A. (Holdingstruktur und Standortwahl, 1996): Holdingstruktur und Standortwahl unter besonderer Berücksichtigung der Schweiz und der Staaten der Europäischen Union, Bamberg 1996

Hakelmacher, S. (Die Wirtschaftsprüfung 1992): Hält die Holding, was von ihr gehalten wird?, in: Die Wirtschaftsprüfung 1992, 122-127

Halphen, C./Schneider, R. A. (The Tax Adviser 1998): Withholding and Reporting Requirements for Payments to Foreign Partnerships, in: The Tax Adviser 1998, 220-222

Hamaekers, H. (European Taxation 2000): Tackling Harmful Tax Competition - a Round Table on the Code of Conduct, in: European Taxation 2000, 398-400

Hamill, J. R./White, C. G. (Taxes 2001): When "Checking The Box" Can Lead To Corporate Tax Savings, in: Taxes 2001 (February), 36-43

Hammer, M. (Journal of International Taxation 2002): Germany Is More Than Attractive For Holding Companies After Reforms, in: Journal of International Taxation 2002 (September), 36-38

Hannes, S. P./Riedy, J. A. (Tax Notes 2001): Time to Move to a Worldwide Group Approach For Apportioning Interest, in: Tax Notes 2001, 1305-1317

Hansen, A. O. (European Taxation 2001): Denmark - Holding Company Regime Amendments, in: European Taxation 2001, 229-231

Haris, K. L./Wirtz, F. J. (Tax Management International Journal 1991): Has the Tax Court Endorsed Special Allocations Under Section 902?: Vulcan Materials Co. v. Comr., in: Tax Management International Journal 1991, 462-467

Hariton, D. P. (Tax Notes International 1998): Notice 98-11 Notwithstanding, What Should Be Done With Subpart F?, in: Tax Notes International 1998 (6 April), 1089-1091

Hariton, D. P. (Tax Notes International 1998): U.S. Notice 98-11 and the 'Logic' of Subpart F: a Response to Professor Avi-Yonah, in: Tax Notes International 1998 (15 June), 1881-1883

Harrington, D./Frediani, M. (Tax Management Memorandum 2000): A Big Year for Partnerships: Partnership Tax Developments at the Turn of the Millennium, in: Tax Management Memorandum 2000, 119-132

Hartmann, J. (International Tax Review 2000): Germany, in: International Tax Review 2000, Tax Developments, 9-13

Haun, J. (Hybride Finanzierungsinstrumente im deutschen und US-amerikanischen Steuerrecht, 1996): Hybride Finanzierungsinstrumente im deutschen und US-amerikanischen Steuerrecht - eine Analyse ihres grenzüberschreitenden Einsatzes aus steuersystematischer und ökonomischer Sicht, Frankfurt a. M./Berlin/Bern u.a. 1996

Hawksworth, J. (Journal of International Taxation 1999): The Slow Process Of Business Tax Harmonization In The New Europe, in: Journal of International Taxation 1999 (September), 36-45

Hayden, J. R./Mogenson, H. (Tax Management International Journal 1991): Tax-Free Transfers to Foreign Partnerships and the IRS' Ruling Policy on Hybrid Foreign Entities, in: Tax Management International Journal 1991, 503-513

Heinze, M. (Zeitschrift für Unternehmens- und Gesellschaftsrecht 2002): European Company Law Review: Die Europäische Aktiengesellschaft, in: Zeitschrift für Unternehmens- und Gesellschaftsrecht 2002, 66-95

Hendricks, B. (European Taxation 2000): Germany - A View on Tax Harmonization and the Code of Conduct, in: European Taxation 2000, 413-414

Hensley, A. D. (Mertens Law of Federal Income Taxation, 2002): Chapter 45E. Controlled Foreign Corporations, in: Mertens Law of Federal Income Taxation, New York 2002

Herold, C. (Gestaltende Steuerberatung 2001): Deutsche „Gewerbesteuer-Oasen", in: Gestaltende Steuerberatung 2001, 67-68

Herrmann, H. (Einordnung ausländischer Gesellschaften, 2001): Die Einordnung ausländischer Gesellschaften im deutschen, US-amerikanischen und europäischen Internationalen Steuerrecht, Lohmar/Köln 2001

Herzig, N. (Hrsg.) (Harmonisierung der Körperschaftsteuersysteme in den EU-Staaten, 1994): Harmonisierung der Körperschaftsteuersysteme in den EU-Staaten, herausgegeben von Herzig, N., mit Beiträgen von Müller-Dott, J.-P./Herzig, N./Rädler, A., u.a., Köln 1994

Herzig, N. (Resümee, 1996): Resümee, in: Herzig, N., Advance Pricing Agreements (APAs) - Ein neues Instrument zur Vermeidung von Verrechnungspreiskonflikten?, Köln 1996, 83-95

Herzig, N. (Besteuerung der Unternehmen in Europa, 1996): Besteuerung der Unternehmen in Europa - Harmonisierung im Wettbewerb der Systeme, in: Lehner, M. (Hrsg.): Steuerrecht im Europäischen Binnenmarkt: Einfluss des EG-Rechts auf die nationalen Steuerrechtsordnungen, herausgegeben im Auftrag der Deutschen Steuerjuristischen Gesellschaft e.V., Köln 1996, 121-149

Herzig, N. (Die Wirtschaftsprüfung 1998): Globalisierung und Besteuerung, in: Die Wirtschaftsprüfung 1998, 280-296

Herzig, N./Förster, G. (Der Betrieb 1992): Steueränderungsgesetz 1992: Die Umsetzung der Fusionsrichtlinie in deutsches Steuerrecht (Teil II), in: Der Betrieb 1992, 959-963

Herzig, N./Griemla, S. (Steuer und Wirtschaft 2002): Steuerliche Aspekte der Europäischen Aktiengesellschaft/Societas Europaea (SE), in: Steuer und Wirtschaft 2002, 55-77

Hey, F. E. F. (Recht der Internationalen Wirtschaft 1992): Gesellschafts- und steuerrechtliche Aspekte der Limited Liability Company - Zugleich ein Beitrag zur Qualifizierung ausländischer Rechtsgebilde, in: Recht der Internationalen Wirtschaft 1992, 916-923

Hey, J. (Harmonisierung der Unternehmensbesteuerung in Europa, 1997): Harmonisierung der Unternehmensbesteuerung in Europa, Köln 1997

Heyvaert, W./Springael, B. (Intertax 2002): Luxembourg Tax Reform Acts of 21 December 2001 - International Aspects for Corporations and Businesses, in: Intertax 2002, 326-331

Hinchman, G. (Financial Executive 2001): It's Time To Repeal Corporate AMT, in: Financial Executive 2001, 67

Hines, J. R. Jr. (National Tax Journal 1999): The Case against Deferral - A Deferential Reconsideration, in: National Tax Journal 1999, 385-404

Hintzen, B. (Die deutsche Zwischenholding als Gegenstand der internationalen Steuerplanung, 1997): Die deutsche Zwischenholding als Gegenstand der internationalen Steuerplanung, Frankfurt a.M./Berlin/Bern/u.a. 1997

Hirschler, K. (Rechtsformplanung im Konzern, 2000): Rechtsformplanung im Konzern: Ertragsteuerlich motivierte Rechtsformentscheidungen im grenzüberschreitend tätigen Konzern, Wien 2000

Hirschler, K./Sulz, G. (Steuer & Wirtschaft International 1997): Die internationale Schachtelbeteiligung nach dem Abgabenänderungsgesetz 1996, in: Steuer & Wirtschaft International 1997, 216-223

Hishikawa, A. (Boston College International and Comparative Law Review 2002): The Death of Tax Havens?, in: Boston College International and Comparative Law Review 2002 (Spring), 389-417

Hjortshøj, J./Bjørnholm, N. (The International Tax Journal 2000): New Danish Tax-Efficient Holding Structure, in: The International Tax Journal 2000, Vol. 26, Iss. 1, 65-81

Höhn, E. (Internationale Steuerplanung, 1996): Internationale Steuerplanung: eine Einführung in die Steuerplanung für internationale Unternehmen mit Bezug zur Schweiz, Bern/Stuttgart/Wien 1996

Hoffman, W. H. Jr./Gately, M. S. (Journal of Taxation 1986): Post-1984 Act Planning To Avoid Taxation Of Foreign Personal Holding Company Income, in: Journal of Taxation 1986, 92-95 and 98-99

Hoffmann, W.-D. (Steueroptimales Ausschüttungsverhalten und Repatriierungsstrategien, 2000): Steueroptimales Ausschüttungsverhalten und Repatriierungsstrategien, in: Grotherr, S. (Hrsg.), Handbuch der internationalen Steuerplanung, herausgegeben von Grotherr, S., Herne 2000, 513-532

Hoke, W. D. (Tax Notes International 1992): Tax Aspects of Multinational Acquisitions and Combinations, in: Tax Notes International 1992 (19 October), 836-851

Hoke, W. D./Dablain, D. A. (Tax Notes 1998): Taxpayer Relief Act of 1997: Impact on Foreign Taxable Restructurings, in: Tax Notes 1998, 1169-1182

Hollingswood, T. (Journal of Accountancy 1997): Check-the-Box: Choosing an Entity's Tax Classification, in: Journal of Accountancy 1997, 24

Hollingsworth, G./Fuller, C. (Tax Planning International mergers & acquisitions 2002): Tax Planning for M&As Involving Irish Companies, in: Tax Planning International mergers & acquisitions 2002, Vol. 1, No. 3, 3-7

Horwood, R. M./Hechtman, J. A. (Journal of Corporate Taxation 1995): Global Warning: Review the Subpart F Rules Before Going Abroad, in: Journal of Corporate Taxation 1995, 366-378

Howlett, K./Reed, M./Sylvester, C. (Journal of International Taxation 2000): U.K. Budget 2000: A Bitter Pill For U.K. Multinationals?, in: Journal of International Taxation 2000 (July), 16-21 and 62-64

Howlett, K./Rudd, A./Sylvester, C. (Journal of International Taxation 1999): 1999 U.K. Budget: For Smaller Enterprise?, in: Journal of International Taxation 1999 (July), 38-49

Huber, M. F./Kapalle, U./Koch, M. (Steuer Revue 2001): Entwicklungen im internationalen Steuerrecht, in: Steuer Revue 2001, 390-402

Huber, M. F./Kapalle, U./Kubaile, H. (Steuer Revue 2002): Entwicklungen im internationalen Steuerrecht, in: Steuer Revue 2002, 366-379

Hudson, B. D. (The Tax Adviser 1997): Franchise Tax Board to Defer Actions on S Corporation Conformity and Check-the-Box Regulations, in: The Tax Adviser 1997, 217

Hufbauer, G. C. (U.S. Taxation, 1975): A Guide to Law and Policy, in: U.S. Taxation of American Business Abroad, American Enterprise Institute, Hoover Institution Policy Study No. 16, 1975

Huffman, R./ Fischl, A. (The Tax Adviser 2000): Sec. 904 - Base Difference vs. Timing Difference for Foreign Taxes, in: The Tax Adviser 2000, 484-485

Huyghe, A./Meeus, L. (Tax Notes International 2002): Belgian Council of State Considering Corporate Income Tax Reform Draft, in: Tax Notes International 2002 (17 June), 1257-1260

IBFD (European Tax Handbook, 2000): European Tax Handbook 2000, Amsterdam 2000

IBFD (Annual Report 2001-2002, 2002): Annual Report 2001-2002, Amsterdam 2002

Immerman, L. A. (Tax Notes International 2002): U.S. IRS Applies Section 482 to Partnership Contributions: Was It Necessary?, in: Tax Notes International 2002 (4 March), 1005-1018

Infanti, A. C. (Tax Management International Journal 2001): The Proposed Domestic Reverse Hybrid Entity Regulations: Can the Treasury Department Override Treaties?, in: Tax Management International Journal 2001, 307-314

Isenbergh, J. (International Taxation, 2000): International Taxation, New York 2000

Isenbergh, J. (International Taxation: U.S. Taxation of Foreign Taxpayers and Foreign Income, 2002): International Taxation: U.S. Taxation of Foreign Taxpayers and Foreign Income, 3rd ed., New York 2002

Jackel, M. A./Dance, G. E. (Tax Notes 1998): Elective Entity Conversion under proposed check-the-box regs, in: Tax Notes 1998, 595-601

Jackstein, C. D. (Das deutsche Steuerrecht im Wettbewerb mit ausländischen Steuersystemen, 1997): Das deutsche Steuerrecht im Wettbewerb mit ausländischen Steuersystemen, in: Burmester, G./Endres, D. (Hrsg.): Aussensteuerrecht, Doppelbesteuerungsabkommen und EU-Recht im Spannungsverhältnis, Festschrift für Helmut Debatin zum 70. Geburtstag, München 1997, 179-206

Jacobs, O. H. (Hrsg.) (Internationale Unternehmensbesteuerung, 2002): Internationale Unternehmensbesteuerung – Deutsche Investitionen im Ausland; ausländische Investitionen im Inland, bearbeitet von Jacobs, O. H./Endres, D./Spengel, C., 5., neubearbeitete und erweiterte Aufl., München 2002

Jacobs, O. H./Spengel, C. (European Tax Analyzer 1996): European Tax Analyzer: EDV-gestützter Vergleich der Steuerbelastung von Kapitalgesellschaften in Deutschland, Frankreich und Großbritannien, Baden-Baden 1996

Jacobs, O. H./Spengel, C. (Intertax 2000): Measurement and Development of the Effective Tax Burden of Companies - An Overview and International Comparison, in: Intertax 2000, 334-352

Jacobs, O. H./Spengel, C. (Effective Tax Burden in Europe, 2002): Effective Tax Burden in Europe - Current Situation, Past Developments and Simulations of Reforms, ZEW Economic Studies, Vol. 15, Heidelberg/New York 2002

Jaeger, C. (Die Körperschaftsteuersysteme in Europa, 2001): Die Körperschaftsteuersysteme in Europa: eine europarechtliche und betriebswirtschaftliche Analyse, Lohmar/Köln 2001

Jahn, A./Herfs-Röttgen, E. (Der Betrieb 2001): Die Europäische Aktiengesellschaft - Societas Europaea, in: Der Betrieb 2001, 631-638

Jann, M./Schuch, J./Toifl, G. (Austria, 2001): Austria, in: IBFD, The Taxation Of Companies In Europe, Binder *, Last Supplement No. 162, April 2002

Jennings, R. (The National Public Accountant 1997): Choosing the Entity: LLC or S Corporation, in: The National Public Accountant 1997, 25-29

Jensen, P./Spikes, P./Carter, D. (The International Tax Journal 1998): International Provisions of the Taxpayer Relief Act of 1997, in: The International Tax Journal 1998, Vol. 24, Iss. 3, 1-11

Jesse, L. (Errichtung internationaler Holdingstrukturen durch Anteilstausch, 1997): Errichtung internationaler Holdingstrukturen durch Anteilstausch, in: Klein, F./Stihl, H. P./Wassermeyer, F. (Hrsg.): Unternehmen Steuern: Festschrift für Hans Flick zum 70. Geburtstag, Köln 1997, 831-856

Jodoin, C. E. (Tax Management International Journal 1998): Federal Budget Proposal - February 24, 1998, in: Tax Management International Journal 1998, 197-204

Johnsen, K. M. (The CPA Journal 1993): Limitation Of Foreign Tax Credit Upheld, in: The CPA Journal 1993, 81

Johnsen, K. M./Lipton, J. A. (Tax Management International Journal 1991): Maximizing Foreign Tax Credit Utilization: The Fair Market Value Method for Interest Expense Allocation, in: Tax Management International Journal 1991, 235-243

Jonas, B. (Die Steuerkonsolidierung als Instrument der internationalen Konzernsteuerplanung, 2000): Die Steuerkonsolidierung als Instrument der internationalen Konzernsteuerplanung, in: Grotherr, S. (Hrsg.), Handbuch der internationalen Steuerplanung, herausgegeben von Grotherr, S., Herne 2000, 217-221

Jong, C. E. de (Internationale Wirtschaftsbriefe, Fach 5, Niederlande, Gruppe 2, 2001): Steuerliche Aspekte des Unternehmenskauf in den Niederlanden, in: Internationale Wirtschaftsbriefe, Fach 5, Niederlande, Gruppe 2, 2001, 309-320

Joris, J.-L. (International Financial Law Review 2002): Will the European company work?, in: International Financial Law Review 2002, Vol. 21, Iss. 2, 19-23

Josephs, S. R. (The Tax Adviser 1998): Treatment of Hybrid Arrangements under Subpart F, in: The Tax Adviser 1998, 294-295

Jouanjan, A. (Tax Notes International 2000): France Plans FRF 120 Billion in Tax Cuts Over Three Years - What the Plans Entails, in: Tax Notes International 2000 (18 September), 1298-1299

Joyce, T. B. (Tax Management International Journal 1992 I): Section 904(f) - Losses and the Foreign Tax Credit Limitation, Part I, in: Tax Management International Journal 1992, 55-77

Joyce, T. B. (Tax Management International Journal 1992 II): Section 904(f) - Losses and the Foreign Tax Credit Limitation, Part II, in: Tax Management International Journal 1992, 115-130

Joyce, T. B./Parks, S. M. (Tax Management International Journal 1990 I): The Foreign Tax Credit - Separate Limitations (Part I), in: Tax Management International Journal 1990, 323-341

Joyce, T. B./Parks, S. M. (Tax Management International Journal 1990 II): The Foreign Tax Credit Limitation - Part II, in: Tax Management International Journal 1990, 407-429

Joyce, T. B./Parks, S. M. (Tax Management International Journal 1990 III): The Foreign Tax Credit Limitation - Part III, in: Tax Management International Journal 1990, 451-468

Kam, F. de (Tax Notes International 1994): The Tax System of the Netherlands, in: Tax Notes International 1994 (19 September), 903-924

Karp, J. J. (The International Tax Journal 2001): Effect of OECD and Similar Initiatives on Multinational Operations, in: The International Tax Journal 2001, Vol. 27, Iss. 3, 12-22

Kaufmann, R. (Steuer & Wirtschaft International 2001): Controlled Foreign Companies(CFC)-Gesetzgebung - Übersicht über die Rechtslage in den EU-Mitgliedstaaten, CFC-Legislation - An Overview on the National Laws in the EU Member States, in: Steuer & Wirtschaft International 2001, 16-20

Kaupa, A. (Österreichische Steuer-Zeitung 1998): Fremdkapitalzinsen beim Beteiligungserwerb bedingt abzugsfähig, in: Österreichische Steuer-Zeitung 1998, 315-320

Kawada, G. (Intertax 1989): An outline of Japanese anti-tax avoidance provisions, in: Intertax 1989, 361-363

Kaye, T. A. (Boston College International and Comparative Law Review 1996): European Harmonization and the Implications for U.S. Tax Policy, in: Boston College International and Comparative Law Review 1996 (Winter), 109-171

Keller, T. (Der Betrieb 1991): Die Einrichtung einer Holding: Bisherige Erfahrungen und neuere Entwicklungen, in: Der Betrieb 1991, 1633-1639

Keller, T. (Unternehmensführung mit Holdingkonzepten, 1993): Unternehmungsführung mit Holdingkonzepten: Wege in ein Holdingkonzept, rechtliche Rahmenbedingungen und Rechtsformwahl, Verbundintegration, Lösung struktur- und führungsorganisatorischer Problemstellung, 2. Auflage, Köln 1993

Kessler, W. (Internationales Steuerrecht 1993): Internationale Organschaft in Dänemark, in: Internationales Steuerrecht 1993, 303-310

Kessler, W. (Internationales Steuerrecht 1995): Holdingstandort Luxemburg, in: Internationales Steuerrecht 1995, 11-16

Kessler, W. (Die Euro-Holding, 1996): Die Euro-Holding: Steuerplanung, Standortwahl, Länderprofile, München 1996

Kessler, W. (Überlegungen zur Standortwahl einer Euro-Holding aus steuerlicher Sicht, 1997): Überlegungen zur Standortwahl einer Euro-Holding aus steuerlicher Sicht, in: Grenzüberschreitende Aktivitäten deutscher Unternehmen und EU-Recht, herausgegeben von Fischer, L., Köln 1997, 130-164

Kessler, W. (Holdinggesellschaften und Kooperationen in Europa, 1998): Holdinggesellschaften und Kooperationen in Europa, in: Steuerrecht und steuerorientierte Gestaltungen im Konzern, herausgegeben von Schaumburg, H., Köln 1998, 177-126

Kessler, W. (Grundlagen der Steuerplanung mit Holdinggesellschaften, 2000): Grundlagen der Steuerplanung mit Holdinggesellschaften, in: Grotherr, S. (Hrsg.), Handbuch der internationalen Steuerplanung, herausgegeben von Grotherr, S., Herne 2000, 187-216

Kessler, W. (Steuer Revue 2001): Holdinggesellschaften in Europa, in: Steuer Revue 2001, 768-774

Kessler, W. (Internationale Holdingstandorte, 2002): Internationale Holdingsstandorte, in: Schaumburg, H./Piltz, D. J. (Hrsg.), Holdinggesellschaften im Internationalen Steuerrecht, Köln 2002, 67-108

Kessler, W./Dorfmueller, P. (Praxis Internationale Steuerberatung 2001): Gestaltungsstrategien bei internationaler Steuerplanung mit Holdinggesellschaften, in: Praxis Internationale Steuerberatung 2001, 177-185

Kessler, W./Dorfmueller, P. (Journal of International Taxation 2002), The Tax Jungle of Working Cross-Border in Europe - The European Company as a Potential Pilot Project?, in: Journal of International Taxation 2002 (October), 51-56

Kessler, W./Dorfmueller, P. (Tax Planning International European Union Focus 2002), EU Company Taxation: The European Company as a Pilot Project?, in: Tax Planning International European Union Focus 2002, Vol. 4., No. 9, 3-7

Kessler, W./Dorfmueller, P. (Internationales Steuerrecht 2003): Holdingstandort Großbritanntien - eine attraktive Alternative?, in: Internationales Steuerrecht 2003, forthcoming

Kessler, W./Dorfmueller, P./Schmidt, W./Teufel, T. (Tax Notes International 2001): European Holding Entities in Germany: Partnerships as Attractive Alternatives, in: Tax Notes International 2001 (3 September), 1217-1223

Kessler, W./Dorfmueller, P./Schmitt, C. P. (Praxis Internationale Steuerberatung 2001): Änderungen der Hinzurechnungsbesteuerung durch den Entwurf eines UntStFG, Praxis Internationale Steuerberatung 2001, 318-329

Kessler, W./Dorfmueller, P./Schmitt, C. P. (International Tax Report 2001): Controlled Foreign Companies - Germany to make fundamental changes, in: International Tax Report 2001 (December), 2-6

Kessler, W./Schmalz, A. (Praxis Internationale Steuerberatung 2002): EU-Kommission – Wege zur Harmonisierung der Körperschaftsteuer in der EU, in: Praxis Internationale Steuerberatung 2002, 210-212

King, M. A./Fullerton, D. (The Taxation from Income of Capital, 1984): The Taxation from Income of Capital: A Comprehensive Study of the United States, the United Kingdom, Sweden, and West Germany, Chicago/London 1984

Kingson, C. I. (Columbia Law Review 1981): The Coherence of International Taxation, in: Columbia Tax Review 1981, 1151-1229

Kingson, C. I. (Brooklyn Journal of International Law 2001): Symposium International Tax Policy in the New Millennium, Panel III: U.S. Multinational and International Competitiveness, Leonardo Da Vinci and the 861 Regulations, in: Brooklyn Journal of International Law 2001, 1565-1577

Kirwin, J. (Daily Tax Report 2001): International Taxes - European Commission Seeks Modernization Of Corporate Tax System for Single Market, in: Daily Tax Report 2001 (October 25), G-2

Kischel, D. (Internationale Wirtschaftsbriefe, Fach 5, Irland, Gruppe 2, 2000): Übersicht über die direkten Steuern in Irland, in: Internationale Wirtschaftsbriefe, Fach 5, Irland, Gruppe 2, 2000, 77-86

Kischel, D. (Internationale Wirtschaftsbriefe, Fach 5, Dänemark, Gruppe 2, 2000): Übersicht über die direkten Steuern Dänemarks, in: Internationale Wirtschaftsbriefe, Fach 5, Dänemark, Gruppe 2, 2000, 137-146

Kleemann, F. (Österreichische Steuer-Zeitung 1997): Richtlinienshopping: Voraussetzungen für die KESt-Entlastung nach § 94a EStG, in: Österreichische Steuer-Zeitung 1997, 114-119

Klein, S. I./Looney, S. R. (Business Entities 2000): Final Check-the-Box Regulations Describe How Elective Changes in Classification of Business Entities are Treated for Tax Purposes, in: Business Entities 2000 (January/February), 48-49

Klöne, H. (Steuerplanung, 1980): Steuerplanung, Neuwied 1980

Kloot, N. van der/Subramaniam, A. I. S./Ganz, M. (International Tax Review 1997): United States, in: International Tax Review 1997, Supplement: Tax Development Yearbook 1997, 91-99

Kluge, V. (Das Internationale Steuerrecht, 2000): Das Internationale Steuerrecht: Gemeinschaftsrecht, Außensteuerrecht, Abkommensrecht, 4. Auflage, München 2000

Könen, R. (Internationale Wirtschaftsbriefe, Fach 5, Luxemburg, Gruppe 2, 1998) Die Holdinggesellschaft im Großherzogtum Luxemburg, in: Internationale Wirtschaftsbriefe, Fach 5, Luxemburg, Gruppe 2, 1998, 145-150

Koifman, L. (The CPA Journal 1993): Case Clarifies Calculations Of Pre-86 Foreign Tax Credit, in: The CPA Journal 1993, 78

Kohlhepp, K. (Recht der Internationalen Wirtschaft 1989): Die Europäische Aktiengesellschaft, in: Recht der Internationalen Wirtschaft 1989, 88-90

KPMG (2001 WTD 164-2): Luxembourg Presents Key Measures of Draft Budget for 2002, in: 2001 WTD 164-2

KPMG (2001 WTD 206-7): Luxembourg Parliament Considering Extensive Tax Reform Package for 2002, in: 2001 WTD 206-7

Kral, K. H./Katz, S. B. (International Tax Review 2001): United States, in: International Tax Review 2001 (January 1), 7985

Kral, K. H./Serota, J. (Journal of Accountancy 1996): The Check-the-Box Proposal: Simpler Classification for Both Foreign and U.S. Companies, in: Journal of Accountancy 1996, 34-36

Kral, K. H./Serota, J./Mandell, J. (International Tax Review 1995): US CFC rules cast a wide net, in: International Tax Review 1995, Vol. 6, Iss. 2, 40-43

Kral, K. H./Serota, J. /Weiss, J. (Journal of Accountancy 1995): Determining Foreign Income Tax Credit, in: Journal of Accountancy 1995, 25

Kral, K. H./Serota, J./Weiss, J. (Journal of Accountancy 1995): Brown Group Decision Reversed, in: Journal of Accountancy 1995, 26-27

Kral, K. H./Tilevitz, O. (International Tax Review 1998): Mergers & Acquisitions, in: International Tax Review 1998, Supplement: North America Tax Guide, 13-17

Kral, M. E. (The Tax Adviser 1999): Final loss allocation regs. result in increased FTC limitations, in: The Tax Adviser 1999, 222-224

Kramer, J.-D. (Tax Management International Forum 2002): Germany, in: Tax Management International Forum 2002, Vol. 23, No. 1, 23-27

Kratz, P. (Steuerplanung internationaler Unternehmungen, 1986): Steuerplanung internationaler Unternehmungen: Systeme und Modelle, Bern/Stuttgart 1986

Krehbühl, H.-H. (Das Steueranrechnungsverfahren in den USA, 1997): Das Steueranrechnungsverfahren in den USA - Ein Vorbild für Deutschland?, in: Kley, M. D./Sünner, E./Willemsen, A. (Hrsg.): Steuerrecht, Steuer- und Rechtspolitik, Wirtschaftsrecht und Unternehmensverfassungen: Festschrift für Wolfgang Ritter zum 70. Geburtstag, Köln 1997, 147-166

Kriegbaum, K. E. (Tax Planning International Review 2000): Denmark - Budget 2000/2001, in: Tax Planning International Review 2000, Vol. 27, No. 11, 25-26

Kriegbaum, K. E./Petersen, C. M. (Internationale Wirtschaftsbriefe, Fach 5, Dänemark, Gruppe 2, 2001): Steuerliche Rahmenbedingungen für Unternehmenskäufe in Dänemark, in: Internationale Wirtschaftsbriefe, Fach 5, Dänemark, Gruppe 2, 2001, 147-156

Kroniger, A./Thies, A. (Internationales Steuerrecht 2002): Anwendung des check the box-Systems auf die KGaA als Joint Venture-Vehikel, in: Internationales Steuerrecht 2002, 397-405

Kroppen, H.-K. (Internationale Wirtschaftsbriefe, Fach 8, USA, Gruppe 2, 1994): Advanced Pricing Agreement in den USA, in: Internationale Wirtschaftsbriefe, Fach 8, USA, Gruppe 2, 1994, 795-798

Kroschel, J. (Federal Income Tax, 2000): Die Federal Income Tax der Vereinigten Staaten von Amerika, Düsseldorf 2000

Kuhlmann, C. (Steuerplanung bei Direktinvestitionen in der Bundesrepublik Deutschland, 1998): Steuerplanung bei Direktinvestitionen in der Bundesrepublik Deutschland - Vorteilhaftigkeit der Handlungsalternativen in Abhängigkeit vom Steuersystem des Wohnsitzstaates, in: Theisen, M. R. (Hrsg.), Der Konzern im Umbruch, Stuttgart 1998, 3-31

Kuntz, J. D./Peroni, R. J. (U.S. International Taxation, 2002): U.S. International Taxation, 3rd ed., Boston 1996, Current Through 2002 Supplement No. 3

Laffie, L. S. (The Tax Adviser 1997): Check-the-Box Prop. Regs., in: The Tax Adviser 1997, 749

Laffie, L. S. (The Tax Adviser 1998): Hybrid Entities, in: The Tax Adviser 1998, 517

Lainoff, S. R. (Tax Management International Journal 1992): Designating International Issues for Litigation, in: Tax Management International Journal 1992, 23-27

Laity, E. T. (Cornell International Law Journal 1998): The Foreign Base Company Sales Income of Controlled Foreign Corporations, in: Cornell International Law Journal 1998, 93-151

Lam, E. W. (DePaul Business Law Journal 1996): The Treasury's Panacea Against Abusive Partnerships - Anti-Abuse Regulation Section 1.701-2: Tax Planning In The Wake Of Brown Group Inc. v. Commissioner, in: DePaul Business Law Journal 1996 (Fall/Winter), 65-107

Lampreave, P. (Verkehrsteuer, 2000): in: Courage, C./Dechant, R.-M./González, D./u.a.: Steuerfibel Spanien: Erläuterungen zum spanischen Steuerrecht, Deutschsprachige Wiedergabe wichtiger steuerlicher Regelungen, Steuerliche Formulare, Steuerliches Glossarium, 1. Auflage, Frankfurt am Main 2000, 65-72

Lang, J. M./Stack, R. B./Charnovitz, S./Brady, J. T. (Tax Management International Journal 2000): What Tax Lawyers Should Know About Trade Law, in: Tax Management International Journal 2000, 566-581

Lang, M. (Internationales Steuerrecht 2002): CFC-Gesetzgebung und Gemeinschaftsrecht, in: Internationales Steuerrecht 2002, 217-222

Langer, M. J. (Tax Notes International 2000): Harmful Tax Competition: Who are The Real Tax Havens?, in: Tax Notes International 2000 (18 December), 2831-2839

Larkins, E. R./Oakley, E. F./Winkle, G. M. (The Tax Adviser 1999): Tax and Accounting Aspects of Global Expansion, in: The Tax Adviser 1999, 416-422

Lau, P. C./Soltis, S. L. (Journal of Taxation 2001): Planning For Foreign Corporations Using Partnerships To Take The Plunge Into U.S. Markets, in: Journal of Taxation 2001, 105-117

Laursen, J. (Internationales Steuerrecht 1999): Die neue dänische Holdingbesteuerung, in: Internationales Steuerrecht 1999, 717-719

Leary, W. F. (Tax Management International Journal 1998): Wrestling With Advance Corporation Tax In Post-'86 Years - TAM 9817001, in: Tax Management International Journal 1998, 346-353

Leblang, S. E. (Tax Management International Journal 1998): Deferred Gratification: A More Rational Approach for Taxing U.S. Multinationals, in: Tax Management International Journal 1998, 539-554

Lee, P. T./Kowallik, A. (Internationale Wirtschaftsbriefe, Fach 8, USA, Gruppe 2, 2001): Steuerliche Rahmenbedingungen des Unternehmenskaufs in den USA, in: Internationale Wirtschaftsbriefe, Fach 8, USA, Gruppe 2, 2001, 1085-1100

Lefebvre, F. (Fiscal, 2000): Mémento Pratique Francis Lefebvre Fiscal 2000, Paris, 2000

Leffers, I. (Germany, 2000): Germany, in: IBFD, Guides to European Taxation Volume II. The Taxation of Companies in Europe, Amsterdam 1972, Last Supplement December 2000

Lehner, M. (Steuer und Wirtschaft 1998): Wettbewerb der Steuersysteme im Spiegel europäischer und U.S.-amerikanischer Steuerpolitik, in: Steuer und Wirtschaft 1998, 159-173

Lemein, G. D./McDonald, J. D. (Taxes 2001): International Tax Watch - Proposed Regulations Regarding Domestic Reverse Hybrid Entities, in: Taxes 2001 (May), 5-8 and 45

Lethaus, H. J./Mohr, H. (Bulletin for International Fiscal Documentation 2000): The Taxation of German Partnerships, in: Bulletin for International Fiscal Documentation 2000, 397-404

Lettl, T. (Deutsches Steuerrecht 1997): Betriebswirtschaftliche Vor- und Nachteile bzw. Gefahren der Unternehmensorganisation in Form der Holding-Struktur, in: Deutsches Steuerrecht 1997, 1016-1020

Levenson, A./Shapiro, A./Reynolds, B. (Tax Notes International 1996): IRS Finalized Check-the-Box Regulations, in: Tax Notes International 1996 (23 December), 2097-2098

Levey, M. M. (Journal of International Taxation 1997): U.S. Distribution Companies of Foreign Multinationals Can Present Difficult Transfer Pricing Issues, in: Journal of International Taxation 1997 (December), 540-547

Levey, M. M./Pollack, L. A. (Journal of International Taxation 1990): Should Your Foreign Corporation Be A CFC?, in: Journal of International Taxation 1990 (November/December), 204-208

Levey, M. M./Teigen, R. D. (Journal of Taxation 1996): International Implications of 'Check-the-Box', in: Journal of Taxation 1996, 261-266

Levy, D. F. (Florida Tax Review 1997): Towards Equal Tax Treatment Of Economically Equivalent Financial Instruments: Proposals For Taxing Prepaid Forward Contracts, Equity Swaps, and Certain Contingent Debt Instruments, in: Florida Tax Review 1997, 471-543

Lier, P./Paardekooper, W. J. (Tax Management International Forum 2002): Netherlands, in: Tax Management International Forum 2002, Vol. 23, No. 1, 34-38

Lindonk, C. van (Tax Planning International Review 2001): Dutch Fiscal Proposal Focuses on Anti-Abuse Provisions, in: Tax Planning International Review, Vol. 28, No. 11, 9-10

Lipton, R. M./Thomas, J. T. (Journal of Partnership Taxation 1996): Proposed Check-the-Box Business Classification Regulations Simplify Rules, in: Journal of Partnership Taxation 1996, 195-217

Lipton, R. M./Thomas, J. T. (Journal of Partnership Taxation 1997): Impact of Final Check-the-Box Regulations Awaits Further IRS Guidance and States' Input, in: Journal of Partnership Taxation 1997, 91-118

Lodin, S.-O. (European Taxation 2001): The Competiveness of EU Tax Systems, in: European Taxation 2001, 166-171

Lodin, S.-O./Gammie, M. (European Taxation 1999): The Taxation of the European Company, in: European Taxation 1999, 286-294

Lodin, S.-O./Gammie, M. (Home State Taxation, 2001): Home State Taxation, Amsterdam 2001

Lohuis, H./Rubbens, B. (Internationale Wirtschaftsbriefe, Fach 5, Niederlande, Gruppe 2, 2001): Steueränderungen in den Niederlanden zum 1.1.2002, in: Internationale Wirtschaftsbriefe, Fach 5, Niederlande, Gruppe 2, 2001, 327-328

Long, Y./Leffers, I. (Internationale Wirtschaftsbriefe, Fach 5, Frankreich, Gruppe 2, 2001): Unternehmenskäufe in Frankreich, in: Internationale Wirtschaftsbriefe, Fach 5, Frankreich, Gruppe 2, 2001, 1265-1278

López-Muñoz, G. de Arce (International Tax Report 2000): Spain's holding company regime, in: International Tax Report 2000 (September), 4-6

Loukota, H. (Internationales Steuerrecht): Internationales Steuerrecht: Einführung, Wien 2000

Lowell, C. H./Burge, M./Briger, P. L. (International Transfer Pricing, 2002): US International Transfer Pricing, 2nd ed., Boston 1998, Current Through 2002 Supplement No. 2

Lowell, C. H./Governale, J. P. (International Taxation, 2002): US International Taxation: Practice and Procedure, Boston 1997, Current Through 2002 Supplement No. 2

Lubkin, G. (Tax Management International Journal 2001): Extraterritorial Exclusions and the WTO: Everything Is Still in Play, in: Tax Management International Journal 2001, 482-487

Lüdemann, P./Echevarria, A./Hruschka, F. (Steuerfolgen gewerblicher Unternehmen in Spanien, 1999): Steuerfolgen gewerblicher Unternehmen in Spanien: Investitionsmodelle nach spanischem und deutschem Ertragsteuerrecht, Heidelberg 1999

Lüthi, D. (Intertax 1989): Countering the abuse of tax treaties - A Swiss view, in: Intertax 1989, 336-340

Lutter, M. (Erscheinungsformen und der für dieses Buch maßgebende Rechtsbegriff der Holding, 1995): Erscheinungsformen und der für dieses Buch maßgebende Rechtsbegriff der Holding, in: Lutter, M. (Hrsg.): Holding-Handbuch, Recht - Management - Steuern, 2. Auflage, Köln 1995, 1-30

Lutter, M. (Holding Handbuch): Holding-Handbuch, Recht - Management - Steuern, 2. Auflage, Köln 1995

Lutter, M. (Betriebs-Berater 2002): Europäische Aktiengesellschaft - Rechtsfigur der Zukunft?, in: Betriebs-Berater 2002, 1-7

Luttermann, C. (Internationales Steuerrecht 1994): Unitary Taxation und U.S. Supreme Court - Die Entscheidung Barclays Bank PLC/Colgate-Palmolive Company v. Franchise Tax Board of California, in: Internationales Steuerrecht 1994, 489-493

Luttermann, C. (Recht der Internationalen Wirtschaft 1996): Besteuerung multinationaler Konzerne in den Vereinigten Staaten von Amerika. Zur Geschichte, Rechtslage und jüngeren Entwicklung des „formulary apportionment"-Prinzips im Lichte der Entscheidung Barclays Bank: Unitary taxation auch auf Bundesebene?, in: Recht der Internationalen Wirtschaft 1996, 935-948

MacLachlan, J. E. (Tax Planning International Review 2001): "Harmful" Taxation: Its Impact On Group Financing Company Locations, in: Tax Planning International Review 2001, Vol. 3, No. 3, 17-20

Maguire, N./Anolik, S. (Tax Notes 2000): Subpart F And Source Of Income Issues In E-Commerce, in: Tax Notes 2000, 1767-1778

Malherbe, J. (Tax Competition, 2000): Harmful Tax Competition and the Future of Financial Centres in the European Union, in: Kirchhof, P./Lehner, M./Raupach, A./Rodi, M. (Hrsg.): Staaten und Steuern: Festschrift für Klaus Vogel zum 70. Geburtstag, Heidelberg 2000, 1125-1135

Malherbe, J. (Tax Notes International 2000): Harmful Tax Competition and the European Code of Conduct, in: Tax Notes International 2000 (10 July), 151-155

Malherbe, J./Pauw, B. de (Tax Management International Forum 2002): Belgium, in: Tax Management International Forum 2002, Vol. 23, No. 1, 3-6

Manasterli, J. B. (Tax Notes International 2000): Offshore Financial Centers and Harmful Tax Regimes Trigger Flurry of International Developments, in: Tax Notes International 2000 (4 December), 2541-2546

Marantelli, A. (Steuer Revue 2000 I): Die Schweiz als Baustein US-amerikanischer Steuerplanung? - Teil 1, in: Steuer Revue 2000, 11-22

Marantelli, A. (Steuer Revue 2000 II): Die Schweiz als Baustein US-amerikanischer Steuerplanung? - Teil 2, in: Steuer Revue 2000, 92-99

Marcus, D. (The CPA Journal 1997): "Check-the-box" Regulations, in: The CPA Journal 1997, 61

Martin, K. (International Corporate Law 1995): Stricter Criteria for Partnerships, in: International Corporate Law 1995, 44-45

Martin, K. (International Tax Review 2000): IRS Blocks Box Options, in: International Tax Review 2000, Vol. 11, Iss. 2, 27-28

Martin, W. J. (Tax Management International Journal 1998): Treaty Tax-Sparing Credits, in: Tax Management International Journal 1998, 444-465

Martín Jiménez, A. J. (Tax Notes International 2001): Tax Planning Opportunities Under Spain's New PE Regime, in: Tax Notes International 2001 (2 July), 91-99

Matthews, K. (Tax Notes International 1989): U.S. Tax Officials Update International Tax Practitioners On Recent U.S. Developments at Cannes Conference, in: Tax Notes International 1989 (December), 575-579

May, T. R. (Tax Notes International 1999): Warning: Hybrid Entities - Proceed With Caution, in: Tax Notes International 1999 (20 December), 2357-2367

Mayor, J. (International Tax Report 2002): Holding Companies - Luxembourg ups the stakes with tax revamp proposals to enhance regime, in: International Tax Report 2002 (January/February), 10

Mayor, J./Davezac, C. (International Tax Report 2002): Holding Companies - Luxembourg tax reform adopts improvements to enhance regime, in: International Tax Report 2002 (March), 2-5

McCormick, J. M./Curlee, W. B. (The Tax Adviser 1997): Don't Check the Box Without First Checking SALT Ramifications, in: The Tax Adviser 1997, 698-701

McDaniel, P. R./Ault, H. J. (Introduction to United States International Taxation, 1998): Introduction to United States International Taxation, in: Series on International Taxation, No. 10, 4th ed., Deventer/Boston 1998

McDaniel, P. R./McMahon, M. J. Jr./Simmons, D. L. (Federal Income Taxation of Business Organizations, 1999): Federal Income Taxation of Business Organizations, 3rd ed., New York 1999

McDonald, J. (Northwestern Journal of International Law and Business 1995): Anti-Deferral Deferred: A Proposal for the Reform of International Tax Law, in: Northwestern Journal of International Law and Business 1995, 248-283

McIntyre, M. J. (Tax Notes International 1994): Viewpoint: U.S. Tax Court's Brown Group Decision Threatens Subpart F, in: Tax Notes International 1994 (17 October), 1225-1230

McIntyre, M. J. (Tax Notes International 1996): Separate Basket Limitations in Theory and in Practice, in: Tax Notes International 1996 (1 January), 56-64

McKee, W. S./Nelson, W. F./Whitmire, R. L. (Federal Taxation of Partnerships and Partners, 2002): Federal Taxation of Partnerships and Partners, 3rd ed., Boston 1997, Current Through 2002 Supplement No. 4

McLaughlin, M. (The CPA Journal 1998): The Consolidated Return And Limited Liability Companies After The Check-The-Box Regulations, in: The CPA Journal 1998, 60

McLoughlin, K. (Tax Notes International 2001): Irish Budget Contains Significant Business Provisions, in: Tax Notes International 2001 (17 December), 1140-1141

McLure, C. E. (Corporate Income, 1979): Must Corporate Income Be Taxed Twice?, Washington D.C. 1979

McLure, C. E. Jr. (The State Corporation Income Tax, 1984): Defining Unitary Business: An Economist's View, in: Mc Lure, C. E. Jr. (editor), The State Corporation Income Tax: Issues in Worldwide Unitary Combination, Stanford 1984, 89-126

McLure, C. E. Jr. (editor) (The State Corporation Income Tax, 1984): The State Corporation Income Tax: Issues in Worldwide Unitary Combination, Stanford 1984

McLure, C. E. Jr. (European Taxation 1989): Economic Integration and European Taxation of Corporate Income at Source: Some Lessons from the U.S. Experience, in: European Taxation 1989, 243-250

McLure, C. E. Jr. (EC Tax Review 1992): Coordinating Business Taxation in the Single European Market: The Ruding Committee Report, in: EC Tax Review 1992, 13-21

McLure, C. E. Jr./Zodrow, G. R. (National Tax Journal 1998): The Economic Case For Foreign Tax Credits For Cash Flow Taxes, in: National Tax Journal 1998, Vol. 51, Iss. 1, 1-22

McNulty, J. K. (Limited Liability Companies, 1995): A Tax Experiment In the United States Federal System: Limited Liability Companies As An Escape From the Unintegrated Corporate Income Tax, in: Lang, J. (Hrsg.): Die Steuerrechtsordnung in der Diskussion: Festschrift für Klaus Tipke zum 70. Geburtstag, Köln 1995, 683-705

McNulty, J. K. (Brief Look at the Early History of the Unintegrated Corporate and Individual Income Taxes in the U.S.A., 2000): Brief Look at the Early History of the Unintegrated Corporate and Individual Income Taxes in the U.S.A., in: Kirchhof, P./Lehner, M./Raupach, A./Rodi, M. (Hrsg.): Staaten und Steuern: Festschrift für Klaus Vogel zum 70. Geburtstag, Heidelberg 2000, 873-886

Meldgaard, H. (International Tax Report 1993): Danish Holding Company Regime Offers Variety of Tax Benefits, in: International Tax Report 1993 (May), 7-10

Meldman, R. E./Schadewald, M. S. (A Practical Guide to U.S. Taxation of International Transactions, 2000): A Practical Guide to U.S. Taxation of International Transactions, 3rd ed., Chicago 2000

Menger, J./Kahl, I. (Journal of International Taxation 2001): Still More German Tax Reforms, in: Journal of International Taxation 2001 (October), 26-33

Mens, H. van/Porquet, F. G. (European Taxation 2001): European Union - Current European Tax Issues, in: European Taxation 2001, 335-338

Meyer, D. I./Outman, W. D. II (Journal of International Taxation 2002): U.S. Tax And Customs Consequences Of Dealing With A Related Foreign Supplier - Part 2, in: Journal of International Taxation 2002 (January), 16-27 and 60-62

Middleton, C. I. (Journal of Partnership Taxation 1999): Use of a Partnership in International Dealings can be Beneficial for Both Inbound and Outbound Transactions, in: Journal of Partnership Taxation 1999, 306-335

Milhac, E./Bayle, P./Gerner, F. (Journal of International Taxation 1999): Mixed-Bag 2000 French Finance Bill: Corporate Tax Increases and Decreases, New Limits on Avoir Fiscal, in: Journal of International Taxation 1999 (December), 18-25

Mintz, J. M. (CESinfo Forum 2002): European Company Tax Reform: Prospects for the Future, CESinfo Forum 2002 (Spring), 3-9

Möller, M. A. (Der Holdingstandort Schweiz, 1998): Der Holdingstandort Schweiz: Ermittlung der steuerlichen Attraktivität im Vergleich zu Deutschland, Wiesbaden 1998

Mössner, M. (Hrsg.) (Steuerrecht international tätiger Unternehmen, 1998): Steuerrecht international tätiger Unternehmen, herausgegeben von Mössner, M., 2. Auflage, Köln 1998

Moetell, M. C. (Tax Management International Journal 1997): IRS Issues Final Regulations Under Section 902, in: Tax Management International Journal 1997, 111-120

Mogenson, H./Benson, D. M. (Tax Notes International 1996): IRS Issues Final Check-the-Box Regs - Tax Simplification Creates Planning Opportunities, in: Tax Notes International 1996 (30 December), 2159-2163

Molenaars, M./Bongers, E. (Journal of International Taxation 2001): Dateline - the Netherlands: Despite Capital Tax Rate Deductions, Netherlands Focuses on Exemptions, in: Journal of International Taxation 2001 (September), 42-47

Morris, A. (Tax Notes International 1992): Spanish Implementing Legislation for EC Parent/Subsidiary Dividend Directive Examined, in: Tax Notes International 1992 (17 August), 323-325

Mors, M. (CESinfo Forum 2002): Conference on "Corporate and Capital Income Taxation in the European Union", Mons, 7-8th December 2001, Summary , CESinfo Forum 2002 (Spring), 21-23

Moussallem, S. (Die Besteuerung der US-corporation, 2001): Die Besteuerung der US-corporation - eine ökonomische Analyse, Frankfurt am Main/Berlin/Bern, u.a. 2001

Mueller, J. (Internationale Wirtschaftsbriefe, Fach 11, Europäische Gemeinschaften, Gruppe 2, 2001): Mitteilung der Europäischen Kommission zur Unternehmensbesteuerung in der EU, in: Internationale Wirtschaftsbriefe, Fach 11, Europäische Gemeinschaften, Gruppe 2, 2001, 475-478

Müller, K. (Verwirklichung von Gerechtigkeit und Entscheidungsneutralität, 2001): Verwirklichung von Gerechtigkeit und Entscheidungsneutralität in den Einkommen- und Körperschaftsteuersystemen der EU-Mitgliedsstaaten: eine Analyse unter Berücksichtigung des Einkommens und des Konsums als alternative Anknüpfungspunkte der Besteuerung, Lohmar/Köln 2001

Müssener, I. (Internationale Wirtschaftsbriefe, Fach 5, Niederlande, Gruppe 2, 2002): Das Steuersystem der Niederlande im Überblick, in: Internationale Wirtschaftsbriefe, Fach 5, Niederlande, Gruppe 2, 2002, 331-350

Mukadi Nogy, J. (Journal of International Taxation 2001): The Paradox of Tax Havens: Consequences of the Subjective Approach, in: Journal of International Taxation 2001 (January), 34-43 and 61-64

Mullerat, R./Kolff, A. Q. (Intertax 2002): Goodwill Deduction and Other Good Things from Spain, in: Intertax 2002, 252-254

Mullerat, R./Rodriguez, R. (Tax Notes International 2000): Spain Introduces New Participation Exemption Rules, in: Tax Notes International 2000 (14 August), 681-684

Musgrave, P. B. (Economic Analysis, 1963): Taxation of Foreign Investment Income: An Economic Analysis, Baltimore 1963

Musgrave, P. B. (U.S. Taxation, 1969): United States Taxation of Foreign Investment Income: Issues and Arguments, Cambridge 1969

Neffati, S./Gutknecht, M. (Internationale Wirtschaftsbriefe, Fach 5, Luxemburg, Gruppe 2, 2002): Luxemburger Steuerreform 2002, in: Internationale Wirtschaftsbriefe, Fach 5, Luxemburg, Gruppe 2, 2002, 159-166

Newberry, K. J. (Foreign Tax Credit Limitations, 1994): Foreign Tax Credit Limitations and Public Issuances by U.S. Multinationals - New Evidence of Tax Clienteles, Arizona State University 1994

Newberry, K. J. (Journal of Accounting Research 1998): Foreign Tax Credit Limitations and Capital Structure Decisions, in: Journal of Accounting Research 1998, 157-166

Newberry, K. J./Dhaliwal, D. S. (Journal of Accounting Research 2001): Cross-Jurisdictional Income Shifting by U.S. Multinationals: Evidence from International Bond Offerings, in: Journal of Accounting Research 2001, 643-662

New York State Bar Association Tax Section (Tax Notes International 1998): Notice 98-11: Tax Treatment of Hybrid Entities in the U.S., in: Tax Notes International 1998 (25 May), 1669-1676

Nijkamp, H. (International Tax Review 2001): Tax Competition - EU stands up to harmful tax regimes, in: International Tax Review 2001, Vol. 12, Iss. 3, 35-39

Noren, D. G. (Tax Law Review 2001): Commentary The U.S. National Interest In International Tax Policy, in: Tax Law Review 2001, 337-351

Not, N. (Tax Planning International Review 2001): Are French Thin Capitalisation Rules Compatible with OECD Model Convention?, in: Tax Planning International Review 2001, Vol. 28, No. 9, 16-24

Obluda, S. (Internationale Wirtschaftsbriefe, Fach 5, Niederlande, Gruppe 2, 1998): Das Steuerrecht der Niederlande, in: Internationale Wirtschaftsbriefe, Fach 5, Niederlande, Gruppe 2, 1998, 269-296

O'Brien, C. (International Tax Review 1999): Ireland, in: International Tax Review 1999, Tax Developments Yearbook, 23-46

O'Connor, W. F./Toyoda, Y. (The International Tax Journal 2000): What Will "Control" Mean in International Taxation in the Next Millennium?, in: The International Tax Journal 2000, Vol. 26, Iss. 1, 82-88

OECD (The OECD Observer 2000): Towards world tax co-operation, in: The OECD Observer 2000, Iss. 221-222, 88-90

Oestreicher, A. (Konzern-Gewinnabgrenzung, 2000): Konzern-Gewinnabgrenzung: Gewinnabgrenzung - Gewinnermittlung - Gewinnaufteilung, München 2000

Offermanns, R. (Belgium, 2001): Belgium, in: IBFD, The Taxation Of Companies In Europe, Binder *, Last Supplement No. 162, April 2002

Offermanns, R. (Luxembourg, 2001): Luxembourg, in: IBFD, The Taxation Of Companies In Europe, Binder ***, Last Supplement No. 162, April 2002

Ogley, A. (Journal of International Taxation 1996): International Financing Options Include Overseas Finance Companies, in: Journal of International Taxation 1996 (January), 22-32

O'Grady, E. (Tax Notes International 2002): World Tax Conference Comes to London, in: Tax Notes International 2002 (3 June), 1058-1066

O'Grady, J. E. (Tax Notes International 1992): Apple and IRS Enter Into First Transfer-Pricing Arbitration Under U.S. Tax Court Rule, in: Tax Notes International 1992 (16 March), 518-519

O'Mahony, G. (International Tax Review 2001): Ireland maintains its charm, in: International Tax Review 2001, Vol. 12, Iss. 2, 36-39

Ottosen, A. M./Hansen, L. C. (Journal of International Taxation 2002): Denmark Tightens Rules on CFCs, Holding and Captive Insurance Companies, in: Journal of International Taxation 2002 (February), 44-46

Owens, J. (Tax Planning International e-commerce 2002): Unco-operative Tax Havens, in: Tax Planning International e-commerce 2002, Vol. 4, No. 5, 11-12

Palacios, J./Bootello, V. (Journal of International Taxation 2002): Tax Advantages in New Measures for 2002, Expected Reform for 2003, in: Journal of International Taxation 2002 (September), 39-41

Pantaleo, N. (European Holding and Financing Companies, 2001): European Holding and Financing Companies, in: CTF, Report of Proceedings of the Fifty-Second Tax Conference, 2000 Conference Report, Toronto 2001, 13:1-13:42

Patton, M. F./Wood, K. W. (Tax Management International Journal 1997): Rev. Proc. 96-53: Continuous Quality Improvement of the APA Process, in: Tax Management International Journal 1997, 80-90

Pernegger, R. (Österreichische Steuer-Zeitung 1999): Die Beteiligungsertragsbefreiung bei internationalen Schachtelbeteiligungen, in: Österreichische Steuer-Zeitung 1999, 429-433

Peroni, R. J. (University of Miami Law Review 1997): Back to the Future: A Path to Progressive Reform of the U.S: International Income Tax Rules, in: University of Miami Law Review 1997, 975-1011

Peroni, R. J. (Brooklyn Journal of International Law 2001): Symposium International Tax Policy in the New Millennium, Panel III: U.S. Multinational and International Competitiveness, The Proper Approach for Taxing the Income of Foreign Controlled Corporations, in: Brooklyn Journal of International Law 2001, 1579-1593

Peroni, R. J. (Texas Law Review 2001): Deferral of U.S. tax on international income: End it, don't mend it - why should we be stuck in the middle with Subpart F, in: Texas Law Review 2001, 1609-1620

Peroni, R. J./Fleming, J. C. Jr./Shay, S. E. (SMU Law Review 1999): Getting Serious About Curtailing Deferral Of U.S. Tax On Foreign Source Income, Symposium on 'Time, Tax, and Money', in: SMU Law Review 1999, 455-525

Peter, M. (Fortentwicklung des Betriebsstättenprinzips, 2002): Fortentwicklung des Betriebsstättenprinzips, Frankfurt am Main/Bern/Bruxelles/u.a. 2002

Pflüger, H. (FR 1996): Ein Organisations- und Belastungsvergleich zwischen dem US-amerikanischen und deutschen Steuersystem, in: FR 1996, 204-211

Pillow, R. F./Rooney, J. J. (Journal of Taxation 2000): Check-the-Box: Final Conversion Regs. Add Clarification While New Prop. Regs Add Some Uncertainty, in: Journal of Taxation 2000, 197-206

Phillips, B. (The National Public Accountant 1998): „Check the box" Final Regulations Explained, in: The National Public Accountant 1998, Vol. 43, Iss. 6, 8-9

P. M. D. (Journal of International Taxation 2000): From the Editor, in: Journal of International Taxation 2000 (September), 4

Pöllath, R. (Unternehmensbesteuerung nach dem DBA-USA, 1990): Unternehmensbesteuerung nach dem DBA-USA, in: Kramer, J.-D. (Hrsg.), Grundzüge des US-amerikanischen Steuerrechts, Stuttgart 1990, 241-276

Polito, A. P. (Virginia Tax Review 1998): Borrowing, Return Of Capital Conventions, And The Structure Of The Income Tax: An Essay In Statutory Interpretation, in: Virginia Tax Review 1998 (Winter), 467-575

Pollack, L. A./Porter, D./Corrie, F. (International Tax Review 1998 I): US planning for ACT - part one, in: International Tax Review 1998, Vol. 9, Iss. 8, 75-81

Pollack, L. A./Porter, D./Corrie, F. (International Tax Review 1998 II): US planning for ACT - part two, in: International Tax Review 1998, Vol. 9, Iss. 9, 23-25

PricewaterhouseCoopers (International Transfer Pricing 1999-2000, 2001): International Transfer Pricing 1999-2000, Bicester 2001

PricewaterhouseCoopers (Tax Notes International 2002): Danish Parliament Approves Corporate Tax Incentives, in: Tax Notes International 2002 (3 June), 1040-1041

Pugh, E. O. T. (Tax Notes International 1993): The Interaction of the U.S. Deemed Paid Foreign Tax Credit and the German Integration System, in: Tax Notes International 1993 (6 December), 1429-1437

PwC Deutsche Revision (Unternehmenssteuerreform 2001, 2000): Unternehmenssteuerreform 2001 - Analyse aller wesentlichen Änderungen mit Praxishinweisen, Gestaltungsempfehlungen und Checklisten, Freiburg/Berlin/München 2000

Quinn, T. F./Garre, K./Hangebrauck, W. (The International Tax Journal 2001): Foreign partnerships - Rules, issues, and planning opportunities regarding U.S. filing requirements, in: The International Tax Journal 2001, Vol. 27, Iss. 2, 1-46

Quirke, L./Walsh, A. (International Tax Review 1999): Ireland: Ireland as a Holding Company Regime, in: International Tax Review 1999, Vol. 10, Iss. 6, 46

Qvist, H. (Area Development Sites & Facility Planning 1998): Denmark: A New Approach to a New Europe, in: Area Development Sites & Facility Planning 1998, Vol. 33, Iss. 11, 87-89

Raedel, J./Cohen, H./Chan, D. (The Tax Adviser 1998): Regulations Issued for Notice 98-11, in: The Tax Adviser 1998, 378-381

Rädler, A. (Vorstellung des EG-Sachverständigenausschusses zur Unternehmensbesteuerung (Ruding-Ausschuß), 1994): Vorstellung des EG-Sachverständigenausschusses zur Unternehmensbesteuerung (Ruding-Ausschuß), in: Harmonisierung der Körperschaftsteuersysteme in den EU-Staaten, herausgegeben von Herzig, N., mit Beiträgen von Müller-Dott, J.-P./Herzig, N./Rädler, A., u.a., Köln 1994, 1-20

Rädler, A. J./Lausterer, M./Blumenberg, J. (Der Betrieb 1996, Beilage 3): Steuerlicher Missbrauch und EG-Recht - Verstößt die generelle Anwendung von § 42 AO auf die Beteiligung deutscher Unternehmen an Tochterkapitalgesellschaften im irischen IFSC gegen Gemeinschaftsrecht? -, in: Der Betrieb 1996, Beilage 3, 1-12

Raineri, W. T. (Tax Notes International 1996): Thin Capitalization Issues in the United States, in: Tax Notes International 1996 (18 November), 1716-1732

Raventós Calvo, S./Cueva González-Cotera, A. de la (Spain, 2001): Spain, in: IBFD, The Taxation Of Companies In Europe, Binder ****, Last Supplement No. 162, April 2002

Reich, M. (Steuer & Wirtschaft International 2001): Reform der Unternehmensbesteuerung in der Schweiz - Reform of Business Taxation in Switzerland, in: Steuer & Wirtschaft International 2001, 486-490

Reimer, M. (Die steuerliche Erfassung privater Veräußerungsgewinne, 2001): Die steuerliche Erfassung privater Veräußerungsgewinne: Reformüberlegungen für die deutsche Besteuerung unter Berücksichtigung der Rechtslage in Österreich, Großbritannien und den USA, Frankfurt a.M. 2001

Reynolds, B. W./Denovio, N. J./Mundstock, G. (Journal of International Taxation 1994): RRA '93 Anti-Deferral Provisions Create Planning Hurdles For CFCs, in: Journal of International Taxation 1994 (February), 52-60

Reynolds, B. W./Melcer, G. J. (Journal of International Taxation 1995): New Subpart F Regs. Impose Data-Gathering Burdens on Shareholders, in: Journal of International Taxation 1995 (December), 532-545

Ricketts, R./Masselli, J. (Taxes 2001): Tax Consequences Of Partnership Breakups, in: Taxes 2001 (April), 39-49

Riedweg, P. (Internationales Steuerrecht 1998): Die Schweizer Holding nach der Reform im internationalen Vergleich, in: Internationales Steuerrecht 1998, 585-594

Rodriguez, A. E. (The International Tax Journal 2001): Data Reduction Techniques in the Allocation of Operational Expenses under I.R.C. Section 861: A Structural Approach, in: The International Tax Journal 2001, Vol. 27, Iss. 2, 84-109

Rodríguez, P./Briones, L. (Tax Management International Forum 2002): Spain, in: Tax Management International Forum 2002, Vol. 23, No. 1, 38-42

Rödder, T. (Die Wirtschaftsprüfung 1991): Bilanzierung und Besteuerung der Europäischen Aktiengesellschaft - Regelungen und Auswirkungen des Statut-Entwurfes der EG-Kommission (Teil 1), in: Die Wirtschaftsprüfung 1991, 200-208

Roin, J. A. (Virginia Law Review 1989): The Grand Illusion: A Neutral System for the Taxation of International Transactions, in: Virginia Law Review 1989 (August), 919-969

Rollinson, M. (Tax Management International Journal 1998): A Wish List for U.S. Multinationals - The Houghton/Levin Bill, in: Tax Management International Journal 1998, 519-525

Romano, C. (European Taxation 1999): Holding Company Regimes in Europe: A Comparative Survey, in: European Taxation 1999, 256-269

Rose, G./Glorius-Rose, C. (Steuerplanung und Gestaltungsmissbrauch, 2002): Steuerplanung und Gestaltungsmissbrauch: Eine Auswertung der jüngeren Rechtsprechung des BFH zu § 42 AO, 3. Auflage, Bielefeld 2002

Rosenbach, G. (Steuerliche Parameter für die Internationale Standortwahl und ausländische Holdingstandorte, 1995): Steuerliche Parameter für die Internationale Standortwahl und ausländische Holdingstandorte, in: Lutter, M. (Hrsg.): Holding-Handbuch, Recht - Management - Steuern, Köln 1995, 679-737

Rosenbloom, H. D. (Tax Law Review 2000): The David R. Tillinghast Lecture - International Arbitrage and the International Tax System, in: Tax Law Review 2000, 137-166

Rosenbloom, H. D. (Brooklyn Journal of International Law 2001): Symposium International Tax Policy in the New Millennium, Panel III: U.S. Multinational and International Competitiveness, From the Bottom Up: Taxing the Income of Foreign Controlled Corporations, in: Brooklyn Journal of International Law 2001, 1525-1554

Rosenbloom, H. D./Booth, C. W. (Case Western Reserve Journal of International Law 1993): Some unconventional thinking about foreign tax credits and the Advance Corporation Tax, in: Case Western Reserve Journal of International Law 1993, 1-22

Ross, S. G. (Tax Notes International 1990): U.S. International Tax Policy: Where Are We? Where Should We Be Going, in: Tax Notes International 1990 (July), 781-785

Rousslang, D. J. (National Tax Journal 2000): Deferral and the Optimal Taxation of International Investment Income, in: National Tax Journal 2000, 589-600

Rsm International Tax Committee/Lorence, R. D. (Journal of International Taxation 1996): Will The World Follow The U.S. Lead On Limitation Of Treaty Benefits?, in: Journal of International Taxation 1996 (March), 124-129

Ruchelman, S. C./Asbeck, E. van/Canalejo, G./et. al. (Journal of International Taxation 2000): A Guide to European Holding Companies - Part 1: Luxembourg, Denmark, and Switzerland, in: Journal of International Taxation 2000 (August), 40-49

Ruchelman, S. C./Asbeck, E. van/Canalejo, G./et. al. (Journal of International Taxation 2001 I): A Guide to European Holding Companies - Part 2: Belgium, The Netherlands, and Spain, in: Journal of International Taxation 2001 (January), 24-33 and 59-60

Ruchelman, S. C./Asbeck, E. van/Canalejo, G./et. al. (Journal of International Taxation 2001 II): A Guide to European Holding Companies - Part 3: United Kingdom, in: Journal of International Taxation 2001 (March), 20-33

Ruding, H. O. (Journal of International Taxation 1994): U.S. Tax Policy is Hurting U.S. Multinationals Operating in the EC, in: Journal of International Taxation 1994 (January), 4-9

Ruding, H. O. (Tax Law Review 2000): The David R. Tillinghast Lecture - Tax Harmonization in Europe: The Pros And Cons, in: Tax Law Review 2000, 101-109

Ruding-Bericht (Der Betrieb 1992, Beilage 5): Die Schlussfolgerungen und Empfehlungen des Rudingausschusses, in: Der Betrieb 1992, Beilage 5

Runge, B. (Wettbewerb nationaler Steuerrechte, 1997): Wettbewerb nationaler Steuerrechte, in: Klein, F./Stihl, H. P./Wassermeyer, F. (Hrsg.): Unternehmen Steuern: Festschrift für Hans Flick zum 70. Geburtstag, Köln 1997, 957-969

Ryder, D. R./Yoder, L. D. (International Tax Review 1997): Final Rules Offer New Opportunities, in: International Tax Review 1997, Vol. 8, Iss. 7, 35-39

Ryser, W. (Intertax 1975): Some Reflections on the Unilateral Measures taken by Switzerland against the Abuse of Treaties for the Avoidance of Double Taxation, in: Intertax 1975, 60-66

Salmon, J. J./Gander, F. R. (Tax Notes International 1990): Refining Subpart F To Make U.S. Firms More Competitive After 1992, in: Tax Notes International 1990 (January), 97-101

Salzberger, W. (Internationales Steuerrecht 1999): Unitary Taxation - Vorbild für eine Konzernbesteuerung in der Europäischen Union, in: Internationales Steuerrecht 1999, 97-103

Sams, J. (The Tax Adviser 1998): Treasury Fulfills Promise to Issue *Brown Group* Partnership Regulations, in: The Tax Adviser 1998, 374

Sanders, T./Clancy, F. (International Tax Review 2002): Is the UK going Dutch?, in: International Tax Review 2002, Vol. 13, Iss. 3, 22-26

Sandison, F. G. (Tax Management International Forum 2002): United Kingdom, in: Tax Management International Forum 2002, Vol. 23, No. 2, 38-42

Saunders, G. (Tolley's Taxation in the Republic of Ireland 2000-01, 2000): Tolley's Taxation in the Republic of Ireland 2000-01, Croydon 2000

Schaumburg, H. (Internationales Steuerrecht, 1998): Internationales Steuerrecht: Außensteuerrecht, Doppelbesteuerungsrecht, 2. Auflage, Köln 1998

Schaumburg, H./Jesse, L. (Die internationale Holding aus steuerrechtlicher Sicht, 1995): Die internationale Holding aus steuerrechtlicher Sicht, in: Lutter, M. (Hrsg.): Holding-Handbuch, Recht - Management - Steuern, 2. Auflage, Köln 1995, 606-678

Scheucher, R. (Österreichische Steuer-Zeitung 1998): Steuerliche Behandlung von Zinsen für die Anschaffung von nationalen und internationalen Schachtelbeteiligungen, in: Österreichische Steuer-Zeitung 1998, 158-150

Scheuchzer, M. (Recht der Internationalen Wirtschaft 1995): Zur Notwendigkeit einer Europäisierung der Organschaft, in: Recht der Internationalen Wirtschaft 1995, 35-48

Schiffer, K. J./Wahlers, U. (Steuern und Bilanzen 2001): Die Europäische Aktiengesellschaft (SE) - Erfolgsmodell für die Praxis, in: Steuern und Bilanzen 2001, 467-468

Schjelderup, G. (International Journal of the Economics of Business 1999): Multinationals, intra-firm trade and the taxation of foreign-source income, in: International Journal of the Economics of Business 1999, 93-105

Schneider, H. (Internationale Wirtschaftsbriefe, Fach 5, Österreich, Gruppe 2, 2000): Gesellschaftsteuer bei österreichischen Beteiligungen, in: Internationale Wirtschaftsbriefe, Fach 5, Österreich, Gruppe 2, 2000, 485-488

Schnieder, E.-A. (Internationales Steuerrecht 1997): Die spanische Körperschaftsteuerreform 1995 unter Berücksichtigung der neuen Holding-Regelung, in: Internationales Steuerrecht 1997, 68-73

Schreiber, C./Dorfmueller, P. (CTF, 2001): Germany (Pantaleo, N., New Developments for European Holding and Financing Companies), in: CTF, Report of Proceedings of the Fifty-Second Tax Conference, 2000 Conference Report, Toronto 2001, 13:10-13:14

Schreiber, C./Meiisel, P. (Internationales Steuerrecht 2002): Auswirkungen des § 14 Abs. 1 Nr. 5 KStG auf die Nutzung von Organträgerverlusten, in: Internationales Steuerrecht 2002, 581-586

Schreiber, U. (Steuer und Wirtschaft 1994): Unternehmensbesteuerung im europäischen Binnenmarkt, in: Steuer und Wirtschaft 1994, 238-254

Schulz, A./Eicker, K. (Intertax 2001): The European Company Statute - the German View, in: Intertax 2001, 332-341

Schulz, A./Geismar, B. (Deutsches Steuerrecht 2001): Die Europäische Aktiengesellschaft - Eine kritische Bestandsaufnahme, in: Deutsches Steuerrecht 2001, 1078-1086

Schulz, A./Petersen, S. (Deutsches Steuerrecht 2002): Die Europa-AG: Steuerlicher Handlungsbedarf bei Gründung und Sitzverlegung, in: Deutsches Steuerrecht 2002, 1508-1517

Schuth, M. R. (The Tax Adviser 2001): The Dual-Consolidated-Loss-Trap, in: The Tax Adviser 2001, 593-596

Schwarz, J. S. (Journal of International Taxation 1992): EC Directive Attempts To Harmonize Use Of Cross-Border Losses, in: Journal of International Taxation 1992 (March/April), 370-373

Scott, C. (Tax Notes International 2001): OECD Answers 17 Questions, Tax Havens Say Problems Still Remain, in: Tax Notes International 2001 (3 September), 1127-1129

Sellers Smith, R. (Tax Law Dictionary, 2002): West's Tax Law Dictionary: Definitions of Terms, Words, and Phrases Used in Modern American Law, 2002 ed., St. Paul 2002

Shakow, D. J. (The Taxation of Corporations, Partnerships, and Their Owners, 1997): The Taxation of Corporations, Partnerships, and Their Owners, 2nd ed., New York 1997

Shapiro, A./Mantegani, B. (Tax Notes International 1997): From Morrissey to Check-the-Box: can You Get There From Here?, in: Tax Notes International 1997 (10 February), 513-519

Sharp, W. M. Sr. (Tax Notes International 1998): Establishing a Multinational Operating Structure: Hybrid and Other 'Outbound' Planning Considerations, in: Tax Notes International 1998 (2 March), 689-713

Shelton, N. (European Taxation 1999): Denmark - Holding Company Regime Introduced, in: European Taxation 1999, 33

Shelton, N. (International Tax Report 2001): Danish tax change postponed, in: International Tax Report 2001 (March), 4

Shelton, N. (Tax Planning International Review 2002): Denmark: New Tax Law for Holding Companies, in: Tax Planning International Review 2002, Vol. 29, No. 6, 22

Shelton, N. (International Tax Report 2002): Holding Companies - Denmark's new law means positive changes for international tax planning, in: International Tax Report 2002 (September), 10-11

Shepherdson, D. P. (Case Western Reverse Journal of International Law 1985): The Simplification of Subpart F, in: Case Western Reverse Journal of International Law 1985, 459-487

Sheppard, L. A. (Tax Notes International 1998): U.S. Cross-Border Tax Arbitrage, 'Hybridity,' Mules, and Hinnies, in: Tax Notes International 1998 (23 February), 579-585

Sheppard, L. A. (Tax Notes 1998): Sweet Tax Nothings; Rethinking Treasury's Foreign Policy, in: Tax Notes 1998, 145-147

Sheppard, L. A. (Tax Notes 1998): Notice 98-11 Withdrawn: Who Won?, in: Tax Notes 1998, 1671-1678

Shields, C. C. (Tax Notes International 2002): Different Conclusions Regarding the Subpart F Problem, in: Tax Notes International 2002 (11 March), 1113-1117

Sider, V./Maiorano, R./Beaulne, D./Zive, J. (Journal of International Taxation 2000): A Practitioner's Guide To Corporate Distributions In Canada and the U.S. - Part 3: Domestic And Cross-Border Distributions, in: Journal of International Taxation 2000 (February), 22-39

Sieker, K. (Internationale Wirtschaftsbriefe, Fach 8, USA, Gruppe 2, 1993): Die Besteuerung von S-Corporations in den USA, in: Internationale Wirtschaftsbriefe, Fach 8, USA, Gruppe 2, 1993, 719-722

Siemaszko, D. J./Windsor, J. G. (The Tax Adviser 1996): MNCs Should Start Addressing Sec. 404A Issues, in: The Tax Adviser 1996, 411-413

Sinclair, B./Kopstein, R. (Guaranteed to Enlighten: The Impact of Guarantees on Financing Arrangements, 2001): Guaranteed to Enlighten: The Impact of Guarantees on Financing Arrangements, in: CTF, Report of Proceedings of the Fifty-Second Tax Conference, 2000 Conference Report, Toronto 2001, 22:1-22:40

Small, D. G. (Internationales Steuerrecht 1996): USA: Das neue Wahlrecht zur Klassifizierung von Kapital- und Personengesellschaften, in: Internationales Steuerrecht 1996, 280-282

Smith, M./Laudan, D. (International Tax Review 1999): German Rules Pierce Corporate Veil, in: International Tax Review 1999, Vol. 10, Iss. 8, 61-65

Sparagna, G. T./Chase, R. (Tax Management International Journal 2000): Regulations Proposed to Nullify Certain „Disregarded Entity" Elections, in: Tax Management International Journal 2000, 131-140

Spencer, D. E. (Journal of International Taxation 1998): OECD Report Cracks Down on Harmful Tax Competition, in: Journal of International Taxation 1998 (July), 26-35

Spencer, D. E. (Journal of International Taxation 2000): Recent U.S. Tax Treaties Raise The Stakes For Withholding Rate Exceptions, in: Journal of International Taxation 2000 (October), 28-33 and 61-64

Spencer, D. E. (Journal of International Taxation 2001 I): Stepping up the Pressure on Tax Havens: An Update (Part 1), in: Journal of International Taxation 2001 (April), 26-35 and 62

Spencer, D. E. (Journal of International Taxation 2001 II): Stepping up the Pressure on Tax Havens: An Update (Part 2), in: Journal of International Taxation 2001 (May), 37-44

Spencer, D. E. (Journal of International Taxation 2002 I): OECD Project on Tax Havens and Harmful Tax Practices (Part 1), in: Journal of International Taxation 2002 (April), 8-17 and 57

Spencer, D. E. (Journal of International Taxation 2002 II): The OECD Proposals: A Status Report, in: Journal of International Taxation 2002 (July), 15-16 and 60-64

Spengel, C. (Europäische Steuerbelastungsvergleiche, 1995): Europäische Steuerbelastungsvergleiche: Deutschland - Frankreich - Großbritannien, Düsseldorf 1995

Spengel, C./Lammersen, L. (Steuer und Wirtschaft 2001): Methoden zur Messung und zum Vergleich von internationalen Steuerbelastungen, in: Steuer und Wirtschaft 2001, 222-238

Springael, B. (Tax Notes International 2002): Luxembourg Enacts Tax Reform to Enhance International Standing, in: Tax Notes International 2002 (18 March), 1245-1249

Sprohge, H./Burt, C. J. (Management Accounting 1994): Dodging the S Corporation's Silver Bullet, in: Management Accounting 1994, 34-40

Spudowski, M. A./Sutro, P. J. (Journal of International Taxation 1999): Foreign-Source Capital Gains and the Foreign Tax Credit: Debugging the Anomaly, in: Journal of International Taxation 1999 (September), 16-21 and 48

Stark, K. J./Zolt, E. M. (European Taxation 2000): United States Partnership Taxation: Current Structure and Proposals for Reform, in: European Taxation 2000, 326-338

Steenholdt, S./Josephsen, N. (European Taxation 1999): The New Holding Company Regime - The Best of Both Worlds, in: European Taxation 1999, 146-156

Steichen, A. (Internationale Wirtschaftsbriefe, Fach 5, Luxemburg, Gruppe 2, 1997): Das Steuerrecht Luxemburgs, in: Internationale Wirtschaftsbriefe, Fach 5, Luxemburg, Gruppe 2, 1997, 117-144

Steichen, A. (Internationale Wirtschaftsbriefe, Fach 5, Luxemburg, Gruppe 2, 1999): Änderungen des luxemburgischen Steuerrechts, in: Internationale Wirtschaftsbriefe, Fach 5, Luxemburg, Gruppe 2, 1999, 151-158

Stevens, M. G. (The Practical Accountant 1998): Pay Attention To The Tax Changes In The Spending Bill, in: The Practical Accountant 1998, 37-38

Stoffregen, P. A./Lipeles, S. R. (Tax Notes International 1994): The Impact of Section 956a and Related Legislative Changes on U.S. Multinationals, in: Tax Notes International 1994 (16 May), 1325-1337

Stok, E. van der (International Tax Review 2001): Netherlands Corporate Income Hit by Tax Plan 2002 II, in: International Tax Review 2001, Vol. 12, Iss. 10, 38

Streu, V. (Der Einsatz einer inländischen Zwischenholding in der internationalen Konzernsteuerplanung, 2000): Der Einsatz einer inländischen Zwischenholding in der internationalen Konzernsteuerplanung, in: Grotherr, S. (Hrsg.), Handbuch der internationalen Steuerplanung, herausgegeben von Grotherr, S., Herne 2000, 169-186

Strub, A. (Internationales Steuerrecht 1993): Die Europäische Aktiengesellschaft - Lagebericht, in: Internationales Steuerrecht 1993, 179

Sunley, E. M. (CESinfo Forum 2002): The Pros and Cons of Formulary Apportionment, CESinfo Forum 2002 (Spring), 36-37

Swanick, M. F. (Tax Management International Journal 1995): IRS Issues Guidance for Section 936 Companies, in: Tax Management International Journal 1995, 474-477

Swanick, M. F./Leary, W. (Tax Management International Journal 2000): IRS Clarifies the Treatment of U.K. ACT Refunds, in: Tax Management International Journal 2000, 291-300

Tardivy, P./Schiessl, M./Haelterman, A./et. al. (International Tax Review 2002): Parent subsidiary directive: the long reach of Athinaiki, in: International Tax Review 2002 (March), 11-18

Taylor, J. C./Hannum, C. E. (Tax Notes International 1997): Spanish Holding Company Legislation Eclipses Netherlands and Luxembourg, in: Tax Notes International 1997 (14 July), 91-96

Tello, C. P. (Tax Management International Journal 1999): Basic Tax Considerations for Conducting Ongoing Business Activities Abroad, in: Tax Management International Journal 1999, 11-23

Tello, C. P. (Tax Management International Journal 2001): The Upside Down World of Corporate Inversion Transactions, in: Tax Management International Journal 2001, 161-173

Tello, C. P. (Tax Management International Forum 2002): United States, in: Tax Management International Forum 2002, Vol. 23, No. 2, 43-51

Teufel, T. (Steuerliche Rechtsformoptimierung, 2002): Steuerliche Rechtsformoptimierung - Gestaltungsversuche im Gesellschafts-Gesellschafter-Verhältnis, Frankfurt am Main/Bern/Bruxelles/u.a. 2002

Thiele, C. (Einführung in das US-amerikanische Steuerrecht, 1997): Einführung in das US-amerikanische Steuerrecht, Wien 1997

Thömmes, O./Tomset, E. (EC Tax Review 1992): Issues of the Implementation of the Merger Directive in the EC Member States, in: EC Tax Review 1992, 228-240

Tillinghast, D. R. (Tax Law and Practice, 1994): The Life And Times Of Brown Group: Judicial Repeal Of Subpart F And Regulatory Re-Enactment (?), in: Practising Law Institute (editor), Tax Law And Estate Planning Course Handbook Series - Tax Law and Practice, WL 1994, 641-652

Tillinghast, D. R. (Tax Notes 1998): An Old-Timer's Comment On Notice 98-11, in: Tax Notes 1998, 1739-1740

Tillinghast, D. R. (Florida Tax Review 1999): Taxation Of Electronic Commerce: Federal Income Tax Issues In The Establishment Of A Software Operation In A Tax Haven, in: Florida Tax Review 1999, 339-379

Tillmanns, W. (Internationale Wirtschaftsbriefe, Fach 5, Frankreich, Gruppe 2, 1999): Das Steuerrecht Frankreichs - Teil 3, in: Internationale Wirtschaftsbriefe, Fach 5, Frankreich, Gruppe 2, 1999, 1197-1212

Tillmanns, W. (Internationale Wirtschaftsbriefe, Fach 5, Frankreich, Gruppe 2, 2001): Steueränderungen in Frankreich 2000/2001, in: Internationale Wirtschaftsbriefe, Fach 5, Frankreich, Gruppe 2, 2001, 1257-1262

Timokhov, V. (Tax Notes International 2002): Using the U.S. Foreign Tax Credit System as an Investment Incentive in Developing Countries, in: Tax Notes International 2002 (13 May), 775-784

Tinner, H. (Konzernstruktur und Steuerplanung, 1984): Konzernstruktur und Steuerplanung - Strukturierung und Umstrukturierung von schweizerischen internationalen Konzernen aus steuerlicher Sicht, Landquart 1984

Tipke, K. (Die Steuerrechtsordnung I, 1993): Die Steuerrechtsordnung, Bd. I, Wissenschaftsorganisatorische, systematische und grundrechtlich-rechtsstaatliche Grundlagen, Köln 1993

Tischer, F. (Die Betriebswirtschaft 1993): Anrechnungsüberhänge bei ausländischen Einkünften und das Steuerrecht in Deutschland und den USA, in: Die Betriebswirtschaft 1993, 209-219

Triplett, C. (International Tax Review 1994): US leads in advance pricing agreements, in: International Tax Review 1994, Supplement February, 33-39

Tuerff, T. T./Gordon, R. A. (Journal of International Taxation 1994): Brown Group, Anti-Abuse Rules Create Uncertainty In Using Partnerships, in: Journal of International Taxation 1994 (July), 292-299

Valat, A./Bouzidi, C. (France, 2002): France, in: IBFD, The Taxation Of Companies In Europe, Binder **, Last Supplement No. 162, April 2002

Vanistendael, F. (EC Tax Review 1992): Comments on the Ruding Report, in: EC Tax Review 1992, 3-13

Veltins, M. A. (Das Recht der U.S. partnership und limited partnership einschließlich ihrer Besteuerung, 1984): Das Recht der U.S. partnership und limited partnership einschließlich ihrer Besteuerung - eine systematische Darstellung des Gesellschafts- und

211

Steuerrechts der Personengesellschaften in den Vereinigten Staaten von Amerika, Herne/Berlin 1984

Vlaanderen, P. (Tax Notes International 2002): Why Exempt Foreign Business Profits?, in: Tax Notes International 2002 (11 March), 1095-1102

Vorwold, G. (GmbH-Rundschau 2001): Wahl und Besteuerung von Kapitalgesellschaften in den USA, in: GmbH-Rundschau 2001, 19-21

Vorwold, G. (Recht der Internationalen Wirtschaft 2002): „Cash"- versus „accrual"-Methode - Paradigmenwechsel der US-amerikanischen „tax accounting"?, in: Recht der Internationalen Wirtschaft 2002, 235-247

Vrouwenvelder, M. (Tax Management International Journal 2001): Tax Planning to Reduce Foreign Taxes for U.S. Multinationals - An EU and Netherlands Tax Update, in: Tax Management International Journal 2001, 403-414

Wagner, F. W./Dirrigl, H. (Die Steuerplanung der Unternehmung, 1980): Die Steuerplanung der Unternehmung, Stuttgart/New York 1980

Warco, D./Nyari, L. (International Tax Review 2001): Subpart F, in: International Tax Review 2001, Vol. 12, Iss. 1, 37-46

Ward, J. (Ireland, 2001): Ireland, in: IBFD, The Taxation Of Companies In Europe, Binder **, Last Supplement No. 162, April 2002

Warner, J. P. (Tax Management International Forum 2002): United States, in: Tax Management International Forum 2002, Vol. 23, No. 1, 48-56

Warner, P./Allgaier, D. (International Tax Review 2001): Why the US-Luxembourg Treaty Brings Long-Awaited Benefits, in: International Tax Review 2001, Vol. 12, Iss. 9, 10-14

Warner, R./Cussons, P. (International Financial Law Review 2002): United Kingdom: The European Company Statute and Taxation Update, in: International Financial Law Review 2002, Vol. 21, Iss. 2, 53

Weerth, J. de (Internationales Steuerrecht 2001): Anmerkung - BMF, Schrb. v. 19.3.2001, IV B4 - S 1300 - 65/01, in: Internationales Steuerrecht 2001, 228 und 232

Weiner, J. M. (Tax Notes International 2001): EU Commission Study on Company Taxation and the Internal Market Considers Comprehensive Company Tax Reform, in: Tax Notes International 2001 (29 October), 511-518

Weiner, J. M. (Tax Notes International 2002 I): European Parliament Issues Report on EU Tax Policy, in: Tax Notes International 2002 (22 April) 252-254

Weiner, J. M. (Tax Notes International 2002 II): EU Commission, Member States Commit to EU-Wide Company Taxation, Formulary Apportionment, in: Tax Notes International 2002 (6 May) 515-520

Weiner, J. M. (CESinfo Forum 2002): Formulary Apportionment and the Future of Company Taxation in the European Union, CESinfo Forum 2002 (Spring), 10-20

Wells, B. (Tax Executive 2001): Interest Allocation - The Dog Days of Summer, in: Tax Executive 2001, 365-372

Wenzl, H. (Holding, 1996): Holding - Eine Chance für kleine und mittlere Unternehmen, Eschborn 1996

Wiesner, P. M. (GmbH-Rundschau 2001): Europa-AG: Steuerneutralität der Fusionsgründung soll erst in der nächsten Legislaturperiode angegangen werden - wird der EuGH die Rechtsform für nichtig erklären?, in: GmbH-Rundschau 2001, R461

Willens, R. (Journal of Taxation 1999): Rationalizing The Reorg. Provisions: IRS Abandons The Bausch & Lomb Doctrine, in: Journal of Taxation 1999, 69-77

Willis, A. B./Pennell, J./Postlewaite, P. F./Lipton, R. (Partnership Taxation, 2002): Partnership Taxation, 6th ed., Boston 1997, Current Through 2002 Supplement No. 4

Windholtz, T. F./Bernot, J. E. (Journal of International Taxation 1991 I): International Related-Party Debt: Part I, in: Journal of International Taxation 1991 (July/August), 85-91

Windholtz, T. F./Bernot, J. E. (Journal of International Taxation 1991 II): International Related-Party Debt: Part II, in: Journal of International Taxation 1991 (September/October), 147-155

Wittendorff, J./Graff, T. (Tax Notes International 2001): Denmark Introduces New Withholding Tax on Dividends, in: Tax Notes International 2001 (16 April), 1893

Wrappe, S. C. (Tax Management International Journal 1997): Working with the New IRS Procedures: A Silver Lining in the Transfer Pricing Cloud, in: Tax Management International Journal 1997, 27-34

Wuermli, R. J. (Internationale Wirtschaftsbriefe, Fach 5, Schweiz, Gruppe 2, 1993): Das neue Stempelsteuergesetz in der Schweiz, in: Internationale Wirtschaftsbriefe, Fach 5, Schweiz, Gruppe 2, 1993, 395-398

Yanoshak, J. (The Tax Adviser 1995): Rethinking the S Election, in: The Tax Adviser 1995, 42-48

Yoder, L. D. (Tax Management International Journal 1995): Final and Proposed Subpart F Regulations: Determination of FBCI, Definitions of FPHCI and the Earnings and Profits Limitations (Part One), in: Tax Management International Journal 1995, 571-592

Yoder, L. D. (Tax Management International Journal 1996 I): Final and Proposed Subpart F Regulations: Determination of FBCI, Definitions of FPHCI and the Earnings and Profits Limitations (Part Two), in: Tax Management International Journal 1996, 3-25

Yoder, L. D. (Tax Management International Journal 1996 II): Bausch & Lomb: The "Manufacturing" Exception to Foreign Base Company Sales Income, in: Tax Management International Journal 1996, 427-433

Yoder, L. D. (Tax Management International Journal 1996 III): Section 1248: Treatment of Gain from the Disposition of Stock in a Controlled Foreign Corporation (Part One), in: Tax Management International Journal 1996, 483-497

Yoder, L. D. (Tax Management International Journal 1996 IV): Section 1248: Treatment of Gain from the Disposition of Stock in a Controlled Foreign Corporation (Part Two), in: Tax Management International Journal 1996, 589-603

Yoder, L. D. (Tax Management International Journal 1997 I): Subpart F Potpourri: Tax-Exempt Interest, the E&P Limitation and Other Rules Modified by T.D. 8704, in: Tax Management International Journal 1997, 203-231

Yoder, L. D. (Tax Management International Journal 1997 II): Proposed Amendments to Subpart F, in: Tax Management International Journal 1997, 259-271

Yoder, L. D. (Tax Management International Journal 1998 I): Hybrid Branches: Temporary Regulations Create Something Out of Nothing for Subpart F Purposes, in: Tax Management International Journal 1998, 219-248

Yoder, L. D. (Tax Management International Journal 1998 II): Notice 98-35 - Subpart F Hybrid Entity Regulations In Suspense, in: Tax Management International Journal 1998, 427-443

Yoder, L. D. (Tax Management International Journal 1998 III): The Application of Subpart F to Structures and Transactions Involving Partnerships, in: Tax Management International Journal 1998, 603-644

Yoder, L. D. (Journal of International Taxation 1998): Contract Manufacturing Proposed Regs. Add Fuel To The Fire: What Changed?, in: Journal of International Taxation 1998 (May), 10-15 and 44

Yoder, L. D. (Tax Management International Journal 1999 I): TAM 9906035: A Contorted Application of Section 1248, in: Tax Management International Journal 1999, 339-356

Yoder, L. D. (Tax Management International Journal 1999 II): Proposed Subpart F Hybrid Entity Regulations: A Further Retreat, But No White Flag, in: Tax Management International Journal 1999, 707-724

Yoder, L. D. (Tax Management International Journal 2000): Prop. Regs. Address the Application of Subpart F to a CFC's Distributive Share of Partnership Income, in: Tax Management International Journal 2000, 667-691

Yoder, L. D. (Tax Management International Journal 2001): Planning Techniques Described in the Treasury's Subpart F Study, in: Tax Management International Journal 2001, 221-240

Yoder, L. D./Everson, S. L. (Tax Management International Journal 2000 I): Sale of Lower-Tier CFC: IRS Advises that Branch Election Does Not Avoid Subpart F, in: Tax Management International Journal 2000, 3-35

Yoder, L. D./Everson, S. L. (Tax Management International Journal 2000 II): Proposed CTB Regulations Void Branch Elections: Subpart F and Other Consequences, in: Tax Management International Journal 2000, 301-326

Yoder, L. D./Everson, S. L. (Tax Management International Journal 2001): FSA 200046008: Another Branch Attack, in: Tax Management International Journal 2001, 14-32

Yoder, L. D./Kahn, J. H. (Tax Management International Journal 1999): Buyers Electing Section 338 for CFC Targets: Sellers Beware, in: Tax Management International Journal 1999, 531-562

Yoder, L. D./McGill, S. P. (Tax Management International Journal 1997): Treatment of CFC Loans to U.S. Affiliates: The Sword and Sickle of Subpart F, in: Tax Management International Journal 1997, 454-477

Yoder, L. D./Waimon, R. L. (Journal of International Taxation 2001): Seagate: Tax Court Holds Restricted Stock Gains are Subpart F Income, in: Journal of International Taxation 2001 (April), 40-49

Yu, A./Chan, D. F. (International Tax Review 1999): United States, in: International Tax Review 1999, Supplement: Tax Development Yearbook 1999, 43-47

Yu, A./Lisecki, C. (Tax Notes International 2002): Recharacterization of Payments by Domestic Reverse Hybrid Entities, in: Tax Notes International 2002 (19 August), 945-950

Yu, A./McClellan, E. (Tax Management International Journal 1997): Notice 97-18: Some Results Unforeseen, in: Tax Management International Journal 1997, 325-331

Zagaris, B. (Tax Notes International 1998): OECD Report on Harmful Tax Competition: Strategic Implications for Caribbean Offshore Jurisdictions, in: Tax Notes International 1998 (16 November), 1507-1519

Zagaris, B. (Tax Management International Journal 2000): The OECD Report Identifying Harmful Tax Practices and Tax Havens Solidifies the Momentum of the Harmful Tax Competition Initiative, in: Tax Management International Journal 2000, 521-530

Zettler, H. (Treaty-shopping nach Inkrafttreten des § 50d Ia EStG, 2001): Treaty-shopping nach Inkrafttreten des § 50d Ia EStG - Anwendung der deutschen Abwehrvorschrift und ihre Konsequenzen für die Internationale Steuerplanung mit Zwischengesellschaften, Hannover 2001

Zink, W. J. (The Tax Adviser 1997): Check-the-Box: European Options, U.S. and European Consequences, in: The Tax Adviser 1997, 79-81

Zink, W. J./Mezzo, L. J. (The Tax Adviser 1989): Subchapter S Corporations in the International Business Arena, in: The Tax Adviser 1989, 105-108

Zois, A. (Cardozo Journal of International and Comparative Law 1999): Corporate Tax Planning: Spain Offers Advantages Over Luxembourg and the Netherlands, in: Cardozo Journal of International and Comparative Law 1999, 179-204

Zschiegner, H. (Die Besteuerung von Gesellschaften, 1990): Die Besteuerung von Gesellschaften, in: Kramer, J.-D. (Hrsg.), Grundzüge des US-amerikanischen Steuerrechts, Stuttgart 1990, 115-145

Zschiegner, H. (Internationale Wirtschaftsbriefe, Fach 8, USA, Gruppe 2, 1995): Zuordnung von Einkünften und Betriebsausgaben zwischen Nahestehenden in den USA, in: Internationale Wirtschaftsbriefe, Fach 8, USA, Gruppe 2, 1995, 799-808

Zschiegner, H. (Internationale Wirtschaftsbriefe, Fach 8, USA, Gruppe 2, 1997 I): Steuerliche Klassifizierung in- und ausländischer Unternehmen als Kapital- oder Personengesellschaft („Check-the-Box"-Richtlinien), in: Internationale Wirtschaftsbriefe, Fach 8, USA, Gruppe 2, 1997, 885-894

Zschiegner, H. (Internationale Wirtschaftsbriefe, Fach 8, USA, Gruppe 2, 1997 II): Besteuerung einer US Limited Liability Company und ihrer Gesellschafter, in: Internationale Wirtschaftsbriefe, Fach 8, USA, Gruppe 2, 1997, 895-902

Zschiegner, H. (Internationale Wirtschaftsbriefe, Fach 8, USA, Gruppe 2, 1998 I): Das Einkommensteuerrecht der USA - Teil I, in: Internationale Wirtschaftsbriefe, Fach 8, USA, Gruppe 2, 1998, 919-942

Zschiegner, H. (Internationale Wirtschaftsbriefe, Fach 8, USA, Gruppe 2, 1998 II): Das Einkommensteuerrecht der USA - Teil II, in: Internationale Wirtschaftsbriefe, Fach 8, USA, Gruppe 2, 1998, 943-958

Zschiegner, H. (Internationale Wirtschaftsbriefe, Fach 8, USA, Gruppe 2, 1998 III): Das Einkommensteuerrecht der USA - Teil III, in: Internationale Wirtschaftsbriefe, Fach 8, USA, Gruppe 2, 1998, 959-984

Zschiegner, H. (Internationale Wirtschaftsbriefe, Fach 8, USA, Gruppe 2, 1998 IV): Das Einkommensteuerrecht der USA - Teil IV, in: Internationale Wirtschaftsbriefe, Fach 8, USA, Gruppe 2, 1998, 985-996

Zschiegner, H. (Internationale Wirtschaftsbriefe, Fach 8, USA, Gruppe 2, 1998 V): Änderungen der „Check-the-Box"-Richtlinien und deren Auslegung in den USA, in: Internationale Wirtschaftsbriefe, Fach 8, USA, Gruppe 2, 1998, 997-1000

Zschiegner, H. (Internationale Wirtschaftsbriefe, Fach 8, USA, Gruppe 2, 1998 VI): Mißbrauch bei Steuergutschriften für ausländische Ertragsteuern in den USA, in: Internationale Wirtschaftsbriefe, Fach 8, USA, Gruppe 2, 1998, 1003-1004

Zschiegner, H. (Internationale Wirtschaftsbriefe, Fach 8, USA, Gruppe 2, 2000 I): Status und Tendenz der US-Verrechnungspreisrichtlinien, in: Internationale Wirtschaftsbriefe, Fach 8, USA, Gruppe 2, 2000, 1021-1032

Zschiegner, H. (Internationale Wirtschaftsbriefe, Fach 8, USA, Gruppe 2, 2000 II): US-Verrechnungspreiszusagen im Vorhinein - IRS Jahresbericht 2000 -, in: Internationale Wirtschaftsbriefe, Fach 8, USA, Gruppe 2, 2000, 1047-1064

Zschiegner, H. (Internationale Wirtschaftsbriefe, Fach 8, USA, Gruppe 2, 2001): Senkungen für 2001 beim Einkommensteuerrecht der USA, in: Internationale Wirtschaftsbriefe, Fach 8, USA, Gruppe 2, 2001, 1133-1136

TABLE OF DOUBLE TAX TREATY LAW

Double Tax Treaty Argentina/Spain	Dated July 21, 1992 Official State Gazette, dated September 9, 1994
Double Tax Treaty Argentina/U.S.	Not yet in force; Protocol signed http://www.natlaw.com/treaties/taxtreat/arusa1.htm Download: May 24, 2002
Double Tax Treaty Austria/Switzerland	Dated January 30, 1974 Ö-BGBl. 1975/64
	Revised by the Protocol Amending the Convention between the Republic of Austria and Switzerland for the Avoidance of Double Taxation with Respect to Taxes on Income and Capital, dated July 20, 2000 Ö-BGBl. III 2001/204
Double Tax Treaty Austria/U.S.	Dated May 31, 1996 S. Doc. No. 104-31
Double Tax Treaty Belgium/Ireland	Dated June 24, 1970 B.S./Mon.B. February 19, 1974
Double Tax Treaty Belgium/U.S.	Dated July 9, 1970 23 U.S.T. 2687
	Revised by the Supplementary Protocol Modifying and Supplementing the Convention between the United States of America and the Kingdom of Belgium for the Avoidance of Double Taxation and the Prevention of Fiscal Evasion with Respect to Taxes on Income, dated December 31, 1987
Double Tax Treaty Cyprus/U.S.	Dated March 19, 1984 1989-2 C.B. 280
Double Tax Treaty Czech Republic/U.S.	Dated September 16, 1993 S. Doc. No. 103-17
Double Tax Treaty Denmark/Switzerland	Dated November 23, 1973 BEK 117, dated October 31, 1974
Double Tax Treaty Denmark/U.S.	Dated August 19, 1999 S. Doc. No. 106-12
Double Tax Treaty Estonia/U.S.	Dated January 15, 1998 S. Doc. No. 105-55
Double Tax Treaty France/Ireland	Dated March 21, 1968 J.O., dated September 10, 1971
Double Tax Treaty France/U.S.	Dated August 31, 1994 S. Doc. No. 103-32
Double Tax Treaty	Dated October 17, 1962

Germany/Ireland	BGBl. II 1964, 267
Double Tax Treaty Germany/U.S.	Dated August 29, 1989 BGBl. II 1991, 355
Double Tax Treaty Hungary/U.S.	Dated February 12, 1979 1980-1 C.B. 333
Double Tax Treaty Ireland/Italy	Dated June 11, 1971 S.I. 1973 No. 64
Double Tax Treaty Ireland/Luxembourg	Dated January 14, 1972 S.I. 1973 No. 65
Double Tax Treaty Ireland/U.S.	Dated July 28, 1997 S. Doc. No. 105-31
Double Tax Treaty Japan/U.S.	Dated March 8, 1971 1973-1 C.B. 630
Double Tax Treaty Latvia/U.S.	Dated January 15, 1998 S. Doc. No. 105-57
Double Tax Treaty Lithuania/U.S.	Dated January 15, 1998 S. Doc. No. 105-56
Double Tax Treaty Luxembourg/Switzerland	Dated January 21, 1993 AS 1994 333
Double Tax Treaty Luxembourg/U.S.	Dated April 3, 1996 S. Doc. No. 104-33
Double Tax Treaty The Netherlands/Switzerland	Dated November 12, 1951 Trb. 1951, No. 148
	Revised by the Protocol Amending the Convention between the Kingdom of the Netherlands and Switzerland for the Avoidance of Double Taxation with Respect to Taxes on Income and Capital, dated June 22, 1966 Trb. 1966, No. 177
Double Tax Treaty The Netherlands/U.S.	Dated December 18, 1992 S. Doc. No. 105-8
Double Tax Treaty Poland/U.S.	Dated October 8, 1974 1977-1 C.B. 416
Double Tax Treaty Romania/U.S.	Dated December 4, 1973 1976-2 C.B. 492
Double Tax Treaty Slovak Republic/U.S.	Dated October 8, 1993 S. Doc. No. 103-18
Double Tax Treaty Slovenia/U.S.	Dated June 31, 1999 S. Doc. No. 106-9

Double Tax Treaty Spain/U.S. Dated February 22, 1990
          Official State Gazette, dated December 22, 1990

Double Tax Treaty   Dated May 7, 1965
Sweden/Switzerland   AS 1967 90

Double Tax Treaty   Dated October 2, 1996
Switzerland/U.S.   S. Doc. No. 105-8

Double Tax Treaty Turkey/U.S. Dated March 28, 1996
          S. Doc. No. 104-30

TABLE OF TREASURY RULINGS

Germany
BMF-Schreiben
19.03.2001	IV B4 - S 1300 - 65/01	BStBl. I 2001, 243

Spain
Royal Decree
05.07.1991	1080/1991	Official State Gazette, dated July 13, 1991

USA
Revenue Procedures
Rev. Proc.	91-22	1991-1 C.B. 26
Rev. Proc.	2000-13	2000-6 I.R.B. 515

Revenue Rulings
Rev. Rul.	71-388	1971-2 C.B. 314
Rev. Rul.	74-351	1974-2 C.B. 144
Rev. Rul.	75-341	1975-2 C.B. 308
Rev. Rul.	81-290	1981-2 C.B. 108
Rev. Rul.	87-14	1987-1 C.B. 181
Rev. Rul.	89-72	1989-1 C.B. 257
Rev. Rul.	90-31	1990-1 C.B. 147
Rev. Rul.	90-112	1990-2 C.B. 186
Rev. Rul.	99-5	1999-6 I.R.B. 8
Rev. Rul.	99-6	1999-6 I.R.B. 6

Notices
Notice	94-47	1994-19 I.R.B. 9
Notice	95-14	1995-1 C.B. 297
Notice	96-39	1996-32 I.R.B. 8
Notice	98-5	1998-3 I.R.B. 49
Notice	98-11	1998-6 I.R.B. 18
Notice	98-35	1998-27 I.R.B. 25

TABLE OF CASES

Germany

Bundesverfassungsgericht

Date	File number	Citation
14.04.1959	1 BvL 23, 34/57	BVerfGE 9, 237

Bundesfinanzhof

March 16, 1993	XI R 52/90	BStBl. II 1993, 562
January 19, 2000	I R 94/97	BStBl. II 2001, 222
January 19, 2000	I R 117/97	*Internationales Steuerrecht* 2000, 182

Austria

Verwaltungsgerichtshof

July 6, 1967	ZI 1278/66	ÖStZB 1967, 170
June 8, 1988	87/13/0068	ÖStZB 1989, 15
December 10, 1991	89/14/0064	ÖStZB 1992, 662
October 10, 1996	94/15/0187	*Österreichische Steuer-Zeitung* 1998, 158
November 20, 1996	96/15/0188	*Österreichische Steuer-Zeitung* 1999, 623

The Netherlands

Hoge Raad

February 23, 2000	BNB 2000/215
February 23, 2000	BNB 2000/216
February 23, 2000	BNB 2000/217
March 14, 2001	BNB 2001/210

USA

U.S. Supreme Court

U.S. v. Basye	410 U.S. 441 [1973]
Morrissey v. Commissoner	296 U.S. 344 [1935]
U.S. v. Goodyear Tire & Rubber Co.	110 S. Ct. 462 [1989]

U.S. Court of Appeals, U.S. States Emergency Court of Appeals

Brown Group Inc v. Commissioner	77 F. 3d 217 (8th Cir. 1996)

Caruth Corp. v. United States	865 F.2d 644 (5th Cir. 1989)
Commissioner v. American Light & Traction Co.	156 F.2d 398 (7th Cir. 1946)
Keasbey & Mattison Co. v. Rothensies	133 F.2d 894(3rd Cir. 1942)
Roth Steel Tube Co. v. Commissioner	800 F.2d 325 (6th Cir. 1986)
Textron Inc v. U.S.	561 F.2d 1023 (1st Cir. 1977)
Young & Rubicam Inc v. The United States	410 F.2d 1233 (Ct.Cl. 1969)

U.S. District Courts

Apple Computer v. Commissioner	No. 2178-90 T.C. [1993]
Bausch & Lomb Inc v. Commissioner	71 T.C.M. 2031 [1996]
Brown Group Inc v. Commissioner	102 T.C. 616 [1994]
Brown Group Inc v. Commissioner	104 T.C. 105 [1995]
Columbian Rope Co. v. Commissioner	42 T.C. 800 [1964]
International Multifoods Co. v. Commissioner	108 T.C. 25 [1997]
Textron Inc v. C.I.R.	117 T.C. 67 [2001]
Vulcan Materials Co. v. Commissioner	96 T.C. 410 [1991]

Treasury Decision

T.D.	8697	61 Fed. Reg. 66584
T.D.	8767	63 Fed. Reg. 14613
T.D.	8827	1999-30 I.R.B. 120
T.D.	8844	1999-50 I.R.B. 661
T.D.	8889	2000-30 I.R.B. 124

MISCELLANEOUS

Agencia Tributaria (Taxation): Taxation of Non Residents, Appendum 3 Tax Havens, http://www.aeat.es/normlegi/noreside/irnr/ingles/anexos.htm#3 (Download: May 14, 2002)

Baker & McKenzie (Effective Tax Burden, 2001): The Effective Tax Burden of Companies in the Member States of the EU - The Perspective of a Multinational Investor, March 2001, http://www.bakernet.com/BakerNet/Resources/Publications/Recent+Publications/ (Download: October 31, 2001)

Baker & McKenzie (Effective Tax Burden - Summary, 2001): The Effective Tax Burden of Companies in the Member States of the EU, Summary, London 2001, http://www.bakernet.com/NR/rdonlyres/ev4ssvp2rley3f5ogleehwydyepsrs6vppfab4sznvc a4w5eq2qrfzjhfo7chhclpc7526nfjlnfsg/1%2beurotax_final2.pdf (Download: October 31, 2001)

BDO (SOPARFI, 2001): SOPARFI holding companies, http://www.cflux.lu/domino/html/cfwebenEX.nsf/pages/societesoparfi (Download: February 14, 2002)

Bolkestein, F. (Internal Market, 2002): Towards an Internal Market without Tax Obstacles, Speech at the European Commission conference on company taxation in the European Union, Brussels, April 29, 2002, http://europa.eu.int/comm/taxation_customs/speeches/29apr2002_en.htm (Download: May 5, 2002)

Della Vedova, B. (Choice of Approach, 2002): Towards an Internal Market without tax obstacles - A strategy for providing companies with a consolidated corporate tax base for their EU-wide activities, Speech at the European Commission conference on company taxation in the European Union, Brussels, April 29, 2002, http://europa.eu.int/comm/taxation_customs/taxation/company_tax/docs/della.pdf (Download: May 15, 2002)

Department of the Treasury (Subpart F, 2000): Treasury Department Policy Study Deferral of Income Earned Through U.S. Controlled Foreign Corporations - The Deferral of Income Earned Through U.S. Controlled Foreign Corporations, A Policy Study, December 29, 2000, http://www.treas.gov/taxpolicy/library/subpartf.pdf (Download: March 2, 2002)

Department of the Treasury (U.S. Tax Treaties, 2001): U.S. Tax Treaties, Publication 901, April 2001, http://www.intltaxlaw.com/FORMS/2001/p901.pdf (Download: March 13, 2002)

Department of the Treasury & Internal Revenue Service (PS-43-95, 1996): Notice of Proposed Rulemaking and Notice of Public Hearing, Simplification of Entity Classification, 26 CFR Part 301, PS-43-95, 1996-24 I.R.B. 20, http://www.unclefed.com/Tax-Bulls/1996/PS-43-95.PDF (Download: April 25, 2002)

Department of the Treasury & Internal Revenue Service (REG-113909-98, 1999): REG-113909-98, RIN 1545-AW63: Withdrawal of Guidance Under Subpart F Relating to Partnerships and Branches and Issuance of New Guidance Under Subpart F Relating to Certain Hybrid Transactions, July 13, 1999, 64 Fed. Reg. 37727

Department of the Treasury & Internal Revenue Service (REG-112502-00, 2000): REG-112502-00, RIN 1545-AY45: Guidance Under Subpart F Relating to Partnerships, September 20, 2000, 65 Fed. Reg. 56836

Department of the Treasury & Internal Revenue Service (REG-107101-00, 2001): REG-107101-00, RIN 1545-AY13: Treaty Guidance Regarding Payments With Respect to Domestic Reverse Hybrid Entities, February 27, 2001, 66 Fed. Reg. 12445

Deutscher Bundesrat (Drucksache 324/02): Gesetzentwurf der Bundesregierung: Entwurf eines Gesetzes zu dem Revisionsprotokoll vom 12. März 2002 zu dem Abkommen vom 11. August 1971 zwischen der Bundesrepublik Deutschland und der Schweizerischen Eidgenossenschaft zur Vermeidung der Doppelbesteuerung auf dem Gebiete der Steuern vom Einkommen und dem Vermögen, Drucksache 324/02, 19.04.02

Deutscher Bundestag (Drucksache 14/9201): Gesetzentwurf der Bundesregierung: Entwurf eines Gesetzes zu dem Revisionsprotokoll vom 12. März 2002 zu dem Abkommen vom 11. August 1971 zwischen der Bundesrepublik Deutschland und der Schweizerischen Eidgenossenschaft zur Vermeidung der Doppelbesteuerung auf dem Gebiete der Steuern vom Einkommen und dem Vermögen, Drucksache 14/9201, 03.06.02

Deutscher Bundestag (Entwurf StSenkG, 2000): Entwurf eines Gesetzes zur Senkung der Steuersätze und zur Reform der Unternehmensbesteuerung (Steuersenkungsgesetz - StSenkG), Bundestag-Drucksache 14/2683 vom 15.02.2000

EBIT (Tax Analysis, 2002): EBIT Key Messages and Tax Analysis, Contribution to the European Conference on Company Taxation 29/30 April 2002, Brussels, http://europa.eu.int/comm/taxation_customs/taxation/company_tax/docs/ebit.pdf (Download: April 27, 2002)

Embassy of the United States of America (2001 Statement): Argentina - 2001 Investment Climate Statement, http://usembassy.state.gov/posts/ar1/wwwhaics.html (Download: May 24, 2002)

Ernst & Young (TNI 2000): United States - Treatment of Dividends Under Tax Treaty with the United Kingdom, in: TNI, 2-3, http://www.ey.com/global/vault.nsf/EYPassport/United_States_TNI_June_2000/$file/Jun e_2000_TNI_-_United_States.pdf (Download: March 31, 2002)

Ernst & Young (Spain, 2001): Doing Business in Spain, Madrid 2001, http://www.ey.com/global/vault.nsf/EYPassport/DBI_Spain/$file/DBI%20Spain.pdf (Download: May 14, 2002)

EU (Proposal, 1970): Proposal for a Council Regulation Embodying a Statute for the European Company, COM/70/600FINAL, Official Journal of the European Communities, No. C 124, dated October 10, 1970

EU (EU Merger Directive, 1990): Council Directive No. 90/434 on the common system of taxation applicable to mergers, divisions, transfers of assets and exchanges of shares concerning companies of different Member States, dated July 23, 1990, Official Journal of the European Communities, No. L 225, dated August 8, 1990, 1

EU (EU Parent-Subsidiary Directive, 1990): Council Directive No. 90/435 on the Common System of Taxation Applicable in the Case of Parent Companies and Subsidiaries of Different Member States, dated July 23, 1990, Official Journal of the European Communities, No. L 225, dated August 8, 1990, 6

EU (Proposal, 1990): Proposal for a Council Directive Concerning Arrangements for the Taking into Account by Enterprises of the Losses of their Permanent Establishments and Subsidiaries

223

Situated in other Member States, COM/90/595FINAL, dated December 6, 1990, Official Journal of the European Communities, No. C 53, dated February 28, 1931, 30

EU (Code of Conduct, 1997): Council, Conclusions of the ECOFIN Council Meeting on 1 December 1997 concerning taxation policy, Conclusions No. 98/C 2/01, http://europa.eu.int/comm/taxation_customs/publications/official_doc/com/taxation/Dec1 997_Council_conclusions/texte/en.pdf, Annex 1: http://europa.eu.int/comm/taxation_customs/publications/official_doc/com/taxation/Dec1 997_Council_conclusions/annexe1/en.pdf, Annex 2: http://europa.eu.int/comm/taxation_customs/publications/official_doc/com/taxation/Dec1 997_Council_conclusions/annexe2/en.pdf (Downloads: May 15, 2002)

EU (Enlargement, 2001): Enlargement of the European Union - An historic opportunity: A general overview of the enlargement process and the pre-accession strategy of the European Union, 2001, http://europa.eu.int/comm/enlargement/docs/pdf/corpusen.pdf (Download: May 31, 2002)

EU (SE Statute, 2001): Statute for a European Company (SE), Council Regulation (EC) No. 2157/2001 of October 8, 2001, Official Journal of the European Communities, No. L 294/1, dated November 10, 2001, http://europa.eu.int/eur-lex/pri/en/oj/dat/2001/l_294/l_29420011110en00010021.pdf (Download: May 15, 2002)

EU (SE Statute Supplement, 2001): Council Directive 2001/86/EC of 8 October 2001 supplementing the Statute for a European company with regard to the involvement of employees, Official Journal of the European Communities, No. L 294/22, dated November 10, 2001, http://europa.eu.int/eur-lex/pri/en/oj/dat/2001/l_294/l_29420011110en00220032.pdf (Download: May 15, 2002)

EU Commission (Communication, 2001): Communication from the Commission to the Council, the European Parliament and the Economic and Social Committee, COM(2001) 582 FINAL, October 23, 2001, http://europa.eu.int/comm/taxation_customs/publications/official_doc/IP/ip1468/commun ication_en.pdf (Download: October 24, 2001)

EU Commission (Memo, 2001): Commission Company Tax Strategy - Frequently Asked Questions, MEMO/01/335, October 23, 2001, http://europa.eu.int/rapid/start/cgi/guesten.ksh?p_action.gettxt=gt&doc=MEMO/01/335|0| AGED&lg=EN&display= (Download: October 24, 2001)

EU Commission (Study, 2001): Company Taxation in the internal market, SEC(2001) 1681, October 23, 2001, http://europa.eu.int/comm/taxation_customs/publications/official_doc/IP/ip1468/compan y_tax_study_en.pdf (Download: October 24, 2001) Annexes: http://europa.eu.int/comm/taxation_customs/publications/official_doc/IP/ip1468/Annexes .pdf (Download: May 21, 2002)

EU Commission (Memorandum, 2002): Conference on company taxation supports further work on an EU-wide consolidated tax base, MEMO/02/84, April 30, 2002, http://europa.eu.int/rapid/start/cgi/guesten.ksh?p_action.gettxt=gt&doc=MEMO/02/84|0| RAPID&lg=EN&display= (Download: May 3, 2002)

European Court of Justice (Lankhorst-Hohorst GmbH v. Finanzamt Steinfurt, 2002): Judgment of the Court (Fifth Chamber) C-324/00, http://www.curia.eu.int/jurisp/cgi-bin/gettext.pl?lang=en&num=79978787C19000324&doc=T&ouvert=T&seance=ARRET&where=() (Download: December 13, 2002)

Folketinget (Bill L99, 2002): L99 (som vedtaget): Forslag til lov om ændring af afskrivningsloven, aktieavancebeskatningsloven, ligningsloven, personskatteloven, selskabsskatteloven, virksomhedsskatteloven og andre love (Strukturtilpasninger m.v. og lempelse af tabs- og underskudsregler) http://www.folketinget.dk/Samling/20012/MENU/00672242.htm (Download: June 10, 2002)

Handelsblatt (52/2002): Chemie- und Pharmakonzern verpasst sich neue Organisationsstruktur - Aus Bayer Alt wird Bayer Neu, in: Handelsblatt, No. 52, 2002, 13

Hey, J. (German Perspective, 2002): Tax Competition in Europe: The German Perspective, EATLP Annual Congress, 7 June 2002, Lausanne, http://www.eatlp.org/Germany02.PDF (Download: June 20, 2002)

Internal Revenue Service (International Taxpayer): International Taxpayer - Items of Interest, http://www.irs.gov/businesses/small/intltaxpayer/display/0,,i1%3D2%26i2%3D23%26i3%3D37%26genericId%3D79871,00.html (Download: May 27, 2002)

Joint Committee on Taxation (Alternative Minimum Tax, 2002): Background Materials on Alternative Minimum Tax and Capital Cost Recovery Prepared for the House Committee on Ways and Means Tax Policy Discussion Series (JCX-14-02), March 8, 2002, http://www.house.gov/jct/x-14-02.pdf (Download: May 28, 2002)

Kondo, S. (Ending, 2002): Ending Tax Haven Abuse, dated April 18, 2002, http://www.oecd.org/pdf/M00028000/M00028566.pdf (Download: June 11, 2002)

Lannoo, K./Levin, M. (EU Company, 2002): An EU Company without an EU Tax - A Corporate Tax Action Plan for Advancing the Lisbon Process, CEPS Research Report, Contribution to the European Conference on Company Taxation 29/30 April 2002, Brussels, http://europa.eu.int/comm/taxation_customs/taxation/company_tax/docs/corporate_taxation.pdf (Download: April 27, 2002)

Makhlouf, G. (Exchange, 2002): OECD Work on Harmful Tax Practices and Improving the Exchange of Information - A statement by Gabriel Makhlouf, Chair of the OECD's Committee on Fiscal Affairs, dated January 31, 2002, http://www.oecd.org/EN/document/0,,EN-document-127-3-no-12-25339-0,00.html (Download: June 11, 2002)

Makhlouf, G. (Statement, 2002): The OECD List of Unco-operative Tax Havens - A statement by the Chair of the OECD's Committee on Fiscal Affairs, dated April 18, 2002, http://www.oecd.org/EN/document/0,,EN-document-99-3-no-12-28549-0,00.html (Download: June 11, 2002)

Malherbe, J./Neirynck, O. (Belgian Measures, 2002): Harmful Tax Competition: Belgian Measures Considered Tax Harmful, EATLP Annual Congress, 7 June 2002, Lausanne, http://www.eatlp.org/Belgium02.PDF (Download: June 20, 2002)

Ministére des Finances (Reforme, 2001): Reforme Fiscale 2002 - entreprises, 2001, http://www.etat.lu/FI/reforme_fiscale_presentation_291101_entreprises.pdf (Download: February 14, 2002)

Molenaars, M. L./Bongers, E. (The Netherlands, 2002): Recent International Tax Developments - The Netherlands, American Bar Association, New Orleans Meeting, Foreign Lawyers Forum, January 19, 2002

OECD (Harmful Tax Competition, 1998): Harmful Tax Competition - An Emerging Global Issue, Paris 1998, http://www1.oecd.org/daf/fa/harm_tax/harmfultax_eng.pdf (Download: March 25, 2002)

OECD (Global Tax Co-operation, 2000): Towards Global Tax Co-operation - Report to the 2000 Ministerial council Meeting and Recommendations by the Committee on Fiscal Affairs - Progress in Identifying and Eliminating Harmful Tax Practices (http://www.oecd.org/pdf/M000014000/M00014130.pdf (Download: March 25, 2002)

OECD (Model Tax Convention, 2000): Articles of the OECD Model Tax Convention on Income and on Capital, Paris, 2000, http://www1.oecd.org/daf/fa/treaties/MTCArticles.pdf (Download: April 9, 2002)

OECD (Progress Report, 2001): The OECD's Project on Harmful Tax Practices: The 2001 Progress Report, http://www.oecd.org/pdf/M00021000/M00021182.pdf (Download: March 25, 2002)

OECD (Agreement, 2002): Agreement on Exchange of Information on Tax Matters, dated April 18, 2002, http://www.oecd.org/pdf/M00028000/M00028528.pdf (Download: June 10, 2002)

OECD (List, 2002): List of Unco-operative Tax Havens, dated April 18, 2002, http://www.oecd.org/EN/document/0,,EN-document-103-3-no-12-28534-103,00.html (Download: June 10, 2002)

OECD (Model Agreement, 2002): OECD Releases Model Agreement on Exchange of Information in Tax Matters, dated April 18, 2002, http://www.oecd.org/EN/document/0,,EN-document-103-3-no-12-28532-0,00.html (Download: June 11, 2002)

President's 1961 Tax Recommendations (H.R. 10650): The Revenue Act of 1962, Hearings before the House Comm. on Ways and Means on the Recommendations of the President Contained in his Message Transmitted to the Congress, April 20, 1961, 87th Cong., 1st Sess. (Vol. I) 303, 343 (1962)

PricewaterhouseCoopers (Tax Guide, 2000): Luxembourg Financial Products and Services -The Tax Guide, 2000, http://www.pwcglobal.com/lu/eng/ins-sol/publ/pwc_taxguide.pdf (Download: December 24, 2001)

PricewaterhouseCoopers (Holding Companies, 2002): Holding Companies in Luxembourg, http://www.pwcglobal.com/lu/eng/ins-sol/publ/pwc_holding_uk.pdf, (Download: February 14, 2002) with addendum: Tax Reform 2002, http://www.pwcglobal.com/lu/eng/ins-sol/publ/pwc_holding_taxreform.pdf (Download: April 15, 2002)

PricewaterhouseCoopers (Tax Data, 2002): Tax Data, 2002, http://www.pwcglobal.com/ie/eng/ins-sol/publ/pwc_taxdata02.pdf (Download: January 31, 2002)

Ruding, H. O. (Remarks, 2002): Remarks, European Conference on Company Taxation 29/30 April 2002, Brussels, http://europa.eu.int/comm/taxation_customs/taxation/company_tax/docs/ruding.pdf (Download: May 15, 2002)

Schön, W. (General Report, 2002): Tax Competition in Europe: General Report, EATLP Annual Congress, 7 June 2002, Lausanne, http://www.eatlp.org/GeneralReportSchoen.PDF (Download: June 20, 2002)

Spahn, P. B. (Reflections, 2002): The Need for Corporate Tax Reform in the EU: Reflections on an International Conference European Company Taxation, http://europa.eu.int/comm/taxation_customs/taxation/company_tax/docs/pb-spanh.pdf (Download: June 3, 2002)

The House of Representatives (H.R. 83-1337): P.L. 83-891, Report on the 1954 Code, 83d Cong., 2d Sess. 65 (1954), 1954 WL 6063 (Leg.Hist.)

The House of Representatives (H.R. 3838): Tax Reform Act 1986, P.L. 99-514, H.R. 3838, 99th Cong., 2d Sess. (1986), 100 Stat. 2085

The House of Representatives (H.R. 2014): Taxpayer Relief Act of 1997, P.L. 105-34, H.R. 2014, 105th Cong., 1st Sess. (1997), 111 Stat. 788

The House of Representatives (H.R. 4173): International Tax Simplification for American Competitiveness Act of 1998, 105th Cong. 2d Sess., http://frwebgate.access.gpo.gov/cgi-bin/getdoc.cgi?dbname=105_cong_bills&docid=f:h4173ih.txt.pdf (Download: April 11, 2002)

The House of Representatives (H.R. 2018): International Tax Simplification for American Competitiveness Act of 1999, 106th Cong. 1st Sess., http://www.nftctax.org/MemberSection/HR2018.pdf (Download: April 11, 2002)

Thiel, S. van (Removal, 2002): Removal of income tax barriers to market integration: harmonization or litigation? - A summary of the impact of the Court's case law on the features of any future system of income taxation in the European Union, Contribution to the European Conference on Company Taxation 29/30 April 2002, Brussels, Geneva 2002, http://europa.eu.int/comm/taxation_customs/taxation/company_tax/docs/freiburg.pdf (Download: May 15, 2002)

Troup, E./Le Floc'h Louboutin, H./Juchum, G./Bijl, J. van der (Choice of Approach, 2002): The Choice of Approach, European Conference on Company Taxation 29/30 April 2002, Brussels, http://europa.eu.int/comm/taxation_customs/taxation/company_tax/docs/troup.pps (Download: May 15, 2002)

UNICE (Reaction, 2002): UNICE's Reaction to the European Commission communication and report on company taxation in the internal market: "Towards an Internal Market without tax obstacles", COM (2001) 582 final, Contribution to the European Conference on Company Taxation 29/30 April 2002, Brussels, http://europa.eu.int/comm/taxation_customs/taxation/company_tax/docs/unice_en.pdf (Download: April 27, 2002)

U.S. Senate (P.L. 83-591): Internal Revenue Code Of 1954, P.L. 83-591, S. Rep. No. 1622, 83d Cong., 2d Sess. 89 (1954), 954 WL 6064 (Leg.Hist.)

U.S. Senate (P.L. 87-834): Revenue Act Of 1962, P.L. 87-834, S. Rep. No. 1881, 87th Cong., 2d Sess. 84 (1962), 1962 WL 4862 (Leg.Hist.)

U.S. Senate (P.L. 99-514): Tax Reform Act of 1986 Senate Finance Committee Report to Accompany H.R. 3838, Summary of Estimated Budget Effects of H.R. 3838, as Approved by the Conference Committee, P.L. 99-514, S. Rep. No. 99-313, 99th Cong., 2d Sess. 518-19 (1986), 1986-3 (Vol. 3) C.B. 1

Vanden Abbele, M. (Closing Remarks, 2002): Closing Remarks, European Conference on Company Taxation 29/30 April 2002, Brussels,

http://europa.eu.int/comm/taxation_customs/taxation/company_tax/docs/conclusions_mva
.pps (Download: May 15, 2002)

WAK-N (Unternehmensbesteuerung, 2000): Ausweitung des Steuerpakets 2001 auf die
Unternehmensbesteuerung, Pressemitteilung,
http://www.parlament.ch/D/Pressemitteilungen/01_04/PM14_24_04_01_D.htm
(Download: March 15, 2002)

Winther-Sørensen, N. (Danish National Report, 2002): Tax Competition in Europe: Danish National
Report, EATLP Annual Congress, 7 June 2002, Lausanne,
http://www.eatlp.org/Denmark02.PDF (Download: June 20, 2002)

INDEX